ADVANCES IN
HEADACHE RESEARCH

Editor

F. Clifford Rose

*Academic Unit of Neuroscience, Charing Cross and
Westminster Medical School, Charing Cross Hospital,
London W6 8RF, UK*

The cover illustration by courtesy of
Dr. J. Schoenen (Chapter 4).

ADVANCES IN HEADACHE RESEARCH

Proceedings of the 6th International
Migraine Symposium

Edited by
F. CLIFFORD ROSE

John Libbey
LONDON · PARIS

British Library Cataloguing in Publication Data

International Migraine Symposium *(6th)*
  Advances in headache research: proceedings
  of the 6th International Migraine Symposium.
  —(Current problems in neurology,
  ISSN 0268–6252).
  1. Migraine
  I. Title   II. Rose, F. Clifford   III. Series
  616.8′57   RC392

ISBN 0–86196–097–1

First published in 1987 by
John Libbey & Company Ltd
80/84 Bondway, London SW8 1SF, England. (01) 582 5266
John Libbey Eurotext Ltd
6 rue Blanche, 92120 Montrouge, France. (1) 47 35 85 52

Phototypeset by Dobbie Typesetting Limited, Plymouth, Devon.
Printed in Great Britain by
Whitstable Litho Ltd, Whitstable, Kent.

PREFACE

The first symposium organized by the Migraine Trust took place in 1966. Initially held annually, for the past 12 years the symposia have been planned every two years; during this time most of the participants and speakers have come from outside the UK making the Symposia indeed truly International.

The 6th International Migraine Symposium, on which this volume is based, held in London in October, 1986, broke new ground in several respects. Firstly, it lasted for three days instead of two; secondly, the number of participants exceeded 500, partly due to mini-symposia as well as satellite meetings of the International Headache Society and World Federation of Neurology Migraine and Headache Research Group. Most of the success of the Symposium was due to the tremendous work of the Head Office of the Migraine Trust and, in particular, its most able and energetic Director, Commander Oliver Wright.

It is a pleasure to thank my colleagues on the Symposium Committee for their help in the selection of contributors to this volume which is divided into five sections. The first three deal with migraine viz pathogenesis, vascular and therapeutic aspects, the fourth with cluster headache and the fifth with other types of idiopathic headache eg tension, muscle contraction and mixed headaches. Its contents provide the latest insights into the pathogenesis of headache and confirm that its differential diagnosis is becoming more accurate, its therapy increasingly effective and its research no longer a neglected area of the neurosciences.

London
1987

F. Clifford Rose

CONTENTS

III. Migraine therapy

IV. Cluster headache

V. Chronic headache

1

CRITERIA FOR THE

DIAGNOSIS OF COMMON MIGRAINE

Seymour Solomon and Karen Guglielmo Cappa

Headache Unit of Montefiore Medical Center
Albert Einstein College of Medicine, New York, USA

Summary

The symptoms of 100 patients diagnosed as having common migraine were compared with migraineurs reported in three large series, and marked concordance was found. We then compared the prevalence of symptoms in 100 patients with common migraine with 100 patients diagnosed as having chronic daily headaches. The following features occurred significantly ($P < 0.001$) more often in patients with common migraine than chronic daily headache: nausea, vomiting, unilateral site, throbbing quality, photophobia, phonophobia, increase of headache with menstruation, and family history of migraine. Severe, but not moderate, pain was significantly ($P < 0.01$) more common in migraine than chronic daily headache. Except for degree of pain, the above features were incorporated into a set of criteria for the diagnosis of migraine. These criteria and others were retrospectively applied to patients diagnosed as having migraine and those with chronic daily headache, and the advantages and deficiencies of these sets of criteria are discussed.

Introduction

Clinical criteria must be relied upon to make the diagnoses of migraine and tension headache, for there are no laboratory tests or biological markers to link or differentiate the two. The definition of common migraine used for the past quarter of a century is vague and inaccurate[1]. There is a need to establish new operational criteria for the diagnosis of common migraine. Such criteria are essential for further research in this field, for the daily care of our patients, and to allow those interested in the field to have a common language.

This study is an attempt to define the criteria for the diagnosis of common migraine. Classical migraine is not difficult to define but the features of common migraine are not unique and occur with other kinds of benign headache[2]. It is for this reason that questions have been raised regarding the dichotomy of common migraine and tension headache[2,3] which, most would agree, should be considered as separate entities, at least until their pathophysiology is better understood.

Material and methods

Patients were drawn from the Headache Unit of Montefiore Medical Center and the history and examination was performed by one of two senior neurologists. A study which attempts to establish criteria for the diagnosis of a specific entity is best approached retrospectively. Therefore, the last 100 patients diagnosed as having common migraine and the last 100 patients diagnosed as having chronic daily headache with certain exclusion criteria were studied. The diagnosis of these two headache types was not based on a set of criteria but, as is the practice of most headache specialists, upon the gestalt, the overall clinical picture of the patient. To help eliminate underlying organic disease, patients with either type were excluded if their headache onset was after the age of 60, and if their headaches followed head trauma or illness.

We set out to compare cases of common migraine with those of tension headache and found that most of our patients diagnosed as having tension headache had headaches every day. We, therefore, further narrowed our comparison group to patients with chronic daily headaches. Because a large percentage of cases of chronic daily headache evolve from many years of migraine, a common mechanism may be present[4]. Nevertheless, most agree that the two conditions are separate clinical entities. The diagnosis of chronic daily headache required a history of daily or almost daily headaches (at least six per week) without organic causes, of more than 2 months duration. Patients diagnosed as having common migraine were excluded if they had headaches for less than 2 months and experienced more than four headaches per month. Symptoms of common migraine and tension headache sometimes occur within one headache pattern, and these patients with mixed headache were excluded. Tension headaches may occur between attacks of migraine, so called interval headaches. The migraine headaches of such patients were studied if the interval headaches were clearly distinguishable, minor, and infrequent.

In order to validate our concepts of migraine, we compared the features of our 100 patients diagnosed as having common migraine with three large series of classical and common migraine reported in the past[5,6,7]. (There are no large studies of the features limited to common migraine.)

We studied symptoms commonly used to differentiate migraine from tension headache. These included: features of the headache (laterality of site, throbbing quality, degree of pain [moderate or severe]); associated symptoms (nausea, vomiting, anorexia without nausea or vomiting, photophobia, phonophobia, osmophobia); and other factors that may enter into the diagnostic process (increase in headache with menstruation or with ingestion of alcoholic beverages, decrease of headache during pregnancy, and family history of migraine). The percentage of occurrence of each item in common migraine and chronic daily headache was compared using the chi-square method.

Because all of the features of common migraine may be seen in patients with tension headache[8] or chronic daily headache[9] the criteria for the diagnosis of common migraine must emphasize those features that are not only highly prevalent, but also occur significantly more often in migraine than in chronic daily headache. Using those items that occurred significantly more ($P < 0.001$) with common migraine than with chronic daily headache,

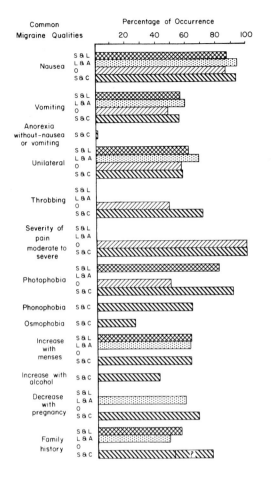

Figure. *Qualities of migraine.* S & L, see reference 5; L & A, see reference 6; O, see reference 7; S & C, Solomon & Cappa: present study.

criteria were promulgated for the operational diagnosis of migraine. With these, and sets of criteria formulated by Tfelt-Hansen and Olesen[10], and by the committee on classification of headache of the International Headache Society, our patients were retrospectively re-evaluated to determine what percentage of the two headache groups would have conformed to these criteria.

Results

Features of migraine in four series

The prevalences of features of our 100 patients with common migraine showed great concordance with those of three large series of common and classical migraine[5,6,7] (Figure). The approximate prevalences were as follows. Nausea occurred in about 90% of patients in all four series; vomiting in more than half. We found only one patient with anorexia without nausea or vomiting. Throbbing quality and unilateral site were noted in about half to two thirds of the patients in these series. Pain was moderate to severe in almost all cases. Photophobia ranged from about 50 to 90%. We noted phonophobia and osmophobia in two thirds and one fourth of patients respectively. Headaches increased

Table 1. *Qualities of common migraine.* 100 patients with common migraine compared to 100 patients with chronic daily headache.

	Percentage of occurrence	
	Migraine *(HA < 4/month* *onset < 60 years* *mean duration 17.2 years)*	*Chronic daily headache* *(HA > 2 months* *onset < 60 years* *mean duration 7.8 years)*
Nausea	93	31*
Vomiting	57	6*
Anorexia without nausea or vomiting	1	7§
Unilateral	57	7*
Throbbing	68	28*
Severity		
moderate	19	27§
severe	79	58†
combined	98	85†
Photophobia	91	35*
Phonophobia	65	40*
Osmophobia	28	16§
Increases with menses	62	21*
	(50 of 81)	(15 of 70)
Decrease with pregnancy	64	42§
	(18 of 28)	(5 of 12)
Increases with alcohol	41	27§
+ Family history	77	39*
definite	46	7*
questionable	31	32§
Male	19	30§
Female	81	70§

*, $P < 0.001$; †, $P < 0.01$; ‡, $P < 0.05$; §, not significant.

by menstruation were noted in almost two thirds of the series. About 40% of our patients noted aggravation of migraine after drinking alcohol. Headache was decreased during pregnancy in two thirds of two series. About half of the patients had a family history of migraine; we noted an additional third of families with headaches that were questionably migraine.

Features of common migraine compared to chronic daily headache

All of the features associated with common migraine were found in the patients diagnosed as having chronic daily headache (the two groups are compared in Table 1). Significant differences ($P < 0.001$) were noted for nausea, vomiting, unilateral site, throbbing quality, photophobia, phonophobia, increase of headache with menstruation, and family history of migraine.

The prevalence of headache of moderate severity was not significantly different in patients with migraine and those with chronic daily headache. Severe headache and moderate and severe degrees of headache considered together, occurred significantly more often in common migraine than in chronic daily headache, $P < 0.01$, but the combined ratio was 98:85. There were no significant differences in the occurrence of anorexia without nausea or vomiting, osmophobia, women who noted decrease in headache with pregnancy, and patients who noted aggravation of headache after alcoholic ingestion.

Table 2a. *Criteria of common migraine (Solomon & Cappa).*

Any two   1. Nausea with or without vomiting
               2. Unilateral
               3. Throbbing
               4. Photophobia or phonophobia
               5. Increase with menses and family history of migraine

Retrospectively applied to patients with:

Common migraine	99/100
Chronic daily headache	38/100

Table 2b. *Criteria of common migraine (Tfelt-Hansen & Olesen)*[10].

Nausea and one other
               1. Unilateral
               2. Pulsating
               3. Photophobia
               4. Phonophobia

Retrospectively applied to patients with:

Common Migraine	93/100
Chronic daily headache	24/100

Table 2c. *Criteria of common migraine proposed for International Headache Society (Sept. 1986).*

Any one   1. Unilateral
               2. Pulsating
               3. Moderate or severe pain

               and

Any one   a. Nausea
               b. Vomiting
               c. Photophobia
               d. Phonophobia

Retrospectively applied to patients with:

Common migraine	99/100
Chronic daily headache	58/100

Criteria for diagnosis of common migraine

On the basis of our data, a simple standard of operational criteria for the diagnosis of common migraine was formulated (Table 2a). All of the features found significantly more prevalent in migraine than in chronic daily headache were included in the criteria except severity of pain. Degree of pain is the most subjective feature and moderate or severe pain occurs in a very high percentage of patients with chronic daily headache as well as migraine. Our criteria are very similar to the standards recently proposed by Tfelt-Hansen and Olesen[10] (Table 2b). These tables also show how the two criteria, when applied retrospectively, fit our cases of migraine and chronic daily headache.

Criteria proposed by a committee of the International Headache Society were also applied to our cases of migraine and chronic daily headache (Table 2c). That formula would permit classification of headaches as migraine if the recurrent headaches were only of moderate severity with photophobia or phonophobia. Such criteria were noted in 15 patients diagnosed as having chronic daily headache, but in none with common migraine. Moreover, these criteria would not permit the diagnosis of migraine in a patient with severe headaches of unilateral site and pulsating quality; nor with nausea, vomiting, photophobia and phonophobia.

Discussion

Concordance of features of our patients diagnosed as having common migraine with three other series[5,6,7] is pleasantly surprising. Studies have shown that no combination of features are unique to migraine[8,11]. We similarly noted the presence of features typical of migraine in patients with chronic daily headache. In establishing operational criteria for the diagnosis of migraine, several combinations of features were considered before reaching the proposed set.

In our criteria, we list nausea with or without vomiting, as a single criterion because they usually occur together, are both manifestations of a common mechanism, and the couple should not be considered as the only criteria of migraine. For the same reasons, photophobia or phonophobia were grouped as a single criterion. The criterion of headaches: increased with menstruation and a positive family history of migraine, are weak because not all migraineurs menstruate and family history is subject to error. In our series, however, this criterion never occurred with only one other feature and could be eliminated without altering our statistics (Table 2a).

The main differences between our criteria and those of Tfelt-Hansen and Olesen[10] is the latter's requirement of nausea. A gastrointestinal symptom is the feature which conventionally most clearly differentiates migraine from tension headache and other benign headache, but we believe that nausea is not absolutely necessary for the diagnosis of migraine. From 5 to 14% of patients diagnosed as having common migraine in the four series (Figure) did not have nausea. In our cases without nausea, the diagnosis of migraine was based upon recurring idiopathic headache with associated features of unilateral site and throbbing pain (one case), unilateral site and photophobia or phonophobia (two cases), throbbing pain and photophobia or phonophobia (three cases). (Two of the six cases had a third criterion to further support the diagnosis.)

We believe that the diagnosis of migraine is warranted with our criteria, but only six of the 99 cases that matched our criteria would be eliminated by limiting the criteria to those of Tfelt-Hansen and Olesen[10]. If chronic headache is a form of tension headache, insisting on nausea as an invariable feature of migraine would reduce the potential error of diagnosing tension headache for migraine. For purposes of clinical drug trials, the narrower criteria of Tfelt-Hansen and Olesen[10] would be best. For the day to day management of clinical practice, we believe our wider set of criteria are appropriate.

References

1 Ad Hoc Committee on Classification of Headache (1962): *J. Am. Med. Ass.* **179**, 717–718.
2 Drummond, P. D. & Lance, J. W. (1984): Clinical diagnosis and computer analysis of headache symptoms. *J. Neurol. Neurosurg. Psychiat.* **47**, 128–133.
3 Saper, J. R. (1983): *Headache disorders. Current concepts and treatment strategies*, pp. 125–130. Boston: John Wright-PSG.
4 Mathew, N. T., Stubits, E. & Nigam, M. P. (1982): Transformation of episodic migraine into daily headache: analysis of factors. *Headache* **22**, 66–68.
5 Selby, G & Lance, J. W. (1960): Observations on 500 cases of migraine and allied vascular headache. *J. Neurol. Neurosurg. Psychiat.* **23**, 23–32.

6   Lance, J. W. & Anthony, M. (1966): Some clinical aspects of migraine — a prospective study of 500 patients. *Arch. Neurol.* **15**, 356–361.

7   Olesen, J. (1978): Some clinical features of the acute migraine attack. An analysis of 750 patients. *Headache* **18**, 268–271.

8   Nikiforow, R. (1981): Features of migraine — comparison of a questionnaire study and a neurologist-examined random sample. *Cephalalgia* **1**, 157–166.

9   Sjaastad, O. (1985): Chronic daily headache (Cefalea cronica quotidiana). *Cephalalgia* **5** (Suppl. 2), 191–193.

10   Tfelt-Hansen, P. & Olesen, J. (1985): Methodological aspects of drug trials in migraine. *Neuroepidemiol.* **4**, 204–236.

11   Ziegler, D. K., Hassanain, R. S. & Couch, J. R. (1982): Headache syndromes suggested by statistical analysis of headache symptoms. *Cephalalgia* **2**, 125–134.

I

MIGRAINE PATHOGENESIS

2

REDUNDANT PAIN TRANSMISSION

FROM FUNCTIONAL DEAFFERENTATION

Federigo Sicuteri and Maria Nicolodi

Institute of Internal Medicine and Clinical Pharmacology
Florence University, Viale Morgagni, 85, 50134 Florence, Italy

Summary

Central pains are currently considered dependent on partial or total deafferentation (DAF) which occurs in the spinal cord and/or in the brainstem. Migraine pain exhibits the same symptomatic characteristics of organic DAF, in particular the overreaction provoked from even inadequate (emotional, sensorial) stimuli. In addition, the migraine attack is characterized by a train of stereotypical vegetative phenomena, identical to those of acute opiate abstinence, where a pain, central in nature, emerges later and at different sites. A common mechanism (a functional and pharmacological DAF) may explain the nature of these '*sine materia*' pains as well as that of the vegetative manifestations which occur both during migraine and abstinence.

Introduction

Migraine, in spite of an increased awareness of its chemical and pharmacological properties, still hides the secret of its mechanism; the critical analysis of a single clinical phenomenon, and its interdependence or interindependence with other phenomena, remains even today the best tool for speculation. The typical migraine attack is characterized by three orders of phenomena: affective (anxiety or depression), vegetative (multiple in their nature) and nociceptive. The non-pain phenomena, such as yawning, vomiting or depression, can sometimes manifest itself before the pain emerges, so excluding these phenomena as consequences of the pain. A common mechanism for the three (affective, vegetative, nociceptive) orders of phenomena is the first uncontestable assumption derived from clinical analysis. A second irrefutable assumption is that they are per se not pathological (as are, for example, the seizure of epilepsy and delirium of psychosis). In fact the migraine phenomena are normal expressions of physiological function but, on the other hand, their automaticity is pathological, since they fire apparently without any stimulus or driving force. Rarely, pathological manifestations such as paralysis or total amnesia can arise in association with an attack, but these are true complications. Based on these two assumptions, the nature of the common denominator capable of triggering intermittently and simultaneously the detonation of the three (affective, vegetative, nociceptive) different functions can only be speculated. The direct implication of a 'common' transmitter (for instance, noradrenaline, dopamine, substance P) for these functions can be difficult to propose, since these functions have different (aminic and peptidic) transmitters. A simultaneous release of different transmitters for multiple functions is also difficult to conceive.

It is possible to postulate the involvement of only one transmitter (or only one neuronal system) which controls different neurons having different transmitters, as in inhibitory systems which modulate different functions, which, when activated, simultaneously perform a complex and integrated design. A classic example of this is that of defense, where multiple functions are instantaneously fired to preserve individual survival.

Some years ago it was suggested that impairment of one of the most important inhibitory systems, the endogenous opioid system (EOS)[1], could play a major role in the migraine mechanism for two main reasons: EOS

(a) controls those functions (nociception included) which appear, during an attack, interindependently (simultaneously) activated;

(b) could involve the same three orders of functions (affective, vegetative, nociceptive) in human pathology, eg where the opiate (mainly 'mu') receptors are heavily and persistently stimulated as happens in opiate addiction. Here the different aminergic and peptidergic opioid dependent neuron (ODNs) are persistently unsettled in their function because of an excess of inhibition: the interneuronal as well as the terminal synapses of ODNs are expected to be markedly damaged in function. Thus, the acute abstinence syndrome represents, *in vivo*, the most reliable topographic and functional map of the ODNs in man. The maintenance of addiction correlates with the necessity of restraining the emerging abstinence, which depends mainly on intermittent increased inhibition of the ODNs. The pivot of this argument is that the synaptic activity of ODNs during addiction is not the same as that of naive neurons, since the hyperinhibition of ODNs impair the release of their 'common transmitter' so evoking a post-synaptic compensatory supersensitivity. This supersensitivity is clearly demonstrated in tolerant animals, *in vivo* and *in vitro*, and in iris and dorsal hand vein in human addicts[2,3]. In addiction, an increasing pharmacological inhibition is required to maintain the same effect of the first opiate administration. The mechanism of avoiding the phenomena of abstinence could be as follows: a condition of gradual synaptic hyposecretion with consequent gradual supersensitivity of post-synaptic receptors of ODNs, a sort of pharmacological denervation of ODNs. Since ODNs are efferent (vegetative) and afferent (nociceptive), a condition of deefferentation (DEF) and deafferentation (DAF) will be established and maintained through the addiction with the teleological aim of preserving functional homeostasis.

An analogy between the mechanisms of the clinical manifestations of abstinence and migraine attacks may be drawn, since, effectively, the post-synaptic supersensitivity to monoamines of iris and vein detected in opiate abstinence has been found in migraine[3,4]. Nevertheless, the nature of EOS involvement in the migraine attack remains uncertain. More than one hypothesis can be considered:

(a) a hypertonus of EOS, creating self-addiction, a condition which strictly minimizes the opiate addiction. However, naloxone, even in high doses (10–20 mg) injected as an i.v. bolus, does not precipitate the attack in migraine sufferers and the lowered or normal levels of opioids found in migraine sufferers do not support this hypothesis;

(b) a hypotonus of EOS which creates a lack of modulation of ODNs, the final result being a lack of specific transmitter in ODNs and consequently a post-synaptic compensatory supersensitivity of the subserved neurons. This second hypothesis seems more acceptable.

The substance P-empty neuron (SPEN) as substrate of the pain arising from deafferentation

An infallible method of depleting a nerve of its transmitter is that of severing the nerve. The effect of this denervation on the content of pain transmitter has been studied initially only in vegetative and motor (skeletal muscle) efferent nerves. Recently, however, the neural content of the pain transmitter, substance P (sP), following section (or damage) of primary and secondary order sensory fibres has been evaluated in animal and man. The following observations have been made:

(1) the content of sP in the ipsilateral spinal dorsal horn (where sensory fibres enter the grey matter) dramatically declines[5];

(2) in the same area, proliferation of sP receptors occurs[6];

(3) reactivity of the second order sensory neurons when stimulated mechanically, electrically or chemically (local application of sP) appears strongly amplified[7]. This hyperreactivity is deduced from the behavioural signs of pain and from electrical hyperactivity (expressed continuously and/or as epileptic-like bursts).

The generation of these nociceptive quasi-epileptic foci (QEF) occurs not only ipsimetamerically to the deafferentation: in fact, QEFs disseminate rostrally, to the thalamus[8,9,10] and even to the cortex[11], Clearly, the afferent nerves even have (through sP secretion?) a neurotrophic function related to maintenance of the anatomical and functional organization of the pain transmitting system[12]. In fact, nociceptive homeostasis is compromised organically and functionally, even permanently, by a reduction or suppression of sensory imput. The DAF pain strictly depends on the number, as well as, contiguity of the deafferentated fibres. Neuronal plasticity and reorganization are sufficient to maintain the nociceptive homeostasis when the DAF interests only one or few, but not contiguous, sensitive fibres[12]. Even in the case of 'clinically silent' DAF (section of one or few non-contiguous fibres) an anatomical damage of the pain transmission system is demonstrated rostrally to the deafferentated metamer. Anatomofunctional studies have been carried out in animals particularly on tooth DAF, since tooth sensitivity concerns only pain sensation. Partial tooth DAF (removal of coronal portion of tooth pulps) induces changes in receptive field location and extension, with disruption of somatotopic organization: many neurons of trigeminal nuclei exhibit both spontaneous and unusual responses to the stimulation[13]. Another investigation, in leg deafferentated macacus, concerns the rostral dissemination of QEFs from the ipsimetameric spinal cord, up to the thalamus: this experiment suggests that the loss of afferents alters not only the ipsimetameric cordal neurons activity (local QEFs) but even the rostral pain transmitter system, along with sensory pathways of the deafferentated field[9]. The autotomy (or autocannibalism) of the limb of the deafferentated animal[14] reflects an instinctual behaviour finalized to:

(a) eliminate insensitive body parts or

(b) liberate itself of an excruciating pain. However, even in this second case the insensitivity to bites facilitates autocannibalism. In the mechanisms of both functional hypernociception and electrical (QEFs) hyperactivity, the major role could be played by the anatomofunctional unit of sP-ergic or other pain transmitting empty neurons (Fig. 1).

In spite of the interruption of sensory fibres (and then axonal flow of sP), it is not difficult to believe that sP receptors can arrive from more than one source on supersensitive sP-ergic receptors: from intermetameric sP-ergic connections, from residual fibres not

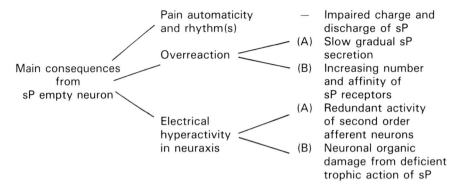

Fig 1. *Functional and organic damages from deafferentation (DAF).*

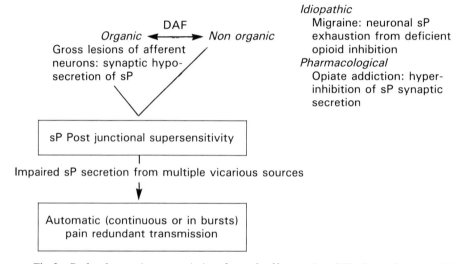

Fig 2. *Redundant pain transmission from deafferentation* (NB,sP = pain transmitters).

completely sectioned or damaged (a frequent situation in accidental DAF), from new sP-ergic fibres (sprouting, reorganization and regeneration processes) or from functionally silent neurons and synapses[12,13]. The final result in DAF can be:

(a) insufficient pain transmission: if no pain is felt, because the amount of sP impacting receptors is insufficient, in spite of supersensitivity, to fire pain signals;

(b) A redundant pain transmission, when the amount is sufficient. In this last case the perceived pain is expected to have the characteristics of (DAF) central pain.

Pharmacological DAF

A pharmacological inhibition of neuronal sP secretion along the pathways of first and second order fibres of the pain transmitting system could provoke a condition of sP receptor supersensitivity; consequently a silhouette of SPEN can be theoretically considered. The most powerful inhibitors of sP secretion in the grey matter of spinal cord and brainstem are the opiates (morphine) and EOs[15,16,17]. The acute inhibition of sP secretion could be the (or one of the) mechanisms of opiate analgesia[18].

During acute opiate abstinence, addicts constantly complain of pain originating from flanks, back and neck. The mechanism of abstinence pains can be correlated with:
(a) a secretion of sP from disinhibited sP neurons;
(b) an amplified effect of sP on post-synaptic sites, because of sP post-synaptic supersensitivity;
(c) a deficiency of the endogenous opioid system, due to a feed-back mechanism from the chronic excess of opiate with consequent failure of endogenous analgesia when opiate administration is discontinued (Fig. 2). The hypernociception during abstinence in an opiate tolerant rat is remarkable and proportional to the entity of the addiction; this reaction can be suggested as one of the parameters of the entity of opiate tolerance[19].

The afferent (nociceptive) neurons are only a part of the neurons inhibited by the opiates, in fact, multiple vegetative neurons (mainly noradrenergic ones) are modulated by opioids and indirect evidence has recently been adduced in man[20], recently confirmed by extensive investigations[21]. Concerning the existence of vegetative empty neurons in migraine sufferers, some indirect evidence has been obtained in our laboratory and the results confirmed recently in a comprehensive study. There opiates induce, through the reduced secretion of the main transmitter, a sort of pharmacological DEF, as proved by the florid autonomic manifestations during abstinence.

The neuromuscular junction of the dilator muscle of the iris of addicts behaves in the pattern of the empty neuron: supersensitivity (enhanced midriatic response) to phenylephrine (a pure alpha adrenoceptor agonist) and apparent normosensitivity (in spite of supersensitivity of post-synaptic receptor) to tyramine, a noradrenaline releaser[2]. The silhouette of the sympathetic empty neuron in the neuromuscular junction of vein is evident under the same conditions: increased (in some cases dramatic) sensitivity to noradrenaline, and normoreactivity to tyramine[3]. The acute abstinence in addicts is a faithful guide to the topographic map of opiate receptors as well as of their influence on multiple functions, mainly vegetative, affective and nociceptive. Abstinence could be considered as a sort of syndrome from acute disinhibition of neurons impaired by a persistent hyposecretion, consequent to hyperstimulation of chronic opiate receptors. It is suggested that this pharmacological DAF (addiction) has clinical and pharmacological links with migraine[1,??].

Functional DAF

Pain in migraine (especially if seriously 'decompensated') exhibits certain characteristics which define its nature:
(1) almost apparent spontaneity, in fact, even after hundreds or thousands of attacks, signs of damage are not detectable;
(2) overreaction, that is a pain which after a stimulus remains stable even for hours and later explodes into a full spontaneous-like attack, significantly different from nociceptive physiological pain;
(3) evocation or exacerbation from inadequate stimuli. Emotive, sensory (visual, auditory, olfactory), physical (cold, warm), and mechanical (repetitive head jolting) stimuli are inadequate to evoke headache in healthy (headache-free) subjects. It is a common observation, especially in decompensated migraine, that there is an increased capacity of these inadequate stimuli to precipitate or exacerbate the headache. The characteristics of points (2) and (3) strictly intercorrelate: a pain having the typical course of overreaction is provoked by an inadequate stimulus (emotion, for example) (Fig. 3).

The difference between functional and organic DAF is quantitative rather than qualitative: the vegetative manifestations so florid in the first condition are practically absent in the second. It is significant that the autonomic phenomena are present and stereotypically

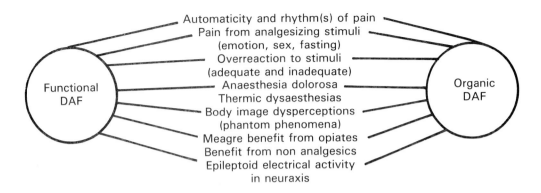

Fig. 3. *Analogous phenomena from different deafferentations.*

analogous in both functional and pharmacological DAF, which is in agreement with their underlying mechanism.

Evidence for functional DAF

The main evidence which supports the present concept of functional DAF (sP empty neuron) in the mechanism of migraine pain are:
(a) overreaction to nitroglycerine; in migraine sufferers, but not in headache free (personal and familial) subjects, nitroglycerine provokes a mild headache which after 1–2 h (when vasomotor and chemical reactions to the drug are long since exhausted) can increase even dramatically until assuming the physiognomy of a full migraine attack. This delayed reaction corresponds to the phenomenon of overreaction. Healthy (headache-free) sons of migrainous sufferers can exhibit following nitroglycerine administration a delayed long-lasting headache which is here seen as an overreaction, a typical phenomenon of central pain[23]. These results are indirect evidence that a genetic predisposition to migraine can be unmaskable even in apparently healthy subjects.
(b) Another indirect evidence in favour of a DAF theory is that of the 'phantom tooth' during migraine attacks. Patients who have lost one or more (specially if contiguous) teeth, in the upper jaw ipsilateral to the headache, frequently complain of aches irradiating to the absent tooth, feeling that it should be present. The avulsion of a tooth in the newborn rat is followed by alterations of neurons in the brain stem and cortex along afferent pathways[13]. It has been suggested that these lesions after tooth DAF may remain asymptomatic in man, because of the plasticity and reorganizational processes: if in the same sensitive field is superimposed a process of DAF the phenomenon of phantom tooth pain can occur[13].

During cluster headache, pain can be projected to the same area of an eye previously enucleated or deafferentated. The phenomenon of 'true eye phantom pain' in cluster headache merits particular consideration; if confirmed it could be an almost determinant support to the interpretation[24-27] of cluster headache as a 'quasi phantom eye pain'.

Acknowledgements—The authors would like to thank Mr Michael Fusco for language revision of the text and Ms Anna Bassi for typing the manuscript. The work was supported by a grant from CNR, Rome (Italy): target program 'Chimica fine e secondaria'.

References

1   Sicuteri, F. (1972): Natural opioids in migraine. In *Advances in Neurology*, vol. 33 eds M. Cricthley *et al.* pp. 65–74. New York: Raven Press.

2   Pietrini, U., Geppetti, P., Fanciullacci, M. & Sicuteri, F. (1982): Iris adrenergic hyperresponsiveness in opiate addicts. In *XXI Congr. Ital. Soc. Pharmac. Naple (Italy)*, vol. Abstract p. 334.

3   Sicuteri, F., Del Bianco, P. L. & Anselmi, B. (1979): Morphine abstinence and serotonin supersensitivity in man: analogies with mechanism of migraine. *Psychopharmacol.* **65**, 205–209.

4   Fanciullacci, M., Pietrini, U. & Boccuni, M. (1982): Disruption of iris adrenergic transmission as an index of poor endorphin modulation in headache. In *Advances in neurology*, Vol. 33, eds M. Cricthley *et al.* pp. 365–374. New York: Raven Press.

5   Zseli, J., Horvath, J., Szücs, J. & Hollo, I. (1982): Substance P and enkephalins in spinal cord after limb amputation. *Lancet* **i**, 1023.

6   Wright, D. M. & Roberts, M. H. T. (1978): Supersensitivity to substance P analogue following dorsal root section. *Life Sci.* **22**, 19–24.

7   Nakata, Y., Kusaka, Y. & Segawa, T. (1979): Supersensitivity to substance P after dorsal root section. *Life Sci.* **24**, 1651–1654.

8   Levitt, M. & Levitt, J. M. (1981): The deafferentation syndrome in monkeys: dysesthesias of spinal origin. *Pain* **10**, 129–147.

9   Levitt, M. (1983): The bilateral symmetrical deafferentation syndrome in macaque after bilateral spinal lesions: evidence for dysesthesias resulting from brain foci and considerations of spinal pain pathways. *Pain* **16** (2), 167–184.

10 Lombard, M. C., Nashold, B. S. & Pelissier, T. (1979): Thalamic recordings in rats with hyperalgesia. In *Advances in pain research and therapy*, vol. 5, eds J. J. Bonica *et al.* pp. 767–772. New York: Raven Press.

11 Albe-Fessard, D., Condés-Lara, M., Sanderson, P. & Levante, A. (1984): Tentative explanation of paleospinothalamic projection in patients with deafferentation pain syndromes. In *Advances in pain research and therapy*, ed L. Kruger & G. C. Liebeskind, vol. 6, pp. 167–182. New York: Raven Press.

12 Wall, P. D. (1983): Alterations in the central nervous system after deafferentation: connectivity control. In *Advances in pain research and therapy*, vol. 5, pp. 677–689. New York: Raven Press.

13 Dostrovsky, D. O., Ball, G. J., Hu, J. W. & Sessle, B. J. (1982): Functional changes associated with partial tooth removal in neurons of the trigeminal spinal tract nucleus and their clinical implications. In *Anatomical, physiological and pharmacological aspects of trigeminal pain*, eds B. Matthews & R. G. Hill, pp. 293–309. Amsterdam: Excerpta Medica.

14 Albe-Fessard, D., Nashold, B. S. J., Lombard, M. C., Yamaguchi, Y. & Boreau, F. (1979): Rat after dorsal rizothomy, a possible animal model for chronic pain. In *Advances in pain research and therapy*, vol. 3, pp. 761–772. New York: Raven Press.

15 Lamotte, C., Pert, C. B. & Snyder, S. H. (1976): Opiate receptors binding in primate spinal cord: distribution and changes after dorsal root section. *Brain Res.* **112**, 407–412.

16 Yaksh, T. L., Jessel, T. M., Mudge, A. W. & Leeman, S. E. (1980): Intrathecal morphine inhibits substance P release from mammalian spinal cord in vivo. *Nature* **286**, 155–157.

17 Jessel, T. M. & Iversen, L. L. (1977): Opiate analgesic inhibit substance P release from trigeminal nucleus. *Nature* **286**, 594–551.

18 Terenius, L. (1982): Endorphin and modulation of pain. In *Advances in neurology*, eds M. Cricthley, A. P. Friedman, G. Gorini & F. Sicuteri, vol. 33, pp. 59–64. New York: Raven Press.

19 Tilson, H. A., Rech, R. H. & Stolman, S. (1973): Hyperalgesia during withdrawal as a means measuring the degree of dependence in morphine dependent rats. *Psychopharmacol.* **28**, 287–300.

20 Fanciullacci, M., Del Bianco, P. L. & Sicuteri, F. (1978): Iris and vein adrenoceptors in migraine and central panalgesia. In *Recent advances in pharmacology of adrenoceptors*, eds E. Szabadi, C. M. Bradshaw & P. Bevan, pp. 295–303. Amsterdam: Elsevier Biomedical Press.

21 Gotoh, F., Kamatsumoto, S., Araki, N. & Gomi, S. (1984): Noradrenergic nervous activity in migraine. *Arch. Neurol.* **41** (9), 951–955.

22 Sicuteri, F., Gatto, G. & Panconesi, A. (1985): Hallmarks of deficient opioid homeostasis: Migraine as a quasi self (endorphin) acute abstinence. In *Updating in headache*, eds V. Pfaffenrath *et al.*, pp. 249–263. Berlin: Springer Verlag.

23 Sicuteri, F., Poggioni, M., Del Bene, E. & Bonazzi, L. (1986): Unmasking latent dysociception in healthy subjects. *Headache* (in press).

24 Sicuteri, F. (1983): Quasi phantom eye pain and 'Janus effect' of substance P in cluster headache. *Cephalalgia* **5**, 370–371.

25 Sicuteri, F. (1985): Quasi phantom eye pain: an evolution of the substance P theory of cluster headache. *Headache* **25**, 447–451.

26 Sicuteri, F. (1986): Changing trends in migraine and cluster headache: the concept of functional deafferentation. *IRCS Medical Science* **14**, 1062–1065.

27 Sicuteri, F. (1986): Quasi phantom head pain from functional deafferentation. *Clin. J. Pain* (Boston) (In press).

3

ON THE INFERRED RELATIONSHIP OF

MIGRAINE AND SPREADING DEPRESSION

Aristides A. P. Leão

The Institute of Biophysics,
Federal University of Rio de Janeiro, Brazil

Introduction

Of the two entities whose relations are considered, spreading depression (SD) is relatively unfamiliar and so, to guard against misunderstanding, we will review this experimental phenomenon.

Spreading depression was first noted in the exposed cerebral cortex of the rabbit, as a reaction to various modes of local stimulation of the cortical tissue. The reaction was essentially characterized by a profound depression of neuronal activity, which appears first at the stimulated site, and then spreads in all directions for a greater and greater distance from it[1].

Subsequently, it was found that the hippocampus, striatum, cerebellum, and other neuronal aggregations of the brain of all classes of vertebrate, may also undergo SD. Interestingly, the reaction has never been observed in the grey matter of the spinal cord[2], but we are here concerned with SD in the cerebral cortex:

(1) SD occurs only in certain conditions, which render the tissue susceptible to it. The more susceptible the tissue, the lower the threshold of stimulation, the faster the spread, and the more deeply affected the activity.

(2) The speed of the spread is on the order of 3 mm/min, and at any site the profound depression lasts for 1–3 min. Thus, the distance that the advancing front of a cortical SD moves tangentially away from a given site, during the time that the activity at that site is profoundly depressed, does not exceed some 8–10 mm.

(3) The spread is self-sustained. Once a SD is set up, its spread depends only on the local conditions of the tissue, as regards susceptibility to the reaction. If it happens that some parts of the sheet of cortical tissue are more susceptible than others, the spread through those parts is faster. If it happens that only a part of the sheet is susceptible, the spread is restricted to that part. Sulci constitute an obstacle to the spread: SD may be retarded in crossing them, or make a circuit around them. Thus, especially in convoluted cortices, the advancing edge of a SD may come to be of a very irregular shape.

(4) Although all intrinsic and evoked neuronal activity are depressed, abnormal activity may occur locally in the course of cortical SD. At any site, at the onset of the depression, the neurones usually generate a brief (1–3 s) burst of discharges, and within some 30 s of this burst, abnormal activity of the same kind as cortical seizure activity may erupt, and last for more than 20 s. This eruption depends on the local conditions, and in a single cortical SD it may occur at some sites and not at others.

(5) At any site, SD is followed by an absolutely refractory period of at least 1 min. Two or more SDs can be initiated at the same time in different sites, but when the advancing front of one comes into the refractory period of another, it is annihilated. At any site, recovery from SD is to a large extent effected in a few minutes, but it may well take more than 1 hour for the tissue to be fully restored to its pre-SD state.

Symptoms

The symptoms that would be expected in the occurrence of cortical SD in man compare with the symptoms arising from the cerebral cortex in the aura of classic migraine. Since at any one time during SD, only a narrow band of tissue is deeply affected, one would expect transient, focal symptoms—as are those of the migraine aura.

Visual symptoms

Visual symptoms are the most detailedly described by migraine sufferers and, by mapping and timing his own scotomata as they drifted across his visual field, Lashley came to the conclusion that a disturbance was advancing at a speed of about 3 mm/min over his visual cortex[3]. This is the speed of propagation of SD and, in a study of the duration of fortification spectra, Hare has given reasons for the acceptance of this speed as typical of the aural cortical disturbance[4]. As for the kind of visual symptoms, one would expect from SD, signs of abnormal activity followed by depressed activity, or of just depressed activity. This is what is indicated by the typical aural symptoms consisting of fortification spectra (scintillations) followed by blindness, or of purely negative scotomata. Most often the visual symptoms begin near the point of central vision, and the patients who make a sketch of their fortification spectra draw the zig-zag lines of increasing size as they move towards the periphery, and report that as they grow larger, these lines move with increasing speed. This is precisely what one would expect from SD, that is, from a disturbance of function in a narrow band of the visual cortex, moving in the direction from the occipital pole to the temporal lobe, at constant speed. The increasing size and speed of the zig-zag lines is simply due to the fact that the linear millimetres of cortex related to 1 degree of visual field diminishes progressively as one moves from the field's central region to its periphery. Interestingly, it has been reported that in some cases, in which somatosensory symptoms precede the visual, these move from the periphery of vision towards the centre, and the speed of drift decreases as they approach the centre[5]. This is what is to be expected from a SD spreading from the somatosensory to the visual area, entering it near its temporal border, and proceeding towards the occipital pole.

It seems well established that an essential part of the mechanism of SD is transmission of a disturbance of cell membrane function, from one cell to its neighbours, by diffusion of substances in the extracellular fluid. Therefore, close proximity of the cells certainly facilitates SD. The density of packing of the cells varies with the region of the cortex, and is by far highest in the visual area. Thus, one would expect this area to be the most liable to suffer from SD, and in fact visual symptoms are the most frequent in the migraine aura. They may be the only symptoms (SD restricted to the visual area), and if they are not the only ones, they most often precede the other symptoms (SD originated in the visual area and propagated to other areas).

Somatosensory symptoms

Of the symptoms that may follow the visual ones, the most often reported by the patients are somatosensory symptoms. As with the visual symptoms, they indicate both abnormal activity (paraesthesiae) and depressed activity (anaesthesiae), and commonly move from one to another part of the body in conformity with the sequence of cortical representation. Considering that the farther a SD spreads, the more irregular may be its advancing edge, it can be expected from SD that any part of the somatosensory cortical strip along the postcentral gyrus may happen to be the first attained by a SD originated near the occipital pole. The probability of this part being related to sensation about the mouth or on the fingers would, of course, be higher, because of the greater extent of the cortical representation of these portions of the tactile field. Thus, what could be expected from SD actually occurs in the migraine aura: the somatosensory symptoms most commonly begin about the mouth or in the fingers, but may begin in any other part of the body.

Such remarks as have been made with regard to the visual and somatosensory symptoms may be applied to the other symptoms arising from the cerebral cortex during the migraine aura: auditory hallucinations or loss of hearing, dysphasia, motor disorders, etc.

In fact, the symptoms of cortical origin typical of the aura of migraine do not just resemble in some respects the symptoms that are to be expected from cortical SD; they are definitely similar in all respects. Objections to this statement generally derive from the kaleidoscope of migraine being contrasted with an oversimplified, lacunar, view of SD. Unless it is realized how complex may be the spread of SD over the extensive cerebral cortex of man, it would not be realized how well SD accounts for the immense variety of auras.

Evidence for SD occurring in migraine

Another kind of evidence supporting the view that SD occurs in migraine is given by the findings of Olesen and Lauritzen, and their colleagues. As is well known, in measurements of regional cerebral blood flow in patients with classic migraine, they found, during the attacks, a wave of reduced blood flow, originating in the posterior part of the brain and progressing anteriorly at a speed of the same order of magnitude as that of SD. This 'spreading oligemia', as they called it, reaches the somatosensory area after symptoms from that area have begun and persists there long after the symptoms have disappeared[6,7]. This led them to suggest that the spreading oligemia is a consequence of cortical SD, and to undertake parallel experiments on rats. In these experiments they found that a persistent, moderate reduction of cortical blood flow occurs in the wake of cortical SD, lasting at least 1 hour[8]. Following this up, they found that the blood flow response to changes in the arterial blood CO_2 tension is similarly reduced during the oligemia of migraine and of SD[9]. It should be noted that by using emission tomography after inhalation of Xenon-133, these authors were able to demonstrate that the blood flow changes of migraine are, like those of SD, purely cortical[10].

Further evidence for a relationship between migraine and SD is given by the similarity of the effect of CO_2 on the two phenomena. As is well known, Wolff and his colleagues have shown that inhalation, during the aura, of a mixture of 10% CO_2–90% O_2 produces clearing of the visual symptoms[11]. Intrigued by this finding, Gardner-Medwin undertook experiments on rats, and found that inhalation of such a mixture after initiation of a cortical SD can abolish its spread[12].

There is, in my judgement, sufficient evidence for it to be accepted that SD occurs in the aura of migraine, but direct proof is difficult. Reference should be made to other manifestations of SD, which are of use in detecting its presence. What we know of SD strongly suggests that there occurs a transient, nonspecific increase in the permeability of the membrane of the cells; this increase, the mechanism of which has not yet been clarified, leads to severe depolarization of the membrane, with flow of ions along electrochemical gradients into and out of the cells. It has already been established that K^+ leaves cells, its concentration in extracellular fluid rising to a level of between 30 and 60 mM, and that a large fraction of the Cl^-, Na^+ and Ca^{2+}, present in this fluid, and also water, enter the cells[13]. In relationship with membrane depolarization (of both neurons and glia) the local extracellular potential goes through a large change, the characteristic feature of which is a negative wave of 10–30 mV, lasting at least 0.5–1 min. In relationship with the water movement, physical properties of the tissue, such as its electric impedance and its luminous transmittance, go through large local changes. In relationship to the work of restoration of the normal distribution of ions and the integrity of the cell membranes, energy metabolism increases, and the tissue content of substances involved in this metabolism (O_2, glucose, lactic acid, etc) go through local changes. In the cerebral cortex, and apparently also in relation to its recovery from SD, the local blood flow increases considerably for about 1.5–3 min.

Notwithstanding all the manifestations of SD, a direct proof of its presence in man is, as said, difficult, the reason being that at any time they occur in only a small part of the cortex. Thus, the electric manifestations would escape detection by conventional electro-encephalography, in which the required spatial resolution is not achieved. Again, because of the limited spatial and temporal resolution of the available techniques for recording regional blood flow changes in man, the just mentioned brief increase in cortical blood flow would not show up clearly in the records.

To say that SD occurs in the aura of migraine is not to say that it is an essential link in the classic migraine headache process; this is a larger question, to be answered in the future. As pointed out by Gardner-Medwin[14], SD, though responsible for the focal neurological symptoms of the aura, may have no part in the process leading to the headache. This is possible but, even if it is so, SD remains relevant to migraine research. Even if SD and the process leading to the headache are distinct entities, their coincident occurrence shows that there are certain conditions which favour the triggering of one as well as of the other. Investigation of the conditions which favour the triggering of SD may therefore contribute to the elucidation of the determinants of the classic migraine attack.

There are several points in this connection.

(1) Experimenting on cats and macaque monkeys, Marshall and co-workers showed that, as a rule, SD does not occur immediately after exposure of the dorso-lateral surface of the brain, but that prolonged exposure to room air renders the cortical tissue susceptible to SD. This finding led to the notion that SD occurs only in badly damaged tissue. One wonders why this notion became so widespread, because the authors themselves stated that 'slow deterioration is not a necessary condition for the reaction'[15]. The reason for this statement is that the authors had found exceptional cases in which a typical SD occurred immediately after the exposure. These cases are of considerable significance, because they indicate that the incidence of SD may be influenced by factors (metabolic, hormonal, or others) operative under physiological circumstances in the intact organism—as is the incidence of a migraine attack. In being rendered susceptible to SD, the tissue is not necessarily rendered incapable of accomplishing its normal functional activities. This is demonstrated by the production of learned responses involving cortex fully susceptible to SD (and that had previously undergone a few SDs), as first observed by Bureš and co-workers in their experimental studies of animal behaviour, in which SD was used to achieve a temporary, functional 'decortication' in rats[16].

(2) Another erroneous notion is that the cortex of lower mammals is more susceptible to SD than that of primates. Actually, the relatively smooth cortex of small mammals is more susceptible to SD than the convoluted cortex of large mammals, but this is irrespective of the position of the mammal in the evolutionary tree. Cortical SD is as readily elicited in small primates (eg the marmosets and the squirrel monkey) as in rats or rabbits. There is not the slightest reason to doubt that the cortex of man may become susceptible to, and undergo SD, in the same manner as the cortex of other mammals. There is no report of properly carried out attempts to elicit SD in the neocortex of man, but there is a report, from experienced hands, of its elicitation in the hippocampus and caudate nucleus, during stereotactic surgery in patients with focal epilepsy[17].

(3) A third erroneous notion is that the elicitation of SD requires a noxious, violent stimulus applied to the cortex. On the contrary an important feature of SD is precisely that, if the tissue is highly susceptible, trifling stimuli suffice to trigger it and, in the very first studies of cortical SD, it was shown that just volleys of nervous impulses can trigger it[18,19]. This is the same as in migraine; as is well known, in patients whose attacks occur at fairly regular intervals, gross provocation may elicit a premature attack but, when an attack is nearly due, trifling stimuli will trigger it.

In unanaesthetized rats, cortical SD has effects on a variety of behaviour, and a well studied instance is that on thermoregulatory operant behaviour. The studies indicate clearly that a single, unilateral cortical SD makes the rat feel cold. Further investigation has demonstrated that this is due to overactivity of hypothalamic cold-sensitive neurons, resulting from withdrawal by the SD of a tonic inhibitory action that the frontal cortex exerts on these neurons[20,21]. It is to be expected that such effects, related to altered activity of subcortical centres in consequence of the suspension by SD of the inhibitory or excitatory action exerted on them by the cortex, will be more striking in a small brain than in a large. Nevertheless, it is not inadmissible that some subtle symptoms of the migraine aura, such as alterations of affect and mood, could thus be due to cortical SD.

The study of SD, especially since the introduction of fast-responding ion-selective micropipettes, has certainly brought about a considerable clarification of the underlying events, but the mechanism whereby the tissue becomes susceptible to SD is still completely unknown. We at least know various ways of rendering the tissue susceptible or insusceptible to SD, for example, the simplest of these is to alter the ionic make-up of extracellular fluid by applying to the surface of the tissue modified physiological saline solutions. Thus, the tissue is rendered susceptible, or its susceptibility raised, by solutions with increased $[K^+]$ or decreased $[Na Cl]$, relatively to ordinary Ringer's solution, or even with the Cl^- of the latter replaced by certain other anions, such as acetate or sulphate. Conversely, solutions with increased $[Mg^{2+}]$ or $[Na Cl]$, or, with the Na^+ replaced by certain other cations, such as choline or tetramethylammonium, lower the susceptibility, or even fully prevent the occurrence, of SD. In this connection, while cortical SD can be regularly elicited in animals under the deepest level of anaesthesia with barbiturates or urethane, surgical anaesthesia with ether or ketamine prevents the occurrence of the phenomenon.

Conclusion

In a recent essay on SD, the authors, following speculation on its biological purpose, say 'SD can also be regarded as an evolutionary accident, an inevitable by-product of the massive aggregation of interacting excitable elements, a minor risk, the elimination of which by a more conservative brain organization would be too costly'[22]. This applies equally well to migraine.

Up to the present, only very few studies directed specifically to the relation of SD and migraine have been carried out but, in view of the interest aroused by the finding of 'spreading oligemia', it is hoped that research in this direction will be more extensively undertaken.

References

1 Leão, A. A. P. (1944): Spreading depression of activity in the cerebral cortex. *J. Neurophysiol.*, **7**, 359–390.
2 Somjen, G. (1978): Metabolic and electrical correlates of the clearing of excess potassium in the cortex and spinal cord. In *Studies in neurophysiology*, ed. R. Porter, pp. 181–201. Cambridge: Cambridge University Press.
3 Lashley, K. S. (1941): Patterns of cerebral integration indicated by the scotomas of migraine. *Arch. Neurol. Psychiat., Chicago*, **46**, 331–339.
4 Hare, E. H. (1973): The duration of the fortification spectrum in migraine. In *Background to migraine*, ed. J. N. Cumings, pp. 93–98. London: W. Heinemann Medical Books.
5 Lord, G. D. A. (1986): Clinical characteristics of the migraine aura. In *The prelude to the migraine attack*, ed. W. K. Amery & A. Wauquier, pp. 87–98. London: Ballière Tindall.
6 Olesen, J., Larsen, B. & Lauritzen, M. (1981): Focal hyperemia followed by spreading oligemia and impaired activation of rCBF in classic migraine. *Ann. Neurol.* **9**, 344–352.
7 Lauritzen, M., Skyhøy Olsen, T., Larsen, N. A. & Paulson, O. B. (1983): Changes in regional cerebral blood flow during the course of classic migraine attacks. *Ann. Neurol.* **13**, 633–641.
8 Lauritzen, M., Jorgensen, M. B., Diemer, N. H., Gjedde, A. & Hansen, A. J. (1982): Persistent oligemia of rat cerebral cortex in the wake of spreading depression. *Ann. Neurol.* **12**, 469–474.
9 Lauritzen, M. (1984): Long-lasting reduction of cortical blood flow of the rat brain after spreading depression with preserved autoregulation and impaired CO_2 response. *J. Cereb. Blood Flow Metab.* **4**, 546–554.
10 Lauritzen, M. & Olesen, J. (1984): Regional cerebral blood flow during migraine attacks by Xenon-133 inhalation and emission tomography. *Brain* **107**, 457–461.
11 Marcussen, R. M. & Wolff, H. G. (1950): Studies on headache: (1) Effects of carbon dioxide-oxygen mixtures given during preheadache phase of the migraine attack; (2) Further analysis of the pain mechanisms in headache. *Arch. Neurol. Psychiat., Chicago* **63**, 42–51.
12 Gardner-Medwin, A. R. (1981): The effect of carbon dioxide and oxygen on Leão's spreading depression: evidence supporting a relationship to migraine. *J. Physiol., Lond.* **316**, 23P–24P.
13 Nicholson, C. & Kraig, R. P. (1981): The behaviour of extracellular ions during spreading depression. In *The application of ion-selective microelectrodes*, ed. T. Zeuthen, pp. 217–238. New York: Elsevier/North Holland Biomedical Press.
14 Gardner-Medwin, A. R. (1981): Possible roles of vertebrate neuroglia in potassium dynamics, spreading depression and migraine. *J. Exp. Biol.* **95**, 111–127.
15 Marshall, W. H. & Essig, C. F. (1951): Relation of air exposure of cortex to spreading depression of Leão. *J. Neurophysiol.* **14**, 265–273.
16 Bureš, J., Burešová, O. & Křivánek, J. (1974): *The mechanism and applications of Leão's spreading depression of electroencephalographic activity.* New York: Academic Press.
17 Šramka, M., Brožek, G., Bureš, J. & Nádvornik, P. (1977): Functional ablation by spreading depression. Possible use in human stereotaxic neurosurgery. *Appl. Neurophysiol.* **40**, 48–61.
18 Leão, A. A. P. & Morison, R. S. (1945): Propagation of spreading cortical depression. *J. Neurophysiol.* **8**, 33–46.
19 Marshall, W. H. (1959): Spreading cortical depression of Leão. *Physiol. Rev.* **39**, 239–279.
20 Shibata, M., Hori, T., Kiyohara, T. & Nakashima, T. (1983): Facilitation of thermoregulatory heating behaviour by single cortical spreading depression in the rat. *Physiol. Behav.* **31**, 651–656.
21 Hori, T., Shibata, M., Kiyohara, T. & Nakashima, T. (1982): Effects of cortical spreading depression on hypothalamic thermosensitive neurons in the rat. *Neurosci. Lett.* **32**, 47–52.
22 Bureš, J., Burešová, O. Křivánek, J. (1984): The meaning and significance of Leão's spreading depression. *An. Acad. Brasil. Cienc.* **56**, 385–400.

4

TOPOGRAPHIC EEG MAPPING IN

COMMON AND CLASSIC MIGRAINE

DURING AND BETWEEN ATTACKS

J. Schoenen,* B. Jamart and P. J. Delwaide

Headache Clinic and Department of Neurology-Clinical Neurophysiology, University of Liege, Hôpital de Bavière, 66 Boulevard de la Constitution, B-4020 Liege, Belgium

Summary

Thirty-three migraineurs underwent spectral analysis and topographic EEG mapping. In a case of an induced attack of classic migraine with a complex aura, posterior-anterior spreading of slow activities contralateral to the neurological signs was the prominent finding. This preceded the first clinical symptom and outlasted the attack for at least 24 h. Another patient who developed a spontaneous attack of classic migraine with a visual aura had unilateral reduction of α and, to a lesser degree, of θ power. Six other classic migraineurs were studied between 10 days and 4 months after their last attack; their EEG analyses were normal. In 17 out of 20 patients recorded during an attack of common migraine the only abnormality was markedly reduced α power over one occipital region, usually on the side of the headache. Fourteen of these had concomitantly reduction of θ power in the same location. In all patients, except one, restudied at least 7 days after an attack EEG asymmetries had disappeared. Preliminary results obtained in two cases of menstrual migraine might indicate that electrophysiologic changes can precede the common migraine attack, since slight unilateral depression of α activity was found 24 h before the headache.

Using spectral analysis and topographic mapping, unilateral EEG changes can thus be detected during attacks of both classic and common migraine. The posterior-anterior spreading of slow activities during an induced attack of classic migraine has striking temporal and spatial similarities, with the 'spreading oligemia' reported by Olesen *et al.* (1981)[28]. However, the findings in the case of classic migraine with a strictly visual aura are identical to those observed in most common migraineurs during the attack, ie unilateral reduction of α (and θ) power. This suggests that common, as classic, migraine is associated with

*Senior Research Associate of the NFSR (Belgium).

unilateral disturbances of cortical electrogenesis, which might reflect metabolic abnormalities. The two migraine entities might thus have similar underlying pathophysiologic mechanisms. Whether or not these are related to Leão's spreading depression, where depression of cortical electrical activity is a well-known feature, remains to be determined.

Introduction

According to the literature, the incidence of EEG abnormalities in migraineurs varies between 20%[1] and 70%[2]. Most authors agree that the standard EEG in migraine is non-specific and of poor diagnostic aid[3-6]. In common migraine, the majority of EEG studies have been performed between attacks, 'immature'[7] or 'dysrhythmic'[8-10] patterns being the major findings. Golla & Winter[11] first reported a more consistent EEG abnormality: persistent photic drive to flicker at flash rates exceeding 18 to 20 Hz. Subsequently, this was confirmed in a greater number of patients[12] and with spectral analysis[13,14].

On the other hand, focal EEG slowing is a common finding during attacks of classic migraine[10,15-23], which is usually contralateral to the neurological signs and may outlast the attack for hours or days[19]. The consistency of EEG changes during classic migraine has been questioned by Lauritzen *et al.*[24], who found abnormalities in only two out of ten patients.

Quantitative EEG studies using computer assisted spectral analysis have been performed in a small number of migraineurs. Interhemispheric asymmetrics of α power and α frequency were reported in attack-free intervals[26]. Two brief reports[26,27] mention posterior-anterior spreading of unilateral slow activity in a patient undergoing topographic EEG mapping during an attack of classic migraine.

There is some analogy between EEG abnormalities and cerebral blood flow changes in migraine. Both are prominent during attacks of classic migraine, where spreading unilateral oligemia was reported[28,29] and both may be absent during common migraine[30,31]. The pathophysiologic similarity between these two entities has therefore been questioned[31]. However, most common migraineurs in the forementioned EEG studies were recorded between attacks and with routine techniques. It might thus be premature to conclude that there are no consistent electrophysiologic abnormalities. Modern electrophysiologic techniques offer an excellent opportunity to reinvestigate this question.

We report here the results obtained with such techniques, ie spectral analysis and topographic EEG mapping, in 25 common and eight classic migraineurs during and between attacks.

Materials and methods

The Cadwell 8400 System was used for all patients. The EEG was recorded from 16 channels with Cz as a reference. The following leads of the 10/20 montage were analyzed: Fp1, F7, T3, T5, O1, P3, C3, F3, Fp2, F8, T4, T6, O2, P4, C4 and F4. Traces and colour maps of EEG activity were computed after FFT analyses over 7 s epochs in four different frequency bands: δ, 0.5–3.5 Hz; θ, 4–7.5 Hz; α, 8–12.5 Hz; β, 13–16 Hz. Absolute power and voltage of each frequency band were averaged over 5 min with a decay of eight. Print-outs of colour maps and FFT traces were obtained using an Anadex colour printer and an Oki Data printer respectively.

All recordings were made in a supine position with eyes closed in a light dimmed room. Standard paper EEGs were always recorded during the brain mapping procedure.

Thirty-three outpatients of both sexes were included in the study. They were diagnosed as having classic ($n = 7$) or common ($n = 24$) migraine according to the classification of the Ad Hoc Committee (1962)[32] and to Vahlquist's criteria[33,34]. One patient had attacks of both classic and common migraine. One patient had complicated migraine with a persisting neurological deficit. Nine common migraineurs were recorded during an attack as well as in a headache free interval at least 7 days after an attack. Thirteen common migraineurs were studied only during an attack. Three female patients underwent the procedure just before or during a menstrual migraine. Sequential recordings were performed during the course of an attack of classic migraine in two patients. One had a spontaneous attack with a visual aura. The other had his attack triggered by drinking 1 litre of Coke which was known to be a usual trigger factor; he had a more complex neurological aura. Six classic migraineurs were recorded between 10 days and 4 months after an attack, the patient with complicated migraine during persistent left hemiparesis after the headache phase. Headache intensity was graded on a four point scale, three representing a severe headache that does not allow normal activity.

Results

Classic migraine

Results differed slightly between the two patients recorded during an attack of classic migraine (Table 1). In patient no. 1, there was a more than 50% reduction of α power in right parieto-occipital regions, while he was experiencing a scintillating scotoma in the left visual field. Theta activity was also reduced, though to a lesser degree, in the same area. These findings remained unchanged during right hemicrania after disappearance of the visual. A less than 50% reduction of α power persisted over the right posterior leads 24 h after the attack, while EEG mapping disclosed symmetrical activity 4 days later.

In patient no. 2, slight increase in θ power and voltage was visible in the left occipital region 30 min after ingestion of Coke. Shortly thereafter he had brief teichopsias

Table 1. *Topographic EEG mapping in classic migraine.*

Patient	Timing	*Attack* Neurological signs	Headache	EEG mappping
	(Spontaneous)			
1. Sch...J.	+ 10 min	L. scintillating scotoma	0	R↓↓α, ↓θ
♂ 38 y.o.	+ 30 min	0	R	R↓↓α, ↓θ
	+ 90 min	0	R	R↓α
	+ 24 h	0	0	R↓α
	+ 4 day	0	0	R = L
	(after Coke 1l.)			
2. Fra...J.	+ 30 min	0	0	L↑θ
♂ 20 y.o.	+ 120 min	R. cheiro-oral parasthesias; dysphagia	0	L↑↑θ, ↓α
	+ 140 min	R. tongue parasthesias	L	L↑↑θ, ↑δ, ↓↓α
	+ 150 min	0	L	L↑θ, ↑θ, ↓α
	+ 120 min	0	0	L↑θ, ↓↓α
	+ 24 h	0	0	L↑θ, R = Lα

y.o., years old; L, left; R, right.

in the right visual field. When he experienced marked dysphasia and right cheiro-oral parasthesias, EEG mapping showed marked increase of θ activity over the left hemisphere spreading up to the temporal area (Fig. 1). Concomitantly there was reduction of α power on the same side. At the beginning of the headache phase, unilateral increase of θ and decrease of α activities persisted, but there was in addition increased δ activity over the lcft hcmisphere. The increase of slow activities progressively diminished at the end of the headache, but persisted long after the attack as did the reduction of α activity.

Spectral EEG analysis and mapping showed no significant asymmetries of α, θ or δ activities in six classic migraineurs recorded at a distance from an attack. In the patient with complicated migraine and persistent left hemiparesis, there was reduced α and increased θ-δ activity over the right hemisphere. The patient had a right hypodense lesion on CT-Scan.

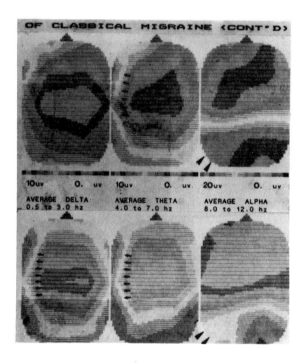

Fig. 1. *Induced attack of classical migraine (patient no. 2). The topographic maps of δ, θ, and α voltage are* shown at 120 minutes after ingestion of Coke (upper traces), when the patient has dysphasia and right cheiro-oral paresthesias, and at 140 minutes (lower traces), when he experiences a left hemicrania. Reduction of posterior α voltage on the left (arrowheads) and increase of δ and θ power over the left hemisphere (arrows) can be seen. In this black and white reproduction, the darker shadings represent the higher power values, the lighter the lower values (see scale).

Common migraine

Table 2 summarizes our results in nine common migraineurs recorded during and between attacks. In six patients with unilateral headache, EEG analysis disclosed a marked (more than 50%) reduction of parieto-occipital alpha power on the side of the headache. Theta power was moderately reduced over the same leads in five of them (Fig. 2). Only patient no. 4 had slightly increased θ activity. In all patients, except no. 9, no significant asymmetry of alpha or theta power was apparent during headache free intervals but, in two patients (no. 5 and 6), α and θ asymmetries persisted respectively 24 and 48 h after the attack. Two patients experienced bilateral headaches, more intense on the left side; both had reduced α and θ power over the right parieto-occipital region, which normalized after the attack.

Among common migraineurs recorded only during an attack (Table 3), eight had a moderate to marked reduction of posterior alpha activity on the side of the headache. Six of these had concomitant reduction, two (no. 7 and 8) increase of θ activity. In two patients

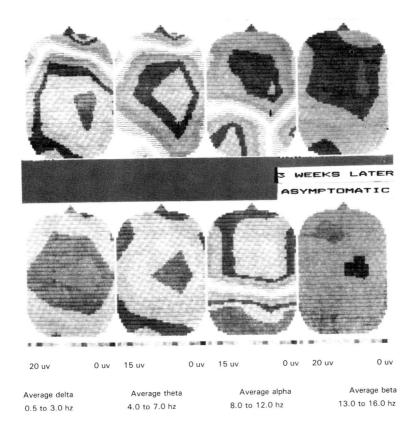

| 20 uv | 0 uv | 15 uv | 0 uv | 15 uv | 0 uv | 20 uv | 0 uv |

| Average delta | Average theta | Average alpha | Average beta |
| 0.5 to 3.0 hz | 4.0 to 7.0 hz | 8.0 to 12.0 hz | 13.0 to 16.0 hz |

Fig. 2. *Spontaneous attack of common migraine.* During the attack with right hemicrania (upper traces), there is a reduction of α voltage over the right parieto-occipital cortex (arrow) and, to a lesser degree, of θ and δ power. Three weeks later (lower traces), when the patient has no symptoms, the topographic EEG map is within normal limits.

Table 2. *Topographic EEG mapping in common migraine.* 1. Patients recorded during and between attacks.

Patient	Duration	Headache Intensity	Localization	EEG mapping During	Between
1. Sch...J. ♂ 38 y.o.	2 h	2	R	R⇊α, ↓θ	R = L
2. Hal...M. ♀ 30 y.o.	6 h	3	R	R⇊α, ⇊θδ	R = L
3. D'Ha...Cl. ♀ 28 y.o.	7 h	1	R	R⇊α, ↓θ	R = L
4. Jeh...JM. ♂ 27 y.o.	15 h	2	L	L↓α, ↑θ	L = R
5. Pon...R. ♀ 26 y.o.	3 h	2	L	L⇊α, ↓θ	L = R
	24 h after	0	(L)	L⇊α, ↓θ	
6. Dec...M. ♀ 35 y.o.	48 h after	0	(L)	L↓α, ↓θ	L = R
7. Mon...G. ♀ 34 y.o.	8 h	3	L > R	R⇊α, ↓θ	R = L
8. Chi...A. ♂ 40 y.o.	3 h	2	L > R	R↓α, ↓θ	R = L
9. Jor...J. ♀ 24 y.o.	5 h	1	R	R⇊α, ↓θ	R slight ↓α

y.o., years old; L, left; R, right.

(no. 9 and 10) with bilateral headache, more intense on the left side, there was increased left posterior θ activity in one, reduced left posterior α and θ activity in the other. One patient (no. 11) with right hemicrania had normal findings. Two patients (no. 12 and 13) recorded 2 and 24 h after an attack showed persistent asymmetries of α and/or θ power.

Three patients with menstrual migraine were studied 1 day before or on the day the headache started (Table 4). In two patients (no. 1 and 2) unilateral reduction of α power was present 24 h before the attack.

There was no obvious correlation between severity of EEG asymmetries and intensity of the headache or duration of the attack (see Tables 2 and 3). In most patients studied here the routine paper EEG would have been considered within normal limits.

Table 3. *Topographic EEG mapping in common migraine*. 2. Patients recorded during attacks.

Patient	Duration	Headache Intensity	Localization	EEG mapping
1. God...M.Cl ♀ 25 y.o.	3 h	2	R	R↓↓α, ↓θ
2. Mas...N. ♀ 23 y.o.	5 h	1	R	R↓↓α, ↓θ
3. Cla...M. ♀ 39 y.o.	4 h	2	R	R↓α, ↓θ
4. Mar...A. ♀ 35 y.o.	7 h	1	R	R↓α, ↓θ
5. Qui...G. ♀ 40 y.o.	7 h	2	R	R↓α, ↓θ
6. Hor...D. ♂ 24 y.o.	5 h	2	L	L↓α, ↓θ
7. Fre...L. ♀ 31 y.o.	10 h	2	L	L↓α, ↑θ
8. Sch...H. ♀ 37 y.o.	2 h	1	L	L↓α, ↓θ
9. Tin...L. ♀ 28 y.o.	6 h	2	L > R	L↑θ
10. Aya...J. ♀ 39 y.o.	5 h	2	L > R	L↓α, ↓θ
11. Leg...N. ♀ 25 y.o.	3 h	1	R	R = L
12. Lho...A. ♀ 50 y.o.	2 h after	0	(L)	R↓α, ↓θ
13. Aub...R. ♂ 40 y.o.	24 h after	0	(L)	L↑θ

y.o., years old; L, left; R, right.

Eye opening or hyperventilation did not cancel the observed EEG asymmetries. Pharmacologic treatments, such as inhalation of orciprenaline or i.v. administration of dihydroergotamine, produced no consistent effects.

Discussion

As reported in the majority of studies available in the literature[10,15-23] we found marked EEG change on the side of the presumed cerebral dysfunctioning in two classic migraineurs during an attack, but there were some striking differences between the two patients. In patient no. 2, who had an induced attack with a complex aura, there was simultaneously reduction of α power and increase of $\theta-\delta$ power contralateral to the neurological symptoms.

Table 4. *Topographic EEG mapping in common migraine.* 3. Menstrual migraine.

| | *Headache* | | *EEG mapping* | |
| | *Beginning* | | | |
Patient	*(day of menses)*	*Localization*	*Day of menses*	*Finding*
1. Mey...M. ♀ 32 y.o.	+2	R	+1	R⇊α, ↓θ
2. Bri...S. ♀ 29 y.o.	+1	R+L	−1	L↓α
3. Ton...L. ♀ 25 y.o.	+3	R	+3	R=L

y.o., years old; L, left; R, right.

Discrete unilateral slow activities appeared before the first clinical sign and topographic EEG mapping suggested that they spread posterior-anteriorly in the course of the attack. The temporal and spatial characteristics of EEG abnormalities are thus very similar to those of cerebral blood flow changes recorded with SPECT[29]. Moreover, lateralized EEG slowing outlasted the attack for at least 24 h, as reported by others[19].

In contradistinction, patient no. 1, who developed a spontaneous attack with a strictly visual aura, had parallel unilateral reduction of α and θ power. This was present during the aura, during the headache on the same side as the pain and outlasted the attack for 24 h. Our findings in this patient differ from those reported by others[15,16,19] of unilateral increase of slow activities during attacks with visual auras but they are similar to those we will discuss later in common migraine. Interestingly, patient no. 1 had rare attacks of classic migraine with scintillating scotomata and more frequent attacks of common migraine without any aura. Quantitative and topographic EEG analyses were identical during both types of attacks.

The most original results of this study were found in the group of common migraineurs. Seventeen out of 20 patients recorded at various stages during an attack had reduction of α power over one occipital region and 14 of these concomitant reduction of θ power. This contrasts with most previous routine EEG studies in common migraine, where changes, if present at all, are usually not lateralized and nonspecific, as mentioned earlier. It is not clear from most publications if, and how many patients are studied during an attack. It is well-known that α activity may be asymmetric on the normal adult EEG but, if so, the higher amplitude is usually found over the non-dominant hemisphere[4]. All the patients included in this study, except three, were right-handed, while in most instances (11 of 17) the lower α activity was on the right side. Moreover, in seven out of eight patients studied during and between attacks symmetric α power returned in the headache free interval. It is thus most unlikely that physiologic EEG asymmetries related to hemispheric dominance may account for our findings, but it must be kept in mind that focal extracerebral mass lesions, eg meningiomas or subdural hematomas, may be responsible for reduced α activity over one hemisphere[4].

In our patient population there is a good correlation between the side of headache and that of reduced α activity (15 out of 18 cases). This result might be biased, since up to now we have mainly selected patients with unilateral headaches. Out of four cases with bilateral, but asymmetric pain, two had EEG changes on the side of maximal intensity of pain, two on the other side. We are now analyzing more patients with bilateral headaches.

As in classic migraine, asymmetry of the EEG in common migraine might persist up to 24 or even 48 h after the attack. This is suggested by our findings in four patients, but needs further investigation. In addition, preliminary results obtained in two cases of menstrual migraine might indicate that electrophysiologic changes can precede the attack, since reduced unilateral α activity was visible 24 h before the headache respectively one day before and on the first day of menses.

In conclusion, with spectral analysis and topographic mapping, unilateral EEG changes can be detected during attacks of classic, but also of common, migraine. The posterior-anterior spreading of slow activities during an induced attack of classic migraine described here, and mentioned by others[26,27], has striking temporal and spatial similarities with the 'spreading oligemia' reported by Olesen *et al.*[29,30]. During attacks of common migraine, posterior α power is unilaterally decreased, usually on the side of headache. This is not accompanied by increased slow activity as reported in some cases of classic migraine[16,17,19], cerebral ischemia[34], one of our classic migraineurs or our observation of complicated migraine, but rather by a decrease of θ power in the same cortical area. Asymmetry of α power and α frequency were among the abnormal features in 50% of migraineurs in a study using EEG computer analysis which did not include patients having an attack during the recording[25]. Moreover, amplitude reduction of the visual evoked potential on the side of the headache was described during migraine attacks[35,36]. Taken together, these findings suggest that common, as well as classic, migraine is associated with unilateral disturbances of cortical electrogenesis, which might reflect metabolic abnormalities. The two migraine entities might thus have similar underlying pathophysiologic mechanisms. They could differ by the severity of cortical dysfunction, which reaches the threshold of clinical expression in classic, but not in common, migraine. The similarity between common and classic migraine is further underlined by the identical EEG abnormalities we found in the same patient during both types of attacks and by recent reports of regional cerebral blood flow changes during attacks of common migraine[37]. Finally, it is worth mentioning that depression of cortical electrical activity is a well-known feature of spreading depression[38,39] which could explain the blood flow changes in classic migraine[40]. Whether spreading depression plays a role in the pathogenesis of migraine remains however to be determined.

References

1 Giel, R., De Vlieger, M. & Van Vliet, A. G. (1966): Headache and the EEG. *Electroenceph. Clin. Neurophysiol.* **21**, 492–495.
2 Kooi, K. A., Rajput, A. G. & De Jong, R. N. (1965): Significance of the paroxysmal electro-encephalogram in the patient with migraine. In *Proceedings of the 6th Congress on electroencephalography and clinical neurophysiology*, pp. 263–266. Vienna: Verlad der Wiener Medizinischen Akademi.
3 Magnus, O. (1968): De waarde van de electro-encephalographie en de echo-encephalographie voor het onderzoek van patienten met hoofdpijn. *Ned. T. Geneesk.* **140**, 718–728.
4 Kiloh, L. G., McComas, A. J. & Osselton, J. W. (1972): *Clinical electroencephalography*, 3rd edn pp. 55 & 179. London: Butterworths.
5 Goldensohn, E. S. (1976): Paroxysmal and other features of the electroencephalogram in migraine. *Res. Clin. Stud. Headache* **4**, 118–128.
6 Aminoff, M. J. (1980): Electrodiagnosis in clinical neurology, 1st edn, p. 55. New York: Churchill Livingstone.
7 Selby, G. & Lance, J. W. (1960): Observations on 500 cases of migraine and allied vascular headache. *J. Neurol. Neurosurg. Psychiat.* **23**, 23.
8 Dow, D. J. & Whitty, C. W. (1947): Electroencephalographic changes in migraine. *Lancet* **ii**, 52–54.
9 Weil, A. A. (1952): EEG findings in a certain type of psychosomatic headache: dysrhythmic migraine. *EEG Clin. Neurophysiol.* **4**, 181.
10 Hockaday, J. M. & Whitty, C. W. (1969): Factors determining the electroencephalogram in migraine: a study of 520 patients, according to clinical type of migraine. *Brain* **92**, 769.
11 Golla, F. L. & Winter, A. L. (1959): Analysis of cerebral responses to flicker in patients complaining of episodic headache. *Electroenceph. Clin. Neurophysiol.* **11**, 539–549.
12 Smyth, V. D. & Winter, A. L. (1964): The EEG in migraine. *Electroenceph. Clin. Neurophysiol.* **16**, 194–202.
13 Simon, R. H., Zimmerman, A. W., Tasman, A. H. & Hale, M. S. (1982): Spectral analysis of photic stimulation in migraine. *Electroenceph. Clin. Neurophysiol.* **53**, 270–276.

14 Nyrke, T. Lang, A. H. (1982): Spectral analysis of visual potentials evoked by sine wave modulated light in migraine. *Electroenceph. Clin. Neurophysiol.* **53**, 436–442.

15 Engel, G. L., Webb, J. B., Ferris, E. B., Romano, J., Ryder, H. Blankenhorn, M. A. (1944): A migraine like syndrome complicating decompression sickness. *War Med.* **5**, 304.

16 Engel, G. L., Ferris, E. B. Jr & Romano, J. (1945): Focal electroencephalographic changes during the scotomas of migraine. *Am. J. Med. Sci.* **209**, 650–657.

17 Engel, G. L., Hamburger, W. W., Reiser, M. & Plunkett, J. (1953): Electroencephalographic and psychological studies of a case of migraine with severe preheadache phenomena. *Psychom. Med.* **15**, 337–348.

18 Symonds, C. L. (1951): Migrainous variants. *Trans. Med. Soc. Lond.* **67**, 237–250.

19 Camp, W. A. & Wolff, H. G. (1961): Studies on headache. Electro-encephalographic abnormalities in patients with vascular headache of the migraine type. *Arch. Neurol.* **4**, 475.

20 Slatter, K. H. (1968): Some clinical and EEG findings in patients with migraine. *Brain* **91**, 85–98.

21 Parsonage, M. J. (1975): Electroencephalographic studies in migraine. In *Modern topics in migraine* J. Pearce pp. 72–84. London: Heinemann Medical.

22 Matthis, H., Perriand, P., Jckiel, M. & Beaumanoir, A. (1980): Serial EEG records during migrainous attacks. In EEG and clinical neurophysiology, (International Congress Series 526) pp. 267–172. eds H. Lechner & A. Aranibar. Excerpta Medica.

23 Christiani, K., Kolker, B. & Soyka, D. (1980): EEG findings in migraine accompagnée. In *EEG and clinical neurophysiology*, (International Congress Series 526) pp. 259–266, eds H. Lechner & A. Aranibar. Amsterdam: Excerpta Medica.

24 Lauritzen, M., Trojaborg, W. & Olesen, J. (1981): EEG during attacks of common and classical migraine. *Cephalalgia* **1**, 63–66.

25 Jonkman, E. J. & Lelieveld, M. H. (1981): EEG computer analysis in patients with migraine. *Electroenceph. Clin. Neurophysiol.* **52**, 652–655.

26 Agnoli, A., Martucci, N. & Manna, V. (1985): Complicated and common migraine: EEG mapping and computed telethermography. *Headache* **25**, 452.

27 Bès, A., Soulages, X., Guell, A., Géraud, G. & Arné-Bès, M. C. (1985): Données nouvelles sur le débit sanguin cérébral dans la migraine. In *Migraines et céphalées*, pp. 43–52. Grec Sandoz Editions.

28 Olesen, J., Larsen, B. & Lauritzen, M. (1981): Focal hyperemia followed by spreading oligemia and impaired activation of r CBF in classic migraine. *Ann. Neurol.* **9**, 344–352.

29 Lauritzen, M. & Olesen, J. (1984): Regional cerebral blood flow during migraine attacks by Xenon-133 inhalation and emission tomography. *Brain* **104**, 447–467.

30 Olesen, J., Lauritzen, M., Tfelt-Hansen, P., Henriksen, L. & Larsen, B. (1982): Spreading cerebral oligemia in classical and normal cerebral blood flow in common migraine. *Headache* **22**, 242–248.

31 Olesen, J., Tfelt-Hansen, P., Henriksen, L. & Larsen, B. (1981): The common migraine attack may not be initiated by cerebral ischemia. *Lancet* **ii**, 438–440.

32 Ad Hoc Committee on Classification of Headache. (1962): Classification of Headache. *J. Am. Med. Ass.* **179**, 717–718.

33 Vahlquist, B. (1953): Migraine in children. *Int. Arch. Allergy* **7**, 348–355.

34 Van Huffelen, A. C., Poortvliet, D. C. J., Van der Wulp, C. J. & Magnus, O. (1980): Quantitative EEG in cerebral ischemia. In *EEG and clinical neurophysiology, International Congress Series 526* eds H. Lechner & A. Aranibar pp. 115–143. Amsterdam: Excerpta Medica.

35 Regan, D. & Heron, J. R. (1970): Simultaneous recording of visual evoked potentials from the left and right hemisphere in migraine. In *Background to migraine* ed. T. Cochrane, p. 66. London: Heinemann.

36 Mac Lean, C., Appenzeller, O., Cordourdo, J. T. & Rhodes, J. (1975): Flash evoked potentials in migraine. *Headache* **14**, 193–198.

37 Soulages, X., Geraud, G., Guell, A. & Bès, A. (1986): Modifications du débit sanguin cérébral au cours des crises de migraine. Abstract. Société Française d'Etudes des Migraines et Céphalées. p. 13.

38 Leão, A. A. (1944): Spreading depression of activity in cerebral cortex. *J. Neurophysiol.* **7**, 359–390.

39 Leão, A. A. & Morrison, R. S. (1945): Propagation of spreading cortical depression. *J. Neurophysiol.* **8**, 33–45.

40 Lauritzen, M. (1984): Spreading cortical depression in migraine. In *The pharmacological basis of migraine therapy*, ed. W. K. Amery, J. M. Van Nueten & A. Wauqnier pp. 149–160. London: Pitman.

5

DOES MIGRAINE RESULT FROM A DECREASE IN TRANSMEMBRANE POTASSIUM CONDUCTANCE?

Helen L. Leathard and N. K. Eccles

Department of Pharmacology, Charing Cross & Westminster Medical School, St Dunstan's Road, London W6 8RF, UK

Summary

In human intracranial artery and uterine vein spiral strips, 17 β-oestradiol or progesterone (1 μM) preferentially reduced contraction elicited by concentrations of potassium chloride ($\leqslant 30$ mM) lower than the intracellular concentration, suggesting that the hormones reduced vascular contractility by increasing transmembrane potassium conductance, as they do in myometrium. Considering these findings in the context of menstrually-related migraine, it seems possible that, in susceptible subjects, migraine occurs when falling levels of the hormones leads to a decrease in membrane potassium conductance, which allows cerebral vascular muscle (and probably also neurones) to become more reactive to a wide range of stimuli, such as noradrenaline, 5-hydroxytryptamine and prostaglandins. The hypothesis that migraine is triggered by a transient or intermittent decrease in membrane potassium channel conductance is unlikely to be restricted to the menstrually-related situation. It is compatible with other current theories of migraine aetiology and might provide a mechanism for the prophylactic action of propranolol in migraine.

Introduction

In recent studies, 17 β-oestradiol or progesterone, at concentrations occurring in pregnancy and at the peaks of menstrual cyclic variations, suppressed spontaneous and evoked contractions of human cerebral arterial muscle strips[1] (and unpublished). The non-selective nature of this inhibition suggests that either transmembrane potassium conductance is being increased, thus stabilizing the vascular smooth muscle cell membranes, or calcium influx or intracellular action is being inhibited, reducing vascular contractility. The first alternative seems probable, because it is the mechanism of the increase in myometrial resting membrane potential and associated reduction in contractility mediated by these hormones during

35

Table 1. *Results of experiments on three spirally-cut strips, of human intracranial arteries, expressed as percentages of contractions to KCl obtained before >60 min incubation with the hormones or control solution.*

	Control propylene glycol 1:1000	17 β-oestradiol 10 μg/ml (37 μM)	Progesterone 10 μg/ml (32 μM)
KCl (27 mM)	50	0	0
KCl (108 mM)	70	15	22

Table 2. *Results of experiments on ten spirally-cut strips of human intracranial arteries and three spirally-cut uterine veins, expressed as in Table 1.*

	Control propylene glycol 1:500		17 β-oestradiol 1 μM		Progesterone 1 μM	
	n	mean	n	mean	n	mean
KCl (<30 mM)	5	75	4	66	4	66
KCl (90 mM)	4	84	3	83	2	94
NA (150–300 nM)	5	102	4	94	3	84

pregnancy[2]. Experiments to differentiate these possible mechanisms have therefore been conducted, following the theory of Clapham and Wilson[3] that, in isolated vascular muscle strips, a drug which increases potassium channel conductance will only inhibit contractions to extracellular potassium concentrations which are lower than those occurring intracellularly, whereas a calcium 'antagonist' will also reduce contractions caused by higher extracellular potassium ion concentrations.

Materials and methods

Strips of human cerebral arteries and uterine veins, which respond similarly, were set-up as described by Eccles & Leathard (1985). Briefly, human cerebral arteries (circle of Willis and branches) were obtained from autopsies carried out 24–96 h after death and veins were obtained fresh from surgical resections of the uterus. The vessels were dissected free of connective tissue and fat and used on the same day or stored overnight at 4°C. Immediately before setting up they were cut into helical strips (3–4 cm length × 2–4 mm width) which were suspended under a load of 0.5 g in isolated organ baths in Krebs' solution at 37°C bubbled with 5% CO_2 in O_2. Responses were recorded through isotonic transducers connected to pen recorders.

The strips were left for 1–2 h to equilibrate before any drugs were added and were judged to have settled down when consecutive doses of noradrenaline (NA) gave consistent submaximal contractions. Contractions were evoked using NA or potassium chloride (KCl) for 1 or 2 min.

The effects of 1 h incubation with 17 β-oestradiol or progesterone were recorded on submaximal contractions to NA and on contractions to low (≤30 mM) and high (>90 mM) concentrations of KCl.

The drugs used were: $(-)$—noradrenaline bitartrate (Levophed), potassium chloride, progesterone and 17 β-oestradiol. Dilutions of NA were made up in 0.9% NaCl containing 100 μg/ml ascorbic acid. KCl was dissolved in distilled water. The sex hormones were dissolved in small volumes of propylene glycol and added to the Krebs' solution reservoirs at a dilution of 1 in 1000 or 1 in 500. Time-matched control experiments were carried out using appropriate concentrations of propylene glycol.

Results

Due to unpredictable and limited availability of the experimental material, the results presented here are only preliminary findings. In one group of experiments (Table 1), 10 μg/ml of either 17 β-oestradiol (37 μM) and progesterone (32 μM) abolished contractions to the low concentration of KCl and substantially inhibited contractions to the high concentration, providing limited evidence of a selective action on potassium channels. Further experiments were therefore carried out using a lower (1 μM) concentration of the hormones, and the results of these are summarized in Table 2. In 13 experiments (ten intracranial artery strips and three urterine vein strips) the hormones clearly reduced contractions to low concentrations of KCl more than contractions to KCl in high concentrations or to NA. Contractions to low concentrations of KCl were also reduced in the control experiments, although less than with the hormones, emphasizing the need for time-matched controls in these studies.

Discussion

Although the results obtained so far are insufficient for statistical analysis, they are consistent with previously published findings[1] and with the possibility that 1 μM 17 β-oestradiol or progesterone preferentially increases transmembrane potassium conductance whereas > 30-fold higher concentrations of either hormone also suppresses contractility by a non-selective mechanism.

Considering these studies in the context of menstrually-related migraine, it seems possible that in susceptible people migraine occurs when falling levels of the hormones (eg progesterone from around 8 ng/ml to < 1 ng/ml premenstrually) leads to a decrease in membrane potassium conductance, which allows cerebral vascular muscle (and probably other tissues such as neurones) to become more reactive to a wide range of stimuli including noradrenaline, 5-hydroxytryptamine and some prostaglandins. This mechanism could explain the migraine-triggering action of vasoactive amines and the therapeutic usefulness of 5-hydroxytryptamine antagonists and inhibitors of prostaglandin synthesis.

The reason why cerebral arteries are more susceptible to transient changes in membrane potassium conductance than other major arteries is probably related to the unique electrophysiological properties of their smooth muscle cells. From the observations of Eccles & Leathard[1] (and unpublished) and those summarized by Creed[4], peripheral arterial muscle has a resting membrane potential around -60 mV, mainly because of its high potassium conductance. It shows little or no inherent tone, is relatively insensitive to 5-hydroxytryptamine and is 'protected' from over-reactivity because small depolarizations (< 10 mV) further increase potassium conductance and decrease membrane resistance. In contrast, muscle from the carotid artery, from which the cerebral circulation is derived, behaves more like venous muscle, having a lower potassium conductance and a resting membrane potential of -44 mV, which is regulated mainly by electrogenic transport processes. Both human intracranial arteries and peripheral veins tend to have inherent muscle tone and be relatively sensitive to 5-hydroxytryptamine, and this is why uterine veins have been included in the present study.

The possibility that migraine is triggered by a transient or intermittent decrease in membrane potassium channel conductance is unlikely to be restricted to the menstrually-related situation, and is compatible with other current theories of migraine aetiology. For example acording to Olesen[5], the spreading depression of Leão, which leads to blood flow changes similar to those seen in classic migraine, is easily elicited by local application of high concentrations of potassium ions or other procedures which all seem able to increase potassium conductance. These apparently contradictory effects of altering vascular muscle membrane potassium conductance are readily explicable, because an increase in outward potassium current will of itself hyperpolarize and stabilize the membrane, but unless this is rapidly removed the extracellular concentration will rise sufficiently to open voltage-operated calcium channels and produce contraction. If the effects observed in these vascular preparations also occur in central neurones and glia, the potassium channel hypothesis is also compatible with the detailed analysis of the pathomechanism of migraine by Bruyn[6]. Finally, this hypothesis might provide a mechanism of the prophylactic action of propranolol in migraine because, in addition to its β-adrenoceptor blocking activity, low concentrations of this substance have been shown to increase background outward potassium current, at least in canine cardiac Purkinje fibres.

Acknowledgement—We thank the histopathologists and surgeons of Charing Cross Hospital for their help in obtaining specimens, and the Migraine Trust for financial support.

References

1 Eccles, N. K. & Leathard, H. L. (1985): 17 β-oestradiol and progesterone on human vascular reactivity. In *Migraine, clinical and research advances*, ed. F. Clifford Rose, pp. 56–65. Basel: Karger.
2 Abe, Y. (1970): The hormonal control and the effects of drugs and ions on the electrical and mechanical activity of the uterus. In *Smooth muscle*, ed. E. Bulbring *et al*. pp. 396–417. London: Edward Arnold.
3 Clapham, J. C. & Wilson, C. (1986): Effects of the novel anti-hypertensive agent BRL 34915 in comparison with nifedipine on rabbit isolated mesenteric artery. *Br. J. Pharmacol.* **87**, 77.
4 Creed, K. E. (1979): Functional diversity of smooth muscle. *Br. Med. Bull.* **35**, 243–247.
5 Olesen, J. (1985): Vascular aspects of migraine pathophysiology. In *Migraine, clinical and research advances*, ed. F. Clifford Rose, pp. 130–137. Basel: Karger.
6 Bruyn, G. W. (1984): The pathomechanism of migraine as a basis for pharmacotherapy: a clinician's epilogue. In *The pharmacological basis of migraine therapy*, eds W. K. Amery, J. M. van Neuten & A. Wauquier, pp. 267–278. London: Pitman.
7 Stagg, A. L. & Wallace, A. G. (1974): The effect of propranolol on membrane conductance in canine cardiac Purkinje fibres. *Circulation* **50**, Suppl. III, 145.

6

THE PLATELET AND THE

NEURON—TWO CELLS IN FOCUS IN MIGRAINE

Rigmor Malmgren and Lena Hasselmark

Department of Experimental Surgery,
Thoracic Clinics, Karolinska Hospital, S-104 01 Stockholm, Sweden

Introduction

Although there have been a number of different hypotheses concerning the primary cause of migraine, it is established that serotonin has a role in migraine aetiology. As the circulating platelets constitute an important and dynamic reservoir of serotonin and are able to rapidly accumulate and secrete serotonin, much interest has been focused on their possible involvement in migraine pathogenesis, and Hanington[1] formulated a hypothesis that migraine was due to a primary platelet disorder. However, the neurological disturbances that occur in connection with attacks are not simply explained by a platelet release of serotonin. Neither does serotonin administration provoke or aggravate migraine[2].

Olesen and co-workers[3], who investigated the regional cerebral blood flow (rCBF) during migraine attacks, have suggested that classic migraine is associated with a spreading depression (SD). This SD can be described as a transient depolarization process in brain tissue, probably caused by disturbance in ionic balance between cellular and extracellular fluid compartments of neuronal tissue[4]. Although there are still many obscurities and the triggering factor/s of SD in migraine remain unknown, this concept is in good accordance with other observations indicating a primary neuronal disturbance[5]. However, no satisfactory explanation has so far been presented that allows incorporation of observed platelet abnormalities in migraine into the cerebral hypothesis.

Sicuteri[6] has pointed out the association between central serotonin depletion and migraine symptoms, and suggested that most of the typical migraine symptoms like pain, nausea, depression and aura phenomena are linked to changes in serotonin dynamics in the CNS. Part of the increased excretion of serotonin metabolites during attacks most likely originates from platelets, but the extent of the excretion implies the occurrence of a parallel depletion of additional serotonin stores[2].

There are intimate relationships between monoaminergic and endogenous opioid systems[7]. The accumulated data indicate that the pain during migraine attacks mainly

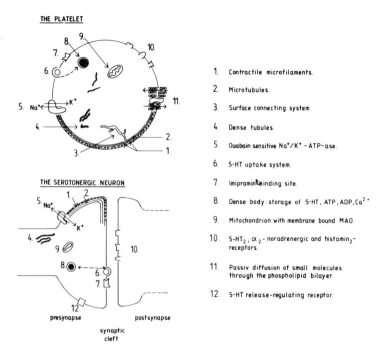

THE PLATELET

1. Contractile microfilaments.

2. Microtubules.

3. Surface connecting system.

4. Dense tubules.

5. Ouabain sensitive Na^+/K^+ - ATP-ase.

6. 5-HT uptake system.

THE SEROTONERGIC NEURON

7. Imipramine binding site.

8. Dense body: storage of 5-HT, ATP, ADP, Ca^{2+}

9. Mitochondrion with membrane bound MAO.

10. $5-HT_2$, α_2 - noradrenergic and histamin$_2$- receptors.

11. Passiv diffusion of small molecules through the phospholipid bilayer.

12. 5-HT release-regulating receptor.

presynapse   postsynapse

synaptic
cleft

Fig. 1. *The platelet as a model for the serotonergic neuron.*

originates from the CNS and is triggered off by a disruption of the anti-nociceptive system that modulates pain perception. It has been suggested that this disruption is caused by a central depletion of serotonin and other nociceptive transmitters[6,8].

The platelet as a model for the serotonergic neuron

We suggest that the alterations in platelet functions observed during migraine attacks reflect processes occurring in the CNS. Platelets and serotonergic nerve endings have an intriguingly large number of common denominators and platelets are considered faithful models for serotonergic neurons[9,10]. The analogy is founded on a proposed common origin from the embryonic ectoderm[10] and on similarities of particular relevance to migraine, such as accumulation and storage of serotonin and the stimulus-response mediated secretion of active substances eg serotonin, catecholamines, and prostaglandins. Both cells types contain monoamine oxidase (MAO)[11]. Their respective outer membranes contain specific imipramine binding sites[12], a similar profile of post-synaptic receptors (α_2, β_2, $5-HT_2$)[9,13], and lipid metabolizing systems[14,15]. The intracellular mediators that promote secretion involve Ca^{2+} and metabolites of the phosphatidylinositol cycle and the prostanoid pathways[14,15].

Platelet abnormalities in migraine

Several investigators have reported an increased aggregability and a lowered threshold for agonist-induced platelet secretion in migraineurs, particularly in association with attacks, while others have failed to confirm these findings (for review, see reference 2). Platelet microaggregates and an enhanced level of the platelet secreted protein, β-thromboglobulin

(BTG), in the circulation have also been observed. Platelet hyperaggregability, circulating microaggregates and increased blood levels of BTG are common findings also in ischemic cerebrovascular disorders[16]. Increased platelet aggregability is one of the aetiological factors in thromboembolism[17], and there are some indications for a predisposition to thrombotic stroke in migraine sufferers[18]. The increased platelet activation in ischemic disorders leads to an increased peripheral destruction of platelets, and consequently also to a shortened megakaryocyte-platelet regeneration time (MPT)[19]. Megakaryocyte-platelet regeneration in classic migraine is however not shortened[20] and the genesis and the clinical consequences of platelet hyperaggregability in migraine thus appears to be different from those of other disorders involving ischemic episodes.

The migraine attack is often associated with a transient depressive episode[6,21]. The involvement of serotonin is central in the monoamine hypothesis of depression[22]. In biological psychiatry, where the platelet is used as a model for the serotonergic neuron, platelet abnormalities are considered to reflect serotonergic dysfunctions in the brain. A lowered V_{max} for the platelet serotonin uptake[23], a reduced number of imipramine binding sites[12], and a lowered platelet MAO activity[22] seem to be consistent findings in endogenous depression. The same platelet abnormalities are found in migraineurs[2,24,25], although in migraine the changes apparently are of a more transient nature.

Several workers have reported a reduced serotonin uptake in platelets from migraine patients and, although some data are contradictory, the deviations from normals seem to be most pronounced in association with attacks (for review, see reference 24). In spite of the apparent resemblances between platelet abnormalities in migraine and depressive disorders, there are important and distinct differences. In migraine, the processes that involve platelet activation are highly implicated, while no such phenomena have been reported in depressive illness. Nevertheless, antidepressants are useful therapy in some migraine patients[2,21]. The beneficial effect is probably not only due to a general mood improvement, since amine uptake inhibitors are known also to elevate nociceptive thresholds[26].

Platelet changes as a reflection of a neuronal event

How should the transient alterations in platelet function in migraineurs be interpreted? It would be easy to assume that if platelet disturbances are not the primary cause of migraine, platelet abnormalities appear as a direct consequence of a neuronal event. Gardner-Medwin and Boullin[27] failed however to ascertain an effect of experimentally induced SD on the platelet serotonin release in the rabbit. Their results are difficult to interpret since no measures were taken to prevent platelet re-uptake of serotonin. Disregarding the methodology used in their investigation, we do however not share the view of a consequential relation between neuronal dysfunction and platelet behaviour.

The recurrent findings of platelet hyperaggregability, the presence of microaggregates and the enhanced sensibility to various agonists rather indicate a generally lowered threshold for stimulus-response in platelets of migraineurs. The suggestion that migraine is associated with SD in particularly vulnerable regions of the brain[3] offers a constructive explanation for the observed platelet abnormalities. It could be that this enhanced cellular response to stimuli is present in both platelets and serotonergic neurons, although their activation may occur independently. Thus, in our opinion, platelet disturbances should not be viewed as a secondary phenomena of a neuronal event, eg SD. Neither could any platelet reactions be held responsible for the initiation of neuronal disturbances of a migraine attack. Thus, although an occurring platelet reaction and a neuronal event may occur simultaneously, they should be viewed as separate, not inter-related, phenomena.

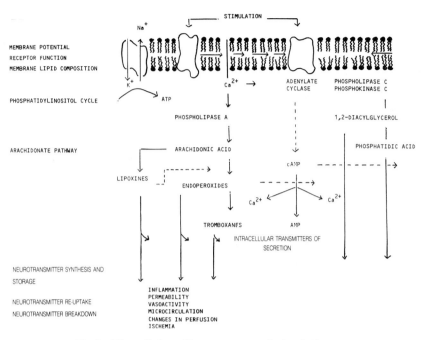

Fig 2. *The cellular effector system of stimulation.*

Antimigraine drugs

The efficacy of antimigraine drugs has been ascribed to their serotonin-antagonistic, vascular and/or antiplatelet properties, which however imperfectly explains their migraine-relieving action. Whether these drugs are used in prophylactic or acute migraine treatment, their common denominator is interference with one or several steps in the pathway for stimulus-response coupling[17]. Although all drugs used in migraine treatment are able to pass the blood-brain barrier[28], comparatively little interest has been devoted to their effects in the CNS. Inhibition of platelet functions in response to drug treatment most likely reflects an analogous pharmacologic effect on serotonergic neurons[26,29]. We suggest that this central effect on a primary neuronal disturbance may account for their main antimigraine action.

Conclusions

In our view, migraine is associated with a lowered threshold for stimulus-response coupling in the serotonergic neurons, comprising an increased sensitivity towards stimuli and changes in the ionic balance of the neuronal environment. This increased sensitivity towards endogenous and/or exogenous stimuli is also present in platelets, as visualized by hyperaggregability and an increased tendency for secretion. Both cell types can thus be considered to have a primary defect, although merely the neuronal abnormality is responsible for the migraine symptomatology.

The various and often contradictory findings concerning platelet function in migraine indicate that the neuronal dysfunction is complex and may be present at different steps and to various degrees in the stimulus-response coupling. The defect may be present in the maintenance of the membrane potential, the membrane lipid composition, and include the mobility and function of receptors. The intracellular response upon stimulation inevitably leads to activation of the phosphatidylinositol cycle and arachidonate pathways. Even a minor deviation in the balance between the intermediaries may lead to uncontrolled and enhanced secretion. On the other hand an imperfect function of mechanisms that regulate secretion will have similar consequences. Enhanced serotonin secretion coupled with a temporarily impeded re-uptake mechanism and impaired enzyme activities will affect the post-synaptic receptor apparatus.

Studies of platelet function in migraine using the platelet as a model for serotonergic neurons may widen our understanding of the neuronal processes that take place during a migraine attack. The model has limitations, since it gives information about possible alterations in serotonergic neurons and the neurological events in migraine are certainly not limited only to serotonergically innervated regions. The substances, or combination of substances, acting as triggering factors can not be expected to be identical in each migraine attack. Consequently we are faced with large intra and inter-individual variations, both in triggering factors and clinical manifestations.

References

1 Hanington, E. (1978): Migraine: a blood disorder? *Lancet* ii, 501–503.
2 Fozard, J. R. (1982): Serotonin, migraine and platelets. In *Drugs and platelets, progress in pharmacology*, 4, eds P. A. Van Zweiten *et al.*, pp. 135–146. Stuttgart: Gustav Fischer Verlag.
3 Olesen, J., Lauritzen, M., Tfelt-Hansen, P., Henriksen, L. & Larsen, B. (1982): Spreading cerebral oligemia in classical- and normal cerebral blood flow in common migraine. *Headache* 22, 242–248.
4 Bruyn, G. W. (1984): The pathomechanism of migraine as a basis for pharmacotherapy: a clinician's epilogue. In *The pharmacological basis of migraine therapy*, eds W. K. Amery *et al.*, pp. 267–278. London: Pitman.
5 Pearce, J. M. S. (1984): Migraine: a cerebral disorder. *Lancet* ii, 86–89.
6 Sicuteri, F. (1978): Endorphins, opiate receptors and migraine headache. *Headache* 17, 253–256.
7 Basbaum, A. I., Moss, M. S. & Glazer, E. J. (1983): Opiate and stimulation-produced analgesia: the contribution of the monoamines. In *Advances in pain research and therapy*, eds J. J. Bonica *et al.*, pp. 323–339. New York: Raven Press.
8 Sicuteri, F. (1982): Natural opioids in migraine. In *Advances in neurology*, eds M. Critchley *et al.*, pp. 65–74. New York: Raven Press.
9 Pletcher, A. & Laubscher, A. (1980): Blood platelets as models for neurons: uses and limitations. *J. Neural Trans.* 2 (Suppl.), 7–16.
10 Campbell, I. C., Marangos, P. J., Murphy, D. L. & Pearse, A. G. E. (1981): Neurone specific enlase (NSE) in human blood platelets: implications for the neuronal model. *Rec. Adv. Neuropsychopharm.* 31, 203–211.
11 Murphy, D. L. & Donnelly, C. H. (1974): Monoamine oxidase in man: enzyme characteristics in platelets, plasma, and other human tissues. In *Neuropsychopharmacology of monoamines and their regulatory enzymes*, ed E. Usdin, pp. 71–85. New York: Raven Press.
12 Langer, S. Z., Zarifian, E., Briley, M., Raisman, R. & Sechter, D. (1981): High affinity binding of ³H-imipramine in brain and platelets and its relevance to the biochemistry of affective disorders. *Life Sci.* 29, 211–220.
13 Exton, J. H. (1981): Molecular mechanisms involved in alpha-adrenergic responses. *Mol. Cell. Endocrinol.* 23, 233–264.
14 Marcus, A. J. (1982): Platelet lipids. In *Hemostasis and thrombosis: basic principles and clinical practice*, eds R. W. Colman *et al.*, pp. 472–485. Philadelphia, Toronto: J. B. Lippincott Co.
15 Birkle, D. L. & Bazan, N. G. (1985): Metabolism of arachidonic acid in the central nervous system. The enzymatic cyclooxygenation and lipoxygenation of arachidonic acid in the mammalian retina. In *Phospholipids in the nervous system*, Vol 2: *Physiological roles*, eds L. A. Horrocks *et al.*, pp. 193–208. New York: Raven Press.

16 Aushri, Z., Berginer, V., Nathan, I. & Dvilansky, A. (1983): Plasma thromboglobulin and platelet aggregation index in transient ischaemic attack: effect of aspirin and dipyridamole therapy. *Int. J. Clin. Pharm. Res.* **3**, 339–342.

17 Packham, M. A. (1983): Platelet function inhibitors. *Thromb. Haemost.*, **50**, 610–619.

18 Featherstone, H. J. (1986): Clinical features of stroke in migraine: a review. *Headache* **26**, 128–133.

19 Hamberg, M., Svensson, J., Blombäck, M. & Mettinger, K. L. (1981): Shortened megakaryocyte-platelet regeneration time in patients with ischemic cerebrovascular disease. *Thromb. Res.* **21**, 675–679.

20 Malmgren, R., Svensson, J. & Hannerz, J. (1985): Prolonged megakaryocyte-platelet regeneration time in patients with classic migraine. In *Migraine, clinical and research advances*, ed F. Clifford Rose, pp. 109–114. Basel: Karger.

21 Couch, J. R., Ziegler, D. K. & Hassanein R. (1976): Amitriptyline in the prophylaxis of migraine. *Neurology* **26**, 121–127.

22 Garver, D. L. & Davis, J. M. (1979): Minireview: biogenic amine hypotheses of affective disorders. *Life Sci.* **24**, 383–394.

23 Rotman, A. (1983): Blood platelets in psychopharmacological research. *Prog. Neuro. Psychopharm. Biol. Psych.* **7**, 135–151.

24 Waldenlind, R., Ross, S. B., Sääf, J., Ekbom, K. & Wetterberg, L. (1985): Concentration and uptake of 5-hydroxytryptamine in platelets from cluster headache and migraine patients. *Cephalalgia* **5**, 45–54.

25 Geaney, D. P., Rutterford, M. G., Elliott, J. M., Schächter, M., Peet, K. M. S. & Grahame-Smith, D. G. (1984): Decreased platelet ^{3}H-imipramine binding sites in classical migraine. *J. Neurol. Neurosurg. Psychiat.* **47**, 720–723.

26 Ögren, S. O., Holm, A. -C. (1980): Test-specific effects of the 5-HT reuptake inhibitors alaproclate and zimelidine on pain sensitivity and morphine analgesia. *J. Neural Transm.* **47**, 253–271.

27 Gardner-Medwin, A. R. & Boullin, D. J. (1985): Platelet function during spreading depression: implications for migraine. In *Migraine, clinical and research advances*, ed F. Clifford Rose, pp. 126–129. Basel: Karger.

28 Raskin, N. H. (1981): Pharmacology of migraine. *A. Rev. Pharmacol. Toxicol.* **21**, 463–478.

29 Åberg-Wistedt, A., Alvariza, M., Bertilsson, L., Malmgren, R. & Wachtmeister, H. (1985): Alaproclate a novel antidepressant? *Acta psychiat. scand.* **71**, 256–268.

7

PLATELET-BASOPHIL

INTERACTIONS IN MIGRAINE

P. T. G. Davies, M. Sitsapesan, T. J. Steiner,
O. Cromwell* and F. Clifford Rose

*The Princess Margaret Migraine Clinic, Academic Unit of Neuroscience,
Charing Cross and Westminster Medical School,
London, W6 8RF, UK and *Cardiothoracic Institute, Brompton Hospital,
London, SW3 6HP, UK*

Summary

Human platelets release a soluble factor of molecular weight $> 10\,000$ daltons when stimulated with thrombin. In four identical experiments this factor *in vitro* produced a dose-dependent release of histamine from a basophil-enriched leucocyte preparation when both platelets and leucocytes were derived from migraineurs; much smaller or negligible responses were seen for age and sex-matched controls. We propose that platelets can act as pro-inflammatory agents in migraine.

Introduction

Two blood cell types stand out as possible candidates for a role in migraine pathophysiology, the platelet and the basophil. The part played by the platelet has not been determined but, between attacks, platelets from migraineurs are hyperaggregable *in vitro* to both ADP and adrenaline[1], high levels of circulating platelet microaggregates occur in migraineurs[2], and the platelet-specific alpha-granule proteins, β-thromboglobulin (β-TG) and platelet factor 4 (PF4), are elevated in the circulation[3]. All these are findings of enhanced platelet activation in migraineurs between attacks.

Like the platelet, the basophil contains pre-packed vasoactive agents and has attracted much interest in the study of migraine. Plasma histamine levels are significantly elevated in migraineurs between attacks[4], with increased urinary excretion of histamine[5] and histamine metabolites[6]. The discovery that many neuropeptides, eg substance P, can

45

release histamine from basophils through non-immunologic mechanisms has renewed interest in how release of this histamine is controlled.

During a migraine attack a platelet release reaction occurs[7], and serum taken from migraineurs at this time can enhance histamine release from basophils taken from normal control subjects[8]. The recent report that a factor released from stimulated human platelets can induce histamine release from basophils[9] establishes a link between platelet and basophil of possible relevance to migraine. This study aims to confirm this report, and for the first time to compare this reaction in migraineurs and controls.

Patients

Four migraineurs (three female, one male, two common, two classical) were studied with age and sex-matched controls. All gave informed consent. Diagnoses of migraine were secure by Vahlquist's criteria. All patients were having one or more attacks per 2 months, were without regular medication, free of aspirin and aspirin-like drugs for 2 weeks and of headache for at least 3 days prior to blood sampling, and had no history of atopy. The controls were healthy hospital personnel.

Materials and methods

A number of solutions were obtained or prepared for the experiment (Table 1).

Migraineurs and their controls were studied in parallel. Venesection was carried out on two occasions in each subject, the first for the preparation of platelet-derived supernatant, the second for basophil-enriched leucocytes.

Preparation of platelet-derived supernatant

Blood (72 ml) was taken into 3.1% sodium citrate (8 ml) and mixed, and platelet-rich plasma (PRP) obtained by spinning at $150\,g$ for 10 min; the platelets were washed twice in platelet washing buffer (PWB) and resuspended in 20 ml of (PACG) and the final platelet count was determined in a Coulter-S4 automated counter. These washed platelets were incubated at 37°C with constant stirring and maximally stimulated with thrombin (final concentration 0.2 U/ml). After 3 min the platelet membrane debris was removed by

Table 1. *Solutions and preparations.*

Platelet washing buffer (PWB):

NaCl	6.60 g/l	$NaH_2PO_4.H_2O$	3.4 g/l
K_2HPO_4	0.75 g/l	Glucose	1.0 g/l
$Na_2HPO_4.12H_2O$	1.54 g/l	EDTA	1.3 g/l
		pH 6.8	

Platelet buffer (PIPES — albumin — $CaCl_2$ — glucose: PACG):

PIPES	7.6 g/l	$CaCl_2$	0.25 g/l
NaCl	6.4 g/l	Bovine serum albumin (BSA)	30 mg/l
KCl	0.37 g/l	Glucose	1.0 g/l
NaOH (10 M)	4.2 ml/l		
		pH 7.4	

Phosphate buffered saline (Dulbecco 'A') with 0.5% BSA (PBS/BSA)
Human thrombin (Sigma Chemicals) 10 U/ml
Lymphoprep (Na metrizoate/Ficoll solution) (Nyegaard & Co.)

centrifugation at 1 000 g for 10 min. The platelet release products of molecular weight > 10 000 daltons were concentrated 20-fold by millipore ultrafiltration and this platelet-derived supernatant concentrate was frozen at − 70°C. Aliquots of this concentrate were periodically analysed for histamine content, pH, ionic concentration and osmolality.

Preparation of the basophil-enriched leucocyte samples

Blood (20 ml) was taken into EDTA as anticoagulant (final concentration 0.01%), layered over an equal volume of lymphoprep and spun at 400 g for 25 min according to the method of Miroli *et al.*[10], yielding a basophil-enriched leucocyte layer. This was aspirated, and the cells washed twice in PBS/BSA and resuspended in the same in a concentration of 25 000 ± 5000 basophils/ml (toluidine blue stain for counting).

Incubation of platelet-derived supernatant and basophil-enriched leucocyte preparation

Experiments were performed in duplicate whenever possible. Aliquots of the basophil-enriched leucocyte preparation were incubated at 37°C. Platelet-derived supernatant was added at a final concentration in the range $5 \times 10^8 - 3 \times 10^9$ platelet equivalents per ml. After 30 min the cells were spun down at 1000 g for 3 min and the supernatant stored at − 70°C prior to histamine assay. The pelleted cells were lysed with 2% perchloric acid and stored likewise.

Histamine assay

An automated spectrofluorimetric method was used. Histamine release was expressed as a percentage of the total white cell histamine.

Results

Dose-response curves for percentage histamine release induced by platelet-derived supernatant in the four matched pairs of subjects (patient and control) are shown in the figure.

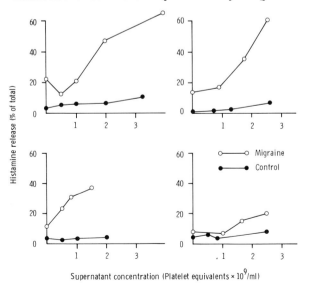

Figure. *Dose-response curves for the four migraineurs and their matched controls, showing histamine release from the basophil-enriched leucocyte preparation in response to concentrations of platelet-derived supernatant, expressed in platelet equivalents (released substances of MW > 10 000 daltons per thrombin-activated platelet) per ml, both from the same subject.* Histamine release is expressed as a percentage of the total leucocyte histamine (see text).

Values in most cases are means from duplicated experiments. The dose-related response apparent in all migraineurs and marked in three out of four was consistently negligible in controls. There was no measurable difference between common and classical migraineurs.

The platelet-derived supernatant contained negligible histamine and was physiological in terms of pH, ionic concentration and osmolality.

Discussion

We have shown that the release reaction initiated by thrombin in platelets of migraineurs produces a soluble factor (or factors) able to release histamine from basophils from the same patient.

Our dose-response curves indicate measurable effects of release products equivalent to around 1.5×10^9 platelets per ml, a concentration that may easily occur *in vivo* in a platelet microaggregate. Other workers have shown that collagen and platelet activating factor, both physiological platelet activators, achieve similar effects in normals[9], but we saw very little in our controls.

The kinetics of histamine release from basophils in response to platelet release factors, studied by Orchard *et al.*[9], make it clear that this is not a cytotoxic effect. Since it is held back by a 10 000 dalton molecular weight filter, the factor responsible for histamine release must have a molecular weight of at least this figure. Putative candidates include previously described platelet peptides such as β-TG and PF4, both of uncertain physiological function. Reports of PF4 prepared by acid extraction possessing basophil histamine-releasing properties were not confirmed by more recent work[9]. We do not yet know if the factor acts by binding directly to the basophil.

The scale of histamine release from basophils of migraineurs in comparison with controls (Figure 1), if borne out in a larger series, should ideally be explained in the context of the pathogenesis of migraine. The difference would be explained by differential platelet production or release of the responsible factor, but this does not appear to be the case. Platelet-derived supernatant from all patients so far studied by Lichtenstein's group has had quantitatively similar effects on samples of responsive basophils (D. Proud, personal communication), suggesting that the response is determined at the level of the basophil. Its enhancement in migraineurs may parallel the increased sensitivity of these patients' platelets to ADP and adrenaline, possibly indicating an alteration of membrane transduction mechanisms. Apart from this, there are no adequate explanations at present. We have no evidence that the platelet factor acts on mast cells to release histamine, although, if it did, it would help to explain the degranulation of mast cells seen in the scalp during the headache phase of a migraine attack[11], giving platelets a pro-inflammatory role in this situation. As our ignorance in one area is replaced by uncertainty in another, it appears increasingly that interactions between different cell types will better explain the biochemistry of migraine than any postulate of altered activity of one cell type alone[12].

Acknowledgements—P. T. G. Davies was supported by the Migraine Trust; M. Sitsapesan by Gist-Brocades, N.V.

References

1 Kalendovsky, Z. & Austin, J. A. (1975): "Complicated migraine" its association with increased platelet aggregability and abnormal plasma coagulation factors. *Headache* 15, 18–35.
2 Deshmuk, S. V. & Meyer, J. S. (1977): Cyclic changes in platelet dynamics and the pathogenesis and prophylaxis of migraine. *Headache* 17, 101–108.

3 D'Andrea, G., Cananzi, A. R., Toldo, M. & Ferro-Milone, F. (1986): Platelet activation and migraine: A study with flunarizine. *Headache* **26**, 339–342.

4 Heatley, R. V., Denburg, J. A., Bayer, N. & Bienenstock, J. (1982): Increased plasma histamine levels in migraine patients. *Clin. Allergy* **12**, 145–149.

5 Sjaastad, O. & Sjaastad, O. V. (1970): The histaminuria in vascular headache. *Acta Neurol. Scand.* **46**, 311–342.

6 Loisy, C., Arnaud, J. L. & Amelot, A. (1972): Contribution to the study of histamine metabolism in migrainous subjects. *Res. Clin. Stud. Headache* **3**, 252–259.

7 Gawel, M., Burkitt, M. & Clifford Rose, F. (1979): The platelet release reaction during migraine attacks. *Headache* **19**, 323–327.

8 Selmaj, K. (1984): Histamine release from leucocytes during migraine attacks. *Cephalalgia* **4**, 97–100.

9 Orchard, M. A., Kagey-Sobotka, A., Proud, D. & Lichtenstein, L. M. (1986): Basophil histamine release induced by a substance from stimulated human platelets. *J. Immunol.* **6**, 2240–2244.

10 Miroli, A. A., James, B. M. B. & Spitz, M. (1986): Single step enrichment of human peripheral blood basophils by Ficoll-Paque centrifugation. *J. Immunol. Methods* **88**, 91–96.

11 Sicuteri, F. (1963): Mast cells and their active substances: their role in the pathogenesis of migraine. *Headache* **3**, 86–92.

12 Steiner, T. J., Joseph, R. & Clifford Rose, F. (1985): Migraine is not a platelet disorder. *Headache* **25**, 434–440.

8

EFFECTS OF 17-β-OESTRADIOL ON AGGREGABILITY OF PLATELETS FROM MIGRAINE SUFFERERS AND NORMALS, AND THE POSSIBLE RELEVANCE TO MENSTRUAL MIGRAINE

N. K. Eccles, M. Sitsapesan*, P. T. G. Davies*,
Helen L. Leathard, T. J. Steiner* and F. Clifford Rose*

*Department of Pharmacology, and *The Princess Margaret Migraine Clinic,
Charing Cross and Westminster Medical School,
St. Dunstans Road, London W6 8RP, UK*

Summary

The *in vitro* effects of 17-β-oestradiol on platelet aggregation in response to adrenaline were monitored in platelet-rich plasma (PRP) using the optical method.

Adrenaline induced aggregation of platelets harvested between days 1 and 4 of menses, from 12 female migraineurs and nine female normal control subjects was estimated. The threshold adrenaline concentration for secondary platelet aggregation was significantly reduced in migraineurs. In a high concentration of 10 μg/ml 17-β-oestradiol inhibited secondary aggregation of platelets from migraineurs and controls. Lower concentrations (10 and 100 ng/ml) enhanced secondary aggregation of platelets from control subjects but usually inhibited it in platelets from migraineurs. These differences between migraineurs and non-migraineurs may be important in the menstrual predisposition to migraine.

Introduction

Reactivity of human isolated blood vessel strips is suppressed by 17-β-oestradiol or progesterone at relatively high concentrations[1], whereas much lower concentrations of the oestrogen, but not of progesterone, sometimes enhance responsiveness (Eccles & Leathard, unpublished). However, few blood vessels are obtained from migraine sufferers, so differences in response to these hormones that may exist between migraine sufferers and non-sufferers cannot be investigated in this way. Blood platelets, readily obtainable from migraine patients and control subjects, are a suitable alternative for a comparative study, especially in view of evidence that platelet activity plays a major role in migraine pathophysiology[2,3]. The effects of 17-β-oestradiol have therefore been studied on adrenaline-induced aggregation of platelets from female migraineurs and control subjects.

The reported abnormalities of platelet behaviour in migraine have been reviewed recently by David and De Clerk[4], who conclude that migraineurs' platelets are hyper-aggregable. The well-known 5-HT-release associated with migraine is also indicative of platelet activity since platelets store 5-HT in the circulation.

The female sex hormones are also implicated in the aetiology of migraine, a condition more common in women, in whom it often begins with the onset of ovulation[5]. Symptoms tend to be aggravated by combined oral contraceptives and relieved during pregnancy[6,7], and many women affected whilst younger experience remission after the menopause. Oestrogen receptors have been demonstrated on human platelets[8], so a direct interaction between oestrogens and platelets would not be surprising; the investigations by Plotka *et al.*[9], in humans, indeed suggest this.

Methods

These investigations were based on *in vitro* platelet aggregation measured as changes in the optical density[10] of platelet-rich plasma.

Adrenaline bitartrate, the inducer, was made up as a 10 mM stock solution in 0.9% NaCl containing 100 μg/ml ascorbic acid. 17-β-oestradiol was dissolved in propylene glycol and added to PRP samples in micro-litre quantities.

Subjects

The subjects were all female, 12 migraineurs (mean age 34 years, range 23–43) and nine controls (mean age 31 years, range 21–39). Of the patients three had classical and nine had common migraine, according to the conventional classification. All subjects had regular predictable periods, were non-smokers and were not taking oral contraceptives, aspirin-like drugs or any other medication regularly. All migraineurs had been headache-free for at least 5 days at the time of venepuncture for platelet sampling. The controls were healthy.

Blood samples

Between days 1 and 4 of each subject's menses, with endogenous hormone levels at their lowest, a 50 ml venous blood sample was taken into 5 ml of 3.1% sodium citrate. Platelet-rich plasma was obtained by centrifugation (150 g for 10 min) and the platelet count standardized to 250 000/μl ± 4% by dilution with platelet-poor plasma (PPP). The PPP was obtained by centrifugation of the PRP-depleted blood (500 g for 10 min). The PRP was divided into four × 5 ml aliquots, two of which were incubated at room temperature with different concentrations of 17-β-oestradiol (10 and 100 ng/ml) and two with appropriate concentrations of propylene glycol, the hormone solvent, and one additional 3 ml aliquot incubated with 10 μg/ml of 17-β-oestradiol. After 60 min, platelet aggregation to adrenaline (0.25–10 μM) was measured in a Payton dual-channel aggregometer, monitoring increased transmission of light through a sample of PRP as platelets aggregated[10]. Each dose of

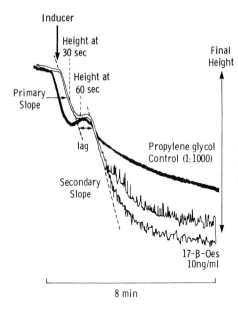

Fig. 1. *Measured indices of platelet aggregation.* Primary slope, height at 30 sec and height at 60 sec were indices of primary aggregation. Lag, secondary slope and final height indicated secondary aggregation.

adrenaline was added in parallel to two platelet samples (30 seconds apart), one hormone-treated, the other a propylene glycol time-matched control, with aggregation in both monitored simultaneously for 8 min. Hormone and control samples were alternated between the two aggregometer channels to obviate channel bias. When a hormone effect was observed at a particular adrenaline concentration, usually at or near the threshold concentration for secondary aggregation, one or two slightly higher or lower adrenaline concentrations were tested to check repeatability of the effect. The time taken from blood collection to completion of each experiment was 4–4.5 h.

Analysis

Aggregation was quantified by direct measurement of the recorded traces, using standard indices to represent both primary (primary slope, height at 30 sec and height at 60 sec) and secondary responses (lag, secondary slope and final height) (Fig. 1). Results were analysed statistically using Student's *t*-test or Mann-Whitney test.

Results

Figure 1 shows a typical control response to adrenaline and the effects of 17-β-oestradiol at 10 ng/ml on platelets from a control subject. Responses to adrenaline were typically biphasic: the first phase, primary or reversible aggregation, resulted directly from adrenaline stimulation. This might be followed by secondary or irreversible aggregation due to the release from the platelets of other aggregating agents (eg ADP, ATP, 5-HT and calcium) or potentiators of aggregation. A variable lag time occurred between these two phases. Adrenaline at 10 μM usually produced maximal aggregation of platelets from migraineurs or control subjects, but the threshold concentration for secondary aggregation was significantly lower for migraineurs (mean 1.3 μM) than for controls (mean 2.6 μM; $P<0.05$, Mann-Whitney test).

17-β-oestradiol in concentrations of 10 or 100 ng/ml had no effect on primary aggregation of platelets from either migraineurs or control subjects, but at 10 μg/ml there was

Table 1. *Effects of 17-β-oestradiol on primary platelet aggregation.* No effect was seen in any of the measured indices with 17-β-oestradiol at 10 or 100 ng/ml, in control subjects or migraineurs. At 10 µg/ml, 17-β-oestradiol significantly reduced all three indices of primary aggregation in platelets from migraineurs but not in platelets from control subjects.

	Primary aggregation	*P*
Control subjects (n = 9)		*(t-test)*
17-β-oes. 10 ng/ml	No change	
17-β-oes. 100 ng/ml	No change	
17-β-oes. 10 µg/ml	No change	
Migraine patients (n = 12)		
17-β-oes. 10 ng/ml	No change	
17-β-oes. 100 ng/ml	No change	
17-β-oes. 10 µg/ml	27%↓slope	<0.01
	37%↓height at 30 s	<0.02
	23%↓height at 60 s	<0.02

significantly suppressed primary aggregation of platelets from migraineurs but not from controls (Table 1). 17-β-oestradiol at 10 or 100 ng/ml enhanced secondary aggregation to adrenaline of control platelets (Fig. 1): this was observed as reduced lag, increased slope (rate of aggregation) and increased final height (degree of aggregation), although not necessarily all of these in any one subject. Figure 2 illustrates the influence of 100 ng/ml 17-β-oestradiol on aggregation induced by various concentrations of adrenaline in platelets from control subjects, showing that the greatest potentiation by 17-β-oestradiol was on threshold concentrations of adrenaline.

At 10 µg/ml, 17-β-oestradiol significantly inhibited secondary aggregation of platelets from control subjects: in Fig. 3(a–c) the effects of 17-β-oestradiol on the three measured indices of secondary aggregation are expressed as percentages, relating the responses recorded in the presence of the hormone to those of the time-matched propylene glycol controls.

In contrast to the results from control subjects, 17-β-oestradiol at 10 and 100 ng/ml usually inhibited secondary aggregation to adrenaline in platelets from migraine patients (Fig. 4 a–c). Although in three of the 12 patients there was some evidence of potentiation of secondary aggregation, none of these patients had anything in common: the type of migraine (classical or common) had no bearing on the hormone effect observed. 17-β-oestradiol at 10 µg/ml inhibited secondary aggregation of migraineurs' platelets as in control subjects (Fig. 4c).

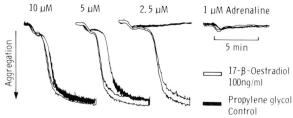

Fig. 2. *Typical tracings of adrenaline-induced aggregation of platelets from control subjects showing response patterns obtained from the dual-channel aggregometer and potentiation of secondary aggregation by 17-β-oestradiol.* Each adrenaline dose was applied to a hormone-treated sample of PRP and 30 sec later to a parallel control sample treated with the propylene glycol solvent. Aggregation is represented by downward displacement of the traces, indicating increased light transmission (arbitrary units). The clearest effect of 17-β-oestradiol was observed with threshold concentrations of adrenaline.

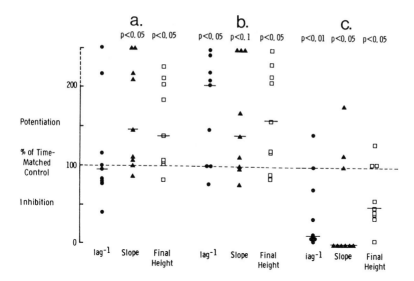

Fig. 3. *Effects of 17-β-oestradiol, at (a) 10 ng/ml, (b) 100 ng/ml and (c) 10 μg/ml, on secondary aggregation of platelets from control subjects, demonstrated by the three measured indices of secondary aggregation, reciprocal of lag, slope (rate of aggregation) and final height (degree of aggregation).* The broken vertical axis above 200% indicates a variable scale of potentiation up to 400% of the time-matched control. Each point represents the measurement in 17-β-oestradiol-treated PRP as a percentage of that in propylene glycol-treated PRP from the same subject, run simultaneously. The bars represent median values. Values of *P* were derived using Student's paired *t*-test. The predominant effect of 17-β-oestradiol in lower doses (a) and (b) is potentiation of secondary aggregation, and in higher doses (c) inhibition.

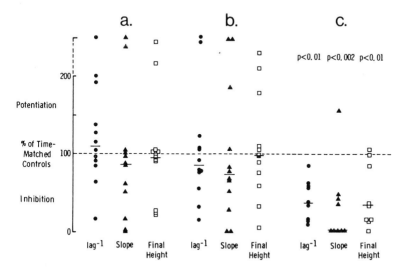

Fig. 4. *Effects of 17-β-oestradiol, at (a) 10 ng/ml, (b) 100 ng/ml and (c) 10 μg/ml, on secondary aggregation of platelets from migraine patients (see legend to Fig. 3 for description).* The predominant effect of 17-β-oestradiol at all concentrations was inhibitory, but statistical significance was achieved only at 10 μg/ml because of occasional potentiation at lower concentrations.

Discussion

In the present study adrenaline evoked a biphasic aggregation response, the threshold concentration for secondary aggregation being significantly lower in platelets from migraineurs than from control subjects. This is consistent with previous reports of enhanced platelet aggregability in migraineurs[11].

The effects of 17-β-oestradiol were studied at room temperature because preliminary experiments showed that platelets incubated at 37°C rapidly lost their ability to aggregate. Furthermore, the concentrations of 17-β-oestradiol studied were more typical of the plasma levels during pregnancy (total oestrogens ~ 50 ng/ml) than of those reached during the menstrual cycle (peak levels ~ 500 pg/ml). As lower hormone concentrations may have greater effect at higher temperatures, the findings can still be relevant to menstrual migraine, especially because platelets *in vivo* are exposed to endogenous oestrogens for much longer than can be achieved with substances added *in vitro*.

The observation of enhanced aggregation in control subjects is consistent with previous findings that synthetic and natural oestrogens can potentiate human platelet aggregation[12-14], and may explain why female platelets are reported to be more sensitive to aggregating stimuli than male platelets[12]. However, inhibition was recorded in platelets from nine out of 12 migraine patients and this finding is not consistent with the concept that increased platelet responsiveness contributes causally to migraine. On the other hand, menstrually-related migraine seems to be associated with falling levels of oestrogen[15], so perhaps increasing platelet aggregability occurs on withdrawal of the inhibitory influence of oestrogen. We have not investigated the effect of oestrogen withdrawal on platelet activity, but this idea is at present tenable since oestradiol appears to bind only loosely to human platelets[9]. A further possibility is that vascular tissue becomes hypersensitive to platelet release products during the period of platelet inhibition and that platelet release on oestrogen withdrawal induces cerebral vasospasm as a consequence. Under normal conditions some platelet release occurs in the circulation[16], and there is evidence that this takes place to a greater extent in migraineurs, between attacks, than in normals[4]. Alternatively, if the role of platelets in migraine is a defensive one, as has been postulated previously[17], whereby platelet aggregation and release counteract vasodilatation, then inhibition of platelet activity might exacerbate the headache.

A quite different way of interpreting our results is that platelets from migraineurs are hypersensitive to a dose-related dual action of 17-β-oestradiol in normals. Thus, secondary aggregation of platelets from both migraineurs and normal control subjects was strongly inhibited by high concentrations (10 μg/ml) of 17-β-oestradiol, but primary aggregation was inhibited only in migraineurs. In this hypothesis, enhancement of aggregation seen in normals with our lower concentrations of 17-β-oestradiol would occur at even lower levels of the hormone in migraineurs. The situation may be that the platelets of migraineurs are under a generally excitatory influence of physiological levels of the oestrogens, but presumably not those of pregnancy, more so than the platelets of non-sufferers.

Two other questions arise: why do normal women not suffer migraine if rising oestrogen levels during the menstrual cycle stimulate platelet aggregation, and why do artificially increased oestrogen levels in women taking oral contraceptives usually aggravate migraine? The answer to the first question may be that platelets have nothing to do with migraine causation[18]; alternatively it may lie in the fact that oestradiol can stimulate the production of prostacyclin in arteries, as demonstrated in rat aorta[19]. The important point is that platelet-vascular interaction occurs, and it is not just the platelets per se that are likely to be involved in migraine. Our findings must be considered in the light of how 17-β-oestradiol may also affect the mechanisms of the vessel wall that protect it against platelet adhesion, and whether this might be different in migraineurs. Nattero *et al.*[20] have reported that plasma levels of 6-keto $PGF_{1\alpha}$, the stable metabolite of prostacyclin, decrease during the late luteal phase in women who suffer from menstrually-related migraine, with a further drop during the attack. This could suggest a decrease in vascular production of anti-platelet prostacyclin in migraineurs under the influence of raised sex hormone levels during the luteal phase. The same group also reported decreased platelet sensitivity to prostacyclin during the migraine attack[21].

The influence of the other major sex hormone, progesterone, must also be considered, and we have shown in control subjects that progesterone at 10 or 100 ng/ml clearly inhibits platelet secondary aggregation to adrenaline (Eccles *et al.*, unpublished). *In vivo*, the balance between the two hormones may be more important than the levels of either alone. A disturbance in this balance might hold the answer to the second question, regarding the exacerbation of migraine by oral contraceptives, but it must be relevant that migraine attacks occur more commonly during the pill-free days[22].

In conclusion, platelets from migraineurs behave differently from those from normal subjects in the presence of 17-β-oestradiol and this may be important in the menstrual predisposition to migraine in many women sufferers.

Acknowledgement—We gratefully acknowledge financial support from the Migraine Trust.

References

1 Eccles, N. K. & Leathard, H. L. (1985): 17-β-oestradiol and progesterone on human vascular reactivity. In *Migraine, clinical and research advances*, ed. F. Clifford Rose, pp. 56–65. Basel: Karger.
2 Hanington, E. (1979): Migraine: a platelet hypothesis. *Biomedicine* **30**, 65–66.
3 Hanington, E. (1982): Migraine as a blood disorder: preliminary studies. *Adv. Neurol.* **33**, 253–256.
4 David, J. L. & De Clerk, F. (1984): Platelets and migraine. In *The pharmacological basis of migraine therapy*, ed. W. K. Amery, J. M. Van Nueten & A. Wauquier. London: Pitman Press.
5 Greene, R. (1975): The endocrinology of headache. In *Modern topics in migraine*, ed. J. Pearce, pp. 64–71. London: Heinemann Limited.
6 Whitty, C. W. M., Hockaday, J. M. & Whitty, M. M. (1966): The effect of oral contraceptives on migraine. *Lancet* **i**, 856–859.
7 Lance, J. W. (1978): In *Mechanism and management of headache*, 3rd edn, pp. 130–158. London: Butterworths.
8 Widder, K. J., Fors, E. M., Liu, K. & Mattani, A. (1983): Oestrogen receptor analysis in human platelets. *Fed. Proc.* **42**, 1355.
9 Plotka, E. D., Nikolai, T. F. & Hague, S. S. (1973): The interaction between oestradiol and human platelets. *Clinica Chimica Acta.* **49**, 287–293.
10 Born, G. V. R. (1962): Aggregation of blood platelets by adenosine diphosphate and its reversal. *Nature (Lond.)* **194**, 927–929.
11 Couch, J. R. & Hassanein, R. S. (1977): Platelet aggregability in migraine. *Neurology* **27**, 843–848.
12 Johnson, M. J., Ramey, E. & Ramwell, P. W. (1975): Sex and age differences in human platelet aggregation. *Nature* **253**, 355–357.
13 Poller, L. (1971). Oral contraception and platelet aggregation. *Acta. Med. Scand. Suppl.* **525**, 197–201.
14 Elkeles, R. S. & Hampton, J. R. (1968): Effects of oestrogens on human platelet behaviour. *Lancet* **ii**, 315–318.
15 Somerville, B. W. (1972): The role of oestradiol withdrawal in the aetiology of menstrual migraine. *Neurology, Minneap.* **22**, 355–365.
16 Kaplan, K. L. & Owen, J. (1981): Plasma levels of a beta-thromboglobulin and platelet factor 4 as indices of platelet activation in vivo. *Blood* **57**, 199–202.
17 Joseph, R., Steiner, T. J., Sitsapesan, M., Das, I., Hadar, U. & Clifford Rose, F. (1986): Platelet release reaction in migraine may be beneficial. *Neurology* **36** (suppl. 1), 100.
18 Steiner, T. J., Joseph, R. & Clifford Rose, F. (1985): Migraine is not a platelet disorder. *Headache* **25**(8), 434–440.

19 Chang, W. C., Nakao, J., Neichi, T., Orimo, H. & Murota, S. I. (1981): Effects of oestradiol on the metabolism of arachidonic acid by aortas and platelets in rats. *Biochim. Biophys. Acta* **664**, 291–297.

20 Nattero, G., Allais, G., De Lorenzo, C., Savi, L., Benedetto, C., Zonca, M., Massobrio, M. & Bocci, A. (1985): Peripheral plasma levels of 6-keto-PGF$_{2\alpha}$, thromboxane B$_2$ and prostaglandin E in patients with menstrual migraine. *Cephalalgia* **5** (suppl. 3), 356.

21 Nattero, G., Allais, G., De Lorenzo, C., Savi, L., Benedetto, C., Zonca, M. Massobrio, M., Foppiani, E., Ancona, M. & Torre, E. (1985): Platelet aggregation and platelet sensitivity to prostacyclin (PGI$_2$) in patients with menstrual migraine. *Cephalalgia* **5** (suppl. 3), pp. 396–397.

22 Biggs, M. J. & Johnson, E. S. (1984): The autonomic nervous system and migraine pathogenesis. In *The pharmacological basis of migraine therapy.* ed. W. K. Amery, J. M. Van Nueten & A. Wauquier, pp. 99–107. London: Pitman Press.

9

NEUROENDOCRINE APPROACH

TO MIGRAINE: THE TRH TEST

M. Daras*, Y. Papakostas,† M. Markianos† and C. Stefanis†

*Department of Neurology, Evangelismos Hospital
Athens, Greece and †Department of Psychiatry
Athens University, Eginition Hospital, Athens, Greece*

Summary

In order to evaluate neuroendocrine involvement in migraine we investigated 16 migraine sufferers using the TRH stimulation test in between attacks. In eight of these patients the test was repeated during a migraine attack. Baseline thyrotropin (TSH), growth hormone (GH) and prolactin values were normal. A blunted TSH response was observed in four cases; three of these four cases were retested during an attack and the response remained blunted in two of those. An unexpected GH response was observed in two patients during in between attacks and three different patients had a similar response during attacks. The mean prolactin response was significantly higher during than between attacks. These findings support the notion of hypothalamic involvement in migraine.

Introduction

The long-standing vascular hypothesis for the pathogenesis of migraine has been recently challenged. Vascular involvement seems to be a secondary phenomenon, the primary being rather a neurological dysfunction involving possibly hypothalamic structures[1,2]. Some migraine sufferers seem indeed to exhibit irregularities of the hypothalamic-pituitary-adrenal axis, including non-suppression after dexamethasone administration[3], not dissimilar to those observed in some depressed patients[4].

In the present study we investigated migraine sufferers using the TRH stimulation test, which also provided the opportunity to study the secretion of prolactin (PRL), which may play a significant role in the pathogenesis of migraine[5].

Table 1. *Clinical data of migraine patients.*

Patients	Age	Age of onset	Family history	Attack frequency per month	Attack duration (h)	Prodromata	Associated symptoms	Precipitating factors	Hamilton score
1	28	20	–	2–3	7–12	Scintillating scotoma	Scintillating scotoma	Menstruation	2
2	38	18	+	1–5	4–6	–	–	Menstruation, alcohol	5
3	29	16	+	3	2–4	Nausea	Tinnitus	Psychic stress	4
4	32	26	+	1	12–24	–	–	Ovulation, psychic stress	1
5	34	26	+	1–3	12–24	Eye pain	Hand tremor, cold sweat	Psychic stress, alcohol, menstruation, contraceptives	4
6	28	18	–	2–3	2–4	Vertigo	Visual scotoma	Psychic stress	8
7	46	18	+	2–3	4–24	Eye pain	Depressed mood	Psychic stress, menstruation, alcohol	8
8	45	13	+	1–3	18–24	–	–	Menstruation	1
9	29	25	–	1–2	12–24	–	–	–	8
10	29	16	+	4–5	24	–	–	Psychic stress	2
11	40	35	–	1–2	24–48	–	–	Menstruation	2
12	49	25	+	1	4–12	–	–	Menstruation	0
13	39	20	+	10	12–16	Nausea	Diarrhoea	Psychic stress, alcohol	15
14	20	19	+	1	3–5	–	–	Menstruation	0
15	32	26	–	1	6–24	–	–	Psychic stress	2
16	46	26	+	4	24	–	Blurred vision	Psychic stress, menstruation, alcohol	5

Table 2. *TRH test in migraine.*

Patient	Attack free state			Migraine attack		
	Δ TSH	Δ GH	Δ PRL	Δ TSH	Δ GH	Δ PRL[‡]
1	13.5	8.2[†]	20.7	8.0	0	35.2
2	22.8	0.2	71.6	21.0	−0.7	83.3
3	4.3*	14.5[†]	36.4	2.3*	−0.3	42.5
4	0.1*	1.1	8.4	0.4*	7.8[†]	19.8
5	6.5	0.2	46.3	9.7	9.9[†]	81.2
6	3.7*	−0.6	39.4	6.7	0.1	59.8
7	19.8	−0.8	83.0	23.0	0.6	93.0
8	11.3	−0.2	14.7	11.0	7.8	13.9
9	4.3*	0.1	51.0			
10	8.6	−6.5	64.5			
11	10.2	−1.1	36.8			
12	14.4	0.2	73.1			
13	14.5	0.1	27.6			
14	25.2	4.4	49.2			
15	11.7	−2.9	68.5			
16	8.7	−0.3	50.0			

Δ , maximal post-TRH (0.4 mg i.v.) value minus baseline value. TSH in μg/ml, GH and PRL in ng/ml.
*Blunted TSH response; [†]unexpected GH response; [‡]mean PRL (attack) higher ($2a < 0.02$) than PRL (attack free).

Patients and methods

A total of 16 women suffering from migraine, 20–49 years of age (mean: 35) were evaluated. According to the criteria of the 'Ad Hoc Committee on Classification of Headache'[6] fourteen suffered from common, and two from classical migraine. The patients had no history of a significant head injury within the year prior to testing nor evidence of endocrine abnormalities. All patients had a normal physical and neurological examination. EEG and CT of the head were normal in all patients. A formal psychiatric examination did not reveal any major psychopathology. The 17 item Hamilton depression scale[7] was also completed in all patients. One patient, who was clinically mildly depressed had a score of 15, while the others scored below 8. The most pertinent clinical data are summarized in Table 1.

After informed consent was obtained, the TRH test was performed between attacks and after a 2 weeks drug-free period. The patients were then instructed to remain drug-free until the end of their participation and come in during an attack and have the test repeated, provided the attack occurred in the morning hours. Thus, the TRH test was always performed between 08.00 and 12.00 h. Eight of the patients were retested during a migraine attack.

Blood samples were obtained, with the patients recumbent, through an indwelling catheter that was kept patent with slow infusion of normal saline. After the first blood sample was obtained (baseline or 'time O' value), 0.4 mg of TRH were given i.v. as a bolus and blood samples were further obtained at 20, 40 and 60 mins. The plasma was separated by centrifugation and stored at −30°C until estimation. Thyrotropin (TSH), Gonatotrophin (GH) and PRL levels were assayed by radioimmunoassay techniques (Biodata kit) and the results were expressed in ng/ml (GH, PRL) and μU/ml (TSH).

For statistical evaluation of data we used the Wilcoxon test for paired differences, the Mann-Whitney U-test for unpaired differences and the Spearman rank correlation coefficient.

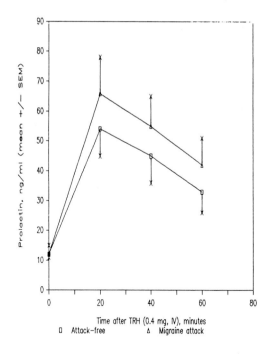

Figure. *Prolactin response to TRH.* Attack-free state vs. migraine attack.

Results

Before TRH administration

The baseline TSH and GH values as well as the thyroid hormones T_3 and T_4 were all within normal range both during and between migraine attacks. The mean baseline PRL value in the 16 migraineurs was higher than in 16 age and sex-matched controls (12 ± 6.5 for the migraineurs as opposed to 9.4 ± 3.9 for the controls) but this difference fell short of reaching statistical significance (Mann-Whitney U-test).

After TRH administration (Table 2)

A blunted TSH response to TRH, defined as maximal TSH increase less than $5 \mu u/ml$[8], occurred in four cases. Three of these patients were retested during a migraine attack and the response remained blunted in two while it normalized in one case. An unexpected GH response was elicited by TRH in two patients but, during migraine attacks, these two patients did not exhibit such a response. Instead, three patients with no GH response to TRH initially exhibited a GH response during the attack. The mean PRL response to TRH, defined as the maximal post TRH value minus baseline value, was higher during the attack (53.6 ± 30.3) than between attacks (40.1 ± 26.5) in the eight patients tested in both states ($2a < 0.02$, Wilcoxon test) (Figure).

No relationship was found between the baseline PRL levels and the PRL response, or the PRL and TSH response in the 16 patients.

Discussion

The view that migraine and depression have certain common features is supported by our findings, since some of the migraine patients respond to TRH administration in a way claimed to be characteristic of a depressed population, that is, an abnormal TSH and GH response[8,9]. A blunted TSH response to TRH has also been reported in patients with chronic post-traumatic pain[10] but not in cluster headache sufferers[11]. Although pain itself, such as organic low back pain[12], can be responsible for a diminished TSH response to TRH, our findings cannot be explained as merely pain related, since the TSH and GH response abnormalities occurred both in pain and pain-free states. Analgesics, which can cause a blunted TSH response[13], were probably not responsible for the abnormalities in our patients, who were drug-free for at least 2 weeks before the testing. Finally, depression per se seems unlikely to be responsible for these findings since only one patient was clinically depressed.

Our findings regarding PRL secretion appear to be more interesting especially in view of the alleged crucial role that PRL may play in the pathogenesis of migraine[5]. Several studies[14-17] have failed to demonstrate a PRL involvement, while others using the L-dopa inhibiting test showed abnormalities in the mechanism of PRL secretion in migraine[18-20]. Our findings of higher PRL response to TRH during the migraine attack as opposed to between attacks indicate an enhanced sensitivity of the PRL secreting mechanisms during the attack. Since baseline PRL levels were similar in both states, this higher PRL response is apparently not due to non-specific factors such as stress or pain.

In conclusion, our data indicate neuroendocrine abnormalities in migraine involving mainly mechanisms responsible for PRL secretion. The GH abnormalities are indicative of a hypothalamic-pituitary derangement rather than merely a local pituitary anomaly[21]. Our findings seem to support the neural hypothesis[1,2], which attributes a significant role in diencephalic-hypothalamic involvement in migraine.

References

1 Blau, J. N. (1984): Migraine pathogenesis: the neural hypothesis reexamined. *J. Neurol. Neurosurg. Psychiat.* **47**, 437–442.
2 Pearce, J. M. S. (1984): Migraine: A cerebral disorder. *Lancet* ii, 86–89.
3 Ziegler, D. K., Hassanein, R. S., Kodanaz, A. *et al.* (1979): Circadian rhythms of cortisol secretion in migraine. *J. Neurol. Neurosurg. Psychiat.* **42**, 741–748.
4 Carroll, B. J., Feinberg, M., Greden, J. F. *et al.* (1981): A specific laboratory test for diagnosis of melancholia: standardization, validation and clinical utility. *Arch. Gen. Psychiat.* **115**, 1367–1374.
5 Horrobin, D. F. (1975): Prolactin. Annual research reviews, pp. 134–150. Montreal: Eden Press.
6 Ad Hoc Committee on Classification of Headache (1962): *J. Amer. Med. Assoc.* **179**, 717–718.
7 Hamilton, M. (1960): A rating scale for depression. *J. Neurol. Neurosurg. Psychiat.* **23**, 56–62.
8 Loosen, P. T. & Prange, A. J. Jr. (1982): The serum thyrotropin (TSH) response to thyrotropin-releasing hormone (TRH) in depression: A review. *Am. J. Psychiat.* **139**, 405–416.
9 Maeda, K., Kato, Y., Ohgo, S. *et al.* (1975): Growth hormone and prolactin release after injection of thyrotropin-releasing hormone in patients with depression. *J. Clin. Endocrinal. Metab.* **40**, 501–505.
10 Mirialdo, G., Polleri, A., Testa, E. *et al.* (1979): Evaluation of pituitary function in chronic posttraumatic headache. In *Headache*, ed. F. Savoldi & G. Nappi, pp. 45–50. Vicenza: Palladio.
11 Boiardi, A., Bussone, E., Martini, A. *et al.* (1983): Endocrinological responses in cluster headache. *J. Neurol. Neurosurg. Psychiat.* **46**, 956–958.
12 Krishnan, K. R. & France, R. D. (1984): TRH stimulation in chronic pain. Abstracts of the American Psychiatric Association, Los Angeles.
13 Wenzel, K. W. (1981): Pharmacological interference with in vitro tests of thyroid function. *Metabolism* **30**, 717–732.
14 Nader, S., Tulloch, B., Blair, C. *et al.* (1974): Is prolactin involved in precipitating migraine? *Lancet* ii, 17–19.

15 Epstein, M. T., Hockaday, J. M. & Hockaday, T. D. R. (1975): Migraine and reproductive hormones throughout the menstrual cycle. *Lancet* **i**, 543–548.

16 Polleri, A., Nappi, G., Maturzo, P. *et al.* (1982): Neuroendocrine approach to headache. *Advances Neurol.* **33**, 173–182.

17 Dorow, R., Horowski, R., Maturzo, P. *et al.* (1983): The role of prolactin in migraine. *Acta Endocrinol. Scand. Suppl.* **102**, 36–37.

18 Vardi, J., Flechter, S., Ayalon, D. *et al.* (1981): L-Dopa effect on prolactin plasma levels in complicated and common migrainous patients. *Headache* **21**, 14–20.

19 D'Andrea, G., Cananzi, A. R., Soffiati, G. *et al.* (1985): Tuberoifundibular dopaminergic transmission in children migraine. *Cephalalgia.* **5** (Suppl. 3), 108–109.

20 Nattero, G., Corno, M., Savi, L. *et al.* (1986): Prolactin and migraine: effect of L-Dopa on plasma prolactin levels in migraineurs and normals. *Headache* **26**, 9–12.

21 Liuzzi, A., Chiodini, P. G., Bottala, L. *et al.* (1977): Inhibitory effect of growth hormone release in acromegalic patients. *J. Clin. Endocrinol. Metab.* **35**, 941–943.

10

SERUM GASTRIN: RELATIONSHIP TO MIGRAINE

G. Nattero*, L. Savi*, P. Piantino† and C. Priolo*

*University of Turin, Department of Biomedicine, Headache Center, Via Genova 3, 10126 Torino, Italy and †Ospedale San Giovanni Battista, Divisione di Gastroenterologia, Torino, Italy

Introduction

Idiopathic headaches are frequently accompanied by alimentary tract problems, mainly loss of appetite, nausea, vomiting and sometimes diarrhoea. Whilst anorexia accompanies most migraine headaches, vomiting can be the most serious component of the syndrome, at times the prevailing symptom, as in the so-called 'cyclical vomiting' of childhood.

Although these symptoms are a clinical criterion of considerable importance in the diagnosis of migraine, it is not easy to obtain the precise incidence of these symptoms, the literature being directed mainly to the neurological symptoms accompanying migraine.

In past and recent studies gastrin has been involved with gastric disturbances during the migraine attack. It might play a much more important role since, like several other hormones of the alimentary tract, it is found in the CNS, particularly in the hypothalamic system and the vagus nerve endings. Because of this, it has been hypothesized that gastrin might act as a neurotransmitter. In patients suffering from peptic ulcer subsequent to a CNS lesion, higher levels of gastrin, pepsin and acid secretion have been observed than in patients with peptic ulcer of different origin and in controls. More recently it was shown that intrahypothalamic injections of gastrin in rats produced an increase in acid gastric secretion.

There are three molecular forms of gastrin which are biologically active: these are 'big gastrin' or G34, 'little gastrin' or G17, and 'mini gastrin' or G14, each having respectively 34, 17 and 14 amino acid residues. Each form has a single tyrosine residue which may be either sulphated (Gastrin II) or not sulphated (Gastrin I). The presence or absence of sulphate groups alters both potency and biological activity of the peptide.

Gastrin is produced and secreted by specific endocrine cells (G cells), which are located in the mucosa of the gastric antrum and to a lesser extent in the proximal duodenum. It is released from G cells into the blood which carries it to the parietal cells where it acts. Under normal circumstances, there are four mechanisms by which gastrin can be released: vagal excitation, gastric distension, food stimulation and blood-borne chemical stimulation.

The release of gastrin is controlled by a negative feedback mechanism in which antral acidification inhibits further release of gastrin. In addition, it is probable that other peptides, ie somatostatin, are also responsible for modulating the feedback control of acid secretion. Acid basal secretion in man shows a circadian rhythm characterized by a high rate in the evening and a low rate in the morning. There is still no consensus as to whether this circadian variation is accompanied by a corresponding change in serum gastrin concentration.

As for the possible role of gastrin in the pathogenesis of the migraine attack the relationship with the other ascertained rings of the migraine pathogenetic chain: serotonin, histamine, catecholamines and also somatostatin might be involved.

In vivo experiments showed that catecholamines directly influence G-cell function, serotonin inhibits basal gastrin output, histamine is released in response to pentagastrin and acetylcholine seems to be a common mediator.

The possible relationship between gastrin and dyspeptic symptoms in migraineurs is worth investigating in view of the fact that it might not only cause alimentary tract disturbances but also reduce the effectiveness of active prophylactic and/or therapeutic agents administered orally to migraineurs.

Previous work done by our research group in 1983 and 1984 had showed an increase in migraineurs' gastrin levels during the migraine attack in comparison with the interictal period.

The aim of the present study is the comparison between serum gastrin levels of migraineurs in the headache-free period and those of controls in order to ascertain if there are statistically significant differences.

Material and method

Serum gastrin levels were determined in a group of 62 migraine patients (47 females and 15 males), age ranging from 14 to 60 years (mean age 34.16), during headache-free periods and in 23 of these during the height of the attack (18 females and five males), age ranging from 14 to 60 (mean age 32.53).

Blood samples were taken in the morning from patients fasting overnight. All these subjects were free from gastrointestinal pathology, especially peptic ulcer. The same evaluation was made in a group of 40 controls, all free of gastric disturbances.

Serum gastrin levels were also determined in a group of 15 migraine children during the headache-free period and in a second group of eight children without migraine. The criteria adopted for patients' selection were as indicated by the 'Ad Hoc Committee for Headache Classification'.

Glass test tubes containing the blood samples were centrifuged and the serum was then stocked in plastic tubes at $-20°C$. Serum gastrin levels were determined by means of Sorin's double antibody radio-immunoassay (RIA) methods.

Results are shown in pg/ml of serum. Normal values in man are lower than 130 pg/ml. Results, in mean values, obtained in the various groups, were then compared together and statistically analysed by means of Student's *t*-test.

Results

Gastrin serum levels were within the normal range in all the cases examined, but a significant difference was observed between migraine patients and controls ($P<0.05$). Mean gastrin levels were 37.38 ± 28.82 pg/ml in migraine patients and of 28.05 ± 14.52 pg/ml in the control group (Fig. 1).

We also found a statistically significant ($P<0.05$) increase in serum gastrin levels during attacks compared to the interictal period. Mean gastrin values resulted of

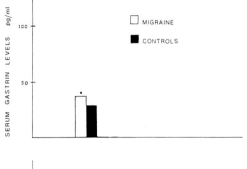

Fig. 1. *Mean gastrin values in migraine patients and controls. *P<0.05.*

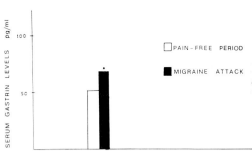

Fig. 2. *Mean gastrin values in migraine patients during headache-free period and during the attack. *P<0.05.*

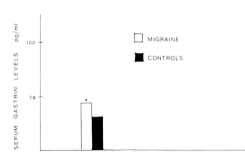

Fig. 3. *Mean gastrin values in migraine children and in controls. *P<0.05.*

52.33 ± 40.02 pg/ml during the headache-free period and of 69.85 ± 56.64 pg/ml during the attack (Fig. 2).

We found the same significant differences ($P < 0.05$) in the childhood group. Mean gastrin values levels were 43.1 pg/ml in migraine children during the headache-free period and 30.3 pg/ml in the controls' group (Fig. 3).

Conclusion

On the basis of the high statistical significance obtained in differences between migraine patients' gastrinemia and that of controls, it may be concluded that these patients must constantly have a high secretion rate of this enterohormone, even between attacks. Even if the constantly high values of gastrinemia stayed within the normal range, it cannot be excluded that a further, periodic increase in blood levels during attacks of this enterohormone might be one of the pathogenetic factors involved in the onset of gastritis and gastric dyspepsia.

Several peptides (including substance P, somatostatin, enkephalin and cholecystokinin) are found both in brain nervous cells and gut endocrine cells. Three components of gastrin were discovered by gel chromatography of extracts from the anterior lobe, posterior lobe and stalk of the pituitary, corresponding to component I, gastrin 34 and gastrin 17.

Results of RIA studies tend to support the hypothesis that gastrin and cholecystokinin might have a physiological role as neurotransmitters in the central nervous system, as well as in the peripheral (vagus) nerve. The constant change in levels of gastrinemia observed in migraine patients might suggest an altered balance in the hypothalamus-pituitary system of the brain-gut polypeptides viz: gastrin, cholecystokinin, substance P, somatostatin, enkephalin etc. and/or of the various fractions I, G17, with different biological activities. For the same reasons, the neurotransmitter gastrin might be directly involved in the pathogenesis of idiopathic headaches, especially migraine.

References

1 Gregory, R. A. (1974): The gastrointestinal hormones: a review of recent advances. *J. Physiol. (Lond.)* **241**, 1–32.
2 Grossman, M. I. (1979): Neural and hormonal regulation of gastrointestinal function: an overview. *A. Rev. Physiol.* **41**, 27–33.
3 Hayes, J. R., Ardill, J., Shanks, R. G. & Buchanan, K. D. (1978): Effects of catecholamines on gastrin release. *Metab. Clin. Exp.* **27**, 385–391.
4 Kleckner, M. S. Jr & Horton, B. T. (1949): The concurrence of migraine and peptic ulcer. *Gasteroenterology* **31**, 141–143.
5 Klimeck, A. (1982): Serum gastrin in patients with migraine and Horton's headache. *Pop. Tyg. Lek.* **37**, 555–557.
6 Krieger, D. T., Martin, J. B. (1981): Brain Peptides. *New Engl. J. Med.* **304**, 876, 944.
7 Nattero, G., Savi, L., Piantino, P., Priolo, C. & Corno, M. (1983): Serum gastrin levels in cluster headache and migraine attacks. 1st International Headache Congress, Munich. Abstr. 70–71.
8 Nattero, G., Savi, L., Piantino, P., Priolo, C. & Corno, M. (1985): Serum gastrin levels and dyspepsia in migraineurs. In *Migraine clinical and research advances*, ed. F. Clifford Rose, pp. 95–102. Basel: Karger.
9 Nattero, G., Savi, L., Piantino, P. & Priolo, C. (1986): Gastrin in cluster headache. International Congress 'Trends in cluster headache', Chieti-Montesilvano (Pe), Abstr. 107.
10 Rehfeld, J. F. (1978): Localization of gastrins to neuro- and adenohypophysis. *Nature* **271**, 771–773.
11 Rehfeld, J. F., Goltermann, N., Larsson, L. I. Emson, P. M. & Lee, C. M. (1979): Gastrin and cholecystokinin in central and peripheral neurons. *Fed. Proc.* **38**, 2325–2329.
12 Saik, R. P. (1981): Serotonin as an inhibitor of gastrin. *Scand. J. Gastroent.* **16**, 337–340.
13 Tepperman, B. L. & Evered, M. D. (1980): Gastrin injected into the lateral hypothalamus stimulates secretion of gastric acid in rats. *Science* **209**, 1142–1143.

   Advances in headache research, ed. F. Clifford Rose. ©*John Libbey & Co Ltd, 1987*

II

VASCULAR ASPECTS

11

CEREBRAL BLOOD FLOW

ASYMMETRIES IN MIGRAINE

Steven R. Levine, K. M. A. Welch, James R. Ewing
and Rajiv Joseph

*Center for Cerebrovascular Disease Research and
Department of Neurology, Henry Ford Hospital,
2799 West Grand Boulevard, Detroit, Michigan 48202, USA*

Summary

We studied regional cerebral blood flow (rCBF) asymmetries in 18 controls, 18 common and 27 classic/complicated migraineurs. All patients had normal neurological and contrast head CT examinations, and had been free of headaches and medication for at least 10 days. Regional cerebral blood flow was performed using ^{133}Xe inhalation with eight homologously situated external collimators over each cerebral hemisphere. Occipital and occipito-parietal probes were designated 'posterior'. Based on normative data, any probe-pair with a difference in actual CBF greater than 7% was designated 'asymmetric'. Migraineurs as a group (16 of 45) more frequently had asymmetric posterior probe-pairs than controls (one of 18) ($P < 0.03$, Fisher's exact test). Although there was no difference in the number of asymmetric anterior probe-pairs, migraineurs had two or more asymmetric probe-pairs (17 of 45) more often than controls (one of 18) ($P < 0.02$, Fisher's exact test). Our results strongly support a difference in rCBF patterns in the headache-free migraineur compared to the non-migraineur. The posterior asymmetries, consistent with the site of activation of many migraine attacks, may be related to more 'labile' control of the cerebral circulation and 'shifting' thresholds to a migraine attack.

Introduction

Cerebral blood flow asymmetries have been reported during the headache-free period in migraine patients[1]. This chapter represents an extension of the previous report in a larger series of migraine patients using measures designed to identify the location and frequency of the previously discovered CBF asymmetries. In addition, we present yet further evidence for instability of cerebral blood flow control in between migraine episodes.

Methods

Regional cerebral blood flow (rCBF) was performed in 63 individuals by use of the non-invasive ^{133}Xe inhalation technique employing home built systems of eight probe pairs (16 total probes) with external collimetry[2]. Probes were carefully matched over homologous regions of the two cerebral hemispheres. Eighteen controls ranging in age from 24–30 years, 18 common migraineurs, mean age 44.9 ± 9 and 27 classic/complicated migraine patients, mean age 27.9 ± 14 were studied. The classic and complicated migraine group constituted patients with a diagnosis of migraine plus transient neurological deficit.

Patients had their rCBF performed at least two weeks after the last migraine attack. Aspirin containing products, non-steroidal anti-inflammatory drugs or caffeine had not been taken for at least 10 days prior to their rCBF study. All 63 patients had normal neurological examinations and all migraine patients had normal contrast infused head CT scans. All migraineurs satisfied the criteria set forth by the Ad Hoc Committee on the classification of headache[3].

The mean rCBF value for each of the three groups was calculated using the initial slope index (ISI) method of Risberg *et al.*[4]. The regional percentage interhemispheric difference was calculated from the difference of the paired ISI values, divided by their mean value, and expressed as a percentage of the denominator. Based on the control population data, the mean plus two standard deviations of each probe-pair difference always fell within 7%. Therefore, if a probe-pair difference greater than 7% was measured, it was designated 'asymmetric'. Six probe pairs were positioned over the anterior circulation (inferior frontal, superior frontal, fronto-temporal, temporal, parietal-temporal and parietal) and two positioned over the posterior circulation (occipital and occipito-parietal).

Statistical plan

We compared controls to migraineurs to evaluate any difference in mean and regional CBF and extent and locations of 'asymmetries'. When significant differences in demographics (sex, age, systolic blood pressure, diastolic blood pressure, hematocrit, and pCO_2) arose, mean CBF data was adjusted and controlled for by regression analysis of continuous variables so that these features could not contribute to differences between groups. Two sample t-tests were performed to compare migraineurs to controls for the continuous variables. Fisher's exact tests were performed for the categorical variables. The significant values were Bonferroni adjusted to allow for multiple testing. The values $P < 0.05$ to 0.03 were regarded as borderline significant; $P < 0.025$ was regarded as significant.

Results

There was no significant difference between mean CBF in control subjects and migraine sufferers although a trend toward lower flow was noted in the latter ($P < 0.05$). When probe-pair asymmetries were analysed, compared to controls two or more asymmetric probe pairs were found more frequently in migraine patients independent of migraine type ($P < 0.02$) (Table 1). No statistically significant differences were seen in the number of patients with asymmetries in the anterior circulation but posterior asymmetries of flow were more evident ($P < 0.03$) (Table 2). Of possible interest, all ten classic/complicated migraineurs found

Table 1. *Number of subjects with two or more asymmetric probe pairs**

Group	Number	%	P value
Controls	1 of 18	6	
All migraineurs	17 of 45	38	$P < 0.02$
Common	7 of 18	39	
Classic/complicated	10 of 27	37	

*An asymmetric probe-pair is defined as an individual pair of probes that differ in their ISI values by greater than 7%.

Table 2. *Asymmetries of rCBF*

Number with asymmetric probe-pair

Group		%	P value
Controls	7 of 18	39	
All migraineurs	29 of 45	64	$P < 0.1$
Common	10 of 18	56	
Classic/complicated	19 of 27	70	

Number with asymmetric posterior probe-pair

Controls	1 of 18	6	
All migraineurs	16 of 45	36	$P < 0.03$
Common	6 of 18	33	
Classic/complicated	10 of 27	37	

Number with asymmetric anterior probe-pair

Controls	6 of 18	33	
All migraineurs	24 of 45	53	$P < 0.18$

to have one asymmetric posterior probe-pair also exhibited further asymmetries in either the anterior or posterior circulation.

Discussion

In a prior publication, the use of a mean asymmetry index of flow during the headache-free period in migraine patients demonstrated the presence of rCBF asymmetries, but only in classic/complicated cases[1]. In the present study, asymmetries were found in both clinical types of migraine and were more frequently located in the posterior circulation. This may be relevant to the spreading oligemia reported during migraine attacks which is generally thought to proceed from the occipital lobes forward[5], analogous to the spreading depression of neuronal function described by Leão[6].

Whether these asymmetries are related to the cause or the effect of migraine is uncertain. There are reports of persistent neurological and neuropsychological deficits resulting from severe or frequent migraine attacks but our patients had normal neurological and head CT examination and flow asymmetries were seen as frequently in common as in classic/complicated migraine. Hockaday and Whitty previously failed to find any correlation between EEG abnormalities and migraine duration or severity[7].

The results do not support our previous contention, namely that testing asymmetries of CBF may distinguish classic/complicated migraine from common migraine nor do they support the concept that these are two different entities. However, if the asymmetries of flow that have now been demonstrated in two separate studies from our laboratory are related to the cause of migraine, this could reflect an instability of CBF control. We have recently proposed that migraine is a biobehaviourally modulated dysautonomia wherein orbito-frontal-brainstem neuronal projections trigger the intrinsic and extrinsic noradrenergic nervous system[8]. Variable function in the noradrenergic nervous system may also be related to an associated purinergic neurotransmitter hypofunction that we have most recently demonstrated[9]. The varying function of this system may influence the threshold for activation of a migraine attack.

Acknowledgements — This work was supported in part by NIH grant # NS23393 and the Henry Ford Hospital Research Fund. We thank Hally Phelps for typing the manuscript.

References

1 Levine, S. R., Welch, K. M. A., Ewing, J. R. & Robertson, W. M. (1986): Asymmetric cerebral blood flow patterns in migraine. *Stroke* **17**, 147.
2 Ewing, J. R., Welch, K. M. A., Robertson, W. M., Brown, G. G., Diaz, F. & Ausman, J. I. (1983): A probe-by-probe identification of focal cerebral ischemia using the 133-Xenon inhalation technique. *J. Cereb. Blood Flow. Metab.* S586–S587.
3 Report of the Ad Hoc Committee on classification of headache (1962): *Arch Neurol.* **6**, 173–176.
4 Risberg, J., Ali, Z., Wilson, E. W. *et al.* (1975): Regional cerebral blood flow by 133-Xenon inhalation. Preliminary evaluation of an initial slope index in patients with unstable flow compartments. *Stroke* **6**, 142–148.
5 Olesen, J., Lassen, B. & Lauritzen, M. (1981): Focal hyperemia followed by spreading oligemia and impaired activation of rCBF in classic migraine. *Ann. Neurol.* **9**, 344–352.
6 Leão, A. P. P. (1944): Spreading depression of activity in cerebral cortex. *J. Neurophysiol.* **7**, 359–390.
7 Hockaday, J. M. & Whitty, C. W. M. (1969): Factors determining the electroencephalogram in migraine: A study of 500 patients, according to clinical type of migraine. *Brain* **92**, 769–788.
8 Welch, K. M. A. (1987): Migraine: A Biobehavioral Disorder. *Arch. Neurol.* **44**, 323–327.
9 Joseph, R., Welch, K. M. A., D'Andrea, G. & Levine, S. R. (1986): ATP hyposection from platelet dense bodies — evidence for the purinergic hypothesis and a marker of migraine. *Headache* **26**, 403–410.

12

CEREBRAL BLOOD FLOW IMAGING IN MIGRAINE PATIENTS WITH 99mTc-HM-PAO AND SINGLE-PHOTON EMISSION TOMOGRAPHY: PRELIMINARY FINDINGS AND A REPORT ON ITS EFFICACY

D. C. Costa*, P. T. G. Davies[†], B. E. Jones[‡],
T. J. Steiner[†], P. J. Ell* and F. Clifford Rose[†]

*Institute of Nuclear Medicine, The Middlesex Hospital Medical School, London UK; [†]The Princess Margaret Migraine Clinic, Academic Unit of Neurosciences, Charing Cross and Westminster Medical School, London UK; and [‡]Department of Nuclear Medicine, Charing Cross Hospital, London, UK

Summary

Changes in cerebral blood flow (CBF) have long been put forward amongst a number of hypotheses to explain the symptoms of migraine. The continuing uncertainty over their role in migraine pathophysiology results largely from methodological difficulties in the measurement of CBF. 99mTc-hexamethylpropyleneamineoxime (99mTc-HM-PAO) is a new radiopharmaceutical for the study of CBF with single-photon emission tomography (SPET). We have used it in seven patients suffering from spontaneous attacks of acute migraine, three classical and four common.

Images showed patterns compatible with normal distribution of CBF in all four common migraine patients, with asymmetries of unknown significance in two. In one of the classical migraine patients, increased CBF in the right frontal lobe corresponded with the site of severe headache and had reverted to normal at a second study 6 days after full recovery. The pattern of CBF was symmetrical in the other two classical patients although uneven in one.

Whilst present results show that the headache phase of acute migraine is not necessarily associated with detectable changes in CBF, other findings were of potential interest. This study of a new method gives a promise of effective future investigations in an area of migraine research that has long resisted scrutiny.

75

Introduction

Although the underlying causes are unknown, changes in CBF apparently occur during attacks of classical migraine. According to the vascular theory of migraine[1], vasoconstriction of cerebral arteries leads to the neurological symptoms and rebound vasodilation of either extra- or intracranial vessels causes the headache.

Direct demonstration of a consistent pattern of CBF changes during migraine has proved technically difficult. Both hypo- and hyperperfusion of cerebral structures during acute attacks have been seen with radionuclide techniques, which have most commonly been planar studies using multiple radiation detectors around the head and, as a tracer, ^{133}Xe by inhalation or intracarotid injection[2-5]. A recent technological advance has been single-photon emission tomography (SPET), with which Lauritzen, still using ^{133}Xe by inhalation, showed a focal decrease in CBF in patients with classical migraine, during acute attacks[6]. No changes in CBF were seen in patients with common migraine.

Whilst SPET offers major advantages over planar imaging in terms of sensitivity, resolution and localization, substantial further improvements are possible with advances in tracer technology. Thus the introduction of ^{99m}Tc-hexamethylpropyleneamineoxime (^{99m}Tc-HM-PAO) as a new tracer for the investigation of cerebral vascular disease with SPET[7] opened new possibilities also for the study of CBF in migraine. We have demonstrated that the brain uptake of ^{99m}Tc-HM-PAO correlates well with the distribution of CBF in young dogs, using radioactive microspheres as the reference method[8]. In man, high resolution images can be obtained, either with a gamma camera computer system or with single-slice multidetector scanners[9]; these show sufficient anatomical detail for the detection of regional changes in CBF.

This study tests this technique for its potential to investigate alterations in CBF during acute migraine and reports its first use in migraineurs.

Patients

Seven patients (2 males, 5 females) presenting to The Princess Margaret Migraine Clinic for symptomatic treatment of spontaneous acute migraine attacks, and admitted to the day ward, were investigated. Their ages ranged from 24 to 62 years. Diagnoses of migraine by Vahlquist's criteria were clinically definite and the patients were classified into two groups (Table 1).

The attacks were themselves characteristic of each patient's usual episodes, and had been present, untreated, for 3 to 12 h at the time of investigation.

Table 1. *Characterization of patients.*

	Patient	Age	Sex
Group 1 (Classical migraine)	1	30	M
	2	31	F
	3	24	M
Group 2 (Common migraine)	4	30	F
	5	62	F
	6	42	F
	7	36	F

M, male; F, female.

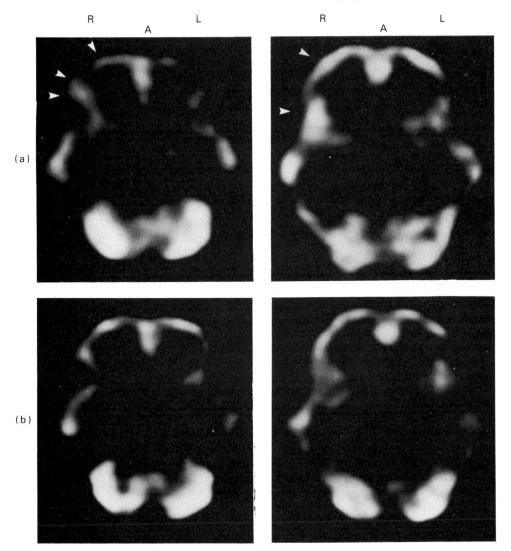

Fig. 1. *CLEON 710 studies in patient 2.* (a) Study 1 at 2 levels during severe right frontal headache showing increased right frontal blood flow. (b) Study 2, at the same levels, showing return to normal after recovery (see text). A, anterior; R, right; L, left.

Three patients (two classical and one common) agreed to and undertook a second study when asymptomatic, 6–14 days later.

Methods

Patients were clinically assessed on presentation before being informed of the project and asked to give consent to their participation. To those agreeable, 7–10 MBq per kg of ⁹⁹ᵐTc-HM-PAO were administered intravenously; immediately afterwards symptomatic treatment for the acute attack of migraine was given.

Table 2. *Instruments used in this study for CBF/SPET studies.*

		Slices			Uniformity	Attenuation
		Direction	No.	Thickness	correction	correction
Single-slice	CLEON 710	Transverse	4–8	12.5 mm	Yes	Yes
Multidetector scanners	NOVO 810	Transverse	4–8	12.5 mm	Yes	Yes
Gamma camera computer system	IGE 400 AC/ STARCAM	Transverse, coronal and sagittal	>16	10–12 mm	Yes	Yes

SPET was undertaken either at Charing Cross Hospital or at the Middlesex Hospital, the patient being transferred by car in the latter case. Studies began 10–90 min post-injection, and one of three available instruments was used (Table 2). With the single-slice multidetector scanners, careful adjustment of the head was performed to obtain transverse slices parallel to the orbitomeatal line.

Results

Table 3 summarizes the qualitative evaluation of the CBF/SPET images in the two groups of patients studied.

Table 3. *Qualitative evaluation of CBF/SPET studies.*

		Study 1 (during attack)	Study 2 (asymptomatic)	
Patient	Symptoms	CBF appearances	Time after study 1 (days)	CBF appearances
1	Visual aura, subsequent mild R frontal headache	Normal		
2	Severe R frontal, throbbing headache	↑R frontal cortex	6	Normal
3	Visual aura and mild L frontal headache	Equivocal (uneven)	14	Unchanged
4	L frontal headache	Normal		
5	L occipitoparietal throbbing headache	Normal		
6	R frontal headache	? normal, with ↓R head of caudate nucleus	10	Unchanged
7	Severe L frontal throbbing headache	? normal, with ↑R, ↓L head of caudate nucleus		

R, right; L, left.

Patient 1, in the aura phase of a classical migraine attack, showed a normal CBF pattern; patient 3 with aura and mild frontal headache showed equivocal changes represented by uneven distribution of CBF throughout the brain, without well-defined areas of increased or decreased perfusion. Only patient 2 in this group had well-established severe headache, which was associated with unequivocally increased cortical uptake of isotope in the same region (right frontal). This pattern of hyperperfusion had reverted to normal when the patient was re-studied 6 days after full recovery (Fig. 1).

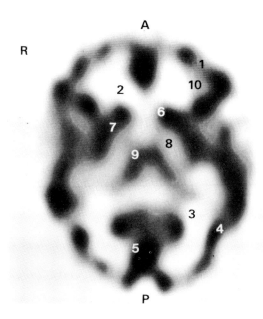

Fig. 2. *NOVO 810 study at 30 mm above the orbitomeatal (OM) line in patient 6 (common migraine), scanned whilst asymptomatic.* A, anterior; P, posterior; R, right side. 1, frontal lobe (grey matter); 2, anterior horn of lateral ventricle; 3, posterior horn of lateral ventricle; 4, parietal lobe (grey matter); 5, occipital lobe (visual cortex); 6, head of caudate nucleus; 7, putamen; 8, internal capsule; 9, thalamus; 10, frontal lobe (white matter).

All patients suffering from common migraine, during or between attacks, showed SPET images compatible with a normal distribution of CBF. An example of the high resolution images that can, at best, be obtained with the technique is exhibited in Fig. 2. With detail of this order, small asymmetries of CBF can become apparent, and were seen in two cases, during attacks, especially in the basal ganglia (head of the caudate nucleus); lower perfusion on the side of the headache was observed in each but we do not yet know its significance.

Discussion

Our work has demonstrated that high resolution CBF/SPET imaging can be carried out in man with ^{99m}Tc-HM-PAO[9]. These studies allow for good anatomical detail, as seen in Fig. 2: grey and white matter are well differentiated, and the head of the caudate nucleus, putamen and thalamus can be seen as separate structures.

To the extent that the distribution of CBF is normal in our images of common migraine patients, our studies of spontaneous migraine attacks are in agreement with others, in which attacks were commonly provoked. If, in two cases of common migraine, the heads of the caudate nuclei showed real asymmetry of CBF, lower on the side of the headache, this is a finding that is difficult to explain. That it has not been reported before, if real, would be a consequence of poorer resolution in past series. Increased CBF in one of the cases of classical migraine, in the right frontal lobe — the site of severe throbbing headache which had completely returned to normal when the patient was studied 6 days after full recovery, are contrary findings to those of Olesen[5], who detected no hyperperfusion in classical migraine. They are supported, on the other hand, by the work of Skinhoj[2]. The study of CBF in provoked migraine attacks or the use of carotid puncture in the study may both introduce artefacts, and our project involved neither. The images from patient 1 of a normal distribution of CBF during the aura phase is also at odds with several previous studies. This patient did not subsequently develop a marked headache and one could speculate, without good evidence at present, that the severity of vasoconstriction in classical migraine determines the severity of the headache.

We believe these preliminary findings of original work are of considerable interest, and indicate that ^{99m}Tc-HM-PAO and SPET will be very useful in studying the behaviour of CBF in acute migraine. Whilst we cannot immediately explain all we see, we now have the means to investigate this long-uncertain area effectively.

References

1   Wolff H. G. (1963): *Headache and other head pain*, 2nd edn. New York: Oxford University Press.
2   Skinhoj E. (1973): Hemodynamic studies within the brain during migraine. *Archs Neurol.* **29**, 95–98.
3   Norris, J. W., Hachinski, V. C. & Cooper, P. W. (1975): Changes in cerebral blood flow during a migraine attack. *Br. Med. J.* **3**, 676–684.
4   Sakai, F. & Meyer, J. S. (1978): Regional cerebral hemodynamics during migraine and cluster headaches measured by the ^{133}Xe inhalation method. *Headache* **18**, 122–132.
5   Olesen, J., Larsen, B. & Lauritzen, M. (1981): Focal hyperemia followed by spreading oligemia and impaired activation of rCBF in classic migraine. *Ann. Neurol.* **9**, 344–352.
6   Lauritzen, M. & Olesen, J. (1984): Regional cerebral blood flow during migraine attacks by Xenon-133 inhalation and emission tomography. *Brain* **107**, 447–461.
7   Ell, P. J., Hocknell, J. M. L., Jarritt, P. H., Cullum, I., Lui, D., Costa, D. C., Nowotnik, D. P., Pickett, R. D., Canning, L. R., & Neirinckx, R. D. (1985): A ^{99m}Tc-labelled radiotracer for the investigation of cerebral vascular disease. *Nucl. Med. Comm.* **6**, 437–441.
8   Costa, D. C., Jones, B. E., Steiner, T. J., Aspey, B. S., Ell, P. J., Cullum, I. & Jewkes, R. F. (1986): Relative ^{99m}Tc-HM-PAO and [113]Sn microspheres distribution in dog brain. *Nuklearmedizin* **25**, A53.
9   Costa, D. C., Ell, P. J., Cullum, I. D. & Jarritt, P. H. (1986): The in vivo distribution of ^{99m}Tc-HM-PAO in normal man. *Nucl. Med. Comm.* **7**, 647–658.

13

SENSORY CONNECTIONS TO CEPHALIC BLOOD VESSELS AND THEIR POSSIBLE IMPORTANCE TO VASCULAR HEADACHES

Michael A. Moskowitz

Stroke Research Laboratory, Neurosurgery and Neurology Services, Massachusetts General Hospital, Harvard Medical School, Boston, MA 02114, USA

Introduction

Most throbbing headaches are presumed to arise from a disturbance in cephalic blood vessels. This notion is inferred from the observations that similar headaches are associated with strokes, aneurysms and arteriovenous malformations, and from the demonstrations by Ray and Wolff[1], Penfield[2], and others that blood vessels are the only structures within the cranium that cause pain when stimulated, and that the symptoms elicited resemble those described by patients with vascular head pain. Unfortunately, no experimental data during the headache experience exist upon which to base confident acceptance or rejection of this notion. Furthermore, firm evidence is lacking regarding the responsible circulation, for example, does pain come from intracranial dural, cerebral or extracranial vessels? Even less is known about initiating stimuli. Numerous studies implicating circulating vasoactive molecules such as histamine, serotonin, and small, biologically active peptides have not been validated. Some exciting and testable clues may come from recent studies on spreading depression[3]. That migraine pharmacology has not yet provided us with significant pathophysiological clues is most disappointing. In other diseases, such clues have been tremendously valuable and have even led to the development of rational treatments for Parkinson's disease and hypertension. Migraine therapy, however, still remains largely empirical. What accounts for such differences remains unexplained.

In our view, vascular pain represents a final common pathway which can arise from multiple causes, all of which activate (depolarize) perivascular sensory axons. It follows, therefore, that a fruitful approach for study should focus on pain producing or nociceptive mechanisms in blood vessels with particular attention to the anatomy, chemistry and physiology of these sensory neural connections. Since pain localizes to the forehead and occiput, the trigeminal and upper cervical nerves appear to be all important. In the first part of this chapter, we review recent information concerning the source and distribution of afferent projections to blood vessels and describe how the established innervation patterns in animals may relate to the localization and referral of vascular headaches in man. In the second part, we suggest a scheme for classifying causes of sensory activation which might underlie headaches. If vascular-sensory connections do represent a final common pathway for the production of headaches, then modulation of this pathway by influences within the vessel wall, along the sensory axon, cell body, root and most importantly central terminations provide a focal point for the pathogenesis and treatment of these conditions.

Sensory connections to cephalic blood vessels

Pial, dural, and extracranial cephalic blood vessels are surrounded by a plexus of nerve fibres some of which derive from sensory ganglia cells[4,5,6]. Studies in the cat indicate that the trigeminal ganglia provides the major sensory projection to blood vessels comprising the circle of Willis (Fig. 1). Cells within the first division send axonal projections which probably reach the major branches of the circle via crossing connections at the level of the cavernous sinus. At the circle, trigeminal fibres distribute themselves to the anterior, middle, posterior, anterior and posterior communicators, rostral basilar and superior cerebellar arteries on the same side[7]. Fibres also cross to innervate the contralateral anterior cerebral artery. Although single fibres do not send axonal branches to both intra and extra-cranial tissues (eg such as those in the trigeminal receptive field)[8,9], recent studies (in rats) indicate that trigeminovascular cells project widely within the cranium[10], so that, for example, the same trigeminal ganglia cell which projects to the middle cerebral artery also sends an axon to innervate the middle meningeal artery. The basilar and vertebral arteries contain fibres which arise from the upper cervical ganglia[11]; the basilar artery also contains projections from the superior vagal ganglia as well[12]. Some of these same pathways were also reported in the guinea-pig[13].

Dural vessels also receive rich trigeminal and upper cervical projections. Mayberg found that the middle meningeal artery is innervated by the ipsilateral trigeminal ganglia, primarily from cells within the first division. He also found that the superior sagittal sinus receives a bilateral innervation, a finding which agrees with other reports in humans. The first and second trigeminal divisions innervate the dura within the anterior fossa, the second and third divisions project to the middle cranial fossa whereas upper cervical nerves (human and cat), as well as vagus and trigeminal ganglia (cat), innervate dural structures within the posterior fossa[5].

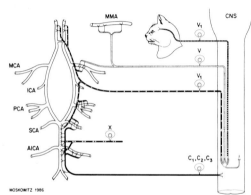

Fig. 1. *Schematic diagram depicting the sensory innervation of cephalic blood vessels.* Except for the divergent trigeminal projection (rat) to the middle meningeal artery, pathways were described in the cat. (See text for more complete explanation.)

Clinical correlations

The origin and distribution of perivascular afferent fibres suggest several of the following unique explanations for vascular headache patterns experienced by man.

(1) The predominantly ipsilateral distribution of trigeminal fibres explains the strictly ipsilateral distribution of many vascular headaches.

(2) The bilateral innervation of certain vessels (anterior cerebral artery and superior sagittal sinus) suggests the possibility that disturbances within produce bilateral headaches. Previous interpretations emphasized blood or some circulating nociceptor. The discovery of a dual innervation provides at least one alternative to this possibility. Theoretically, a vessel which is bilaterally innervated could also cause a contralateral headache, perhaps an explanation for the 'wrong sided headache of classical migraine'.

(3) The trigeminal innervation of the superior cerebellar artery provides an explanation for the frontal headache experienced by patients with cerebellar tumors.

(4) The dual innervation of the superior cerebellar, as well as the rostral basilar, arteries (ie from upper cervical dorsal roots and trigeminal fibres) provides an anatomical explanation for the co-existence of occipital and frontal headaches, a second alternative to the convergence of descending trigeminal impulses with inputs from upper cervical cord segments.

(5) The observation that some dural and pial arteries receive divergent axon collaterals from single trigeminal neurons may account for the difficulty in distinguishing the source of pain in vascular headaches. The same sensory ganglia cell would discharge with appropriate stimulation in both circulations.

A scheme for activation/modulation of afferent connections

The discovery that cephalic blood vessels contain a network of sensory fibres suggests that these fibres may transmit signals of a nociceptive nature. This notion has been confirmed by recent electrophysiological experiments[14,15] and inferred from the therapeutic benefits of radiofrequency lesions or injections of glycerol into the trigeminal ganglia[16]. Figure 2 schematically depicts a prototypic trigeminovascular neuron with its peripheral axon surrounding a cephalic blood vessel. The cell body resides within the trigeminal ganglia and root fibre terminates within the brain stem trigeminal complex. We suggest that such a fibre can be modulated or even activated at various points along its length, from the blood vessel to the brain stem. Some potential modulators are listed in Tables 1 and 2, which are not meant to be complete, and we have omitted potential modifiers of neurotransmission at the axon, ganglion cell body and root. Nevertheless, these tables outline a scheme for classifying triggers/modulators and treatments of vascular headaches and

ACTIVATION / MODULATION OF A FINAL COMMON PATHWAY

Blood Vessel   Axon   Cell Body   Root

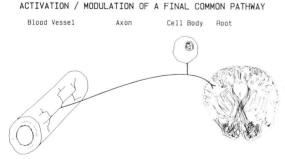

Fig. 2. *The perivascular primary sensory neuron is viewed as a final common pathway subject to activation or modulation by local factors within the vessel wall and also by potential factors influencing the axon, cell body, root and central terminations.*

Table 1. *The blood vessel wall — sensory nerve interaction.*

1. Biochemical modulation:	hormones
	mast cell constituents
	alcohol and drugs
	platelet contents
	foods
2. Mechanical modulation:	stretch
3. Ionic modulation:	spreading depression
4. Neural modulation	opiate-containing fibres
	sympathetic
	parasympathetic

Table 2. *Central modulation of trigeminovascular transmission.*

1. Periaqueductal grey modulation	
2. Special senses:	light, sound
3. Altered physiological states:	sleep, stress
4. Spreading depression?	

by so doing acknowledge the primary sensory nerve fibre as the final common pathway in the genesis of headache. As noted in Table 1, certain biochemical, mechanical, ionic and neural influences may raise or lower sensory fibre threshold at the blood vessel wall. Most of these remain without direct experimental evidence at the present time. Some have been shown to modify sensory transmission in other paradigms, for example, injections of estrogen will enhance the size of the cutaneous receptive field of individual trigeminal fibres by direct effects on sensory nerve endings in the skin[17]. Most assuredly, as we uncover more facts, some listed modulators will be deleted and others added. Moreover, some may act at more than a single locus along the neuron.

Table 2 lists some of the possible central nervous system mechanisms for modifying incoming activity from the trigeminovascular system. Experiments have shown that electrical stimulation within periaqueductal grey (PAG) modulates the responses of brain stem trigeminal units. Using extracellular electrophysiological techniques, Maciewicz and his colleagues demonstrated that stimulation of this 'endogenous pain suppressing region' inhibits the firing of neurons within the trigeminal nucleus caudalis which respond to electrical shock of dural blood vessels[14]. Other listed possibilities (except for spreading depression) are based on clinical observations. The trigeminal nuclear complex possesses rich connections with many brain stem areas including those associated with the regulation of autonomic activity (see for review[18]). Perhaps these connections are responsible for features we often observe during headache. One important question is whether brain stem activity can depolarize afferent fibres or change their threshold. As a corollary, do the reported changes in facial temperature, blood flow, or vessel pulsations in the cutaneous receptive field of the trigeminal nerve develop as a consequence of pain referral from deeper vascular and neural structures?

Conclusion

This chapter has been intentionally selective in its scope and the reader is referred to more detailed reviews on this subject[19,20]. Much more could have been written about the spectrum of neurotransmitters identified within vascular afferent fibres, the effects of sensory fibres on blood vessel calibre and permeability, the electrophysiological data on trigeminovascular fibres and the perivascular afferent fibre in the developing animal. Clearly this review has suggested more areas for future investigation and has raised more questions than it has answered, for example, we know that alternative pain pathways from cephalic blood vessels probably exist (eg via the facial nerve) but we know nothing about them. We must learn about the central terminations of vascular afferents in brain stem, and about the location of projecting second order neurons. We must acquire information about the receptor population which resides on perivascular sensory fibres and learn more about the effects of sensory nerves on the physiology of blood vessels.

We believe that the nature of vascular headaches will be understood eventually if we incorporate emerging information about pain and sensory neurotransmission with information obtained at the bedside. We have suggested some pathophysiological explanations based on emerging principles of sensory neurobiology circa 1987. Perhaps the primary contribution of this review is the acknowledgement of headache's importance as a pain syndrome — something about which our patients have always been eager to tell us.

References

1 Ray, B. S. & Wolff, H. G. (1940): Experimental studies on headache. Pain sensitive structures of the head and their significance in headache. *Arch. Surg.* **41**, 813–856.
2 Penfield, W. (1935): A contribution to the mechanism of intracranial pain. *Res. Nerv. Ment. Dis.* **15**, 399–436.
3 Olesen, J., Larsen, B. & Lauritzen, M. (1981): Focal hyperemia followed by spreading oligemia and impaired activation of rCBF in classic migraine. *Ann. Neurol.* **9**, 344–352.
4 Mayberg, M., Zervas, N. & Moskowitz, M. (1984): Trigeminal projections to supratentorial pial and dural blood vessels demonstrated by horseradish peroxidase histochemistry. *J. Comp. Neurol.* **223**, 46–56.
5 Steiger, H., Tew, J. & Keller, J. (1982): The sensory representation of the dura mater in the trigeminal ganglion of the cat. *Neurosci. Lett.* **45**, 231–256.
6 Penfield, W. & McNaughton, F. (1940): Dural headache and innervation of the dura mater. *Arch. Neurol. Psychiat.* **44**, 43–75.
7 Norregaard, T. V. & Moskowitz, M. A. (1985): Substance P and the sensory innervation of intracranial and extracranial feline cephalic arteries. Implications for vascular pain mechanisms in man. *Brain* **108**, 517–533.
8 Borges, L. & Moskowitz, M. A. (1983): Do intracranial and extracranial trigeminal afferents represent divergent axon collaterals? *Neurosci. Lett.* **35**, 265–270.
9 McMahon, M., Norregaard, T., Beyerl, B., Borges, L. & Moskowitz, M. A. (1985): Trigeminal afferents to cerebral arteries and forehead are not divergent axonal collaterals in cat. *Neurosci. Lett.* **60**, 63–68.
10 O'Connor, T. P. & van der Kooy, D. (1986): Pattern of intracranial and extracranial projections of trigeminal ganglion cells. *J. Neurosci.* **6**, 2200–2207.
11 Saito, K. & Moskowitz, M. A. (1987): Substance P-containing upper cervical sensory ganglia innervate feline pial arteries within the posterior fossa. (In press).
12 Keller, J. T., Beduk, A. & Saunders, M. (1985): Origin of fibres innervating the basilar artery of the cat. *Neurosci. Lett.* **58**, 263–268.
13 Yamamoto, K., *et al.* (1983): Overall distribution of substance P-containing nerves in the wall of the cerebral arteries of the guinea pig and its origins. *J. Comp. Neurol.* **215**, 421–426.
14 Strassman, A., Mason, P., Moskowitz, M. A. & Maciewicz, R. (1986): Response of brainstem trigeminal neurons to electrical stimulation of the dura. *Brain Res.* **379**, 242–250.
15 Davis, K. & Dostrovsky, J. (1986): Activation of trigeminal brainstem nociceptive neurons by dural artery stimulation. *Pain* **25**, 395–401.
16 Onofrio, B. & Campbell, J. K. (1966): Surgical treatment of chronic cluster headache. *Mayo Clin. Proc.* **61**, 537–544.
17 Bereiter, D. A., Stanford, L. R. & Barker, D. J. (1980): Hormone-induced enlargement of receptive fields in trigeminal mechanoreceptive neurons. II. Possible mechanisms. *Brain Res.* **184**, 411–423.

18 Moskowitz, M. A., Beyerl, B. & Henrikson, B. (1986): Central projections of trigeminal neurons: Possible relevance to vascular headaches. In *Prelude to the migraine attack*, ed. W. K. Amery & A. Wauqueir, pp. 150–157. England: Balliere Tindall.
19 Moskowitz, M. A. (1964): The neurobiology of vascular head pain. *Ann. Neurol.* **16**, 157–168.
20 Moskowitz, M. A., Henrikson, B. M. & Beyerl, B. D. (1986): Trigeminovascular connections and mechanisms of vascular headache. In *Handbook of clinical neurology*, Vol. 4, ed. F. Clifford Rose, pp. 107–115. Amsterdam: Elsevier Science Publishers.

14

FUNCTIONAL SIGNIFICANCE OF THE TRIGEMINO-CEREBROVASCULAR INNERVATION: INVOLVEMENT IN CEREBROVASCULAR DISORDERS

Lars Edvinsson*, James McCulloch[†],
Tom A. Kingman[†] and Rolf Uddman[‡]

*Department of Internal Medicine,
University Hospital, Lund, Sweden; †Wellcome Surgical
Institute, University of Glasgow, UK; and ‡Department of
Otolaryngology, Malmö General Hospital, Sweden

Introduction

During recent years there has been a vast increase in the number of putative neuro-transmitters that invest cerebral blood vessels. Some of these transmitter candidates have potent effects on the cerebrovascular bed; these include neurotransmitters/neuromodulators such as noradrenaline, acetylcholine, 5-hydroxytryptamine, vasoactive intestinal peptide, peptide histidine isoleucine, neuropeptide Y, calcitonin gene-related peptide (CGRP), substance P (SP) and neurokinin A (NKA)[1]. However, the functional significance of each perivascular neuronal system in the cerebral circulation has proven elusive. In this chapter we will review in particular one aspect, the trigemino-cerebrovascular system, which originates in the trigeminal ganglion and projects via its ophthalmic division to the cerebral blood vessels[2,3,4], and describe a possible functional significance of this system.

The classic investigations of Wolff and his associates remain crucial in studies on the genesis of vascular head pain and for the involvement of the trigeminal (Vth) cranial nerve. Ray and Wolff (1940)[5] have described painful sensations in patients as a result of mechanical or electrical stimulation of large cerebral arteries, venous sinuses and dural arteries. Further studies have provided evidence that pain sensitive supratentorial structures are applied by nerve fibres from the trigeminal ganglion, whereas subtentorial structures receive few, if any, fibres from this ganglion[6]. Definitive neuroanatomical evidence of trigeminal neuronal projections to intracranial blood vessels was, however, obtained only recently[3], confirming the tentative conclusions of Wolff and his associates. Retrograde axonal transport studies, employing horseradish peroxidase as tracer, demonstrated that cerebrovascular nerves originated in the first division of the ipsilateral trigeminal ganglion[3].

Localization of neuropeptides in cerebrovascular trigeminal nerve fibres

The demonstration of perivascular nerve fibres which contained substance P-like immunoreactivity (SP-LI) around major cerebral arteries has been demonstrated in a number of mammals, including man[7,8,9,10,11]. Based on lesion studies and on neuroanatomical tracing studies, these fibres seem to originate in the ipsilateral trigeminal ganglion[2,4,12]. Although intracerebral SP-LI neurones, particularly in the brain stem, may give rise to dendritic processes which locally supply intracerebral arterioles and capillaries[13,14], the vast majority of the SP fibres in brain vessels originate in the first division of the trigeminal ganglion.

Analysis of the nucleotide sequence of DNA complementary to the SP mRNA has revealed the existence of two different precursors, α- and β-preprotachykinins. The α-form contains the amino acid sequence of SP, whereas the β-form, in addition, contains a second tachykinin, neurokinin A. Trigeminal ganglion cells and perivascular nerve fibres in brain vessels have recently been found to contain both SP-LI and NKA-LI, indicating the presence of the β-form of the preprotachykinin in the trigemino-cerebrovascular system[15].

Another neuropeptide, calcitonin gene-related peptide (CGRP), has been identified from structural analysis of products of the calcitonin gene expression. Alternative processing of mRNA, transcribed from the calcitonin gene, may result in the production in neuronal tissue of a 37 amino acid peptide, CGRP[16]. The presence of CGRP-LI in many regions of the central and peripheral nervous systems, known to contain SP, prompted the examination of the distribution of CGRP in the trigeminal system and in brain vessels. Thus CGRP-LI material has been isolated from feline, bovine and human cerebral vessels and characterized by high performance liquid chromatography (HPLC) and radioimmunoassay[4]. The material is chemically indistinguishable from authentic CGRP. The major cerebral arteries belonging to the circle of Willis and pial arterioles on the cortical surface are invested with fine varicosed nerve fibres which contain CGRP-LI. The trigeminal ganglion contains perikarya in which CGRP-LI is present. Both in the trigeminal ganglion and in the cerebrovascular nerve fibres, the CGRP-LI is at least in part co-localized with SP-LI and NKA-LI. Animals, in which the trigeminal nerve has been surgically divided 2 weeks prior to sacrifice, revealed a market reduction in the number of CGRP-LI and SP-LI immunoreactivity in cerebral blood vessels ipsilateral to the lesion, evidenced both by immunocytochemistry and radioimmunoassay[4,17]. The quantitative data, thus, supports the view that the major origin of the cerebrovascular SP/NKA and CGRP fibres is the ipsilateral trigeminal ganglion.

Vasomotor effects of tachykinins and CGRP on cerebral vessels *in vitro*

SP and CGRP produced relaxation of isolated cat cerebral arteries in nanomolar concentrations. The amount of relaxation was in middle cerebral and convexity pial arteries; SP $17\pm5\%$ and $46\pm10\%$, and CGRP $98\pm23\%$ and $90\pm6\%$ relative to precontraction induced by prostaglandin $F_{2\alpha}$. The concentrations eliciting half maximum relaxation were

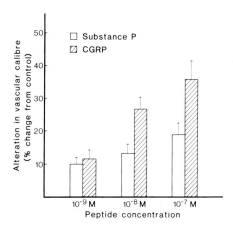

Fig. 1. *Vasomotor responses* in situ *of pial arterioles on the cortical surface.* CGRP elicits the dose-dependent dilatation of cerebral arterioles. The magnitude of the cerebrovascular dilatation to CGRP is significantly greater than that of SP at the same concentrations. The cerebrovascular responses to CGRP are significantly different from those to artificial cerebrospinal fluid at each concentration examined. Data are presented as mean; small bars represent s.e.m. of responses of 7–13 arterioles at each concentration. Preinjection calibre of the arterioles ranged from 36 to 238 μm (with CGRP) and from 34 to 253 μm (with SP).

low, ie 2 nM for SP and 8 nM for CGRP. The SP- and CGRP-induced relaxations were not modified by propranolol (1 μM), atropine (1 μM), or cimetidine (1 μM). The magnitude of the cerebrovascular response to CGRP was, however, considerably greater than that of SP in the cat. Marked species differences were found to exist. Human pial and guinea-pig basilar arteries relaxed upon administration of SP and NKA by 50 between 80% of precontraction, whereas feline major brain arteries elicited only weak responses. The relaxation induced by SP or NKA could be blocked by a group of recently developed SP blockers, eg spantide and (D-Pro[2], D-Trp[7,9])-SP[18]. However, neither of these antagonists modified the CGRP-induced relaxation. In cerebral arteries where the endothelium had been removed the vessels still responded with relaxation upon administration of CGRP whereas the relaxant responses of SP, NKA and acetylcholine were lost[18,19]. Furthermore, CGRP caused a concentration-dependent increase in cAMP accumulation in feline pial vessels whereas SP had no such effect[19]. This indicated that the activation of vessel wall adenylate cyclase was closely linked with the mechanical response to CGRP, whereas for SP it was seen only after maximum relaxation had occurred. Relaxation induced by SP and NKA appeared on the other hand to involve the release of an endothelium-derived relaxing factor[18,20].

Vasomotor responses of cortex pial vessels to the in situ administration of SP and CGRP

In cats anaesthetized with chloralose, the subarachnoid perivascular microapplication of CGRP around individual cortical arterioles provoked a dose-dependent dilatation[17]. The maximum increase in arteriolar diameter was 38 ± 5% from preinjection diameter with the concentration producing half maximal dilatation being 3 nM (Fig. 1). The vasodilatory response to CGRP was more pronounced than that of SP (21 ± 4%). One interesting phenomenon was that SP caused a dose-dependent dilatation of pial veins by up to 16 ± 4%, whereas CGRP did not result in any significant alteration in venous calibre. The cerebrovascular dilatations provoked by CGRP, particularly at the higher concentrations, were prolonged with significant increases in calibre that persisted for over 5 min.

Influence of trigeminal ganglion lesions on pial arteriolar responses in situ

Chronic surgical lesion of the ipsilateral trigeminal nerve did not modify the magnitude of the arteriolar responses to the perivascular microapplication of various vasoactive

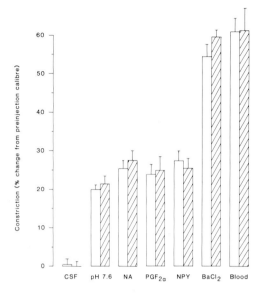

Fig. 2. *Vasomotor responses of feline cortical arterioles* in situ. The magnitude of the vasoconstrictor responses to perivascular microapplication of alkaline CSF, prostaglandin $F_{2\alpha}$, noradrenaline, neuropeptide Y, barium chloride and arterial blood was unaffected by lesions of the ipsilateral trigeminal ganglion.

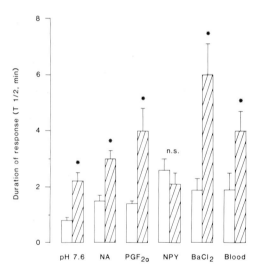

Fig. 3. *Vasomotor responses of feline cortical arterioles* in situ. The duration of the vasoconstrictor responses to alkaline CSF, prostaglandin $F_{2\alpha}$, noradrenaline, barium chloride and arterial blood were significantly prolonged after trigeminal ganglion lesioning as compared to sham-operated controls. The duration of the responses were assessed as the time (mins) for half restoration of preinjection diameter. $P < 0.01$. Responses to neuropeptide Y are generally very long and hence a significant influence by the lesion could not be demonstrated for this vasoconstrictor peptide.

materials (Fig. 2). However, the duration of action of vasoconstrictor responses to microinjections of alkaline CSF (pH 7.6), prostaglandin $F_{2\alpha}$ (10^{-6} M), noradrenaline (10^{-4} M), barium chloride (5%) and arterial blood were significantly prolonged (Fig. 3). The duration of response to vasodilator stimuli, such as microinjection of acidic CSF (pH 6.8) was not altered by lesions to the trigeminal nerve. The standard artificial CSF (pH 7.2) was without significant vasomotor effect both in trigeminal lesioned and sham-operated animals.

Local cerebral blood flow and glucose utilization

Chronic lesions of trigeminal ganglia altered minimally local cerebral blood flow (CBF) and glucose use when compared to sham-operated animals. For example, in cerebral cortex

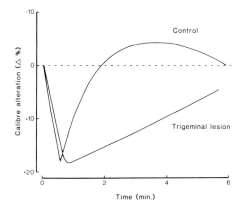

Fig. 4. *Schematic illustration of responses of pial arterioles to the perivascular microinjection of a vasoconstrictor agent in sham-operated and in trigeminal lesioned animals.* The constrictor response has returned to baseline within 2 min in controls while the process is markedly prolonged in lesioned animals. Sometimes a slight overshoot in the response (ie dilatation above baseline) can be seen in sham-operated animals.

(gyrus sigmoideus), which is supplied by blood vessels innervated by trigeminal nerve fibres, CBF was 43 ± 2 ml/100 g^{-1}min^{-1} ipsilateral to the trigeminal lesion and 40 ± 3 ml/100 g^{-1}min^{-1} contralateral to the lesion (data from tissue dissection). The symmetry of CBF in the forebrain could be directly visualized in the autoradiogram and revealed no side-to-side difference. Glucose use in the gyrus sigmoideus was similarly unaltered by trigeminal nerve lesions; 27 ± 3 μmol/100 g^{-1} min^{-1} in the ipsilateral and 30 ± 3 μmoles/100 g^{-1} min^{-1} in the contralateral hemispheres. Trigeminal lesions also failed to alter CBF and glucose use in brain areas whose blood vessels are poorly innervated by nerve fibre originating in the trigeminal ganglion. For example, in the cerebellar hemisphere CBF was 30 ± 1 ml/100 g^{-1} min^{-1} ipsilateral and 36 ± 2 ml/100 g^{-1} min^{-1} contralateral to the lesion; glucose use was 17 ± 3 μmol/100 g^{-1} min^{-1} ipsilateral, and 18 ± 3 μmoles/100 g^{-1}min^{-1} contralateral to the trigeminal lesion. Furthermore, there was an excellent correlation between local oxidative metabolism and cerebral tissue perfusion which was minimally disturbed by unilateral lesion of the trigeminal ganglion.

Pathophysiological importance of the trigemino-cerebrovascular innervation

The cerebral vasculature is innervated by SP-, NKA- and CGRP-containing nerve fibres which originate in the ipsilateral trigeminal ganglion. SP, NKA and CGRP provoke dilatation of feline cerebral arteries *in vitro* and cerebral arterioles *in situ* but marked species variations exist. In cerebral vessels of the cat, dilatation produced by CGRP is more pronounced than that elicited by SP. Furthermore, chronic division of the trigeminal nerve does not alter CBF nor the relationship between oxidative metabolism and CBF. Thus, it appears unlikely that neuronal activity in trigeminal nerves is involved in the moment to moment dynamic regulation of the cerebral circulation. In contrast, the prolonged vasoconstrictor responses which are seen in animals with chronic division of the trigeminal nerve provide evidence that the trigemino-cerebrovascular system is invoked in the detection of excessive cerebral vasoconstriction and facilitates the restoration of normal vascular diameter (Fig. 4).

Although the immunocytochemical localization of neuropeptides and their basic pharmacology can be readily characterized in the cerebral circulation, their physiological role in the regulation of the cerebral circulation has not previously been established. The conceptual approach, hitherto, has been to presume that cerebral vasoconstrictors (such as noradrenaline and neuropeptide Y) provide a mechanism to reduce cerebral blood flow, and that cerebral vasodilators (such as vasoactive intestinal peptide) provide a mechanism to increase cerebral blood flow. Such a view of neurogenically mediated elevations and reductions in CBF conflicts with the established view that local cerebral tissue perfusion is tightly regulated in relation to local cerebral metabolic activity. Our conceptual approach, applied to the trigemino-cerebrovascular neuronal system, has been to examine whether these dilator peptides provide a mechanism to prevent reductions in cerebral tissue perfusion. The physiological role which has been ascribed to the cerebrovascular sympathetic innervation is consistent with this conceptual approach. There is little compelling evidence that the function of the vasoconstrictor sympathetic fibres is to reduce basal levels of CBF; rather, the vasoconstrictor sympathetic fibres provide a neurogenic mechanism to prevent the marked elevations in CBF which would otherwise accompany an excessive increase in perfusion pressure[21,22]. It is unlikely that polypeptides such as SP, NKA and CGRP would be involved in the moment-to-moment regulation of CBF. Our observations that the normal relationship between local CBF and local cerebral glucose utilization is unmodified after chronic trigeminal ganglia lesions provide support for such a view.

If, as we suggest, the trigemino-cerebrovascular system is involved in an axon reflex or in a local response to vasoconstriction which results in the restoration of normal vascular diameter, the system would have important pathophysiological implications. This system may be invoked in attacks of classic migraine with neurological symptoms as well as in subarachnoid haemorrhage where marked reductions of CBF have been observed. The trigemino-cerebrovascular system would provide the brain with a neurogenic mechanism capable of an immediate local, sustained response in emergency conditions where excessive vasoconstriction of the larger arteries threatens the survival of the central nervous system.

Acknowledgements — The work reviewed in this chapter was supported by the Swedish Medical Research Council, the S. and D. Sahlén foundation and the United Kingdom Medical Research Council.

References

1   Edvinsson, L. (1985): Functional role of perivascular peptides in the control of cerebral circulation. *Trends Neurosci.* **8**, 126–131.
2   Liu-Chen, L. -Y., Gillespie, S. A., Norregaard, T. V. & Moskowitz, M. A. (1984): Co-localization of retrogradely transported wheat germ agglutinin and the putative neurotransmitter substance P within trigeminal ganglion cells projecting to cat middle cerebral artery. *J. Comp. Neurol.* **225**, 187–192.
3   Mayberg, M. R., Zervas, N. T. & Moskowitz, M. A. (1984): Trigeminal projections to supratentorial pial and dural blood vessels in cats demonstrated by horseradish peroxidase histochemistry. *J. Comp. Neurol.* **223**, 46–56.
4   Uddman, R., Edvinsson, L., Ekman, R., McCulloch, J. & Kingman, T. A. (1985): Innervation of the feline cerebral vasculature by nerve fibres containing calcitonin gene-related peptide: Trigeminal origin and co-existence with substance P. *Neurosci. Lett.* **62**, 131–136.
5   Ray, B. S. & Wolff, H. G. (1940): Experimental studies on headache. Pain sensitive structures of the head and their significance in headache. *Arch. Surg.* **41**, 813–856.
6   Schumacher, G. A., Ray, B. S. & Wolff, H. G. (1940): Experimental studies on headache. Further analysis of histamine headache and its pain pathways. *Arch. Neurol. Psychiat.* **44**, 701–717.
7   Edvinsson, L., McCulloch, J. & Uddman, R. (1981): Substance P: Immunohistochemical localization and effect upon feline pial arteries in vitro and in situ. *J. Physiol.* **318**. 251–258.
8   Edvinsson, L., Rosendal-Helgesen, S. & Uddman, R. (1983): Substance P: Localization, concentration and release in cerebral arteries, choroid plexus and dura mater. *Cell Tissue Res.* **234**, 1–7.

9 Edvinsson, L. & Uddman, R. (1982): Immunohistochemical localization and dilatory effect of substance P on human cerebral vessels. *Brain Res.* **232**, 466–471.
10 Uddman, R., Edvinsson, L., Owman, C. & Sundler, F. (1981): Perivascular substance P. Occurrence and distribution in mammalian pial vessels. *J. Cereb. Blood Flow Metab.* **1**, 227–232.
11 Yamamoto, K., Matsuyama, T., Shiosaka, S., Inagaki, S., Senba, E., Shimizu, Y., Ishimoto, I., Hayakawa, T., Matsumoto, M. & Tohyama, M. (1983): Overall distribution of substance P-containing nerves in the wall of the cerebral arteries of the guinea-pig and its origin. *J. Comp. Neurol.* **215**, 421–426.
12 Liu-Chen, L. -Y, Han, D. H. & Moskowitz, M. A. (1983): Pia arachnoid contains substance P originating from trigeminal neurons. *Neuroscience* **9**, 803–808.
13 Chan-Palay, V. (1977): Innervation of cerebral blood vessels by norepinephrine, indoleamine, substance P and neurotensin fibres and the leptomeningeal indoleamine axons: Their role in vasomotor activity and local alteration of brain blood composition. In *Neurogenic control of brain circulation*, eds C. Owman & L. Edvinsson pp. 39–53. Oxford. Pergamon Press.
14 Kapadia, S. E. & de Lanerolle, N. C. (1984): Immunohistochemical and electron microscopic demonstration of vascular innervation in the mammalian brainstem. *Brain Res.* **292**, 33–39.
15 Edvinsson, L., Brodin, E., Jansen, I. & Uddman, R. (1987): Presence of neurokinin A immuno-reactive nerve fibres in guinea pig cerebral arteries. *Regul. Pept.* (Submitted for publication).
16 Rosenfeld, M. G., Mermod, J. -J., Amara, S. G., Swanson, L. W., Sawchenko, P. E., Rivier, J., Vale, W. W. & Evans, R. M. (1983): Production of a novel neuropeptide encoded by the calcitonin gene via tissue-specific RNA processing. *Nature* **304**, 129–135.
17 McCulloch, J., Uddman, R., Kingman, T. A. & Edvinsson, L. (1986): Calcitonin gene-related peptide: Functional role in cerebrovascular regulation. *Proc. Natl. Acad. Sci. USA* **83**, 5741–5745.
18 Edvinsson, L. & Jansen, I. (1987): Characterization of tachykinin receptors in isolated basilar arteries of guinea pig. *Brit. J. Pharmac.* **90**, 553–559.
19 Edvinsson, L., Fredholm, B. B., Hamel, E., Jansen, I. & Verrecchia, C. (1985): Perivascular peptides relax cerebral arteries concomitant with stimulation of cyclic adenosine monophosphate accumulation or release of an endothelium-derived relaxing factor. *Neurosci. Lett.* **58**, 213–217.
20 Furchgott, R. F. (1983): Role of endothelium in responses of vascular smooth muscle. *Circ. Res.* **35**, 557–573.
21 Bill, A. & Linder, J. (1976): Sympathetic control of cerebral blood flow in acute arterial hypertension. *Acta Physiol. Scand.* **20**, 91–95.
22 Edvinsson, L., Owman, C. & Siesjö, B. K. (1976): Physiological role of cerebrovascular sympathetic nerves in the autoregulation of cerebral blood flow. *Brain Res.* **117**, 519–523.

15

NEUROPEPTIDES IN HUMAN CEREBRAL

AND TEMPORAL ARTERIES:

OCCURRENCE AND VASOMOTOR RESPONSES

I. Jansen*, L. Edvinsson[†], K. Jensen[‡], J. Olesen[‡] and R. Uddman[§]

*Departments of *Experimental Research and [§]Oto-Rhino-Laryngology, Malmö General Hospital, Malmö, Sweden; Department of [†]Internal Medicine, University Hospital, Lund, Sweden and the Department of [‡]Neuromedicine, KAS, Gentofte, Copenhagen, Denmark*

Summary

Nerve fibres displaying neuropeptide Y (NPY), vasoactive intestinal peptide (VIP), substance P (SP), and calcitonin gene-related peptide (CGRP)-like immunoreactivity were found in the adventitia or at the adventitia-media border of human cerebral (pial) and temporal arteries. NPY constricted human cerebral arteries and, in human temporal arteries, potentiated the contractile response of noradrenaline (NA). Vasoactive intestinal peptide, peptide histidine methionine-27 (PHM-27), SP, neurokinin A (NKA) and human (h) CGRP potently relaxed cerebral and temporal arteries precontracted by prostaglandin $F_{2\alpha}$; the relative potency being hCGRP > SP > VIP > > NKA $\geq$ PHM – 27. The amount of relaxation varied between 55% (SP) and 96% (hCGRP) of the prostaglandin $F_{2\alpha}$ induced contraction.

Introduction

Migraine attacks are conventionally thought to be caused by a dysfunction in the regulation of tone in intra and extra-cranial blood vessels. A number of agents have been suggested as responsible for the vasomotor responses recorded during migraine attacks[1]. Previous histochemical studies have shown that human cerebral arteries are surrounded by adrenergic and cholinergic nerve fibres[2]. In addition, peptide containing nerve fibres, such as neuropeptide Y (NPY), vasoactive intestinal peptide (VIP), substance P (SP) and calcitonin gene-related peptide (CGRP), have been observed around cerebral blood vessels of

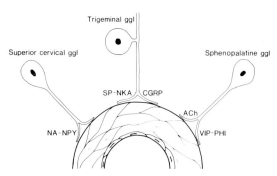

Extrinsic nerve supply

Fig. 1. *Schematic illustration showing the putative organization of perivascular nerve fibres in the cranial circulation.* Sympathetic fibres originate in the superior cervical ganglion (NA, NPY), sensory fibres in the trigeminal ganglion (SP/NKA, CGRP) and parasympathetic fibres in the sphenopalatine ganglion (ACh, VIP/PHM).

laboratory animals[3], for overview see Fig. 1. Few studies have been carried out on human temporal and cerebral arteries[4-7]. In the present study we have examined the distribution of NPY –, VIP –, SP – and CGRP – immunoreactive fibres around human temporal and cerebral arteries and compared the pharmacological effects of these neuropeptides on arterial segments *in vitro*.

Methods

Immunocytochemistry

Human cerebral (cortex pial) arteries were removed from macroscopically intact regions during neurosurgical tumour resections. Temporal arteries were obtained during surgery of the middle ear or in conjunction with neurosurgical tumour resections. Vessel segments were fixed in a mixture of 2% formaldehyde and 15% of a saturated aqueous picric acid solution in 0.1 M phosphate buffer; rinsed in cold Tyrode buffer containing 10% sucrose for 48 h, frozen on dry ice and sectioned in a cryostat at 15 μm thickness. They were processed for immunocytochemical demonstration of NPY, VIP, SP, or CGRP using an indirect immunofluorescence method[8]. The antisera used have been characterized previously[4,5]. Control sections were incubated with antiserum inactivated by the previous addition of excess antigen (10–100 μg/ml diluted antiserum). The absolute identity of the immunoreactive sequence is not certain in that cross reactivity with other peptides containing the same immunoreactive sites cannot be excluded.

Vasomotor responses in vitro

Cerebral (cortex pial) and temporal arterial segments, were examined with a sensitive *in vitro* system[9]. Long arterial segments (2–3 mm) were suspended between two L-shaped metal prongs (0.1–0.2 mm) in small tissue baths containing a buffer solution aerated with 5% CO_2 in O_2, pH 7.4, and kept at 37°C. Mechanical activity were recorded by force displacement transducers (Grass FT03C) connected to a Grass polygraph. The cerebral and temporal vessels were given a passive load of 4 and 6 mN, respectively, and were allowed to stabilize at this tension for 1.5 h before testing. The contractile capacity of the preparations were first tested by exposure to a buffer solution containing 124 mM potassium; this resulted in strong and reproducible contractions which were 12.0 ± 5.2 mN for cerebral and 36.9 ± 5.3 mN for temporal arteries. In experiments with NPY, the peptide was either applied alone in increasing concentrations, or when examining its potentiating capacity, given in a concentration of 10^{-8} M 5 min prior to NA administration. When VIP, SP or human (h) CGRP were tested neither were able to induce relaxation of vessels at the resting level of tension, therefore, the vessels were precontracted with 3×10^{-6} M prostaglandin $F_{2\alpha}$ ($PGF_{2\alpha}$) which induced strong and stable contractions of cerebral arteries 4.2 ± 1.2 mN, temporal arteries 11.8 ± 0.8 mN. The data are expressed below as mean EC_{50} or IC_{50} values (concentration of agonist eliciting half maximum contraction or relaxation, respectively) and as E_{max} or I_{max} (mean of the maximum responses) and given as mean values $\pm$ s.e.m. of responses from a given number (n) of vessel segments (one or two from each patient).

Results and discussion

Neuropeptide Y

Varicose NPY immunoreactive fibres were seen in the wall of the cerebral and temporal arteries[4,5], and were located in the adventitia, sometimes in close apposition to the media. In laboratory animals NPY-like fibres in cerebral blood vessels originate in the superior cervical ganglion and NPY is co-localized with NA, both in ganglion cells and perivascular fibres[10].

In cerebral arteries the administration of NPY elicited concentration-dependent contractions (Fig. 2a). The maximum contraction induced by NPY was $46.8 \pm 13.4\%$ of that elicited by potassium. The NPY induced contraction was thus somewhat stronger in magnitude when compared with that of NA ($26.6 \pm 7.7\%$). NPY was markedly more potent (EC_{50}: $7.0 \pm 2.6 \times 10^{-9}$ M) than NA (EC_{50}: $4.9 \pm 1.5 \times 10^{-7}$ M). The EC_{50} value for NA was, in the presence of NPY, $3.8 \pm 1.6 \times 10^{-7}$ M with an E_{max} of $39.1 \pm 2.9\%$.

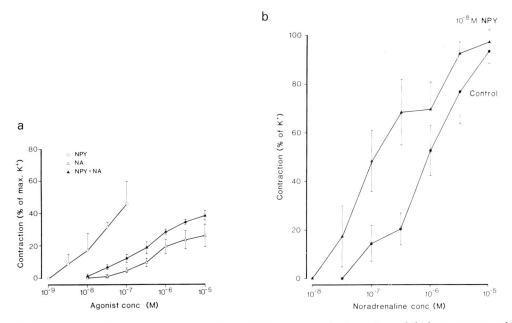

Fig. 2. *Concentration-dependent contractions of (a) human cerebral arteries and (b) human temporal arteries to NPY, to NA, and to NA in the presence of 10^{-8} M NPY. Mean values $\pm$ s.e.m. of five* experiments.

In human temporal arteries NPY did not usually induce contraction. However, vessel segments from one patient (nine patients tested) exhibited contraction (3.6 ± 1.5 mN) when exposed to NPY. Administration of NA, on the other hand, invariably resulted in strong contractions ($86.4 \pm 4.8\%$). Neuropeptide Y (10^{-8} M) significantly potentiated contractions elicited by NA (10^{-8}–10^{-5} M) without changing maximum contraction (Fig. 2b). The EC_{50} for NA was $8.1 \pm 1.8 \times 10^{-7}$ M when tested alone and $1.0 \pm 1.5\ 10^{-7}$ M in the presence of NPY (Student's *t*-test; $P < 0.01$).

In cerebral as well as temporal arteries, the contractile responses to NA were antagonized by the α_1- adrenoceptor blocker prazosin (10^{-7} M). Neither this antagonist nor the 5-hydroxy-tryptamine blocker, ketanserin (10^{-7} M) caused any blockade of contractions induced by NPY nor did they affect the NPY-induced potentiation of NA contraction in temporal arteries.

The NPY induced constriction of human cerebral arteries was somewhat more pronounced than that noted for NA and occurred at much lower concentrations. In human temporal arteries NPY potentiated adrenergically mediated responses, a response that was not seen in experiments performed on human cerebral arteries. Thus, NPY and NA appear to act synergistically in human cerebral arteries since no potentiation of the NA induced contraction was seen. Other studies have shown that NPY-induced contractions in feline cerebral arteries are markedly reduced by calcium antagonists or by calcium depletion, while adrenoceptor or 5-hydroxytryptamine antagonists are without effects[11]. In contrast, the potentiating effect of NPY on peripheral arteries has been shown not to be directly dependent on the extracellular calcium, but is attenuated by oubain and is absent in a sodium-free buffer solution[12]. The present results revealed that there is a different mode of action of NPY on cerebral as compared to temporal arteries. In the cerebrovascular bed NPY may participate with NA in maintaining the upper limit of auto-regulation during acute increases in arterial blood pressure. In temporal arteries NPY may serve as a modulator of adrenergically mediated responses.

Vasoactive intestinal peptide

A sparse to moderate supply of VIP-immunoreactive fibres was seen in the wall of cerebral and temporal arteries. When VIP was given in increasing concentrations to $PGF_{2\alpha}$-contracted arteries, concentration-dependent relaxations occurred (Fig. 3, Table 1). The relaxation was not affected by the β-adrenoceptor antagonist propranolol (10^{-7} M), the histamine H_2-blocker cimetidine (10^{-6} M) or the cholinergic antagonist atropine (10^{-6} M). Recently, it was found that the VIP precursor contains also another peptide, peptide histidine

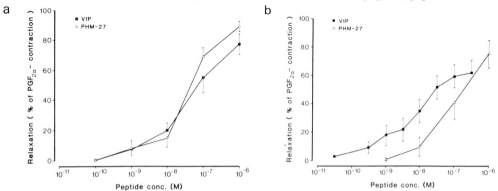

Fig. 3. *Concentration-dependent relaxation of isolated* (a) *human cerebral arteries and* (b) *human temporal arteries following the administration of VIP and PHM-27 to vessels precontracted with* 3×10^{-6} *M* $PGF_{2\alpha}$. Mean values $\pm$ s.e.m. of nine experiments.

Table 1. *Relaxant effect of peptides on human cerebral and temporal arterial segments precontracted by 3×10^{-6} M $PGF_{2\alpha}$ (cerebral arteries: 4.2 ± 1.2 mN; temporal arteries 11.8 ± 0.8 mN). Data are given as means $\pm$ s.e.m., $n =$ number of vessels examined.*

		Cerebral arteries			Temporal arteries	
	n	IC_{50} (M)	I_{max} (%)	n	IC_{50} (M)	I_{max} (%)
VIP	9	$(7.5 \pm 0.2) \times 10^{-9}$ M	62.7 ± 8.6	6	$(2.6 \pm 1.0) \times 10^{-8}$ M	77.0 ± 7.0
PHM $-$ 27	8	$(6.8 \pm 0.9) \times 10^{-7}$ M	75.7 ± 9.6	4	$(3.6 \pm 0.1) \times 10^{-8}$ M	89.3 ± 3.6
SP	11	$(2.6 \pm 2.7) \times 10^{-9}$ M	55.6 ± 9.8	4	$(8.2 \pm 0.3) \times 10^{-9}$ M	67.2 ± 4.3
NKA	7	$(2.7 \pm 1.1) \times 10^{-8}$ M	81.1 ± 15.5	7	$(3.6 \pm 0.2) \times 10^{-8}$ M	76.5 ± 8.4
hCGRP	7	$(6.3 \pm 1.6) \times 10^{-11}$ M	96.0 ± 1.7	6	$(1.5 \pm 4.2) \times 10^{-9}$ M	89.8 ± 2.0

methionine -27 (PHM -27). VIP and PHM -27 are thought to be co-localized with the cholinergic transmitter acetylcholine[13]. In feline cerebral arteries it has been shown that VIP-mediated responses, in contrast to those of acetylcholine, are independent of the removal of the vascular endothelium. These two agents may mediate an increase in the vessel wall adenylate cyclase activity in parallel with producing dilatation[14].

Substance P and calcitonin gene-related peptide

A moderate supply of SP- and CGRP-like immunoreactive nerve fibres was located in the adventitia, sometimes being in close apposition to the media layer. Studies of isolated precontracted arterial segments revealed that the cumulative administration of SP or hCGRP resulted in concentration-dependent relaxations; hCGRP being more potent than SP in both cerebral and temporal arteries (Fig. 4, Table 1). Neither SP nor hCGRP were affected by propranolol (10^{-7} M), cimetidine (10^{-6} M) or atropine (10^{-6} M). SP responses, but not hCGRP responses, were antagonized by the SP-antagonist spantide (10^{-6} M).

Lesion experiments have shown that cerebrovascular SP- and CGRP-immunoreactive fibres originate in the ipsilateral trigeminal ganglion[15,16]. Furthermore, the two peptides are co-localized in trigeminal ganglion cells and in perivascular nerve fibres[16]. The vasomotor response to CGRP occurs concomitant with activation of adenylate cyclase, which is in contrast to that of SP[14]. On the other hand, SP requires an intact endothelium for the dilator responses. The functional role of the trigemino-cerebrovascular system has been examined in some detail in the feline cerebral circulation[17]. Cerebral arterioles respond with vasoconstriction upon administration of eg NA to the same degree in

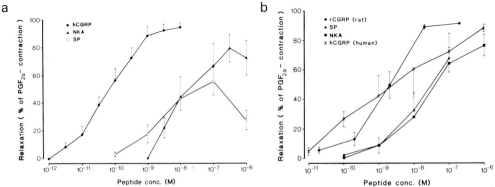

Fig. 4. *Concentration-dependent relaxation of* (a) *human cerebral arteries and* (b) *human temporal arteries to SP, NKA and CGRP in vessels precontracted with 3×10^{-6} M $PGF_{2\alpha}$. Mean values $\pm$ s.e.m. of eleven experiments.*

sham-operated and trigeminal ganglion lesioned animals[17]. However, the return to baseline after constriction is markedly prolonged in lesioned animals. The trigemino-cerebrovascular system may thus have an important role in normalizing the vessel diameter following intense vasoconstriction. This response or 'reflex' may be of particular significance in eg classical migraine where cerebrovascular vasoconstriction reportedly is observed[18].

Acknowledgements—Supported by grants from the Swedish Medical Research Council (no. 5958.6859), the Gunnar Hylténs foundation and the Sahléns foundation.

References

1 Dalessio, D. J. (1980): *Wolffs headache and other head pain.* New York: Oxford University Press.
2 Edvinsson, L., Owman, C. & Sjöberg, N.-O. (1976): Autonomic nerves, mast cells, and amine receptors in human brain vessels. A histochemical and pharmacological study. *Brain Res.* **115**, 337–393.
3 Edvinsson, L. (1985): Role of perivascular peptides in the control of the cerebral circulation. *Trends Neurosci.* **8**, 126–131.
4 Edvinsson, L., Ekman, R., Jansen, I., Ottosson, A. & Uddman, R. (1987): Peptide containing nerve fibres in human cerebral arteries: Immunocytochemistry, radioimmunoassay and in vitro pharmacology. *Ann. Neurol.* **21** (In press).
5 Jansen, I., Uddman, R., Hocherman, M., Ekman, R., Jensen, K., Olesen, J., Stiernholm, P. & Edvinsson, L. (1986): Localization and effects of neuropeptide Y, vasoactive intestinal peptide, substance P and calcitonin gene-related peptide in human temporal arteries. *Ann. Neurol.* **20**, 496–501.
6 Edvinsson, L. & Ekman, R. (1984): Distribution and dilatory effect of vasoactive intestinal polypeptide (VIP) in human cerebral arteries. *Peptides* **5**, 329–331.
7 Allen, J. M., Todd, N., Crockard, H. A., Schon, F., Yeats, J. C. & Bloom, S. R. (1984): Presence of neuropeptide Y in human circle of Willis and its possible role in cerebral vasospasm. *Lancet* **ii**, 550–552.
8 Coons, A. H., Leduc, E. H. & Connolly, J. M. (1955): Studies on antibody production. I. A method for the histochemical demonstration of specific antibody and its application to a study of the hyperimmune rabbit. *J. Exp. Med.* **102**, 49–60.
9 Högestätt, E. D., Andersson, K.-E. & Edvinsson, L. (1983): Mechanical properties of rat cerebral arteries as studied by a sensitive device for recording of mechanical activity in isolated small blood vessels. *Acta Physiol. Scand.* **117**, 49–61.
10 Edvinsson, L., Copeland, J. R., Emson, P. C., McCulloch, J. & Uddman, R. (1987): Nerve fibres containing neuropeptide Y in the cerebrovascular bed: Immunocytochemistry, radioimmunoassay, and vasomotor effects. *J. Cereb. Blood Flow Metab.* **7**, 45–57.
11 Edvinsson, L., Emson, P., McCulloch, J., Tatemoto, K. & Uddman, R. (1983): Neuropeptide Y; Cerebrovascular innervation and vasomotor effects in the cat. *Neurosci. Lett.* **43**, 79–84.
12 Wahlestedt, C., Edvinsson, L., Ekblad, E. & Håkanson, R. (1986): Neuropeptide Y potentiates noradrenaline-evoked vasoconstriction; mode of action. *J. Pharmacol. Exp. Ther.* **234**, 735–741.
13 Hara, H., Hamill, G. S. & Jacobowitz, D. M. (1985): Origin of cholinergic nerves to the rat major cerebral arteries: Coexistence with vasoactive intestinal polypeptide. *Brian Res.* **14**, 179–188.
14 Edvinsson, L., Fredholm, B. B., Hamel, E., Jansen, I. & Verrecchia, C. (1985): Perivascular peptides relax cerebral arteries concomitant with stimulation of cyclic adenosine monophosphate accumulation or release of an endothelium-derived relaxing factor in the cat. *Neurosci. Lett.* **58**, 213–218.
15 Liu-Chen, L. -Y., Han, D. H. & Moskowitz, M. A. (1983): Pia arachnoid contains substance P originating from trigeminal neurons. *Neuroscience* **9**, 803–808.
16 Uddman, R., Edvinsson, L., Ekman, R., Kingman, T. A. & McCulloch, J. (1985): Innervation of the feline cerebral vasculature by nerve fibres containing calcitonin gene-related peptide: Trigeminal origin and co-existence with substance P. *Neurosci. Lett.* **62**, 131–136.
17 McCulloch, J., Uddman, R., Kingman, T. A. & Edvinsson, L. (1986): Calcitonin gene-related peptide: Functional role in cerebrovascular regulation. *Proc. Natl. Acad. Sci. USA* **83**, 5731–5735.
18 Olesen, J. (1985): Migraine and regional cerebral blood flow. *Trends Neurosci.* **8**, 318–321.

III

MIGRAINE THERAPY

16

DICLOFENAC SODIUM IN

THE TREATMENT OF ACUTE MIGRAINE

ATTACK: A DOUBLE-BLIND CLINICAL TRIAL

E. Del Bene*, M. Poggioni* and U. Garagiola[†]

*Migraine Center, Department of Internal Medicine and
Clinical Pharmacology, University of Florence, 50100 Florence, Italy and
[†]Medical Department, CIBA-GEIGY S.p.A., 21040 Origgio (Va), Italy*

Summary

This was a double-blind clinical trial, with a cross-over design, to compare the efficacy of a non-steroidal anti-inflammatory drug, as diclofenac sodium, intramuscularly administered, and placebo in the treatment of migraine attacks.

Forty patients were treated with the two study drugs, each administered once daily for three consecutive attacks. If pain was not relieved within 6 h from administration the patient took a 100 mg diclofenac suppository, in open condition.

Evaluation was performed both by the physician by means of a complete medical examination and by the patient by compiling an especially designed migraine card. Results were analysed after having checked the absence of both period and carry-over effect.

In all the variables examined diclofenac treatment was more effective than placebo ($P < 0.01$). This was confirmed also by the results reported on the migraine cards ($P < 0.001$) and by the preferences expressed by the patients at the end of the trial ($P < 0.001$). Tolerability of the drug was similar to that of placebo.

Introduction

The pathogenesis and pathophysiology of migraine are complex and just beginning to be understood. In idiopathic headache a central dysnociception has been suggested as an aetiopathogenetic hypothesis[1]. According to this assertion, migraine attacks could be considered a 'quasi self-endorphin abstinence syndrome', that is painful crises would be a

Table 1. *Scoring of drug efficacy for each migraine attack.*

Questions		Patient response			
Pain decreased	Yes	Yes	Yes	Yes	No
Pain disappeared	Yes	Yes	No	No	No
Suppository administered	No	Yes	No	Yes	Yes
Final evaluation	Excellent	Good		Scanty	Insufficient
Score	4	3		2	1

consequence of a failure in opioid function[2]. Clinical and pharmacological data demonstrate the analogies between migraine and opiate abstinence[3,4].

There is also considerable evidence that prostaglandins may be involved in the pathogenesis of migraine[5], and several clinical trials have shown that a wide range of prostaglandin inhibitors are effective in alleviating acute migraine attacks[6,7].

Diclofenac sodium appears to be an effective analgesic not only inhibiting prostaglandin biosynthesis[8] but also increasing the release of plasma beta-endorphins[9]. According to this and on the basis of preliminary open clinical observations[10], a double-blind clinical trial was carried out to evaluate the analgesic efficacy of diclofenac sodium in the injectable formulation in controlling the pain in acute migraine attacks.

Material and methods

This was a double-blind, within patient, comparative trial between diclofenac and placebo, each administered once daily intramuscularly for three attacks. The trial included patients of both sexes, aged between 18 and 60 years, affected by migraine (according to the Ad Hoc Committee[11]), with at least one attack per week. The painful crises had to be of severe or very severe intensity, characterized by one or more of the following symptoms: photophobia or phonophobia, nausea, vomiting, sensation of cold, aching limbs. Exclusion criteria were the presence of ophthalmic, hemiplegic or basilar-artery migraine; severe hepatic, cardiac, renal or respiratory failure, or arterial hypertension; present, suspected or previous gastro-duodenal ulcer; asthma (if the subject reported asthmatic attacks), skin rash or acute rhinitis after taking acetylsalicylic acid or other NSAIDs; pregnancy or breast-feeding.

After a wash-out period of at least one month during which no drug for the preventive treatment of migraine had to be taken, patients were treated, according to a randomization list, with diclofenac sodium 75 mg (3 ml), one vial for intramuscular administration, or matched placebo, on three consecutive migraine attacks and then with the alternative preparation on the next three consecutive migraine attacks.

If the migraine attack did not disappear within 6 h since the administration of the study drug, the patient should take a 100 mg-diclofenac suppository, in open condition. The patient could not take any drug for the treatment of migraine except the study drug. A complete medical examination including the pharmacological history of the patient was made at the beginning of the trial.

Patients were seen at the end of each cross-over period: in both occasions patients gave, according to a 3-point scale (1 = unchanged; 2 = improved; 3 = worsened), both a global judgement of their condition and an evaluation of the changes of the individual symptoms. Furthermore for each migraine attack patients recorded at the 6th hour the degree of pain alleviation, the evaluation of 'quality of life' according to a visual analogue scale (0 mm = excellent; 100 mm = very bad) and the need of supplementary analgesic drug on

Table 2. *Associated symptoms' changes in patients who presented them before the treatment.*

| | Diclofenac | | Placebo | |
	↑	↓	↑	↓
Photophobia*	19	10	3	26
Nausea*	21	8	1	28
Vomiting*	17	3	3	17
Sensation of cold*	11	6	1	16
Aching limbs	0	3	0	3

*$P<0.01$ — McNemar Test.
↑, Improved; ↓, unchanged, worsened.

Table 3. *Data showing effectivity of diclofenac treatment.*

	Diclofenac	Placebo
Migraine card score		
Total	308	149
Mean	10.26	4.96
s.d.	2.21	2.44
Quality of life		
Mean	40.15	73.12
s.d.	28.81	22.14

a specially designed migraine card. These data were analysed as shown in Table 1. The scores were summarized every three crises, giving a final result for each treatment period.

Emergent signs and symptoms were recorded at the end of each period. At the end of the trial patients expressed their own preference among the treatments still received, including the previous ones.

Before the analysis of the results, we have checked the absence of both period and carry-over effect in all the variables considered, by means of appropriate tests.

Results

Forty patients, 19 males and 21 females, of mean age 33.3 years (s.d. 8.6) were admitted to the study. Attacks were of severe intensity in 23 patients, very severe in 15; two patients did not specify the degree of attacks severity. Age of onset was 17.2 years (s.d. 8.4), and 32 patients had a family history of migraine. Twelve patients were alcohol consumers and 14 smokers. Photophobia and nausea were the most frequent symptoms, occurring in over 80% of the cases, followed by vomiting and sensation of cold (about 50%) and aching limbs (12.5%).

Homogeneity control of patients distribution between the two sequences as regards demographic characteristics as well as main evaluation criteria were satisfactory.

There were eight drop-outs: three in the first sequence and five in the second one, but all during placebo treatment. These patients were excluded from the statistical analysis. To obtain homogeneity, two patients in the first sequence were excluded at random. In all the variables considered, the analysis showed the absence of both period and carry-over effect.

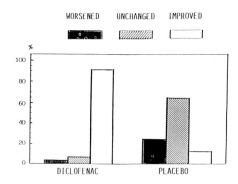

Figure. *Frequence distribution of global evaluation in both the treatments regardless of period and sequence.*

Global evaluations obtained with diclofenac were significantly better than those with placebo ($P < 0.001$) (Figure) (McNemar Test). In all the associated symptoms diclofenac treatment was more effective than placebo ($P < 0.01$) (see Table 2) (McNemar Test). Scores of data recorded in the migraine cards were significantly higher with diclofenac treatment than with placebo ($P < 0.001$), as well as the data of the 'quality of life' were significantly better ($P < 0.001$; t-test) (Table 3).

Preferences expressed by the patients were significantly in favour of diclofenac ($P < 0.001$): 21 against 1 (binomial test). Five patients on diclofenac and two on placebo reported unwanted effects.

Discussion and conclusions

We have performed this clinical trial to evaluate the efficacy of a non-steroidal anti-inflammatory drug, such as diclofenac sodium, intramuscularly administered, in the treatment of acute migraine attack.

Despite the uncommon way of administration (intramuscularly), the drug was well accepted by patients; only eight patients did not conclude the trial, and they all stopped during placebo treatment. The results have shown that a non-steroidal anti-inflammatory drug, such as diclofenac sodium, provides several advantages in the treatment of migraine attack in comparison to standard therapy. The drug was significantly superior to placebo not only in relieving pain but also in reducing the associated symptoms both in number and intensity. Further, the patients themselves indicated a significantly greater preference for diclofenac than for placebo. This is particularly important considering that the tolerability of the drug was similar to that of placebo.

We can conclude that in our patients, affected by migraine attacks, the treatment with a non-steroidal anti-inflammatory drug, such as diclofenac sodium, intramuscularly administered (vial 75 mg/3 ml) o.i.d., was well-accepted and well-tolerated and significantly more effective in resolving the attack than placebo.

References

1 Sicuteri, F. (1976): Headache disruption of pain modulation. In *Advances in pain research and therapy*, eds J. J. Bonica & D. Albe-Fessard, pp. 871–880. New York: Raven Press.
2 Sicuteri, F. (1982): Natural opioids in migraine. In *Advances in neurology*, eds A. P. Friedman, S. Gorini & F. Sicuteri, pp. 65–74. New York: Raven Press.
3 Sicuteri, F. (1979): Headache as the most common disease of the antinociceptive system: analogies with morphine abstinence. In *Advances in pain research and therapy*, Vol 3, eds J. J. Bonica, J. C. Lieberkind & D. Albe-Fessard, pp. 359–365. New York: Raven Press.

4   Sicuteri, F., Gatto, G., Panconesi, A. (1985): Hallmarks of deficient opioid homeostasis: migraine attack as a quasi self (endorphine) acute abstinence. In *Updating in headache*, eds V. Pfaffenrath *et al.*, pp. 249–263. Berlin: Springer Verlag.

5   Horrobin, D. F. (1977): Hypothesis: prostaglandins and migraine. *Headache* **17**, 113–117.

6   Vardi, Y., Rabey, I. M., Strufler, M., Schwartz, A., Linder, H. R. & Zor, U. (1976): Migraine attacks. Alleviation by an inhibitor of prostaglandin synthesis and action. *Neurology* **26**, 447.

7   Hakkarainen, H., Vapaatolo, H., Gothani, G. & Parantainen, J. (1969): Tolfenamic acid is as effective as ergotamine during migraine attacks. *Lancet* ii, 326.

8   Fowler, P. D. (1983): Diclofenac sodium. In *Anti-rheumatic drugs* eds. E. C. Huskisson, pp. 117–121. New York: Praeger Publisher.

9   Martini, A., Bondiolotti, G. P. (1984): Diclofenac increases beta-endorphin plasma concentrations. *J. Int. Med. Res.* **12**, 92.

10 Del Bene, E., Poggioni, M., Borghi, C. & Maresca, V. (1985): Migraine attack treatment with diclofenac sodium. *Cephalalgia* **5** (Suppl. 3), 144–145.

11 Ad Hoc Committee on Classification of Headache (1962): *J. Am. Med. Assoc.* **179**, 127–128.

17

EFFICACY AND SAFETY OF DIHYDROERGOTAMINE AS A NASAL SPRAY FOR COMMON MIGRAINE

P. Tfelt-Hansen, B. Holt Larsen, M. Ingstrup and N. Mygind

*Departments of Neurology and Otorhinopharyngology,
Rigshospitalet, Copenhagen, Denmark*

Summary

Forty-seven common migraine patients entered this double-blind three-way cross-over study comparing dihydroergotamine (DHE) as a nasal spray in initial doses of 1.0 mg and 0.5 mg to placebo in the treatment of migraine attacks. Each treatment was administered twice and a total of six attacks should be treated. Twelve patients were excluded, most often because they treated too few attacks. In the statistically valid patients ($n = 14$) DHE was significantly better concerning duration of attacks and overall judgement of efficacy. When valid and partially valid patients ($n = 21$) were analysed together no significant differences were found between DHE and placebo. Despite these disappointing results in the controlled part of the study, 26 patients continued to treat their migraine attacks (mean 19 and range 1–94) for 1 year, probably because they learned to use the nasal spray more effectively by practising. Ear, nose and throat examinations before and after treatment were normal, and the mucociliary transport times were also unchanged.

Introduction

The extremely low oral bioavailability (less than 1%) of dihydroergotamine (DHE)[1] prevents its use in the treatment of migraine attacks despite the formation of active metabolites during the first-passage effect in the liver[2]. DHE is used as an injection and has — judging from clinical experience but not from controlled clinical trials — some efficacy in the treatment of migraine attacks. Furthermore, the absorption of orally administered drugs is delayed during the migraine attack as has been shown for both aspirin[3] and tolfenamic acid[4]. In order to circumvent both the problem of the first-passage effect in the liver and the problem of delayed oral absorption during a migraine attack a new galenic form of DHE was developed, a DHE nasal spray. In kinetic studies it has been shown that intranasally DHE in a dose of 1 mg and 0.5 mg i.m. DHE result in comparable plasma levels of DHE[5]. Furthermore, in a more formal kinetic study comparable i.v. and intranasal DHE, it was recently shown that the bioavailability of intranasally DHE is 43% and that the absorption is quick but not instantaneous with a $t_{1/2}$ of 18 min (Tfelt-Hansen, unpublished observation).

From a kinetic point of view DHE administered as a nasal spray should be suitable for the treatment of attacks, and preliminary reports have indicated some efficacy of intranasally administered DHE[6]. In the present study we therefore investigated whether DHE administered as a nasal spray is effective in attacks of common migraine.

Dihydroergotamine is generally held to be a rather selective venoconstrictor[7], but it also has an effect of short duration on the arterioles as judged from the pressor effect of the drug after i.v. administration[8]. One major theoretical problem with intranasally DHE is therefore whether administration of this vasoactive drug in the nose could lead to vasomotor rhinitis as is observed after eg ephedrine[9]. The migraine patients included in the trial had an ENT examination (and measurements of mucociliary transport time) before and after the study. Further, 26 patients used the DHE spray openly in a long-term study of 1 year's duration. Local side-effects were noted and the ENT examinations were repeated at the end of the long-term study.

Methods

Forty-seven common migraine patients (41 females and 6 males) with two to six moderate to severe attacks per month were included in this double-blind controlled trial. The patients used 1 mg DHE, 0.5 mg DHE or placebo administered as a nasal spray. Each treatment was given twice in a randomized order. When DHE was given patients could use the spray again (dose 0.5 mg DHE) after 30 and 60 min. Before treatment and after ½, 1, and 2 h , the patients rated severity of headache on a 4 point verbal scale: none, mild, moderate and severe. Escape medication was allowed after 2 h.

Efficacy parameters were: changes in headache severity, the use of escape medication, total duration of attacks, rating of attacks compared to usual attacks: worse, as usual, milder, rating of efficacy of treatment: bad, fair, good, and side-effects.

Statistical method: Friedman's rank analysis of variance.

After the double-blind study the patients were invited to use the DHE nasal spray for 1 year. They recorded attacks, severity and duration of attacks, puffs used, eventual escape medication, and side-effects on a headache diary.

Before, after the double-blind trial, and after the long-term study the patients had an ENT examination and the mucociliary transport time was measured with the saccharine method[9].

Results

Fourteen patients treated all six attacks without any protocol violations. These were considered valid patients for statistical analysis. Twenty-one patients were considered partially valid. They contributed with a mean of 4.8 attacks (range, 3–6) and the most common violations of the protocol were: not using the spray in the randomized order ($n = 8$) and taking additional medication before 2 h ($n = 5$). Two patients stopped because of inefficacy.

Twelve patients were excluded as they only treated one to two attacks.

Most patients used both initial doses and the two optional doses, so the real doses tested were in most cases 2 mg DHE, and 1.5 mg DHE given in 1 h versus placebo.

In the 14 valid patients a significant effect was found for duration of attacks and the patients judgement of the efficacy (Table 1), but when valid and partially valid patients were considered together there was some tendency for better effects of DHE, but no significant result versus placebo (Table 1). For all other efficacy parameters some trends in favour of DHE were found but no statistically significant differences.

Side-effects (local and systemic) occurred in 19 cases with DHE, in three with placebo, and in seven with both DHE and placebo ($P<0.05$). No major side-effects occurred apart from a patient who developed an asthmatic attack with placebo and was excluded.

Twenty-six patients continued in the long-term study and treated a mean of 19 attacks (range 1–94). Most patients used 2 mg DHE = four puffs per attack. One patient twice experienced stuffiness in the nose up to 1 week after use of DHE.

The mean mucociliary transport time (in min) was 15 ± 8 (s.d.) before the double-blind trial and 13 ± 5 after this trial (NS). After 1 year the mean was 15 ± 12. No significant changes were found in the ENT examination at any time.

Table 1. *Effects of DHE as a nasal spray on duration of attacks and rating of efficacy in valid (n = 14) and valid + partially valid (n = 35) patients.*

	Initial doses		
	DHE 0.1 mg	DHE 0.5 mg	Placebo
		Mean duration (h)	
Valid patients	5.17[†]	5.52*	11.87
Valid + partially valid patients	8.10	7.92	10.18
		Mean efficacy[‡]	
Valid patients	2.82*	2.54	2.04
Valid + partially valid patient	2.76	2.43	2.56

*$P<0.05$, [†]$P<0.001$, compared to placebo.
[‡]Rating of efficacy was done on a 4 points verbal scale: 1, don't know; 2, bad; 3, fair; 4, good.

Discussion

In the double-blind trial no convincing effect of DHE as a nasal spray was found. How can we then explain that 27 of 35 (77%) of the patients would use the spray when asked after the double-blind trial, and that 26 patients used it for 1 year? The reason for the patients' willingness to use the spray after their experience in the double-blind trial remains obscure to us. In the long-term study, however, most patients were sure the DHE spray was efficacious, and they explained that they now had learned to use it properly by practising. The device in its present experimental form is rather complicated to use: an ampoule with the DHE solution should first be broken, then the device is assembled, and then refilled with a special manoeuvre by pressing four times, and then the spray is ready for use. One might thus suspect that the patients in the first part of the trial had difficulties in using it correctly. A hint in this direction is the fact that the 'statistically valid' patients, who could be expected to be more meticulous, had some statistical beneficial effects from DHE. Even in supervised volunteers, who had practised with a dummy spray, the DHE bioavailability varied considerably (Tfelt-Hansen, unpublished observation). So for future studies of DHE we would recommend a more simple device for delivering the DHE intranasally.

In general, only minor side-effects were observed and only one patient with a possible 'rebound rhinitis' was found.

The ENT examinations did not show changes even after prolonged use with DHE. The tolerance of DHE as a nasal spray should, however, be judged from large-scale open studies before the tolerance can be judged fairly.

Acknowledgements—The DHE and placebo nasal sprays were kindly provided by Sandoz Ltd, Basel, Switzerland.

References

1 Bobik, A., Jennings, G., Skews, H., Esler, M. & McLean, A. (1981): Low oral bioavailability of dihydroergotamine and first-pass extraction in patients with orthostatic hypotension. *Clin. Pharmacol. Ther.* **30**, 673–679.

2 Maurer, G. & Frick, W. (1984): Elucidation of the structure and receptor binding studies of the major primary metabolite of dihydroergotamine in man. *Eur. J. Clin. Pharmacol.* **26**, 463–470.

3 Volans, G. N. (1975): The effect of metoclopramide on the absorption of effervescent aspirin in migraine. *Br. J. Clin. Pharmacol.* **2**, 57–63.

4 Tokola, R. A. & Neuronen, P. J. (1984): Effects of migraine attack and metoclopramide on the absorption of tolfenamic acid. *Br. J. Clin. Pharmacol.* **17**, 67–75.

5 Aellig, W. H. & Rosenthaler, J. (1986): Venoconstrictor effect of dihydroergotamine (DHE) after intranasal and i.m. administration. *Eur. J. Clin. Pharmacol.* **30**, 581–584.

6 Krause, K.-H. & Bleicher, M. A. (1985): Dihydroergotamine nasal spray in the treatment of migraine attacks. *Cephalalgia* **5**, (suppl. 3) 138–139.

7 Müller-Schweinitzer, E. (1984): What is known about the action of dihydroergotamine on the vasculature in man? *Int. J. Clin. Pharmacol. Ther. Toxicol.* **22**, 677–682.

8 Andersen, A. R., Tfelt-Hansen, P. & Lassen, N. A. (1987): The effect of ergotamine and dihydroergotamine on cerebral blood flow in man. *Stroke* **18**, 120–123.

9 Mygind, N. (1978): *Nasal allergy*. Oxford: Blackwell.

18

PRACTICAL PROBLEMS ASSOCIATED WITH

THE DIETARY MANAGEMENT OF MIGRAINE

A. MacDonald*, W. I. Forsythe[†] and A. M. B. Minford[‡]

*St James's University Hospital, Leeds, West Yorkshire, UK;
[†]St James's University Hospital, Leeds and Leeds General Infirmary,
Leeds, West Yorkshire, UK and [‡]Bradford Children's Hospital,
Bradford, West Yorkshire, UK

Summary

In order to investigate the incidence of food intolerance in migraine, we attempted to start 52 children with common, classical or basilar migraine on an elimination diet. Only 13% had proven food intolerance. A further 25% obtained no benefit from the diet. The remaining 62% of children had numerous unforeseen difficulties with the diet. The practical problems experienced with the elimination diet and migraine will be described.

Introduction

It has been accepted for many years that foods may provoke migraine. Various workers have claimed high rates of success when using elimination diets to identify specific food allergens[1-4], but the exact mechanism linking food to migraine remains unknown.

Foods that have been generally implicated are those containing vasoactive amines, eg chocolate, cheese, citrus fruits and red wine[5,6,7]. More recently, however, Egger *et al.* (1983)[4] demonstrated, by a double-blind controlled trial using an oligoantigenic diet, that almost any food can cause migraine. With the lack of reliable laboratory diagnostic tests, diet remains the only useful tool to identify specific food allergens[7-10]. During the last 5 years, interest has increased in the use of the elimination diet in the treatment of migraine, but little attention has been given to the application and maintenance of such diets. In this study, we present data on the use of elimination diets with 52 children, and the practical problems associated with the dietary management are described in detail.

Patients and methods

From January 1982 to January 1986 we attempted to introduce an elimination diet to 52 children (26 boys and 26 girls) with common, classical or basilar migraine, as defined by Congdon and Forsythe (1979)[11] and Hockaday (1979)[12]. All the patients had headaches at least once a week for the previous 6 months with at least three of the following associated features: aura, nausea, vomiting and a family history of migraine. The patients were referred to two District General Teaching Hospitals and were treated by one paediatrician (WIF) and one paediatric dietitian (AM). The age range of the patients was 4–16 years, mean age 11 years. Twelve of the patients had associated atopic symptoms such as eczema or asthma. A further 12 had no other symptoms but had a strong family history of atopy. Eleven of the patients had already thought that food may be related to their migraine. Common foods implicated included fried foods, citrus fruits, chocolate and ice cream.

The elimination diet consisted of lamb, rice, carrots, a soya-milk substitute, pears, peaches, apricots, sugar, salt, '7-Up' lemonade and Tomor margarine. The basic elimination diet was tried for 3 weeks. If there was only one headache or less during the last 2 weeks of the diet, this was followed by careful food reintroduction. A normal daily portion of one new food was given every 7 days. If there was no improvement in symptoms at the end of 3 weeks the diet was discontinued, and patients were not offered an alternative elimination diet. Vitamin and mineral supplements were given if necessary.

The diagnosis of food intolerance was considered proven if a positive reaction to two open and one blind challenge was obtained. For the blind challenges, special test dishes were prepared. Throughout the study careful records were kept of migraine attacks, viz, severity, frequency and duration of headaches and incidence of nausea, vomiting and aura. Weekly dietetic supervision was also provided during the whole trial.

Results

Of the 52 children included in the study, seven (13%) were proven to have food intolerance. The food most frequently provoking migraine was milk; three children reacted to more than one food. Only one child from this group also suffered from atopic symptoms. Reactions were frequently delayed, patients taking up to 2–3 days before they reacted to foods.

Thirteen patients (25%) obtained no benefit from the 3 week elimination diet. Five of these said their headaches were worse for the full 3 weeks on the basic diet. Of the remaining 32 (62%), numerous unforeseen problems were encountered.

Seven (13%) refused to try the elimination diet either because they considered it would be worse than their migraine or due to social or financial problems which made it almost impossible for the parents to cope with the diet. Eight (15%) had a 'spontaneous remission' as soon as they were shown the diet sheet, even though they had a previous history of frequent migraine attacks from at least 1 to 6 years. Seven (13 per cent) started the diet but failed to comply. Some found the diet restrictive or monotonous; others were hungry and cheated. Three (6%) had complete remissions on the basic diet, but failed to react to any food during reintroduction. Two (4%) responded to the basic diet and on the initial challenge reacted to chocolate and mayonnaise respectively, but on further challenging there were no reactions. Both children are now symptom free on normal diets. A further child reacted to Coca-cola on the initial challenge, but refused to have any further challenges. A further three children (6%) responded to the basic elimination diet, but the migraine attacks returned and were not related to the reintroduction of food. The remaining child appeared to react to a very large variety of foods and always relapsed before the blind challenges were due. The mother was receiving supplementary benefit with an additional £21.00 a week allowance for the diet (estimated cost £16.00 a week). We were satisfied that the child did not have food intolerance.

Other problems

In addition, practical difficulties were experienced with most children. An elimination diet costs two to three times the cost of a normal diet[13] and many parents found the diet expensive. Several parents were receiving supplementary benefit and needed to obtain a high cost dietary allowance before their children could start the elimination diet.

The provision of appropriate school meals, residential meals and indeed any meal away from the home, was particularly arduous. Social eating is important for the older child and was responsible for many dietary indiscretions.

Time was another problem factor. In order to make an elimination diet acceptable, it takes considerable time and effort to produce the special dishes. Virtually no convenience food is suitable and some parents had neither the time, cooking skills or facilities required to prepare the foods for the basic diet.

In general, the older the children the more difficult it was to meet their nutritional needs. Teenagers have high energy requirements and it was hard to achieve these on such a limited diet with the result that weight loss was common during the earlier weeks. Almost all the children refused to drink the soya-milk substitute and required calcium supplements.

Discussion

In contrast to recent published work, 13% of our patients with migraine had proven food intolerance. Although a further 19% improved on the diet, it is possible that some of these had a spontaneous remission of their migraine. It has been suggested that the spontaneous remission rate is between 37% to 43% in 7–16 year-old children[14]. Even with close dietetic supervision, the financial and social limitations of such a rigid diet prevented its introduction or continuation in many patients.

When dealing with children, it is important to provide an acceptable dietary regimen. In order to do this with migraine a modified elimination diet is suggested, ie a diet omitting only milk, eggs, some additives and vasoactive amine containing foods. Although this may fail to diagnose a minority of cases, most children with severe migraine should be able to adhere to this. If the symptoms persist and the child and parents are motivated, a stricter elimination diet should then be tried.

Undoubtedly, the elimination diet is the best diagnostic tool when dealing with multiple food intolerance, but the problems accompanying it are numerous. Thus, it is important to carefully consider all factors before recommending its use for children with migraine.

Acknowledgements—We would like to thank Mrs Linda Tremayne for patiently typing this manuscript.

References

1 Unger, A. H. & Unger L. (1952): Migraine is an allergic disease. *J. Allergy* **23**, 429–440.
2 Grant, E. E. C. (1979): Food allergies and migraine. *Lancet* **i**, 966–969.
3 Monro, J. A. Brostoff, J., Canni, C. & Zilkha, K. (1980): Food allergy in migraine. *Lancet* **ii**, 1–4.
4 Egger, J., Carter, C. M., Wilson, J., Turner, M. W. & Soothill, J. F. (1983): Is migraine food allergy? *Lancet* **ii**, 865–869.

5 Hanington, E. (1983): Migraine. In *Clinical reactions to foods*, ed. M. H. Lessof, pp. 155–180. Chichester: John Wiley and Sons.

6 Monro, J. (1982): Food allergy and migraine. In *Clinics in immunology*, eds J. Brostoff & D. N. Challacombe, vol. 2, no. 1, p. 137–163.
Eastbourne: W. B. Saunders Company Ltd.

7 Lessof, H. M. (Chairman) (1984): Food intolerance and food aversion. *J. R. Coll. Physicians Lond.* **18**, 83–122.

8 Minford, A. M. B., MacDonald, A. & Littlewood, J. M. (1982): Food intolerance and food allergy in children: a review of 68 cases. *Arch. Dis. Child.* **57**, 742–747.

9 David, T. J. (1985): The overworked or fraudulent diagnosis of food allergy and food intolerance in children. *J. R. Soc. Med.* (suppl.) **78**, 21–31.

10 Truswell, A. S. (1985): Food sensitivity. *Br. Med. J.* **291**, 951–955.

11 Congdon, P. J. & Forsythe, W. I. (1979): Migraine in childhood: a study of 300 children. *Develop. Med. Child. Neurol.* **21**, 209–216.

12 Hockaday, J. M. (1979): Basilar migraine in childhood. *Develop. Med. Child. Neurol.* **21**, 455–463.

13 MacDonald, A. & Forsythe, W. I. (1986): The cost of nutrition and diet therapy for low-income families. *Hum. Nutr: Appl. Nutr.* **40 A**, 87–96.

14 Bille, B. (1962): Migraine in school children. *Acta Pediatr.* **51**, Suppl. 36.

19

DECREASED PHENOL AND

TYRAMINE SULPHOCONJUGATION

BY PLATELETS IN DIETARY MIGRAINE

Hany Soliman*, André Pradalier[†],
Jean-Marie Launay*, Jean Dry[†] and Claude Dreux*

*Service de Biochimie et Neuroendocrinologie, Hôpital St Louis,
2 place du Dr Fournier, 75475 Paris Cedex 10, France
and [†]Service de Médecine Interne, Hôpital Rothschild,
33, Boulevard de Picpus, 75571 Paris Cedex 12, France

Summary

Two forms of human platelet phenolsulphotransferase (PST) activity have been described: PST-P and PST-M for which phenol (at low concentrations) and phenolic monoamine neurotransmitters can serve as sulphate acceptor substrates respectively. In this study we confirm a deficit of the 'P' form (substrate: phenol) and we describe a partial deficit (only with tyramine as substrate) of the 'M' form, solely in dietary migraine patients as compared to either non-dietary migraineurs or to control subjects.

Introduction

Many migraine patients believe that the ingestion of certain foodstuffs can precipitate their migraine headaches. In 1967, Hanington[1] drew attention to the similarity between a hypertensive headache following the ingestion of tyramine-rich cheese in patients treated with monoamine oxidase inhibitors (MAOIs) and dietary migraine. Despite some disagreement, the hypothesis that tyramine ingestion can elicit migraine headache in dietary patients appears to have some validity (for review: see Kohlenberg[2]). Platelet MAO studies in dietary and non-dietary migraineurs did not seem to provide a direct implication of a decreased MAO activity in either dietary or non-dietary migraineurs[3,4,5]. Youdim et al.[6] found that tyramine-sensitive migraine patients excreted significantly lower levels of tyramine-O-sulphate after an oral load of tyramine as compared to control subjects and therefore suggested a tyramine conjugation deficit in these patients. Sulphoconjugation of phenolic compounds is catalyzed by phenolsulphotransferase (PST; EC 2.8.2.1.) which is widespread in the human body[7] including blood platelets[8], its highest specific activity being present in gut mucosa[4] which appears important for the detoxification and elimination of potentially toxic dietary phenols[9]. Two forms of the enzyme were characterized: PST-M for which monoamine neurotransmitters and their metabolites can serve as substrates while low concentrations of phenol, p-nitrophenol or salicylamide are substrates for PST-P[10]. Littlewood *et al.*[11] reported a significant decrease of platelet PST-P activity (substrate: phenol) and a slight but not significant reduction of PST-M (substrate : tyramine) in dietary migraineurs as compared to controls or to non-dietary migraine sufferers. We therefore decided to study platelet PST activities in migrainous patients using various substrates and improved methodology.

Methods

Subjects

Common migraine sufferers who are all members of the 'Club Migraine et Céphalées' (Hôpital Rothschild, Paris) were invited to participate in this study. Common migraine was diagnosed according to the criteria defined by the 'Ad Hoc Committee on Classification of Headache'[12]. They were classified into three groups:
(1) 18 dietary attack-free migraine patients (DM) viz those who believed (by repetitive observations) that certain foodstuffs can provoke their headaches, chocolate and cheese being mostly cited;
(2) 13 non-dietary attack-free (NDM) and;
(3) 17 non-dietary during an attack (NDM + A), 13 of whom were all the NDM patients.
The duration of illness was 5 to 42 years, with a frequency of two to eight migraine attacks per month. None of these patients took any medication during 12 days before blood collection, even for an attack. The control subjects consisted of 18 healthy volunteers (Blood Bank, Hôpital Saint Louis). The four groups of subjects (patients and controls) were all females and had a similar age distribution.

Blood samples

Samples (10 ml) were withdrawn from fasting subjects between 7 and 10 am, from cubital fossa vein into plastic containers containing 0.5 ml of 5% Na_2 EDTA, mixed gently and placed in ice. All samples were processed within 2 h after collection.

Platelet isolation

Platelets were isolated from blood by the iterative centrifugation procedure of Corash[13]. Platelets were counted by phase-contrast microscopy.

Platelet PST activities

They were measured by the radio-enzymatic method of Foldes and Meek[14] as modified by Bonham Carter *et al.*[15]. Serotonin (5-HT), 4-hydroxy-3-methoxyphenylglycol (HMPG), dopamine (DA) and p-tyramine in the final concentrations of 10, 800, 30 and 133 μmol/l respectively were used as sulphate acceptor substrates to measure platelet PST-M activity and phenol (30 μmol/l) was used to measure platelet PST-P activity. Enzyme activities were expressed as units: 1 unit represented the formation of 1 nmol of sulphoconjugated substrate/10^8 platelets/h at 37°C.

Data analysis

Two-tailed non-parametric Kolmogorov-Smirnov (KS test) and Spearman rank test (r_s) were used[16].

Results

Platelet PST activities (M and P) in the non-dietary patients either during or between attacks were not significantly different from those of control subjects (Figure).

Dietary patients showed a significantly lower platelet PST-P activity ($P < 0.05$) as compared to either controls or to non-dietary patients with or without an attack (Figure, part E).

A more significant decrease in platelet PST-M activity ($P < 0.01$) was observed in dietary patients only with p-tyramine as substrate (Figure, part D), but with neither of the other PST-M substrates (Figure, parts A, B & C), as compared to either controls or to non-dietary patients.

The significant correlations observed between PST-M activities for control subjects using 5-HT, HMPG, DA and p-tyramine were no longer present for any group of migrainous patients studied (with the exception of a significant correlation between PST activities measured with HMPG and DA in the dietary patients). However, the absence of correlations between PST-M (with any PST-M substrate used) and PST-P (with phenol) was similar for the three groups of patients and for control subjects.

Discussion

In this study, the non-dietary patients (during or between attacks) showed platelet PST-M and P activities not significantly different from those found for controls, which is consistent with previous reports[5,11].

The significantly lower platelet PST-P activity (substrate: phenol) in the dietary patients confirms the observations of Sandler's group[11]. If platelet PST activities were to reflect adequately those elsewhere in the body, then a generalized deficit of PST-P activity in these patients might account for their susceptibility to diets containing as yet unidentified headache triggering phenolic substance(s) which may be substrate(s) for PST-P. However, the identification of these dietary substances and investigating their triggering effects, metabolism and sulphoconjugation seem to be necessary to support the above assumption. The highly significant decrease in platelet PST-M activity solely found with p-tyramine as substrate seems to be of particular interest since it is consistent with a tyramine conjugation defect in tyramine-sensitive migraineurs reported earlier[6]. The slight but not significant reduction of platelet PST activity with tyramine in dietary migraineurs reported by Littlewood *et al.*[11], contrary to our findings, might be explained partly or wholly by one or both of the following:
(1) the presence of subgroups of dietary patients who might be deficient in one or both platelet PST activities;
(2) the absence of correlation between PST-M activities measured in platelets isolated from bloods of the same subjects by iterative centrifugation method (yield 98.28%) and a single centrifugation method (yield 46.15%), as we reported recently[17].

We cannot explain the absence of correlation between PST activities measured with PST-M substrates in all migraine groups studied in contrast to the significant correlations found

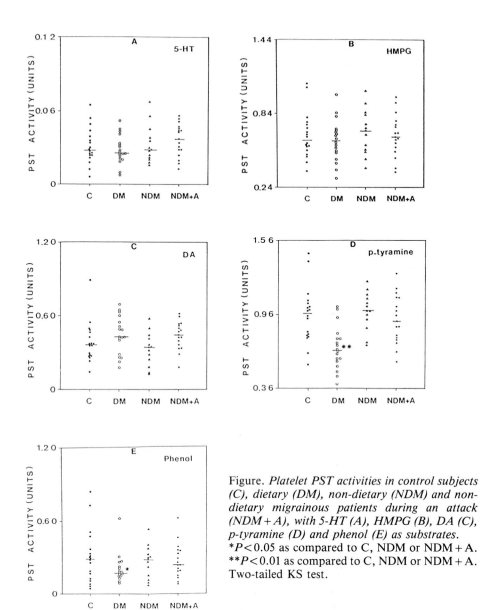

Figure. *Platelet PST activities in control subjects (C), dietary (DM), non-dietary (NDM) and non-dietary migrainous patients during an attack (NDM + A), with 5-HT (A), HMPG (B), DA (C), p-tyramine (D) and phenol (E) as substrates.*
*P < 0.05 as compared to C, NDM or NDM + A.
**P < 0.01 as compared to C, NDM or NDM + A.
Two-tailed KS test.

for normal subjects, while the lack of correlation found with any PST-M and PST-P substrate was observed for all groups of patients as well as controls. A significant correlation between PST-M and PST-P activities was reported in non-dietary patients[11]. Might this represent a general dysregulation of PST activities in these patients? What is its significance in non-dietary patients? It seems not unlikely that PST plays a role in dietary migraine and this warrants further investigation.

Acknowledgements—Members of the 'Club Migraine et Céphalées', Hôpital Rothschild are gratefully acknowledged. H. S. and J. M. L. were supported by a grant from the 'Groupement de Recherche et d'Expérimentation sur les Céphalées'.

References

1 Hanington, E. (1967): Preliminary report of tyramine headache. *Br. Med. J.* **2**, 550–551.
2 Kohlenberg, R. J. (1982): Tyramine sensitivity in dietary migraine: a critical review. *Headache* **22**, 30–34.
3 Glover, V., Peatfield, R., Zammit-Pace, R., Littlewood, J., Gawel, M., Clifford Rose, F. & Sandler, M. (1981): Platelet monoamine oxidase activity and headache. *J. Neurol. Neurosurg. Psychiat.* **44**, 786–790.
4 Glover, V., Littlewood, J., Sandler, M., Peatfield, R., Petty, R. & Clifford Rose, F. (1983): Biochemical predisposition to dietary migraine: the role of phenolsulfotransferase. *Headache* **23**, 53–58.
5 Launay, J. M. & Pradalier, A. (1985): Common migraine attack: platelet modifications are mainly due to plasma factor(s). *Headache* **25**, 262–267.
6 Youdim, M. B. H., Bonham Carter, S. M., Sandler, M., Hanington, E. & Wilkinson, M. (1971): Conjugation defect in tyramine-sensitive migraine. *Nature* **230**, 127–128.
7 Sandler, M. (1981): Phenolsulfotransferases: general introduction. In *Phenol* sulfotransferase in mental health research, eds M. Sandler & E. Usdin, pp. 1–7. London: Macmillan.
8 Hart, R. F., Renskers, K. J., Nelson, E. B. & Roth, J. A. (1979): Localization and characterization of phenolsulfotransferase in human platelets. *Life Sci.* **24**, 125–130.
9 Wardle, E. N. (1982): What does phenolsulfotransferase do? *Lancet* **i**, 691.
10 Rein, G., Glover, V. & Sandler, M. (1982): Multiple forms of phenolsulfotransferase in human tissues, selective inhibition by dichloronitrophenol. *Biochem. Pharmacol.* **31**, 1893–1897.
11 Littlewood, J., Glover, V., Sandler, M., Peatfield, R., Petty, R. & Clifford Rose, F. (1982): Platelet phenolsulfotransferase deficiency in dietary migraine. *Lancet* **i**, 983–986.
12 Ad Hoc Committee on classification of headache (1962): Classification of headache. *J. Am. Med. Ass.* **1979**, 717–718.
13 Corash, L. (1980): Platelet heterogeneity: relevance to the use of platelets to study psychiatric disorders. *Schiz. Bull.* **6**, 254–255.
14 Foldes, A. & Meek, J. L. (1973): Rat brain phenolsulfotransferase — partial purification and some properties. *Biochim. Biophys. Acta.* **327**, 365–374.
15 Bonham Carter, S. M., Glover, V., Sandler, M., Gillman, P. K. & Bridges, P. K. (1981): Human platelet phenolsulfotransferase: separate control of the two forms and activity range in depressive illness. *Clin. Chim. Acta.* **117**, 333–344.
16 Siegel, S. (1956): *Non parametric statistics for the behavioural sciences.* New York: McGraw Hill.
17 Soliman, H., Oset-Gasque, M. J., Callebert, J., Launay, J. M., Tabuteau, F. & Dreux, C. (1987): Isolation of human platelets for sulfotransferase activity determination: the method of choice. *Thromb. Res.* **45**, 279–284.

20

RED WINE AS A MIGRAINE TRIGGER

Julia T. Littlewood*, Celia Gibb*, Vivette Glover*, Pat Hannah*,
M. Sandler*, P. T. G. Davies† and F. Clifford Rose†

*Bernhard Baron Memorial Research Laboratories,
Queen Charlotte's Hospital, Goldhawk Road, London W6 0XG, UK
and †The Princess Margaret Migraine Clinic, Academic Unit of
Neuroscience, Charing Cross and Westminster Medical School,
London W6 8RF, UK

Summary

Patients with migraine who believed themselves sensitive to red wine but not other alcoholic drinks were challenged with either red wine or a vodka and lemonade mixture, both disguised. Red wine provoked a typical migraine attack in nine out of 11 such patients whereas none of the eight challenged with vodka had an attack. Similar challenge produced no such episodes in other migraine subjects or controls. The effect is unlikely to be due to the tyramine content of the wine used as this was very low (less than 1 mg). This is the first objective evidence that red wine contains a migraine provoking agent which is not alcohol or tyramine.

Red wine contains potent *in vitro* inhibitors of the enzyme phenolsulphotransferase. Preliminary evidence from a metabolic experiment suggests that red wine also has an inhibiting effect on sulphoconjugation of phenols *in vivo*, showing that at least some of these inhibitors must be absorbed. We discuss the possibility that it is the phenolic flavonoid component that is responsible for the *in vivo* effects of red wine and for its migraine-inducing properties.

Introduction

Many doctors are sceptical about whether migraine headaches can be induced by food or drink and whether so called 'dietary migraine' exists at all, although many patients are convinced of it.

Of 1310 patients interviewed at the Princess Margaret Migraine Clinic at Charing Cross Hospital, about one quarter thought their migraine attacks could be provoked by articles of diet[1]. Alcoholic drinks, and in particular red wine, headed the list of such dietary factors. We studied this problem objectively to see if red wine really did cause migraine in patients who consider themselves susceptible to this trigger and, if so, what the mechanism might be.

Red wine challenge in migraine patients

For this experiment, we selected 19 patients who suffered regularly from headache and thought they were sensitive to red wine but not to other alcoholic drinks. For the most part, they had already convinced themselves by excluding red wine for several weeks or months from their diet, and on subsequent challenge had found they experienced a migraine attack. The time interval between drinking red wine and experiencing headache was usually brief—anything from ½ to 3 h. They claimed that as little as one or two glasses could trigger a migrainous episode. We also selected some migraine patients who were sure they were not sensitive to red wine or any other alcoholic drink and control subjects from hospital and laboratory staff who did not suffer regularly from headache. All were drug-free at the time of the experiment.

Patients were given either 300 ml of a Spanish red wine or 300 ml of a vodka and lemonade mixture with equivalent alcohol content (w/v) to the red wine. 'Non-dietary' patients and controls were offered red wine only. The drinks were chilled for half an hour to obscure their flavour and drunk from a brown glass bottle with a coloured straw to conceal the colour. Subjects were told they were being given either red wine or a good simulation and seemed genuinely uncertain of what they were drinking. They were observed for a subsequent period of about 3 h to see whether they developed any migrainous symptoms. We attempted to make their environment as relaxed as possible to minimize the stress, and they were offered a video to watch, magazines to read, and were free to wander about the hospital and environs, provided they returned immediately any symptoms developed. They were also telephoned the following day for further discussion of any symptoms.

Vahlquist's[2] criteria were observed to establish whether or not patients had developed a true migraine attack.

Nine out of the 11 migraine patients who considered themselves red wine sensitive developed a migrainous attack after consuming the red wine but none of the eight challenged with vodka did so. The migrainous symptoms experienced by the responders are shown in Table 1. In the group challenged with vodka, two subjects developed mild frontal headache with some nausea but neither developed into a typical migraine attack. The remaining six merely demonstrated symptoms of inebriation.

Table 1. *Response of different patient groups to red wine or vodka challenge.*

Patient group	n	Alcoholic beverage	Number who developed migraine	Number with particular symptoms			
				Headache	Nausea	Photophobia	Numbness
D	11	Red wine	9	9	8	8	3
D	8	Vodka	0[†]	2	0	0	0
ND	5	Red wine	0*	0	0	0	0
C	8	Red wine	0[†]	0	0	0	0

Fisher's Exact Test: *P<0.005; [†]P<0.001; significantly different from group 1.
D, patients who think red wine does induce a migraine;
ND, patients who think it does not;
C, control subjects who do not suffer regularly from headache.

Using Fisher's Exact test for small frequencies, this differential response is highly significant ($P < 0.001$).

None of the non-dietary patients and none of the eight normal controls developed migraine after consumption of red wine. Again, the differential response is highly significant ($P < 0.005$ and $P < 0.001$ respectively).

This study provides the first objective evidence that red wine will induce migrainous episodes in patients who think they are specifically susceptible to it, whereas vodka will not. These data, therefore, militate against the view that it is the alcohol in red wine that is the sole noxious chemical[3] although it may act as a cofactor with some other component. In patients who think that alcoholic drinks in general can initiate their attacks, alcohol itself may of course be more important.

The tyramine content of the wine used was very low (1.9 mg/l) and is extremely unlikely to have had any effect. We have recently analysed several wines for their tyramine content and found that, contrary to popular belief, red wine in general did not have a higher tyramine concentration than white wine (Hannah, Glover and Sandler, in preparation) (Table 2).

We thus have to look beyond both alcohol and tyramine for the chemicals in red wine that provoke migraine.

Table 2. *Tyramine content in wines.*

	n	Free tyramine (mean ± s.d.) (mg/l)
White wine	12	1.22 ± 1.80
Red wine	10	1.36 ± 1.41
Chianti	12	1.48 ± 1.26
Rioja*	1	1.94

*Used in red wine challenge.

Biochemical effects of red wine in vitro and in vivo

A different class of chemicals which may be involved are the phenols, which are substrates for the enzyme phenolsulphotransferase (PST)[4]. Phenolsulphotransferase inactivates a wide range of both exogenous and endogenous phenols by catalysing their conjugation with sulphate[4]. It exists in two forms, PST-M which acts on phenolic monoamines such as tyramine and dopamine and their metabolites, and PST-P which degrades phenol itself and p-cresol[5,6]. The two forms are particularly active in the intestinal wall. We have found that the group of patients who believe that dietary factors (cheese and chocolate) can trigger their migraine have significantly lower mean platelet PST-P activity than controls[7] and this has recently been confirmed by an independent study (Soliman et al., this volume). This suggests that dietary migraine patients may be unable to metabolize phenols efficiently so that they may enter the circulation in higher concentration than normal to become migraine triggers.

Against this background, we looked at ethyl acetate extracts of alcoholic drinks and found that those of red wine contained very potent inhibitors of PST, particularly the P form of the enzyme, when tested *in vitro*[8]. Extracts of white wine inhibited this enzyme to a lesser extent, and extracts of vodka showed very little inhibition. The main difference between red and white wine is in their phenolic flavonoid component. Whereas red wine typically contains 1200 mg/l of these compounds, only about 50 mg/l are present in white

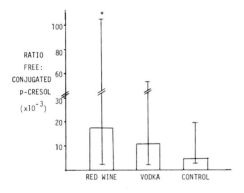

Figure. *Ratio of free : conjugated p-cresol excreted after the consumption of red wine, vodka or water as control.*
*$P<0.05$ (Wilcoxon matched pairs signed rank test).

wine[9]. When this fraction was extracted, it was found to inhibit PST-P potently and specifically (Gibb, Glover and Sandler — unpublished data). Seventy per cent of the phenolic flavonoid fraction is accounted for by large polymeric anthocyanogens which are unlikely to be of importance *in vivo* as they are not absorbed[9]. Catechins and anthocyanins, however, comprise 20% and 10% of this fraction respectively and are absorbed through the gastrointestinal tract in man. We have found catechins to be potent inhibitors of PST-P *in vitro* and that certain anthocyanins, the compounds responsible for the colour of red wine as well as many other fruits and vegetables, can also inhibit this enzyme[10].

Whatever the *in vitro* findings, it is important to establish whether these inhibitors in red wine also have a metabolic effect *in vivo*. To do this, we developed a gas chromatographic assay for measuring urinary excretion of *p*-cresol, a specific substrate for PST-P which is probably generated by the action of gut flora on dietary tyrosine residues. Humans normally excrete 16–39 mg *p*-cresol daily[11], predominantly in sulphoconjugated form (approximately 90%). In this experiment, eight volunteers consumed either 300 ml of red wine, the same variety that was used in the migraine experiment, 88 ml of vodka diluted to 300 ml with water (equivalent alcohol content to red wine, w/v) or 300 ml of water. Three hour urine collections were made. It was found that, after the consumption of 300 ml of red wine, the urinary ratio of free to conjugated *p*-cresol increased significantly compared with control values (Gibb, Glover and Sandler, in preparation) (Figure). Consumption of vodka had no significant effect on *p*-cresol excretion compared with control values.

These preliminary data suggest that red wine is inhibiting the conjugation of *p*-cresol *in vivo* and that this metabolic effect is not due to its alcohol content. Such inhibition was far from total, but even partial inhibition of the conjugation of *p*-cresol and other phenols could result in a build-up of free phenols in the circulation, which may be toxic in several ways. There is evidence that these compounds can inhibit platelet aggregation. They interfere with [^{3}H]noradrenaline uptake and [^{14}C]5-hydroxytryptamine release by platelets[12], and *p*-cresol appears to be neurotoxic to rodents[13].

Whether the migraine-triggering action of red wine stems from a build-up of *p*-cresol and other free phenols or whether red wine affects some other system remains to be established.

Acknowledgements—We are grateful to Dr T. J. Steiner and Dr R. Joseph for their help with these experiments. Julia T. Littlewood was supported by the Medical Research Council. Celia Gibb was supported by the Ministry of Agriculture, Fisheries and Food. R. Joseph and P. T. G. Davies were supported by the Migraine Trust.

References

1 Glover, V., Littlewood, J., Sandler, M., Peatfield, R., Petty, R. & Rose, F. C. (1984): Dietary migraine: looking beyond tyramine. In *Progress in migraine research*, ed. F. Clifford Rose, pp. 113–119. London: Pitman.
2 Vahlquist, B. (1955): Migraine in children. *Int. Arch. Allergy* **7**, 348–355.
3 Anthony, M. (1985): Alcohol and migraine. *Migraine News*, **50**, 2.
4 Sandler, M., Usdin, E. (1981): *Phenolsulfotransferase in mental health research*, eds M. Sandler & E. Usdin. London: Macmillan.
5 Rein, G., Glover, V. & Sandler, M. (1981): Phenolsulphotransferase in human tissue: evidence for multiple forms. In *Phenolsulfotransferase in mental health research*, eds M. Sandler & E. Usdin, pp. 98–126. London: Macmillan.
6 Rein, G., Glover, V. & Sandler, M. (1982): Multiple forms of phenolsulphotransferase in human tissues: selective inhibition by dichloronitrophenol. *Biochem. Pharmac.* **31**, 1893–1897.
7 Littlewood, J., Glover, V., Sandler, M., Petty, R., Peatfield, R. & Rose, F. C. (1982): Platelet phenolsulphotransferase deficiency in dietary migraine. *Lancet* **i**, 983–986.
8 Littlewood, J. T., Glover, V. & Sandler, M. (1985): Red wine contains a potent inhibitor of phenolsulphotransferase. *Br. J. Clin. Pharmac.* **19**, 275–278.
9 Singleton, V. L. & Noble, A. C. (1976): Wine flavour and phenolic substances. In *Phenolic, sulfur and nitrogen compounds in food flavors*, eds G. Charalambous & I. Katz, pp. 47–70. American Chemical Society Symposium, Series No. 26.
10 Gibb, C., Glover, V. & Sandler, M. (1986): Inhibition of phenolsulphotransferase P by certain food constituents. *Lancet* **i**, 794.
11 Bakke, O. M. & Midtvedt, T. (1970): Influence of germ-free status on the excretion of simple phenols of possible significance in tumour promotion. *Experientia* **26**, 519.
12 Mülder, G. J. (1982): Conjugation of phenols. In *Metabolic basis of detoxication*, eds W. B. Jakoby, J. R. Bend & J. Caldwell, pp. 247–269. New York: Academic Press.
13 Veldre, I. (1973): Combined effect of orally administered *p*-cresol and β-napthol on a warm-blooded organism. Gig. Tr. Prof. Patol. Est. SSR 1972; No. 8: 155–64 (Russian): *Chem. Abstr.* **79**, 1334–47.

21

STUDIES ON FEVERFEW

AND ITS MODE OF ACTION

S. Heptinstall*, W. A. Groenewegen*,
D. W. Knight†, P. Spangenberg‡ and W. Loesche‡

*Department of Medicine, University Hospital, Queen's Medical Centre
Nottingham, UK; †Department of Chemistry, University of Nottingham
University Park, Nottingham, UK and ‡Institute of Pathological Biochemistry,
Medical Academy of Erfurt, Erfurt, German Democratic Republic

Introduction

Feverfew is the common name for *Tanacetum parthenium*, a plant with chrysanthemum-like leaves and daisy-like flowers. The plant's leaves are reputed to be of value in a variety of medical conditions and interest among the lay public is such that when a source of information on feverfew was briefly mentioned in a British daily newspaper, 25 000 requests were received[1]. Anecdotal evidence indicates that feverfew may be of value in arthritis, psoriasis and several other conditions, but its chief use among the lay public is as prophylaxis for migraine[2]. Feverfew is commonly taken orally, usually at the rate of two or three fresh leaves per day. Dried leaves are also thought to be effective and there are now several commercial preparations that contain dried feverfew in tablet or capsule form.

Although most reports on the efficacy of feverfew in migraine are anecdotal, the results of a recent clinical trial provide more scientifically reliable evidence that feverfew is of benefit in this condition[3]. Seventeen patients who were already in the habit of taking the herb prophylactically for migraine were asked to stop taking the herb. Eight of the patients were then given capsules containing 50 mg of freeze-dried feverfew powder and nine were given placebo. Those who received placebo had a significant increase in the frequency and severity of headache, nausea, and vomiting, but the group that were given feverfew showed no change in the frequency or severity of symptoms of migraine.

Migraine is associated with abnormal platelet behaviour. Even during a headache-free period platelets adhere to foreign surfaces more readily than do platelets from subjects who do not suffer from migraine. Platelets from migraine sufferers also aggregate more readily than do platelets from normal controls. Serotonin is released from platelets in

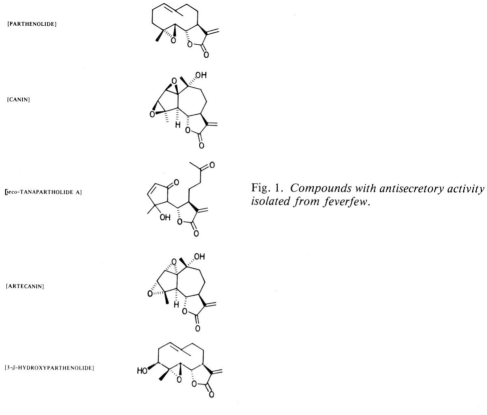

[PARTHENOLIDE]

[CANIN]

[seco-TANAPARTHOLIDE A]

[ARTECANIN]

[3-β-HYDROXYPARTHENOLIDE]

Fig. 1. *Compounds with antisecretory activity isolated from feverfew.*

response to aggregatory stimuli, and this vasoactive amine is implicated in the migraine attack[4]. So it is of some interest that when feverfew leaves are dried and extracted, the extracts so obtained inhibit platelet aggregation and inhibit release of serotonin[5,6]. Extracts of feverfew also inhibit the release of stored materials from leukocytes[6] and this is another possible way in which feverfew may exert its beneficial effect.

After we had found that extracts of feverfew inhibit secretory activity in platelets and leukocytes, we started to ask further questions. What components of feverfew are responsible for antisecretory activity? How does feverfew exert its antisecretory effect? Can we obtain further evidence that feverfew really is of value in migraine and other conditions? Can we obtain further evidence for relationships between cellular secretory activity and migraine? Is feverfew safe? What is the status of commercial preparations of feverfew? In this chapter we indicate the progress made in answering these questions.

What components of feverfew are responsible for antisecretory activity?

In an attempt to identify the components of feverfew responsible for its antiplatelet effects, we fractionated an extract of dried feverfew leaves and examined the fractions obtained[7]. Fractionation was achieved by chromatography on Kieselgel 60 followed by HPLC and fractions were tested for their capacity to inhibit platelet secretory activity. Eleven fractions with antisecretory activity were obtained. These, together with two fractions that were devoid of antisecretory activity, were analysed using thin-layer chromatography, ^{1}H nuclear magnetic resonance spectroscopy, and infra-red spectroscopy. All the active fractions (but

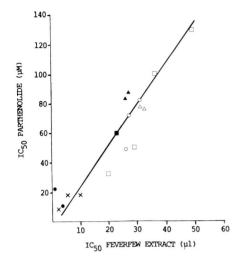

Fig. 2. *A plot of the concentrations of feverfew extract and parthenolide that inhibit serotonin release from platelets by 50%.* The different symbols represent results obtained using different aggregating agents (▲, adenosine diphosphate; ○, adrenaline; □, collagen; △, arachidonic acid; ■, U46619; X, phorbol myristate acetate and ●, 1-oleoyl-2-acetylglycerol).

neither of the inactive fractions) contained compounds with an α-methylenebutyrolactone functionality. Five compounds that contain this functionality were identified. These are parthenolide, 3-β-hydroxyparthenolide, secotanapartholide A, canin and artecanin, all of which are sesquiterpene lactones (Fig. 1). The data strongly suggests that the α-methylenebutyrolactone unit is relevant to the mode of action of the compounds, particularly in view of the other structural diversities within the compounds identified.

To establish more firmly the identity of the components of feverfew responsible for the effects of the herb on platelet behaviour, we have compared the antisecretory effects of a solution of parthenolide and of an extract of feverfew. Platelets were stimulated with a variety of different aggregating agents and the amounts of parthenolide and feverfew extract that were needed to inhibit release of serotonin by 50% were determined. When the results obtained for parthenolide were plotted against those for feverfew extract, a clear relationship was obtained (Fig. 2). We consider it very likely that it is the sesquiterpene lactones that contain an α-methylenebutyrolactone functionality that are responsible for the antiaggregatory and antisecretory activity in extracts of feverfew.

How does feverfew exert its antisecretory effect?

There are reports[5,8,9] that indicate that feverfew extracts can inhibit prostaglandin and thromboxane synthesis through an effect on phospholipase A_2. The latter is an enzyme that cleaves arachidonic acid from the phospholipid in cell membranes prior to its conversion to prostaglandins and thromboxanes. However, in our own studies of the effects of feverfew extract on platelet aggregation and secretion, prostaglandin and thromboxane synthesis was not consistently inhibited[6]. In addition we found that feverfew inhibits the aggregation and secretion induced by exogenous arachidonic acid and by the TXA_2-mimetic U46619. These observations argue for a mode of action other than, or in addition to, inhibition of phospholipase A_2.

The activated methylene group in the α-methylenebutyrolactone unit of sesquiterpene lactones renders it susceptible to nucleophilic attack via Michael addition[10], and we suggested[7] that the antisecretory activity displayed by compounds that contain this unit may be consequent to interaction with molecules that contain sulphydryl groups. We have investigated this possibility using four different approaches. First, compounds that contain sulphydryl groups were examined for their capacity to neutralize the inhibitory effects of feverfew extract on platelet aggregation and serotonin release. Second, the effects of feverfew extract and of parthenolide on acid-soluble (non-protein, mainly reduced glutathione) and acid-insoluble (protein) sulphydryl groups present in platelets were determined, and the amounts of feverfew extract or parthenolide that were needed to reduce the number of sulphydryl groups were compared with the amounts that were required for antisecretory activity. Third, the effects of feverfew extract on the ability of platelets to metabolize exogenous arachidonic acid were investigated. Finally, platelets were treated with feverfew extract in the absence and presence of platelet aggregating agents and the effects of the treatments on the protein composition of platelets were determined by gel electrophoresis. The results of these investigations[11] are all consistent with a mode of action involving sulphydryl groups.

(1) Compounds that contain sulphydryl groups such as cysteine and N-(2-mercapto-propionyl)glycine protected platelets against the inhibitory effects of feverfew extract. This is likely to be through formation of inactive Michael addition products via the α-methylenebutyrolactone unit of the sesquiterpene lactones in the extract. Several other amino acids that we tested (glycine, serine, lysine, ornithine or histidine) which contain nucleophilic groups other than sulphydryl groups (hydroxy and amino groups) did not prevent the inhibitory effects of feverfew extract on platelet behaviour.

(2) Feverfew extract and parthenolide (one of the active components of feverfew) lowered the number of acid-soluble sulphydryl groups in platelets. There was also a small effect on the number of acid-insoluble sulphydryl groups. These effects occurred at concentrations of feverfew extract and parthenolide similar to those that inhibited platelet secretory activity. Again, it was found that cysteine (but not glycine or serine) protected platelets against the sulphydryl-neutralizing effect of feverfew extract.

(3) Feverfew evoked changes in the metabolism of exogenous arachidonic acid. We obtained evidence that hydroperoxy derivatives of arachidonic acid accumulate in the presence, but not in the absence, of feverfew extract. This is likely to be a consequence of removing glutathione from platelets since similar results have been obtained when platelets are depleted of glutathione by other means. Glutathione is a cofactor for glutathione peroxidase which converts hydroperoxy compounds to hydroxy compounds.

(4) Feverfew extract per se did not induce the formation of disulphide-linked protein polymers in platelets but polymer formation occurred when aggregating agents were added to feverfew-treated platelets. Again this is likely to be a consequence of glutathione-depletion.

Despite the marked effect of feverfew extract and of parthenolide on the number of acid-soluble sulphydryl groups (reduced glutathione) in platelets, it is unlikely that this is the explanation of their inhibitory effects on platelet aggregation and secretion. Iodoacetamide also alkylates soluble sulphydryl groups in platelets but has much less effect on platelet behaviour than feverfew extract or parthenolide[12]. 1-Chloro-2,4-dinitrobenzene is another agent that removes reduced glutathione but, unlike feverfew, it is reported to have little effect on platelet behaviour[13]. Although there is only a small change in the number of acid-insoluble (protein) sulphydryl groups in platelets when platelets are treated with feverfew extract or parthenolide, we consider that it is more likely that the inhibitory effects of feverfew extract on platelet behaviour are via neutralization of a small number of sulphydryl groups on specific enzymes or proteins that are fundamental to platelet aggregation and secretion. Clearly attempts should now be made to identify the particular enzymes or proteins that are the target of the sesquiterpene lactones present in feverfew.

Can we obtain further evidence that feverfew really is of value in migraine and other conditions?

In association with colleagues at University Hospital and the City Hospital, Nottingham, we are currently investigating the value of feverfew in migraine, arthritis and psoriasis. The studies are placebo-controlled and double-blind. No data is available for publication at present.

Can we obtain further evidence for relationships between cellular secretory activity and migraine?

In our clinical studies of feverfew in migraine, we are taking blood samples for analysis of cell secretory activity. We hope that these will provide further information in this area.

Is feverfew safe?

Feverfew is used widely by the general public and there is no evidence of any serious consequences resulting from its use. Some subjects who swallow the herb have reported mouth ulceration[2], and there are occasional instances of contact-dermatitis[14]. Information on possible side-effects is being gathered, and routine blood cell counts and measurements of renal and liver function are being performed as part of our therapeutic evaluation of the herb.

What is the status of commercial preparations of feverfew?

In the study reported by Johnson *et al.*[3] feverfew was supplied in capsules that had been prepared by the authors. In view of the possible benefit ascribed to feverfew it is relevant to consider the status of commercial preparations of the herb. Using an assay based on inhibition of secretory activity in platelets we have analysed some commercial preparations and compared the results[15] with those obtained using air-dried leaves taken from feverfew plants grown in the Department of Botany, University of Nottingham. The different commercial preparations of feverfew fall into two categories: herbal and homeopathic preparations. We found antisecretory activity in herbal preparations of feverfew but the activity was always lower than expected and there was some variability. We were unable to detect any activity in homeopathic preparations of feverfew. In view of the problems associated with commercial preparations of the drug, with the help of members of the Department of Botany, University of Nottingham, we prepare our own capsules for the clinical studies in which we are engaged.

Summary and conclusions

In this chapter we have described our ongoing attempts to gain more information on feverfew. We have amassed a considerable amount of information on the antisecretory effects of feverfew, and on the components of feverfew responsible for this activity and their mode of action. Although there are good reasons to believe that the therapeutic effects that are claimed for feverfew relate to its antisecretory effects, at present we have no proof of this. We are currently trying to substantiate previous claims that feverfew is of benefit in migraine and to obtain more information on the way it works.

References

1 Editorial (1985): Feverfew—a new drug or an old wives' remedy? *Lancet* **i**, 1084.
2 Johnson, S. (1984): *Feverfew. A traditional herbal remedy for migraine and arthritis*. London: Sheldon Press.
3 Johnson, E. S., Kadam, N. P., Hylands, D. M. & Hylands, P. J. (1985): Efficacy of feverfew as prophylactic treatment of migraine. *Br. Med. J.* **291**, 569–573.
4 Hanington, E., Jones, R. J., Amess, J. A. L. & Wachowicz, B. (1981); Migraine: a platelet disorder. *Lancet* **ii**, 720–723.
5 Makheja, A. N. & Bailey, J. M. (1982): A platelet phospholipase inhibitor from the medicinal herb feverfew (*Tanacetum parthenium*). *Prostaglandins, Leukotrienes and Med.* **8**, 653–660.
6 Heptinstall, S., Williamson, L., White, A. & Mitchell, J. R. A. (1985): Extracts of feverfew inhibit granule secretion in blood platelets and polymorphonuclear leucocytes. *Lancet* **i**, 1071–1074.
7 Groenewegen, W. A., Knight, D. W., Heptinstall, S. (1986): Compounds extracted from feverfew that have anti-secretory activity contain an α-methylenebutyrolactone unit. *J. Pharm. Pharmacol.* **38**, 709–712.
8 Collier, H. O. J., Butt, N. M., McDonald-Gibson, W. J. & Saeed, S. A. (1980): Extract of feverfew inhibits prostaglandin biosynthesis. *Lancet* **ii**, 922.
9 Capasso, F. (1986): The effect of an aqueous extract of *Tanacetum parthenium L.* on arachidonic acid metabolism by rat peritoneal leucocytes. *J. Pharm. Pharmacol.* **38**, 71–72.
10 Kupchan, S. M., Fessler, D. C., Eakin, M. A. & Giacobbe, T. J. (1970): Reactions of alpha methylene lactone tumor inhibitors with model biological nucleophiles. *Science* **168**, 376–377.
11 Heptinstall, S., Groenewegen, W. A., Spangenberg, P. & Loesche, W. (1986): Extracts of feverfew may inhibit platelet behaviour via neutralization of sulphydryl groups. *J. Pharm. Pharmacol.* (submitted).
12 Bosia, A., Spangenberg, P., Loesche, W., Arese, P. & Till, U. (1983): The role of the GSH-disulfide status in the reversible and irreversible aggregation of human platelets. *Thrombos. Res.* **30**, 137–142.
13 Bosia, A., Spangenberg, P., Ghigo, D., Heller, R., Loesche, W., Pescarmona, G. P. & Till, U. (1985): Effects of GSH depletion by 1-chloro-2,4-dinitrobenzene on human platelet aggregation, arachidonic acid oxidative metabolism and cytoskeletal proteins. *Thrombos. Res.* **37**, 423–434.
14 Vickers, H. R. (1950): Contact dermatitis. *Practitioner* **164**, 226–233.
15 Groenewegen, W. A., Heptinstall, S. (1986): Amounts of feverfew in commercial preparations of the herb. *Lancet* **i**, 44–45.

22

PREVENTION OF MENSTRUAL MIGRAINE BY

PERCUTANEOUS OESTRADIOL TREATMENT

M. G. Bousser*, B. de Lignières†, M. Vincens†, J. L. Mas†
and P. Mauvais-Jarvis†

*Clinique des Maladies du Système Nerveux, Hôpital de la Salpêtrière,
47, Boulevard de l'Hôpital, 75651 Paris Cedex 13, France and
†Department of Reproductive Endocrinology, Hôpital Necker,
149, rue de Sèvres, 75730 Paris Cedex 15, France

Summary

A double-blind placebo controlled cross-over study was performed to evaluate the efficacy of percutaneous oestradiol treatment in the prevention of pure and regular menstrual migraine in women with regular cycles. A 66% decrease in the frequency of attacks was observed ($P<0.01$ between the first and second cycle and $P<0.001$ between the second and third ones). Remaining attacks were less severe and of shorter duration than placebo treated attacks. Mild side-effects were observed in four oestradiol cycles and two placebo cycles. Because of its easy applicability, its tolerance and its efficacy, percutaneous oestradiol offers considerable advantages over oral oestrogens, oestradiol injections and oestradiol implants.

Introduction

Approximately 60% of migrainous women relate the occurrence of their attacks to their menstrual cycles[1] and about one fourth of these have their attacks exclusively at the time of menstruation, most often just prior to or during menstruation[2]. Since the pioneer work of Somerville[3,4], menstrual attacks have been related to the physiological withdrawal of oestradiol which occurs during the premenstrual phase of the cycle and various attempts have been made to prevent menstrual migraine by suppressing this fall in oestradiol[3-6]. However, results have been disappointing either because of lack of efficacy or because of adverse reactions.

The present study is a double-blind placebo controlled cross-over trial of percutaneous oestradiol in the prevention of menstrual migraine.

Patients and methods

Patients were eligible if, in the last 12 months, they had experienced severe, pure, and regular menstrual migraine attacks with regular cycles. Menstrual attacks were defined as attacks of migraine according to the Ad Hoc Committee[7] occurring not earlier than 2 days before menstruation and no later than the last day of the menses. These menstrual attacks had to be:

(1) severe on a 3 step-scale (mild, moderate, severe) and not responding to at least two of the major antimigrainous drugs either acutely or prophylactically.

(2) Pure, with no other attacks during the rest of the cycle.

(3) Regular, occurring always at the same time of the cycle. Regular cycles were defined as cycles not differing from each other by more than two days. Patients were asked for willingness to participate and to give their informed consent.

Prophylactic drug treatment for migraine and oral contraceptives were authorized but only if they had been regularly taken during the three preceding months and if they were not intended to be modified during the trial. In case of failure of the trial medication, patients were asked to treat acute attacks preferentially with aspirin. All other concomitant medications were an exclusion criterion.

The study was a double-blind, placebo-controlled, cross-over, trial on three consecutive cycles, successive patients being randomly allocated to receive either oestradiol-placebo-oestradiol (ten patients) or placebo-oestradiol-placebo (ten patients).

Percutaneous oestradiol treatment consisted of 1.5 mg of oestradiol in 2.5 g of gel. Placebo was indistinguishable but contained only 2.5 g of gel. Treatment was started 48 h before the earliest expected onset of migraine attacks and repeated every day for the next 7 days. Women were instructed to apply the gel to a large surface area of the skin, using the arms, shoulders and abdominal skin but carefully avoiding the breast and to let the gel dry for 5 min before putting on their clothes.

The major efficacy criterion was the presence or absence of menstrual attacks. When attacks occurred, their severity (mild, moderate, severe) and duration were recorded as well as the consumption of acute drug treatment.

Tolerance was assessed by asking the patients to record all possible side-effects and by specifically enquiring about breast soreness, adverse mood changes, and menstrual disorders namely regularity, duration and flow.

Statistical analysis was performed using X^2 test for paired cases (McNemar's test).

Results

Twenty patients entered the study but two were lost to follow up, one in each sequence group. Eighteen patients (mean age 42.5, range 32–53) completed the study but one oestradiol treatment was missed because of amenorrhoea, thus leaving for the efficacy analysis 26 oestradiol (E) cycles and 27 placebo (P) cycles. All patients had menstrual attacks as defined in the protocol and all had common migraine attacks. Five patients were on prophylactic drug treatment (Dihydroergotamine in four, Pizotifen in one). Three patients were on oral contraceptives (oestroprogestagen in two, pure progestagen in one).

Menstrual attacks (Figure) occurred in eight out of 26 oestradiol cycles (30.8%) and in 26 out of 27 placebo cycles (96.3%). The difference between the two treatments is highly significant ($X^2 = 9.1$, $P < 0.01$; comparison between the first and second cycle; $X^2 = 12$ $P < 0.001$; comparison between the second and third cycle).

The severity and duration of attacks occurring despite oestradiol treatment were considerably decreased: all attacks but one were considered as mild or moderate and lasted less than 12 h whereas 24/26 placebo treated attacks were considered as severe and all lasted more than 24 h. Aspirin was taken as acute migraine treatment in three oestradiol-treated attacks and 22 placebo-attacks.

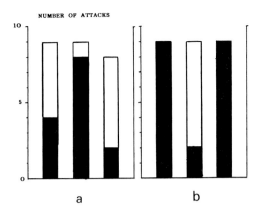

NUMBER OF ATTACKS

a   b

Figure. (a) *Sequence of treatment where oestradiol (O) is given in the first and third cycles and placebo in the second one.*
(b) *Sequence in which P (Placebo) is given first.* □ , no attacks; ■ , attacks.

Tolerance was good. No breast soreness or adverse mood change were observed. Modifications in cycles were observed in 2/27 placebo cycles (amenorrhoea) and in 4/26 oestradiol cycles (amenorrhoea in two, shortened cycle in one and lengthened cycle in one). In one patient, an attack occurred 3 days after stopping oestradiol treatment.

Discussion

Results of this study show a high preventive effect of percutaneous oestradiol on pure and regular menstrual migraine. This supports Somerville's view[3] that menstrual attacks are related to physiological oestradiol withdrawal, which takes place in the 2–3 days preceding menstruation.

Previous attempts to prevent menstrual migraine by suppressing this fall in oestradiol were less satisfactory either because of a lack of efficacy or because of adverse reactions. Injections[3] only delay the attack until the next drop in exogenous oestradiol and they disturb the menstrual cycle. Oral oestrogens only have a marginal beneficial effect[5] possibly due to the 24 h variation in plasma levels[8,10]. Oestradiol implants[6] were reported to have a remarkable beneficial effect on the frequency of menstrual migraine but this study was not controlled and the high levels of oestradiol maintained throughout the menstrual cycle suppressed ovulation and all cyclic ovarian activity.

Percutaneous oestradiol offers considerable advantages over these previous modes of administration in that it possesses excellent efficacy, a good tolerance and it is very easily applicable. This efficacy is probably related to the 24 h stability of plasma levels[11] which contrasts with the initial supraphysiological peak induced by injections[3] and with the brief daily oscillations of the oral route[8,10]. The daily dose of 1.5 mg of percutaneous oestradiol used in the present study has been shown[12] to increase oestradiol plasma levels to a mean of 80 ± 30 pg/ml, which is in the normal range of the early-mid follicular phase. The only moderate increase thus obtained probably accounts for the good tolerance of the treatment. Furthermore at the end of such treatment[12], there is no abrupt fall in plasma levels but a slow decrease over 2–3 days, which presumably explains why attacks occurring at the end of the treatment are so infrequent.

Because of its easy applicability, its remarkable efficacy and its good tolerance, percutaneous oestradiol has become our first choice treatment in this admittedly restricted group of migrainous women who have both regular menstrual cycles and pure and regular menstrual attacks.

References

1 Edelson, R. N. (1985): Menstrual migraine and other hormonal aspects of migraine. *Headache* **25**, 376–379.

2 Stein, M. T., Hockaday, J. M. & Hockaday, T. D. (1978): Migraine and reproductive hormones throughout the menstrual cycle. *Lancet* **i**, 543–545.

3 Somerville, B. W. (1975): Estrogen-withdrawal migraine: 1 — Duration of exposure required and attempted prophylaxis by premenstrual estrogen administration. *Neurology* **25**, 239–244.

4 Somerville, B. W. (1975): Estrogen-withdrawal migraine: 2 — Attempted prophylaxis by continuous estradiol administration. *Neurology* **25**, 245–250.

5 Dennerstein, L., Laby, B., Burrows, G. D. & Hyman, G. J. (1978): Headache and sex hormone therapy. *Headache* **18**, 146–153.

6 Magos, A., Zilkha, K. & Studd, J. (1983): Treatment of menstrual migraine by oestradiol implants. *J. Neurol. Neurosurg. Psychiat.* **46**, 1044–1046.

7 Ad Hoc Committee on classification of headache (1962): *J. Am. Med. Ass.* **179**, 717–718.

8 Stadel, B. W., Sternthal, P. M., Schlesselman, J. J., Douglas, M. B., Hall, W. D., Kaul, L. & Ahluwalia, B. (1980): Duration of ethinylestradiol blood levels among healthy women using oral contraceptives. *Fert. Steril.* **33**, 257–260.

9 Back, D. J., Breckenbridge, A. M. & Crawford, F. E. (1981): Interindividual variations and drug interactions with hormonal steroid contraceptives. *Drugs* **21**, 46–61.

10 Dusterberg, B., & Nishino, Y. (1982): Pharmacokinetic and pharmacological features of estradiol valerate. *Maturitas* **4**, 315–324.

11 Sitruk-Ware, R., de Lignières, B., Basdevant, A. & Mauvais-Jarvis, P. (1980): Absorption of percutaneous oestradiol in postmenopausal women. *Maturitas* **2**, 207–211.

12 Basdevant, A. & de Lignières, B. (1980): Treatment of menopause by topical administration of oestradiol. In *Percutaneous absorption of steroids*, eds P. Mauvais-Jarvis, C. F. H. Vickers & J. Wepierre p. 249. London: Academic Press.

23

DIHYDROERGOTAMINE *VS* FLUNARIZINE *VS* NIFEDIPINE *VS* METOPROLOL *VS* PROPRANOLOL IN MIGRAINE PROPHYLAXIS: A COMPARATIVE STUDY BASED ON TIME SERIES ANALYSIS

E. Scholz*, W. D. Gerber*, H. C. Diener*, H. D. Langohr[†] and M. Reinecke[†]

*Department of Neurology, University of Tübingen, Tübingen and
[†]Department of Neurology, Städtische Kliniken Fulda, Fulda,
Federal Republic of Germany

Summary

In the present study we investigated the prophylactic effectiveness of five different drugs commonly used in the treatment of migraine. Since the same study design was used in five different treatment groups it was possible to compare directly the effects of dihydroergotamine, flunarizine, nifedipine, metoprolol and propranolol. Statistical analysis was based on headache diaries and time series analysis, which permitted the detection of significant treatment responses in individual patients as well as the analysis of group effects. Eighty-five patients suffering from common or classic migraine were treated with any one of dihydroergotamine (DHE), flunarizine, nifedipine, metoprolol and propranolol in a double-blind randomized trial. Treatment extended over a period of 3 to 4 months for the highest dose regimen and a further 3 to 4 months with reduced dosages. The frequency of migraine attacks was best reduced by metoprolol and decreasingly so by DHE, propranolol and flunarizine in that order. DHE led to an increase in headache duration after a treatment period of more than 4 months. Flunarizine reduced the intensity and duration of concomitant headache forms. Nifedipine showed no prophylactic effects with respect to migraine and in some cases even caused additional headaches.

Introduction

Whether propranolol (for a time considered the drug of first choice among other beta-blocking drugs) or different calcium channel blockers should be preferentially used is still a matter of debate. Comparative studies using propranolol and metoprolol showed equivalent therapeutic effectiveness[1,2]. Up to the present no controlled trials using dihydrated ergot derivatives (DHE) were available, although these drugs have been recommended for prophylactic treatment for many years. A recent survey on calcium antagonists indicated no major differences in prophylactic efficacy between diltiazem, flunarizine, nifedipine, nimodipine and verapamil[3]. Comparing different drugs is still nearly impossible since for statistical and methodological reasons it is impossible to directly compare data and results taken from different studies using different designs, treatment strategies and evaluation procedures.

We therefore designed a comparative study using the same protocol and evaluation procedure for five different drugs that had each been reported as being effective in the prophylactic treatment of migraine.

Patients

One hundred and nine patients with common and/or classic migraine and at least two attacks per month were recruited for the study and randomly assigned to the different treatment groups. Eighty-three patients completed the treatment, 26 withdrew in the baseline period prior to treatment. The demographic data are shown in Table 1.

Analysis of variance turned up no significant differences between the five treatment groups for the parameters of age, duration and frequency of migraine.

Table 1. *Demographic data.*

	DHE	*Flu*	*Nif*	*Met*	*Prop*	*Group*
Age (years)						
mean	40.9	42.9	43.2	34.1	37.5	40.4
SD	11.8	12.6	11.8	11.4	9.8	11.9
History of migraine (Years)						
mean	17.8	21.4	22.9	15.2	16.0	19.3
SD	11.9	13.9	13.1	11.7	12.9	12.9

Common migraine $n = 74$, classic migraine $n = 9$.
Female $n = 69$, male $n = 14$.

Methods

Patients were asked to keep a headache diary noting frequency of migraine attacks, attack duration, headache intensity (scored on an analog scale) and other headache types as well as the intake of all kinds of drugs, including analgesics. Furthermore, they monitored their body weight and sleep duration. Side-effects of treatment were not only reported in the diary, but were pinpointed by active questioning at each consultation and additionally registered using a standard questionnaire.

Diary data were evaluated by time series analysis (which included ARIMA-models subjected to modification and further development). For every single patient the relationship between baseline and the different treatment periods was calculated. In this way, significant therapeutic effects during treatment (expressed as z-values) could be distinguished from simple time effects. Responders to treatment were defined by their significant z-values ($z = 1.96$). On the basis of a transformation program (McCall) these single case data could further be computed for group comparisons (ANOVA) and made available for additional conventional statistic analysis.

Treatment

During the baseline of 8 weeks no prophylactic treatment was allowed. Patients were instructed to take their usual abortive migraine medication, which could be taken further during prophylactic treatment. Patients with an overt history of drug abuse involving analgesics or ergotamine were excluded from the trial.

In a 4 week run-in period patients received either nifedipine (20 mg), metoprolol (100 mg) or propranolol (80 mg) once a day. In the following 12 weeks, full dose treatment (nif 40 mg, meto 200 mg, prop 160 mg) was administered. During the following 12 weeks drugs were reduced stepwise (nif 30-20-10 mg, meto 150-100-50 mg, prop 120-80-40 mg). DHE and flunarizine were both immediately started at 10 mg once a day each (DHE 10 mg in the morning, placebo in the evening, flu vice versa). This was maintained for 4 months, thereafter each received 5 mg for a further 3 months. After treatment all patients underwent a 3 month follow-up without prophylactic treatment.

Results

The results are presented in two different ways. First, we present the reduction of the different migraine parameters for the entire treatment group—in a way comparable to conventional statistical analysis using group comparisons. Second, the percentage of patients showing significant improvement during treatment (ie true responders to therapy) is demonstrated on the basis of time series analysis. Frequency and duration of migraine attacks as well as intensity and duration of non-migraine headaches were evaluated.

Dihydroergotamine (DHE)

Thirteen patients were treated with DHE, of whom ten completed the trial and three withdrew from treatment, none of them because of side-effects (Table 2).

Table 2. *Effects of dihydroergotamine.*

Months	Migraine days		Headache intensity		Migraine duration		Headache duration		Abortive medication	
	G	R	G	R	G	R	G	R	G	R
1	43.7	46.2	26.5	23.1	25.1	23.1	9.2	23.1	21.2	15.4
2–4	36.7	30.8	34.1	46.2	21.1	23.1	0.9	23.1	33.5	23.1
5	40.5	33.3	11.5	33.3	23.6	22.2	− 81.7	11.1	44.0	11.1
6	40.5	44.4	21.6	33.3	20.1	22.2	− 115.4	11.1	33.9	11.1
7	45.0	40.0	74.5	40.0	33.0	20.0	−	20.0	65.8	−

G, Improvement percentage for the specific parameter in respect of the entire treatment group (group effect).
R, Responder percentage (as defined by significant z-values).

Table 3. *Effects of flunarizine.*

Months	Migraine days		Headache intensity		Migraine duration		Headache duration		Abortive medication	
	G	R	G	R	G	R	G	R	G	R
1	9.7	16.7	25.6	25.0	20.3	16.7	28.0	41.7	1.0	25.0
2–4	10.6	16.7	34.3	66.7	18.2	8.3	49.3	50.0	40.7	25.0
5	33.8	25.0	60.8	50.0	32.2	12.5	61.6	50.0	67.0	37.5
6	23.8	12.5	55.4	62.5	35.1	12.5	63.1	50.0	83.5	37.5
7	59.9	25.0	68.3	50.0	63.8	12.5	67.8	50.0	68.1	37.5

G, Improvement percentage for the specific parameter in respect of the entire treatment group (group effect).
R, Responder percentage (as defined by significant z-values).

Table 4. *Effects of nifedipine.*

Months	Migraine days		Headache intensity		Migraine duration		Headache duration		Abortive medication	
	G	R	G	R	G	R	G	R	G	R
1	− 24.9	0.0	− 0.9	0.0	− 29.9	11.8	2.8	17.6	50.9	17.6
2–4	5.4	7.7	3.3	0.0	12.1	30.8	11.9	7.7	45.1	38.5
5	37.3	11.1	47.0	0.0	35.1	11.1	40.7	11.1	75.6	33.3
6	28.7	11.1	37.5	11.1	15.8	0.0	39.0	11.1	56.8	22.2
7	5.8	0.0	33.5	0.0	− 11.8	0.0	36.9	11.1	62.2	22.2

G, Improvement percentage for the specific parameter in respect of the entire treatment group (group effect).
R, Responder percentage (as defined by significant z-values).

DHE led to a moderate reduction in migraine frequency and headache intensity. During long-term treatment lasting more than 4 months the duration of headache, however, increased even further, — an effect that resembles chronic headache as a result of ergotamine abuse.

Flunarizine

Twelve patients were treated with flunarizine, of whom two withdrew because of side-effects. Main complaints were fatigue and weight gain (mean 2.4 kg, range 1–5 kg). Although the group effects show a moderate reduction of migraine days, responder rates were low for high-dose (10 mg) as well as low-dose treatment (5 mg). The same holds true for migraine duration, with effects increasing during long-term treatment. This means that only a small number of patients showed a good response concerning their migraine with both reduction in frequency and in duration (Table 3).

Good results were achieved in respect of reduction in headache intensity and with headache duration, once again increasing during long-term treatment.

Nifedipine

Seventeen patients were treated with nifedipine. Eight of them withdrew due to side-effects (one in the run-in and seven in the high-dose phase). Complaints were mainly of increased headaches on the morning following drug intake. This drug-induced headache was different from the kind of headache the patient was accustomed to and was characterized by a constant, dull pain diffused over the whole cranium (Table 4).

On the single patient level migraine frequency was reduced in only one patient (7.7%), while migraine duration was reduced in 30.8% and headache duration in 17.6%.

Nifedipine showed no prophylactic effect but on the contrary led to drug-induced headache.

Metoprolol

Twenty-two patients were treated with metoprolol, six of them withdrew due to side-effects (two during the run-in and four during the high-dose phase of therapy). Side-effects complained of were fatigue and dizziness. Two patients had to be taken off medication in the reduction phase, despite good interim therapeutic effects, because of a drug-induced allergic exanthema (Table 5).

Metoprolol administered in dosages of 100 mg and 200 mg led to a reduction in migraine frequency, migraine duration and headache intensity. The high-dose treatment, however, led to an increasing number of drop-outs. The duration of concomitant headache forms was only moderately influenced.

Table 5. *Effects of metoprolol.*

Months	Migraine days		Headache intensity		Migraine duration		Headache duration		Abortive medication	
	G	R	G	R	G	R	G	R	G	R
1	36.7	40.9	35.3	54.5	37.1	40.9	38.2	27.3	6.6	18.2
2–4	53.7	60.0	40.6	55.0	53.6	60.0	14.3	25.0	40.5	30.0
5	59.3	56.3	62.4	50.0	56.6	37.5	63.9	31.3	75.5	37.5
6	54.5	37.5	52.0	37.5	44.5	25.0	61.9	31.3	46.3	31.3
7	48.6	53.8	70.8	30.8	39.4	38.5	80.1	15.4	70.8	38.5

G, Improvement percentage for the specific parameter in respect of the entire treatment group (group effect).
R, Responder percentage (as defined by significant z-values).

Table 6. *Effects of propranolol.*

Months	Migraine days		Headache intensity		Migraine duration		Headache duration		Abortive medication	
	G	R	G	R	G	R	G	R	G	R
1	16.4	21.1	8.9	21.1	− 10.3	15.8	8.1	10.5	− 8.3	21.1
2–4	29.7	33.3	37.8	33.3	29.2	27.8	36.5	27.8	39.8	38.9
5	18.8	23.5	38.0	23.5	8.1	23.5	41.7	17.6	55.1	23.5
6	− 12.3	26.7	21.2	26.7	− 46.9	20.0	10.8	20.0	23.5	13.3
7	− 3.0	15.4	27.2	15.4	− 12.7	15.4	− 34.0	7.7	37.7	30.8

G, Improvement percentage for the specific parameter in respect of the entire treatment group (group effect).
R, Responder percentage (as defined by significant z-values).

Propranolol

Nineteen patients were treated with propranolol. Three of them withdrew because of side-effects (one during each of the run-in, high-dose and reduction phases). Complaints were the same as for metoprolol, namely fatigue and dizziness. Parallel to the increase in migraine duration, the intake of migraine drugs increased during the run-in phase and decreased during both high-dose and reduction phases. A second increase in migraine duration and frequency was observed after reduction of the dosage to 80 mg, indicating that a dosage of 120 mg or more is necessary for effective treatment (Table 6).

Treatment with propranolol resulted in an only moderate decrease in migraine frequency and migraine duration, as well as headache intensity and headache duration.

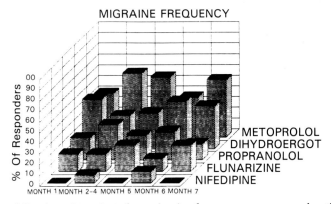

Fig. 1. *The effects of five drugs investigated on migraine frequency are expressed as the percentage of responders.* Best results are obtained with metoprolol (200 mg), while dihydroergotamine, propranolol and flunarizine show less effect at approximately the same amount. Nifedipine shows no prophylactic effects as far as migraine frequency is concerned. For purposes of statistical evaluation we calculated a two-factor analysis of variance and covariance with repeated measures. The analysis of variance showed a significant effect for the factor group and the variable number of migraine days (F = 2.74; $P < 0.05$). For the quantitative assessment of group differences a one-factor analysis of variance (Scheffe test) was calculated. Concerning migraine frequency, significant differences ($P < 0.01$) were obtained for metoprolol and dihydroergotamine as opposed to nifedipine (F = 5.35; $P < 0.01$).

Discussion

In contrast to earlier studies on migraine prophylaxis, we used time series analysis to evaluate the prophylactic efficacy of different drugs in a direct comparison, as well as making use of conventional statistical analysis. We are therefore, for the first time, in the position to calculate responder rates for different migraine and headache parameters on a single patient basis and to exclude simple time effects that interfere with conventional statistic analysis. Another aim of the present study was to compare the prophylactic efficacy of a variety of drugs with completely different pharmacological properties and profiles which had all been reported to be effective in migraine prophylaxis to nearly the same extent. By virtue of applying the same study design and method in all patient groups, we were able for the first time to compare different drugs in respect of migraine prophylaxis.

Nifedipine was included in the study as a representative member of dihydropyridine-type calcium entry blockers. It has been reported to be effective in migraine prophylaxis at a dosage of 60 mg/day[4]. Using a lower dose of 40 mg/day, we were unable to confirm any clinical relevant efficacy. At the applied dosage administered, nifedipine led to a considerable number of side-effects and subsequent dropouts, mainly due to drug-induced headache. This side-effect is well known from the use of nifedipine in antihypertension therapy.

Flunarizine, one of the best documented calcium entry blockers in migraine prophylaxis, has been reported to reduce the frequency of migraine attacks in 83% in a group of 202 patients pooled from several studies[5]. Patients with a migraine history of 4 years or less showed a mean reduction by 54% in attacks. In patients suffering from migraine for more than 30 years the reduction was by only 27%. In our flunarizine group, the frequency of attacks was reduced by 34% after 4 months before increasing to 59.9% after long-term treatment of 7 months, but only a quarter of our patients were responders in the sense of showing a significant therapeutic effect. The mean duration (19 years) of the disease in our group might in part account for that result. Best effects with flunarizine were achieved in terms of reduction in the intensity and duration of concomitant headache, parallel with a considerable reduction in the intake of migraine drugs. Flunarizine might therefore be the choice of drug for patients with a combination headache and/or developing drug abuse.

DHE reduced the frequency of migraine attacks by the same amount as flunarizine after long-term treatment and, as was the case with propranolol, in the course of high-dose treatment. But it had little effect on the duration of migraine attacks and the intensity of the headache. After a treatment period of more than 4 months and with an even lower dosage of 5 mg/day, DHE did, however, lead to an increase in headache duration. This coincides with the experience of ergotamine-induced headaches[6], a headache form which can even be induced by dihydrated ergot derivates[7]. If DHE is given as a prophylactic drug, it should therefore be stopped after a 3-month treatment period.

Best results in terms of reduction of both migraine frequency and duration as well as concomitant headache duration was achieved with metoprolol. The attack frequency per month was reduced from a mean of 7.48 to 3.47, which would appear comparable to the data reported by Kangasniemi & Hedman (1984)[1]. High-dose treatment with 200 mg metoprolol did lead to a considerable amount of side-effects and dropouts, while a number of patients benefited from a lower dosage of 100 mg. This experience prompts us to recommend starting treatment with this dosage and, only after insufficient efficacy has been demonstrated, increasing the amount. Our results suggesting a better effect with metoprolol as compared with propranolol are in contradiction with earlier reports[1,2], which indicate an equivalent therapeutic potency for both drugs. Our treatment groups showed no significant differences in either age or migraine duration and, furthermore, the metoprolol group showed an even higher frequency of migraine attacks at baseline; we are not yet able to give an explanation for this difference.

References

1 Kangasniemi, P. & Hedman, C. (1984): Metoprolol and propranolol in the prophylactic treatment of classical and common migraine. A double-blind study. *Cephalalgia* **4**, 91–96.
2 Olsson, J.-E., Behring, H. C., Forssman, B., Hedman, C., Hedman, G., Johansson, F., Kinnman, J. & Palhagen, S.-E. (1984): Metoprolol and propranolol in migraine prophylaxis: a double-blind multicentre study. *Acta Neurol. Scand.* **70**, 160–168.
3 Solomon, G. D. (1985): Comparative efficacy of calcium antagonist drugs in the prophylaxis of migraine. *Headache* **25**, 368–371.
4 Meyer, J. S., Nance, M., Walker, M., Zetusky, W. J. & Dowell, R. E. (1985): Migraine and cluster headache treatment with calcium antagonists supports a vascular pathogenesis. *Headache* **25**, 358–367.
5 Amery, W. K., Caers, L. I. & Aerts, T. J. L. (1985): Flunarizine, a calcium entry blocker in migraine prophylaxis. *Headache* **25**, 249–254.
6 Tfelt-Hansen, P. (1985): Ergotamine headache. In *Updating in headache*, eds V. Pfaffenrath, P. O. Lundberg & O. Sjaastad, pp. 169–172. Berlin: Springer.
7 Dichgans, J., Diener, H. C., Gerber, W. D., Verspohl, E. J., Kukiolka, H. & Kluck, M. (1984): Analgetika-induzierter Dauerkopfschmerz. *Dtsch. Med. Wschr* **109**, 369–373.

24

BETA-ADRENOCEPTOR FUNCTIONS

AND THE CEREBRAL CIRCULATION

Lars Edvinsson

Department of Internal Medicine,
University Hospital, S-221 85 Lund, Sweden

Introduction

A number of studies have in the past documented that the non-selective beta-adrenoceptor antagonist propranolol has a prophylactic effect in the treatment of migraine (Table 1). The interest in this agent started when patients receiving propranolol for cardiovascular disorders were simultaneously relieved of coexisting migraine[1]. Subsequent clinical studies have amply confirmed this[2,3]. Trials with other beta-adrenoceptor blocking drugs were initially less convincing, but many reports of trials now show that beta$_1$-selective adrenoceptor antagonists, in addition to propranolol, have a beneficial effect in migraine. Practolol seems to have a weak antimigraine effect[4] whereas atenolol[5], metoprolol[6] and timolol[7,8] have now been reported to be as effective as propranolol in the prophylactic treatment of migraine. The reason behind the prophylactic effect of propranolol and the other beta-adrenoceptor antagonists in migraine is still not clear. Since much of migraine symptomatology is linked with the brain circulation, this chapter discusses beta-adrenoceptor functions in the cerebrovascular bed to provide some basis for the understanding of the antimigraine role of beta-adrenoceptor blockers.

Effects of beta-adrenoceptor blockade on the cerebrovascular bed

Several studies have been undertaken to illustrate the influence of various sympathomimetic drugs on the cerebral circulation, but effects obtained have been contradictory with regard to direction and amplitude of responses. Noradrenaline has been found to decrease cerebral blood flow, to have no effect or even to cause an increase in flow[9]. In spite of these contradictory findings, when considering all available data together with a critical appraisal of the techniques used, noradrenaline or sympathetic nerve stimulation may decrease resting cerebral blood flow by about 10–15%. It is not necessary that the degree of vascular

Table 1. *Beta-blockers effective in migraine prophylaxis.*

	Selectivity	ISA	MSA	Lipid soluble
Propranolol	NS	—	+	+ +
Timolol	NS	—	—	unknown
Metoprolol	CS	—	—	$\pm$
Atenolol	CS	—	—	$\pm$

NS, non-selective; CS, cardioselective; ISA, intrinsic sympathomimetic activity; MSA, membrane stabilizing activity.

reactivity obtained at normotension reflects the degree of physiological importance of the cerebrovascular sympathetic nerves. There are several reasons for weak reactions; they may be the result of a mixture of effects in regions with prominent, little or no flow changes[10]; they may be related to the degree of sympathetic innervation[11], the extent of passage through the blood-brain barrier and the degree of neuronal and extraneuronal uptake mechanisms limiting amine effects[12,13]. Furthermore, the amine may simultaneously interact with vascular alpha and beta-adrenoceptors, the flow effect obtained being due to the relative degree of activation of the two types of receptors[14].

Once the amine has penetrated the blood-brain barrier, or if the barrier is circumvented by an intracerebral administration of the agent, marked flow responses are seen as a consequence of the vasodilatation obtained indirectly through activation of amine-sensitive cerebral neuron systems[15]. These aspects of the cerebral circulation have been well-illustrated in a carefully performed series of experiments by MacKenzie *et al.*[16,17], who reported that intracarotid infusion of a small dose of noradrenaline (50 ng/kg min) did not alter cerebral blood flow or cerebral metabolic rates of glucose and oxygen. There was, furthermore, no effect on these variables after an intracarotid bolus injection of hypertonic urea, although this agent resulted in the opening of the blood-brain barrier. Under these circumstances the infusion of noradrenaline in the same dose resulted in significant increases in cerebral blood flow (49%), cerebral oxygen consumption (21%) and cerebral glucose uptake (76%). Also the direct intraventricular administration of noradrenaline (40 μg/kg) resulted in increases in cerebral blood flow (40%), cerebral oxygen consumption (21%) and cerebral glucose uptake (153%). Furthermore, the intraventricular application of reserpine, an agent that causes the release of endogenously stored noradrenaline, resulted in increases in the above mentioned parameters. Taken together, the experiments amply illustrate the fact that responses to noradrenaline depend on the patency of the blood-brain barrier, and that the catecholamine may result in parallel increases in flow and metabolism. These responses may be antagonized by the simultaneous administration of beta-adrenoceptor blockers such as propranolol.

The intra-arterial administration of the beta-adrenoceptor antagonist, propranolol (12 μg/kg $\times$ min), resulted in a small attenuation of cerebral blood flow, while significant reductions were seen in the metabolic parameters of oxygen consumption (40%) and glucose uptake (39%) (Fig. 1). This may be taken as evidence for a tonic influence of a system sensitive to beta-adrenoceptor blockade in the cerebral circulation. In addition, propranolol severely attenuated the cerebrovascular reactivity to increases in arterial CO_2-tensions (Fig. 2). The mechanisms behind this suggests an amine involvement in the hypercapnic response of the cerebral circulation[17].

Characterization of beta-adrenoceptors in cerebral blood vessels

Beta-adrenoceptors are conventionally divided into the beta$_1$ and beta$_2$-subtypes[18,19]. The postsynaptic beta$_1$-adrenoceptors are mainly involved in the regulation of cardiac function.

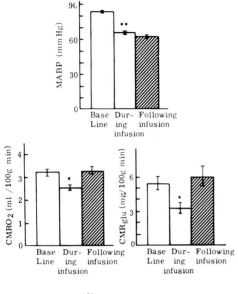

Fig. 1. *Effects of intracarotid infusion of 12 µg/kg × min propranolol on cerebral glucose and oxygen consumption at normocapnia.* Bars indicate 1 s.e. of mean. *P < 0.005, **P < 0.0001[17].

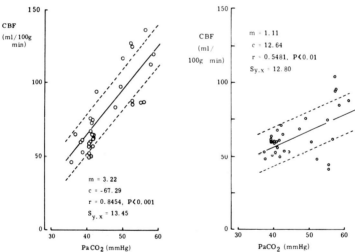

Fig. 2. *Responsiveness of the cerebral circulation to induced hypercapnia in five baboons before the infusion (left) and after the infusion (right) of propranolol (12 µg/kg × min).* m,c = constants that describes the equation $y = mx + c$; r = correlation coefficient; $S_{y,x}$ = standard error of estimate[17].

Upon stimulation, increases in cardiac frequency and contractility are seen. Excitation of beta$_2$-adrenoceptors by their appropriate agonists may induce bronchodilatation, vasodilatation and hyperglycaemia. Classic beta-adrenoceptor agonists, such as iso-proterenol, are non-selective, since they activate beta$_1$ and beta$_2$-adrenoceptors equally well. Beta$_2$-selective adrenoceptor stimulants such as terbutaline and salbutamol predominantly influence the bronchi without causing excessive tachycardia. For this reason they are preferred as bronchospasmolytic agents to the non-selective beta-adrenoceptor agonists (isoproterenol, orciprenaline) which are known to invoke tachycardia and palpitations.

149

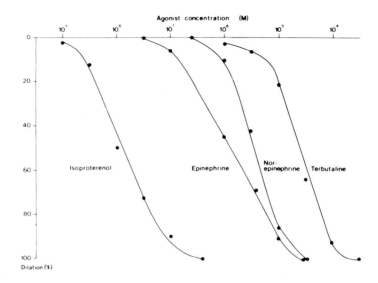

Fig. 3. *Dilatory responses to isoproterenol, adrenaline, noradrenaline and terbutaline obtained in cat middle cerebral arteries precontracted by* $3 \times 10^{-6} M$ *5-hydroxytryptamine*. The alpha-adrenoceptors were blocked by exposure of the vessels to 10^{-6} M dibenamine for 30 min[21].

As a logical consequence of the fact that, in general, vasodilatation can be mediated by beta-adrenoceptor mechanisms, it may be assumed that, at least to some extent, the vasodilatory phase of the migraine attack could be prevented by treatment with beta-adrenoceptor blocking agents. In fact, published results do indicate that beta-sympatholytic drugs have a substantial effect in the management of migraine (Table 1). The result of the beta-adrenoceptor activation during a migraine attack and the blockade of these receptors by drugs will affect both the intra and extracerebral arterial systems because the two vascular areas, both anatomically and functionally, constitute two components of one and the same vascular bed. Moreover, denervation studies in conjunction with histochemical analysis have shown that both vascular systems are innervated by sympathetic adrenergic nerves originating from one and the same ganglion, namely the superior cervical[20].

The first detailed study on the characterization of adrenoceptors in cerebral vessels showed that tonically contracted arteries relaxed upon administration of either of the four amines, isoproterenol (IPNA), adrenaline (A), noradrenaline (NA) and terbutaline (TER)[21]. For the intracranial arteries, the order of potency was IPNA > NA > A > TER (Fig. 3). This pattern of sympathomimetic response is typical for a beta-adrenoceptor functions[18]. In fact this first characterization of beta-adrenoceptor subtypes was based on differences in the potency rank. The beta$_1$-adrenoceptor type is primarily found in the uterus, coronary arteries and in the bronchial tree, whereas most other tissues including the peripheral vascular bed have the beta$_2$-type of adrenergic receptors. A beta$_1$-adrenoceptor is characterized by an NA-to-A ratio of about 1 and an IPNA to TER ratio of about 1000. On the other hand, the IPNA-to-TER ratio is below 150 for the beta$_2$-adrenoceptor type[18].

Feline intracranial arteries have an NA-to-A ratio of 1.2 and an IPNA-to-TER ratio of 2500, suggesting the presence of the beta$_1$-type of adrenoceptors[21]. On the other hand, the IPNA-to-TER ratio is in extracranial arteries of cats only 138, suggesting that this vascular bed is equipped with the beta$_2$-type of adrenoceptors[22]. The reversible antagonist propranolol lowers the sensitivity of the test system to IPNA in both intra- and extracranial

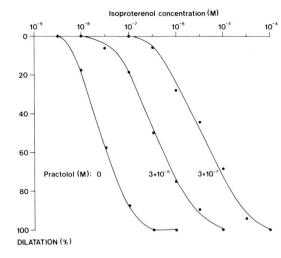

Fig. 4. *Dilatory response to isoproterenol of cat middle cerebral artery precontracted by 3×10^{-6} M 5-hydroxytryptamine.* After the control concentration response curve had been determined and the tissue bath rinsed, practolol was added 20 min before the next determination. During these experiments the buffer bath contained 10^{-6} M cocaine to block neuronal uptake and the alpha-receptor was inactivated by a previous 30 min exposure to 10^{-6} M dibenamine[23].

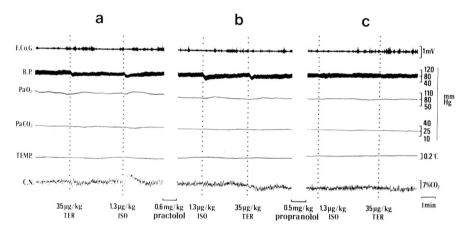

Fig. 5. *Representative experiments performed in a non-anesthetized rabbit, illustrating the different effects of intravenous injections of isoproterenol (ISO) and terbutaline (TER) on the blood flow in the caudate nucleus (C.N.), on the arterial blood pressure (B.P.) and associated variables.* E.Co.G., electrocorticogram; $PaCO_2$ and PAO_2, partial pressure of CO_2 and O_2 in the aorta; Temp, temperature in the caudate nucleus on the opposite side of flow measurements. The calibration is indicated to the right. (a) The B.P. is reduced after addition of the two agonists in non-treated animals, whereas only ISO increases the C.N. blood flow. (b) Practolol inhibits only the cerebrovascular response to ISO, whereas (c) propranolol abolishes all effects[23].

vessels. The dissociation constants are not different for the intracranial and extracranial arteries. This is due to the fact that propranolol is a non-selective beta-adrenoceptor blocking agent.

In another study (*in vitro* and *in situ*) (Figs 4 and 5), it has been noted that cerebrovascular responses to IPNA can be blocked by the beta$_1$-adrenoceptor antagonist practolol[23], supporting the presence of the beta$_1$-type of adrenoceptors in feline cerebral vessels. Furthermore, preliminary experiments *in vitro* have confirmed that also rat cerebral arteries may be equipped with the beta$_1$-subtype of adrenoceptors since metaprolol causes a parallel shift to the right of IPNA induced relaxations (Fig. 6a). On the other hand, human pial

151

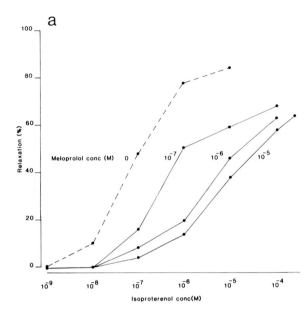

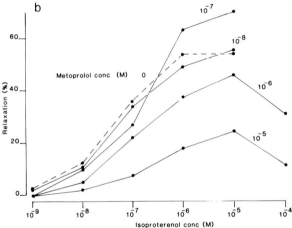

Fig. 6. *Relaxant response of (a) rat basilar artery and (b) human pial artery to increasing concentrations of isoproterenol in prostaglandin $F_{2\alpha}$-precontracted vessels.* This relaxation was blocked to a varying degree by the $beta_1$-adrenoceptor antagonist metoprolol (unpublished observations).

arteries appear to be equipped with a mixture of $beta_1$- and $beta_2$-adrenoceptors as shown in recent *in vitro* tests on fresh human pial arteries (Fig. 6b). This suggestion is supported by recent binding studies on circle of Willis arteries obtained at autopsy[24]. A similar situation appears to exist in porcine cerebral arteries, where both types of beta-adrenoceptors may be involved in IPNA induced relaxation[25].

References

1   Rabkin, R., Stables, D. P., Levin, N. W. & Suzman, M. M. (1966): The prophylactic value of propranolol in angina pectoris. *Am. J. Cardiol.* **18**, 370–383.
2   Weber, R. B. & Reinmuth, O. M. (1972): The treatment of migraine with propranolol. *Neurology* **22**, 366–369.
3   Bruyn, G. W. (1982): Cerebral cortex and migraine. *Adv. Neurol.* **33**, 152–169.
4   Kallanranta, T., Hakkarainen, H., Hokkanen, E. & Tuovinen, T. (1977): Clonidine in migraine prophylaxis. *Headache* **17**, 169–172.

5   Stensrud, P. & Sjaastad, O. (1980): Comparative trial of Tenormin (atenolol) and Inderal (propranolol) in migraine. *Headache* **20**, 204–207.

6   Andersson, P. -G., Dahl, S., Hansen, J. H., Hansen, P. E., Hedman, C., Nygaard Kristensen, T. & de Fine Olivarius, B. (1983): Prophylactic treatment of classical and non-classical migraine with metoprolol — a comparison with placebo. *Cephalalgia* **3**, 207–212.

7   Forssman, B., Lindblad, C. J. & Zbornikova, V. (1983): Atenolol for migraine prophylaxis. *Headache* **23**, 188–190.

8   Standnes, B. (1982): The prophylactic effect of timolol versus propranolol and placebo in common migraine: beta-blockers in migraine. *Cephalalgia* **2**, 165–170.

9   Edvinsson, L. & MacKenzie, E. T. (1977): Amine mechanisms in the cerebral circulation. *Pharmacol. Rev.* **28**, 275–348.

10 Sercombe, R., Aubineau, P., Edvinsson, L., Mamo, H., Owman, C., Pinard, E. & Seylaz, J. (1975): Neurogenic influence on local cerebral blood flow: effect of catecholamines or sympathetic stimulation as correlated with the sympathetic innervation. *Neurology (Minneap)* **25**, 954–963.

11 Edvinsson, L. & Owman, C. (1977): Sympathetic innervation and adrenergic receptors in intraparenchymal cerebral arterioles of baboon. *Acta Physiol. Scand.* **452** (suppl), 57–60.

12 Rapoport, S. I. (1976): *Blood-brain barrier in physiology and medicine.* New York: Raven Press.

13 Hardebo, J. E. & Owman, C. (1980): Barrier mechanisms for neurotransmitter monoamines and their precursors at the blood-brain interface. *Ann. Neurol.* **8**, 1–11.

14 Edvinsson, L., Lacombe, P., Owman, C., Reynier-Rebuffel, A. -M. & Seylaz, J. (1979): Quantitative changes in regional cerebral blood flow of rats induced by alpha- and beta-adrenergic stimulants. *Acta Physiol. Scand.* **107**, 289–296.

15 Edvinsson, L., Hardebo, J. E., MacKenzie, E. T. & Owman, C. (1978): Effect of exogenous noradrenaline on local cerebral blood flow after osmotic opening of the blood-brain barrier in the rat. *J. Physiol.* **274**, 149–156.

16 MacKenzie, E. T., McCulloch, J., O'Keane, M., Pickard, J. D. & Harper, A. M. (1976*a*): Cerebral circulation and norepinephrine: relevance of the blood-brain barrier. *Am. J. Physiol.* **231**, 483–488.

17 MacKenzie, E. T., McCulloch, J. & Harper, A. M. (1976*b*): Influence of endogenous norepinephrine on cerebral blood flow and metabolism. *Am. J. Physiol.* **231**, 489–494.

18 Lands, A. M., Luduena, F. P. & Buzzo, H. J. (1967): Differentiation of receptors responsive to isoproterenol. *Life Sci.* **6**, 2241–2249.

19 Nahorski, S. R. (1981): Identification and significance of beta-adrenoceptor subtypes. *Trends Pharmacol. Sci.* **2**, 95–98.

20 Edvinsson, L. (1975): Neurogenic mechanisms in the cerebrovascular bed. Autonomic nerves, amine receptors and their effects on cerebral blood flow. *Acta Physiol. Scand.* **427** (suppl), 1–35.

21 Edvinsson, L. & Owman, C. (1974): Pharmacological characterization of adrenergic alpha and beta receptors mediating the vasomotor responses of cerebral arteries in vitro. *Circ. Res.* **35**, 835–849.

22 Edvinsson, L. (1985): Beta-adrenoceptor function in the cerebrovascular bed. Implications for a prophylactic effect of beta-adrenoceptor antagonists in migraine. In *Migraine and beta-blockade*, ed J. D. Carroll, V. Pfaffenrath & O. Sjaastad, pp. 62–71. Mölndal: A. B. Hässle.

23 Sercombe, R., Aubineau, P., Edvinsson, L., Mamo, H., Owman, C. & Seylaz, J. (1977): Pharmacological evidence in vitro and in vivo for functional beta$_1$-receptors in the cerebral circulation. *Pflügers Arch.* **368**, 241–244.

24 Tsukahara, T., Taniguchi, T., Shimohama, S., Fujiwara, M. & Handa, H. (1986): Characterization of beta adrenergic receptors in human cerebral arteries and alteration of the receptors after subarachnoid hemorrhage. *Stroke* **17**, 202–207.

25 Wang, J. Y. & Lee, T. J. -F. (1986): Beta-receptor-mediated vasodilation in cerebral arteries of the pig. *Acta Physiol. Scand.* **127** Suppl 552: 41–44.

25

SYMPATHETIC HYPERAROUSAL IN MIGRAINE? EVALUATION BY CONTINGENT NEGATIVE VARIATION AND PSYCHOMOTOR TESTING. EFFECTS OF BETA-BLOCKERS

J. Schoenen*

Headache Clinic, Bavière Hospital, University of Liege, Belgium

Introduction

There is convincing evidence that the primary pathogenetic mechanism in migraine is neural (for review see Rose, 1983)[1]. Excessive central catecholaminergic drive[2] and cortical spreading depression[3] might be crucial steps in the genesis of the migraine attack. Some beta-adrenoreceptor blockers, ie, those devoid of intrinsic sympatheticomimetic activity (ISA), are effective in the prophylactic treatment of migraine (for review see Schoenen, 1984)[4]. Their exact mechanism of action still remains a matter of controversy. Their site of action might be peripheral, since beta-blockers without ISA can reduce cardiac output and thus induce a reflex peripheral vasoconstriction, which would counteract the extracranial vasodilatation of the headache phase[5]. However such an explanation is not quite satisfactory, for total peripheral resistance may remain normal in patients treated with non-ISA beta-blockers[6]. Moreover, the peripheral hypothesis cannot account for the prophylactic effect of beta-blockers on attack frequency and migrainous prodromes, thought to be related to central nervous system (CNS) mechanisms. There might thus be a place for a central action of beta-blockers in migraine.

Possible targets for beta-blockers do exist in the CNS. Intracerebral vessels are innervated by catecholaminergic fibres coming from the superior cervical ganglion (carotid plexus), but also from brain stem nuclei such as the locus coeruleus[7]. Beta-adrenergic receptors are heavily concentrated in the cerebral cortex of rat[8] and man[9]. Moreover, even poorly lipophilic beta-blocking agents penetrate the blood-brain barrier and the brain in considerable amounts[10,11]. Finally, there is convincing, though indirect, evidence from

*Senior Research Associate of the NFSR (Belgium)

animal experiments (for review see Conway *et al.*, 1978)[12] and from their neuropsychiatric effects in man[13,14], that beta-blockers can affect CNS functions.

As long as the exact pathophysiology of migraine remains undetermined, direct evidence for a central action of beta-blockers in migraine prophylaxis will be lacking. Nonetheless, it is of interest to investigate their possible effects on some CNS functions known to be modified in migraineurs. Contingent negative variation, an event-related potential, and psychomotor tests in migraineurs are both thought to be closely controlled by central catecholaminergic systems, which might also play a role in migraine pathogenesis[2]. We have therefore compared the results obtained before and during treatment with beta-blockers.

Results

Contingent negative variation

Contingent negative variation (CNV) is an event-related slow cerebral potential recorded over the scalp with EEG electrodes and an averaging device in a simple reaction time task. There is evidence from animal experiments and from clinical as well as neuroendocrinological correlations in man that CNV is modulated by central catecholaminergic systems[15]. We have previously shown that the amplitude of CNV is significantly increased and its habituation reduced in migraineurs between attacks, while in tension headache CNV is not different from controls[16]. Moreover the amplitude of CNV is positively correlated with plasma levels of noradrenaline in headache patients[17]. During attacks of migraine there is on the contrary a marked reduction of CNV amplitude (unpublished data).

We have now compared CNV in nine patients suffering from common migraine before and after a 2–3 months treatment period with metoprolol (100 mg/day). Before treatment, the mean amplitude of CNV is $-24.8 \pm 7.28 \, \mu V$ in this group of patients. After metoprolol, CNV mean amplitude is significantly reduced ($-15.84 \pm 6.64 \, \mu V$; $P < 0.01$ paired *t*-test). In all these patients, there was also clinical improvement of migraine. By contrast, among six migraineurs, clinically improved by flunarizine (10 mg/day), CNV was significantly modified after a 2–3 months treatment period in only one of them.

Moreover, in 25 migraineurs we have retrospectively compared the clinical response to propranolol or metoprolol, scored from poor to excellent, and the pre-treatment CNV amplitude. A good positive correlation ($r = 0.76$) was found between the amplitude of CNV before treatment and the clinical efficacy of beta-blockers (Fig. 1).

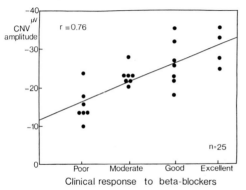

Fig. 1. *Correlation between amplitude of pre-treatment CNV and clinical response to β-blockade (metoprolol or propranolol) in 25 migraineurs.* Excellent: more than 80% improvement of headache severity index; poor: less than 20% improvement.

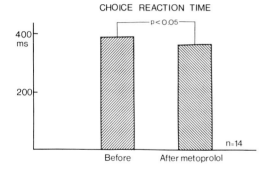

Fig. 2. *Choice reaction time in 14 migraineurs before and during treatment with metoprolol (Student's t-test).*

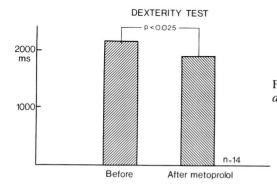

Fig. 3. *Dexterity test in 14 migraineurs before and during treatment with metoprolol.*

Psychomotor tests

Visual reaction time, and dexterity (inserting a plug into five successive holes back and forth) were studied with a custom-built, computer-assisted device. A group of 14 untreated migraineurs (mean age: 35 years) was compared with a group of 13 migraineurs (mean age: 33 years) treated for at least 1 month with metoprolol (100 to 200 mg/day) and with a group of 34 normal sex-matched volunteers (mean age: 48 years).

Mean reaction time in the control group was 204 ± 22.52 ms. Although the mean age of controls was higher than that of migraineurs and reaction time is known to increase with age, the values found in the group of untreated migraineurs are on the average significantly higher ($\bar{m}$ 232.29 ± 42.43 ms; $P < 0.005$). Reaction time tended to be lower in migraineurs treated with metoprolol (212.77 ± 25.69 ms), but this difference was not statistically significant (Student's t-test). Performance on the dexterity test was also significantly better in controls (2094 ± 156 ms) and in migraineurs treated with metoprolol (1982 ± 219 ms) than in untreated migraineurs (2342 ± 208 ms; $P < 0.0005$).

Subsequently, 14 patients suffering from common migraine (mean age: 37.5 years) were studied before, and 2 months after, therapy with metoprolol (100 to 150 mg/day). Visual reaction time, choice reaction time, rapid alternating movements and dexterity were tested with the same device. After treatment there was a clear trend towards better performances for all tests, except rapid alternating movements to the left. This reached the level of significance for choice reaction time to the right (mean before: 390 ms; after: 367 ms; $P < 0.05$) (Fig. 2) and the dexterity test (mean before; 2.157 ms; after: 1934 ms; $P < 0.025$) (Fig. 3). Improvement of reaction time and/or dexterity after metoprolol therapy was not necessarily correlated with clinical antimigraine efficacy, but there was a weak correlation with parameters of peripheral beta-blockade, such as slowing of the pulse rate.

Discussion

It is conceivable that the prophylactic effects of beta-blockers in migraine are in part or totally mediated through an action of these drugs on the CNS. Up to now evidence for a modification of CNS functions by beta-blockers was chiefly indirect but we have shown that these agents can normalize CNS functions, which are abnormal in migraine.

The reduction of CNV amplitude in migraineurs after treatment with a beta-blocker can only be centrally mediated, and it is most probably due to a direct effect on the brain generators of CNV. One cannot definitely rule out that central changes associated with clinical improvement of the migraine play a role, but preliminary results with other effective antimigraine drugs, eg flunarizine, showing no significant reduction of CNV amplitude in spite of clinical improvement, are not in favour of this hypothesis. The finding of a correlation between pre-treatment CNV amplitude and clinical response to beta-blockers could be of interest for the therapeutic choice in migraine. Moreover, it might represent indirect evidence that beta-blockers modify a CNS dysfunction, which could be hyperactivity of central catecholaminergic systems, since both increased CNV amplitude and high peripheral blood levels of noradrenaline can be explained on this basis.

As we have shown, psychomotor tests eg visual reaction time and dexterity, thought to be mediated by the CNS, are impaired in migraineurs and tend to normalize following treatment with beta-blockers. These psychomotor functions are related to performance and arousal and their neurobiological mechanisms are still not fully understood, but it is generally accepted that they depend heavily on central catecholaminergic systems and presumably on subtle interactions between noradrenergic and dopaminergic pathways[18,19]. One may speculate that impairment of psychomotor functions in migraineurs is due to hyperarousal according to Eysenck's principle (1982)[20] (Fig. 4). Central beta-blockade might bring arousal to more favourable levels and thus improve performance.

The data presented here do not solve the question of how beta-blockers exert their therapeutic effect in migraine, nor do they prove that the modifications of CNV and psychomotor tests are directly related to the pathogenesis of this disease. Nevertheless, central catecholaminergic hyperactivity may be a common link between these findings, since it could cause both increased amplitude of CNV and reduced psychomotor performances due to hyperarousal.

One might further speculate that central noradrenergic hyperactivity can induce other neurophysiological and biochemical modifications that have been demonstrated in migraineurs between attacks, for example, according to animal experiments, increased noradrenergic activity is thought to increase signal to noise discrimination, which might explain the increased amplitude of visual evoked potentials observed in migraine[21]. Noradrenaline can decrease activity of dopaminergic and serotonergic neurons, and a long

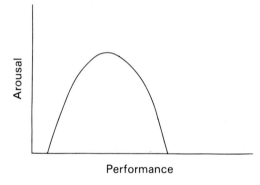

Fig. 4. *Inverted U-shaped relation between level of arousal and performance after Eysenck*[20].

standing inhibition could lead to hypersensitivity of dopamine and serotonin receptors, which has been described in migraineurs[22,23]. These modifications of neurotransmitter systems would moreover offer a plausible explanation for the prophylactic efficacy of antiserotonergics, dopamine agonists (downregulation of receptors) as of beta-blockers. Within the framework of this noradrenergic hypothesis of migraine pathogenesis it remains to be determined why central noradrenergic pathways are hyperfunctioning. A genetic mechanism affecting output of the locus coeruleus (increase), MAO activity (decrease), the hypothalamus, as known from animal genetics, or dysregulation of a cortico-coeruleo-cortical loop[24], are each attractive speculations.

On the other hand, the migraine attack would be triggered by a reduction of central noradrenergic activity, possibly related to hypothalamic dysfunction, neuronal 'exhaustion' ('empty neuron'), stress decompensation, exogenous amines or hormonal changes. This might induce a reduction of brain metabolism (with oligemia and depression of cortical activity), of signal to noise discrimination (with amplitude reduction of visual evoked potentials) and of peripheral sympathetic tone (inducing hypotension). Noradrenergic hypoactivity could also be responsible during the course of the attack for enhanced dopamine activity, suggested by increased levels of HVA in CSF and of dopamine in plasma, by gastro-intestinal disturbances and by the efficacy of dopamine antagonists in acute therapy. Serotonin hyperactivity during the headache phase of the attack, which is indicated by increased levels of 5-HIAA in CSF, might be a consequence of decreased noradrenaline or of brain dysmetabolism. Via 5 HT-3 receptors in the trigemino-vascular system it might lead to activation of substance P and VIP-containing fibres and subsequently to vasodilatation and pain.

Conclusions

The precise mechanism by which beta-blockers, devoid of intrinsic sympathicomimetic activity, are effective in the prophylaxis of migraine remains controversial. Since part of their action might be exerted within the central nervous system, we have studied their effects on CNS functions, which we have previously shown to be modified in migraine. Beta-blockers normalized amplitude of CNV, an event-related cerebral potential, markedly enhanced in untreated migraineurs between attacks. This effect was evident as soon as 2 to 3 weeks after starting treatment, which suggests that it is not an epiphenomenon of clinical improvement. A good positive correlation was found between pre-treatment amplitude of CNV and clinical efficacy of beta-blockers after a 3 months treatment period. Moreover, beta-blockers significantly improved performance in several psychomotor tests, which were impaired in untreated migraineurs. On the basis of the presumed neurobiological mechanisms underlying CNV and psychomotor performance, it can be hypothesized that abnormalities of these CNV functions in migraine are related to central catecholaminergic hyperactivity, which is corrected by beta-blockade. Although these findings do not solve the question of how beta-blockers exert their prophylactic effects in migraine, they demonstrate the possibility of a central action for these agents and initiate speculations about a noradrenergic hypothesis of migraine pathogenesis.

References

1 Rose, F. C. (1983): The pathogenesis of a migraine attack. *TINS* **6**, 247–248.
2 Lance, J. W. (1981): Headache. *Ann. Neurol.* **10**, 1–10.
3 Lauritzen, M. (1984): Spreading cortical depression in migraine. In *The pharmacological basis of migraine therapy*, eds W. K. Amery, J. M. Van Nueten & A. Wauquier, pp. 149–160. London: Pitman.

4 Schoenen, J. (1984): Place des bèta-bloquants dans le traitement de la migraine. In *Migraine et céphalées, GREC*, pp. 85–95. Paris.

5 Rascol, A. & Fanchamps, A. (1984): Antimigraineux. *Sem. Hôp. Paris* **60**, 3137–3161.

6 Man in't Veld, A. & Schalekamp, M. A. (1984): *Mechanism of action of beta blockers in hypertension*, eds J. B. Kostic, E. De Felice pp. 75–131. New York: Raven Press.

7 Edvinsson, L. (1984): Adrenoreceptor mechanisms in migraine therapy. In *The pharmacological basis of migraine therapy*, eds W. K. Amery, J. M. Van Nueten & A. Wauquier pp. 108–117. London: Pitman.

8 Goffinet, A. M. & De Volder, A. (1985): Autoradiographic analysis of adrenergic receptors in the mammalian brain. *Acta Neurol. Belg.* **85**, 82–109.

9 Reznikoff, G. A., Manaker, S., Rhodes, C. H., Winokur, A. & Rainbow, T. C. (1986): Localization and quantification of beta-adrenergic receptors in human brain. *Neurology* **36**, 1067–1073.

10 Cruickshank, J. M., Neil-Dwyer, G., Cameron, M. M. & McAinsh, J. (1980): β-Adrenoreceptor blocking agents and the blood-brain barrier. *Clin. Sci.* **59**, 453s–455s.

11 Taylor, E. A., Jefferson, D., Carroll, J. D. & Turner, P. (1981): Cerebrospinal fluid concentrations of propranolol, pindolol and atenolol in man: evidence for central action of β-adrenoreceptor antagonists. *Br. J. Clin. Pharmac.* **12**, 549–559.

12 Conway, J., Greenwood, D. T. & Middlemiss, D. N. (1978): Central nervous actions of β-adrenoreceptor antagonists. *Clin. Sci. Mol. Med.* **54**, 119–124.

13 Greenblatt, D. J. & Shader, R. I. (1972): On the psychopharmacology of beta adrenergic blockade. *Curr. Therap. Res.* **14**, 615–625.

14 Suzman, M. M. (1981): Use of β-adrenergic receptor blocking agents in psychiatry. *Neuropharmacol. Central Nerv. System Behav. Dis.* **14**, 339–391.

15 Timsit-Berthier, M., Mantanus, H., Ansseau, M., Doumont, A. & Legros, J. J. (1983): Methodological problems raised by contingent negative variation interpretation in psychopathological conditions. *Adv. Biol. Psychiat.* **13**, 80–92.

16 Schoenen, J., Maertens, A., Timsit-Berthier, M. & Timsit, M. (1985): Contingent negative variation (CNV) as a diagnostic and physiopathologic tool in headache patients. In *Migraine: clinical and research advances*, ed. F. C. Rose pp. 17–25. Basel: Karger.

17 Timsit-Berthier, M. (1981): A propos de l'interprétation de la variation contingente négative en psychiatrie. *EEG J.* **11**, 236–244.

18 Robbins, T. W. (1984): Cortical noradrenaline, attention and arousal. *Psychol. Med.* **14**, 13–21.

19 Antelman, S. M. & Caggiula, R. (1977): Norepinephrine-dopamine interactions and behavior. *Science* **195**, 646–653.

20 Eysenck, M. W. (1982): Attention and arousal. Berlin: Springer.

21 Kennard, C., Gawel, M., Rudolph, N. & Clifford-Rose, F. (1978): Visual evoked potentials in migraine subjects. In *Research and clinical studies in headache*, eds A. P. Friedman, M. Granger & M. Critchley pp. 72–80, **6**, Basel: Karger.

22 Bès, A., Geraud, G., Guell, A. & Arne-Bès, M. C. (1982): Hypersensibilité dopaminergique dans la migraine, un test diagnostique. *Nouv. Presse Méd.* **11**, 1475–1479.

23 Del Bianco, P. L., Franchi, G., Anselmi, B. & Sicuterri, F. (1980): Monoamine sensitivity of smooth muscle in vivo in nociception disorders. In *Advances in neurology, vol. 33, headache*, eds M. Critchley, A. P. Friedman, S. Gorini & F. Sicuteri, pp. 391–398. New York: Raven Press.

24 Welch, K. M. (1986): Migraine: a biobehavioral disorder. *Cephalalgia* **6**, (suppl. 4), 103–110.

26

A REVIEW OF THE RELATIONSHIP
BETWEEN BETA-ADRENOCEPTOR
ANTAGONISTS AND THEIR ACTION IN MIGRAINE

R. G. Shanks

Department of Therapeutics and Pharmacology,
The Queen's University of Belfast, Belfast, Northern Ireland

Introduction

Beta-adrenoceptor antagonists were introduced into medicine for the treatment of angina pectoris and cardiac arrhythmias, but have subsequently been shown to be of value in many other conditions including hypertension, hyperthyroidism, migraine, glaucoma, anxiety, hypertrophic obstructive cardiomyopathy and acute myocardial infarction. The value of propranolol in the treatment of migraine was first described by Rabkin in 1966[1] who reported that migraine improved in a patient receiving propranolol for angina pectoris. Many controlled trials have now confirmed that propranolol is effective in the prophylactic treatment of migraine[2].

In this chapter an attempt will be made to determine the possible mechanism of action of beta-blocking drugs in migraine by correlating differences in their properties with their effectiveness in the prophylactic treatment of migraine.

The result of many studies of beta-adrenoceptor antagonists in migraine have been described. As migraine is a variable disease from one patient to another and from one time to another in the same patient, it is essential that double-blind controlled trials are used to assess the effectiveness of beta-blocking drugs. In such trials the following points should receive attention:

(a) A clear definition of migraine must be used to ensure that a homogeneous group of patients are studied.

(b) The selection of patients in studies must be clearly defined as different groups of patients have been used including those who have not responded to other treatments, those who have responded to beta-blocking drugs in an open study, and those who have received no previous prophylactic treatment.

Table 1. *The efficacy of beta-adrenoceptor antagonists in migraine.*

Drug	Effective in migraine
Alprenolol	No
Oxprenolol	No
Propranolol	Yes
Pindolol	No
Nadolol	Yes
Sotalol	—
Timolol	Yes
Acebutolol	No
Atenolol	Yes
Metoprolol	Yes

Table 2. *Efficacy of beta-adrenoceptor antagonists and their pharmacokinetics.*

	Efficacy in Migraine	N-Octanol/water distribution ratio (pH 7.0)*	Plasma protein binding (% bound)	Volume of distribution (l/kg)	Penetration in CNS
Alprenolol	No	3.1 (Lipo)	85	3.0	Yes
Oxprenolol	No	0.7 (Lipo)	80	1.3	Yes
Propranolol	Yes	4.3 (Lipo)	80–90	3.3–5.5	Yes
Pindolol	No	0.2 (Lipo)	60	1.2–2.0	Yes
Nadolol	Yes	NA (Hydro)	30	2.0	No
Sotalol	—	<0.02 (Hydro)	0	1.6–2.4	No
Timolol	Yes	0.3 (Lipo)	80	2.0–2.4	Yes
Acebutolol	No	0.68 (Lipo)	15	1.0	Yes
Atenolol	Yes	<0.02 (Hydro)	3	0.7–1.0	No
Metoprolol	Yes	0.2 (Lipo)	12	5.6	Yes

*Drugs are designated as lipophilic or hydrophilic.

(c) There was considerable variation in the number of patients in trials and in some studies the numbers were so small that it might not have been possible to show a difference between active drug and placebo.

(d) In many studies, a fixed dose of drug was used, although it has been clearly demonstrated that in angina and hypertension the effect is often dose related. Thus the absence of a response in some patients may be due to an inadequate dose of the drug.

(e) As migraine is an episodic condition and patients have been included in trials with an attack frequency of 2 to 4 per month, it is essential that the active treatment period should be at least 8 weeks and preferably 12 weeks, with a pre-trial period of at least 4 weeks during which the frequency, duration and severity of attacks can be documented.

(f) As variability in migraine from patient to patient and from time to time in the same patient can be marked and as the end-points are subjective, it is essential that the effectiveness of a drug is assessed in double-blind controlled trials. Many of the initial observations of beta-blocking drugs in migraine were in open trials but more recently well planned double-blind controlled trials have established the efficacy of these drugs.

(g) Numerous indices have been utilized to facilitate comparison between treatments including number, frequency, duration and intensity of the headache. Additional information for comparison of treatments has involved assessment of the number of days

Table 3. *Efficacy of beta-adrenoceptor antagonists in migraine and the presence or absence of additional properties.*

	Effective in migraine	Lipophilic/ hydrophilic	MSA	Cardioselective	PAA
Alprenolol	No	Lipophilic	Yes	No	Yes
Oxprenolol	No	Lipophilic	Yes	No	Yes
Propranolol	Yes	Lipophilic	Yes	No	No
Pindolol	No	Lipophilic	Yes	No	Yes
Nadolol	Yes	Hydrophilic	No	No	No
Sotalol	—	Hydrophilic	No	No	No
Timolol	Yes	Lipophilic	No	No	No
Acebutolol	No	Lipophilic	Yes	Yes?	Yes
Atenolol	Yes	Hydrophilic	No	Yes	No
Metoprolol	Yes	Lipophilic	Yes	Yes	No

MSA, membrane stabilizing activity; PAA, partial agonist activity.

on which migraine occurred, the consumption of tablets for acute relief of a migraine attack and subjective evaluation of the benefits of treatment.

Efficacy of beta-adrenoceptor antagonists in migraine

Table 1 summarizes the results of studies of beta-blocking drugs in migraine[2,3]. Many double-blind controlled trials have established the efficacy of propranolol in the prophylaxis of migraine. A much smaller number of such trials have demonstrated the effectiveness of nadolol[4], timolol[5], atenolol[6,7] and metoprolol[8]. Double-blind studies have clearly demonstrated that alprenolol[9], oxprenolol[10], pindolol[11,12] and acebutolol[13] are not effective in the treatment of migraine (Table 1).

Correlation of efficacy of beta-adrenoceptor blocking drugs in migraine with differences between the drugs

Pharmacokinetics

There are important differences in the pharmacokinetics of beta-blocking drugs[14], some of which are given in Table 2. The entry of beta-blocking drugs into the central nervous system depends on three factors — protein binding, ionization (pKa) and lipid solubility. Protein binding is important as only free drug in the plasma is available for distribution into brain tissue and cerebrospinal fluid. The protein binding of these drugs varies from almost zero for atenolol to 90% for propranolol. As there is little difference in the pKa values of beta-blocking drugs (range 9.0–9.5) it will not influence their entry to the brain. The third factor determining entry into the brain is the lipid solubility for which there are great differences in beta-blocking drugs. Propranolol, alprenolol, oxprenolol and metoprolol are extremely lipophilic and readily pass into the central nervous system. In contrast, atenolol and sotalol are much more hydrophilic and pass into the central nervous system poorly[15]. From the results in Table 2 there is clearly no correlation between efficacy in migraine and the entry of beta-blocking drugs into the central nervous system. Propranolol, alprenolol

Table 4. *The partial agonist activity and percentage changes of arterial pressure, heart rate, and vascular resistance after long-term treatment with different beta-adrenoceptor antagonists.*

	Partial agonist activity	Arterial pressure	Heart rate	Cardiac output	Vascular resistance
Pindolol	Yes	− 13	− 2	+ 6	− 18
Alprenolol	Yes	− 10	− 9	− 11	− 3
Oxprenolol	Yes	− 11	− 14	− 8	− 2
Acebutolol	Yes	− 6	− 12	− 11	+ 7
Metoprolol	No	− 13	− 22	− 20	+ 8
Atenolol	No	− 17	− 26	− 20	+ 5
Propranolol	No	− 12	− 23	− 21	+ 11
Timolol	No	− 10	− 25	− 23	+ 16

From Man In 'T Veld *et al.*, (1982)[19].

and oxprenolol readily enter the central nervous system but only the first is effective in migraine. In contrast atenolol penetrates the central nervous system poorly but is effective.

Additional properties

Some beta-adrenoceptor antagonists may possess properties in addition to their action in blocking beta-adrenoceptors. Membrane stabilizing activity is a direct effect on peripheral nervous tissue and the heart similar to local anaesthetics and is described as Class 1 anti-arrhythmic drug activity[14]. There is no correlation between efficacy in migraine and the presence or absence of membrane stabilizing activity in beta-blocking drugs (Table 3).

Cardioselective beta-blocking drugs have a greater effect in inhibiting cardiac beta adrenoceptors (beta$_1$) than the receptors (beta$_2$) in bronchi and peripheral blood vessels. There is no correlation between efficacy in migraine and cardioselectivity as propranolol (non-cardioselective) and atenolol (cardioselective) are both effective (Table 3).

Measurement of the binding of several beta-blocking drugs to 5-HT receptors from rat brain has been made[16]. Propranolol had substantial affinity for the 5-HT binding site, being equi-potent with methysergide. Oxprenolol which is not effective in migraine had the same affinity as propranolol; atenolol which is effective in migraine had low affinity. These observations suggest that the effectiveness of some beta-adrenoceptor antagonists in migraine does not result from blockade of 5 hydroxytryptamine receptors.

Partial agonist activity (intrinsic sympathomimetic activity) of beta-blocking drugs has been difficult to demonstrate in man but appears to be of no therapeutic importance[14,17]. The distribution of partial agonist activity amongst beta-blocking drugs and its relationship to their efficacy in migraine is given in Table 3. The beta-adrenoceptor antagonists that are effective are devoid of partial agonist activity. Drugs with partial agonist activity are not effective in migraine. It would appear that partial agonist activity prevents beta-blocking drugs from exerting a beneficial effect. Why should this happen and does it give some insight into the mode of action of these drugs in migraine?

The main difference between beta-blocking drugs with and without partial agonist activity is on the cardiovascular system. Drugs without partial agonist activity produce a greater reduction in resting heart rate[18]. The haemodynamic effects of the long-term (chronic oral dosing from 1 to 24 weeks) administration of beta-blocking drugs have been described by Man In 'T Veld and Schalekamp[19] and are summarized in Table 4. All drugs reduced arterial pressure. The drugs devoid of partial agonist activity (metoprolol, atenolol, propranolol and timolol) produced more marked reductions in heart rate. Pindolol which possesses most partial agonist activity had no effect on resting heart rate; alprenolol and oxprenolol which have less partial agonist activity produced small reductions in heart rate. The changes in cardiac output paralleled those in heart rate. The drugs with partial agonist activity reduced peripheral vascular resistance but those without partial agonist activity increased peripheral vascular resistance.

More detailed comparison of drugs with and without partial agonist activity on peripheral vascular resistance have been made. A comparison of propranolol and oxprenolol in patients with hypertension showed that while both drugs reduced heart rate and blood pressure, propranolol, but not oxprenolol, reduced forearm blood flow[20]. This study and others indicated that drugs devoid of partial agonist activity increase peripheral vascular resistance whereas drugs with this activity reduce peripheral vascular resistance. Thus it would appear that beta-adrenoceptor antagonists that are effective in migraine increase peripheral vascular resistance. It is not known if these drugs have the same effect on the circulation to the brain or localized parts of the brain. At present it is not known if such an effect would prevent the occurrence of migraine but it may provide an important lead to the mechanism of action of these drugs.

Comparison of properties of beta-adrenoceptor antagonists with other drugs effective in migraine

The only demonstrated pharmacological difference between the beta-blocking drugs that are effective or ineffective in the treatment of migraine is the absence or presence of partial agonist activity. Pizotifen, methysergide and cyproheptadine are antagonists of 5 hydroxytryptamine, but some beta-blocking drugs that are effective in migraine (atenolol) do not possess this property. The tricyclic antidepressant, amitriptyline, has been demonstrated to be effective in migraine[21]. The main pharmacological effect of amitriptyline is blockade of the uptake of noradrenaline but it also possesses significant blocking activity at cholinergic, adrenergic and histamine receptors[22]. Although recent studies have demonstrated that amitriptyline is a potent antagonist of 5 hydroxytryptamine receptors[22], its mode of action in migraine is not yet understood. Phenelzine, a mono-amine oxidase inhibitor has also been shown to be effective in migraine. It would appear that there is no pharmacological property common to those drugs that are effective in the treatment of migraine and that the mechanism of action of beta-adrenoceptor antagonists cannot be elucidated by extrapolation from results with other drugs.

Conclusion

Several double-blind studies have clearly established that propranolol is effective in the prophylactic treatment of migraine. A smaller number of studies have shown that nadolol, timolol, atenolol and metoprolol were also effective. The mechanism of action of these beta-blocking drugs in migraine is not understood. The only property possessed by the beta-blocking drugs that were not effective in migraine (alprenolol, oxprenolol, pindolol and acebutolol) was partial agonist activity. The drugs that were effective in migraine increased peripheral vascular resistance but there is no evidence to demonstrate if this occurred in the cerebral circulation. This change in vascular resistance may reduce the responsiveness of the cerebral circulation.

References

1 Rabkin, R., Stables, D. P., Levin, N. W. & Suzman, M. M. (1966): The prophylactic value of propranolol in angina pectoris. *Am. J. Cardiol.* **18**, 370–383.
2 Weersuriya, K., Patel, L. & Turner, P. (1982): β-Adrenoceptor blockade and migraine. *Cephalagia* **2**, 33–45.
3 Turner, P. (1984): Beta-blocking drugs in migraine. *Postgrad. Med. J.* **60**, (Suppl. 2), 1–5.
4 Ryan, R. E. Snr., Ryan, R. E. Jr. & Sudilovsky, A. (1983): Nadolol: its use in the prophylactic treatment of migraine. *Headache* **23**, 26.
5 Briggs, R. S. & Millac, P. A. (1979): Timolol in migraine prophylaxis. *Headache* **19**, 379–381.
6 Forssman, B., Lindblad, C. J. & Zbornikova, A. (1983): Atenolol for migraine prophylaxis. *Headache* **23**, 188.
7 Stensrud, P. & Sjaastad, O. (1980): Comparative trial of tenormin (atenolol) and inderal (propranolol) in migraine. *Headache* **20**, 204–207.
8 Anderson, P. G., Dahl, S., Hansen, J. H., Hansen, P. E., Hedman, C., Nygaard Kristensen, T. & de Fine Olivarius, B. (1983): Prophylactic treatment of classical and non-classical migraine with metoprolol—a comparison with placebo. *Cephalalgia* **3**, 207–212.
9 Ekbom, K. (1975): Alprenolol for migraine prophylaxis. *Headache* **15**, 129–132.
10 Ekbom, K. & Zetterman, M. (1977): Oxprenolol in the treatment of migraine. *Acta Neurol. Scand.* **56**, 181–184.
11 Ekbom, K. & Lundberg, P. O. (1972): Clinical trial of LB46, an adrenergic beta receptor blocking agent in migraine prophylaxis. *Headache* **12**, 15–17.
12 Sjaastad, O. & Stensrud, P. (1972): Clinical trial of a beta receptor blocking agent (LB46) in migraine prophylaxis. *Acta Neurol. Scand.* **48**, 124–128.
13 Nanda, R. N., Johnson, R. H., Grya, J., Keogh, H. J. & Melville, I. D. (1978): A double blind trial of acebutolol for migraine prophylaxis. *Headache* **18**, 20–22.
14 Shanks, R. G. (1983): *Clinical pharmacology of β-adrenoceptor blocking drugs.* L.E.R.S. vol. 1, ed. P. L. Morselli, *et al.* New York: Raven Press.
15 Patel, L. & Turner, P. (1981): Central actions of β-adrenoceptor blocking drugs in man. *Med. Res. Rev.* **1**, 4, 387–410.
16 Middlemiss, D. N., Blakeborough, L. & Leather, S. R. (1977): Direct evidence for an interaction of beta-adrenergic blockers with the 5-HT receptor. *Nature* **267**, 289–290.
17 McDevitt, D. G. (1983): Beta-adrenoceptor blocking drugs and partial agonist activity. Is it clinically relevant? *Drugs* **25**, 331–338.
18 Lysbo Svendsen, T., Hartling, O. & Trap Jensen, J. (1979): Immediate haemodynamic effects of propranolol, practolol, pindolol, atenolol and ICI 89406 in healthy volunteers. *Eur. J. Clin. Pharmacol.* **15**, 223–228.
19 Man In 'T Veld, A. J. & Schalekamp, M. A. D. H. (1982): How intrinsic sympathomimetic activity modulates the haemodynamic responses to β-adrenoceptor antagonists: a clue to the nature of their antihypertensive mechanism. *Br. J. Clin. Pharmac.* **13**, 245s–257s.
20 Vandenburg, M. J. (1982): The acute and chronic effect of oxprenolol and propranolol on peripheral blood flow in hypertensive patients. *Br. J. Clin. Pharmac.* **14**, 733–737.
21 Couch, J. R., Ziegler, D. K. & Hassanein, R. (1976): Amitriptyline in prophylaxis of migraine. *Neurology* **26**, 121–127.
22 Fozard, J. R. (1982): *Basic mechanisms of antimigraine drugs. Advances in Neurology* **33**, ed. M. Critchley *et al.* New York: Raven Press.

 Advances in headache research, ed. F. Clifford Rose. ©*John Libbey & Co Ltd, 1987*

IV

CLUSTER HEADACHE

27

HORNER'S SYNDROME IN CLUSTER HEADACHE

James W. Lance and Peter D. Drummond

Department of Neurology, The Prince Henry Hospital, Sydney, Australia and School of Medicine, University of New South Wales, Sydney, Australia

Summary

Patients with Horner's syndrome following cluster headache showed impairment of tyramine mydriasis similar to that found in third sympathetic neuron lesions, contrasting with the symmetrical dilatation demonstrated in patients with first and second neuron lesions. Thermoregulatory sweating and vasodilatation were impaired over the ipsilateral forehead in six cluster patients, two of whom also showed diminished flushing over the cheek on the affected side. The limited area of defective sweating and flushing was similar to that in three patients with third neuron lesions from internal carotid aneurysms, unlike the wider impairment observed in most patients with first and second neuron lesions. It is concluded that the Horner's syndrome associated with cluster headache is caused by a lesion of the third sympathetic neuron. A further study of flushing and sweating reactions in the cheeks is required to assess whether sympathetic fibres may be compromised in their passage with branches of the external carotid artery as well as in the plexus surrounding the internal carotid artery. The evidence indicates that sympathetic deficit does not play a part in the ocular and nasal vasodilatation that characteristically accompany cluster headache.

Introduction

Romberg[1] described as 'ciliary neuralgia' a syndrome of recurrent pain in the eye which was usually unilateral and associated with photophobia. He continued in the following terms; 'The pupil is contracted. The pain not infrequently extends over the head and face. The eye generally weeps and becomes red. These symptoms occur in paroxysms of a uniform or irregular character, and isolated or combined with facial neuralgia and hemicrania'. This is probably the first description of cluster headache and mentions symptoms that have since been attributed to sympathetic deficit (miosis) and parasympathetic discharge (lacrimation).

Fanciullacci *et al.*[2] examined 45 typical cluster headache patients between attacks, five of whom had a permanent miosis on the affected side. They found that the pupil on the symptomatic side dilated less than the other pupil in response to the instillation of tyramine 2% or cocaine 4% eye drops, even in those patients whose pupils had previously been of equal size. They concluded that a subclinical ocular sympathetic deficit persisted between attacks but could not find evidence of receptor supersensitivity to phenylephrine 1% eye drops. Overactivity of parasympathetic innervation on the affected side was excluded by pupillary asymmetry being maintained during cholinergic blockade with homatropine 0.1% drops. Vijayan and Watson[3] also found evidence of pupillary sympathetic denervation in seven cluster headache patients studied between headaches during a bout. Body heating after application of starch-iodine powder to the face demonstrated a patch of anhidrosis above the affected eye, consistent with a lesion of the third sympathetic neuron. Vijayan and Watson attributed conjunctival injection and nasal stuffiness to sympathetic hypofunction and speculated that the resulting eye pain and conjunctival changes may be sufficient to cause lacrimation and rhinorrhoea as a local irritative phenomenon without having to postulate parasympathetic overactivity.

Sweating in cluster headache patients has been studied extensively by Saunte, Russell and Sjaastad[4]. In 18 patients examined between attacks, sweating induced by body heating or exercise was found to be reduced on the forehead of the symptomatic side in most cases while the injection of pilocarpine 0.1 mg per kg body weight usually evoked excessive sweating over the same area. These data suggest a localized sympathetic deficit with receptor hypersensitivity, which presumably accounts for the excessive sweating noted on the ipsilateral forehead in some patients during cluster headache. Whether the first, second or third sympathetic neurons are impaired in cluster headache remains controversial.

Ekbom and Kudrow[5] stated that they had never observed spontaneous flushing of the face during cluster headache although Horton *et al.*[6] had found an increase in skin temperature of 1–3°C on the affected side. Drummond and Lance[7] used thermography to study heat loss from the face in 11 patients with spontaneous attacks of cluster headache. The affected side was warmer by 0.25°–1.25°C over the orbit in seven patients and by 0.25°–1.5°C over the cheek in ten patients, the mean difference being statistically significant in each case. The area of increased heat loss did not always coincide with the site of pain; for example, orbital temperature increased in only six of the nine patients who experienced pain in the orbit. In 22 patients with induced cluster headache, heat loss was greater from the ipsilateral orbit, nose, cheek and temple at the height of the attack[7].

Flushing of the face in response to body heating or embarrassment has recently been shown by Drummond and Lance[8] to depend on an intact sympathetic nerve supply. Whether sympathetic mechanisms play any part in the increase of facial temperature during cluster headache is unknown.

In the present investigation, pupillary responses to tyramine and forehead flushing and sweating in response to body heating and gustatory stimuli have been examined in six cluster headache patients, as part of a wider study of patients with Horner's syndrome produced by various central and peripheral lesions[8]; to help determine the site of the sympathetic lesion in cluster headache and its possible relationship to vasomotor symptoms.

Patients and methods

Twenty patients with Horner's syndrome, associated with typical episodic cluster headache in six, were studied by the installation into each eye of two drops of tyramine 2% solution and the recording of sweating and capillary pulsation over the forehead and cheek. In the 14 patients without a history of cluster headache, the Horner's syndrome was of first neuron origin in six (brainstem infarction in five, and congenital in one patient with heterochromia iridis and preservation of the cilio-spinal reflex); of second neuron origin in four (preganglionic sympathectomy) and third neuron origin in four (three with internal carotid artery aneurysm and one post-thyroidectomy). Informed consent for the investigation was obtained from all subjects.

Procedures were undertaken in an air conditioned laboratory maintained at $22 \pm 1°C$. Capillary pulsations were recorded by reflectance photoplethysmographs attached to the mid-forehead 2 cm above the eyebrows and to the cheeks 3 cm below the eyes. Pulsations were recorded on a Narco Bio-Systems Mark 1V Physiograph and are reported as a percentage change in amplitude from the baseline measurement.

Evaporation of sweat was measured by a Servo-Med Evaporimeter EPI applied to the forehead 1 cm from the midline above the eyebrows for 20–30 s until a steady reading was obtained, with the output being recorded on a physiograph as above. The rate of evaporation is reported in arbitrary units which are directly proportional to the original calibration in grams of sweat per metre^2 per hour (see reference 8 for details of method).

Body heating was induced by circulating hot air from a fan-forced heater around the patient who was draped in blankets and a plastic cover. Gustatory reactions were provoked by the subjects holding one-half teaspoon of chilli-based Tabasco sauce in their mouths for 30 s.

Results

The installation into each eye of two drops of 2% tyramine (which releases noradrenaline from sympathetic nerve terminals) produced symmetrical pupillary dilatation after 30 min in eight of the ten patients with first and second neuron lesions. One patient was not tested because of glaucoma and one patient with a brainstem infarct responded less on the affected side. The latter patient had also undergone a surgical operation on the middle ear which may have damaged postganglionic sympathetic fibres in the caroticotympanic plexus. The pupillary response to tyramine was reduced on the denervated side in all four patients with third neuron lesions and all five of the patients with cluster headache in whom it was tested. The tyramine test was omitted in one cluster patient because of incipient glaucoma.

After body heating, clinical inspection and Evaporimeter measurements showed that sweating was diminished on the affected side. The asymmetry of sweating was greatest in the supraorbital region in the group with cluster headache (Table 1) and with known third neuron lesions, and was often symmetrical over the upper forehead in these patients.

At the onset of sweating, vascular dilatation was greater on the intact side of the forehead in all 20 patients. In some patients with first and second neuron lesions, a distinct flush

Table 1. *Facial sweating and vascular dilatation in six cluster headache patients with residual Horner's syndrome.*

	Mean change (Standard deviation)			
	Horner's side	Intact side	t-test	P
Body heating				
Forehead sweating	+ 30.0 (4.1)	+ 39.5 (5.4)	4.76	<0.01
Forehead pulsation	+ 21.7% (47.4%)	+ 122.5% (54.3%)	3.78	<0.05
Cheek pulsation	+ 11.3% (17.2%)	+ 23.2% (50.4%)	0.72	–
Taste of chillies				
Forehead sweating	+ 7.7 (8.1)	+ 7.2 (11.6)	0.14	–
Forehead pulsation	+ 34.0% (40.6%)	+ 26.2% (25.3%)	0.36	–
Cheek pulsation	− 3.5% (14.3%)	+ 6.0% (11.2%)	3.86	<0.05

was apparent over the intact half of the face with a sharp line of demarcation being apparent at the midline as the denervated side of the face remained pale. Vascular dilatation was impaired mainly on the medial aspect of the forehead in the cluster headache patients and the three patients with internal carotid artery aneurysms. Flushing of the cheek was also impaired in two patients with cluster headache and one post-thyroidectomy. The pulse amplitude recorded from the cheek on the side of the Horner's syndrome in two cluster headache patients increased by only 22% and 29% respectively, compared with increases of 109% and 53% on the intact side. Asymmetry of cheek pulsations was not significant for the cluster headache group as a whole (Table 1).

Tasting Tabasco sauce resulted in a slight increase in sweating and pulse amplitude on both sides of the forehead in patients with Horner's syndrome. Slight but significant asymmetry was observed in vasodilatation of the cheeks of the six cluster headache patients, the response being greater on the intact side (Table 1). A paradoxical response to a gustatory stimulus was observed in one patient with cluster headache in whom pulse amplitude on the denervated side of the forehead increased by 108% but remained unchanged on the normal side.

Discussion

The pupillary responses to tyramine and the restricted sites of defective sweating in the six patients with cluster headache studied were identical with those of patients with third sympathetic neuron involvement from carotid artery aneurysm, and contrasted with responses found in patients whose Horner's syndrome resulted from first and second neuron lesions.

Drummond and Lance[8] demonstrated that facial vasodilatation after body heating was impaired on the side of Horner's syndrome and suggested that thermoregulatory flushing could be used as a test for an intact sympathetic nerve supply to the facial vasculature. The failure of cluster headache patients to flush over the medial aspect of the forehead is consistent with sympathetic hypofunction in this area as previously demonstrated by diminished sweating[3,4]. Two of the six cluster headache patients examined also showed impaired flushing on the cheek of the affected side which brings up the possibility of sympathetic fibres being compromised in their passage around branches of the external carotid artery before being distributed to the skin with peripheral branches of the trigeminal nerve[9]. This would be compatible with the traditional explanation for the Horner's syndrome in cluster headache being caused by compression of sympathetic fibres in the internal carotid periarterial plexus[10]. The one cluster headache patient who exhibited increased vasodilatation on the denervated side of the forehead after gustatory stimulation may have been an example of parasympathetic salivatory fibres sprouting along the degenerated sympathetic pathway, a phenomenon well known after ganglionic and post-ganglionic lesions of the cervical sympathetic nerves.

Does the sympathetic nervous system play any part in the vasomotor phenomena of cluster headache?

Sympathetic fibres enter the orbit with the ophthalmic division of the trigeminal nerve and are distributed to the skin of the forehead with its frontal and supraorbital branches. We have demonstrated impaired capillary pulsation as well as impaired sweating over the medial aspect of the ipsilateral forehead in patients with a Horner's syndrome resulting from cluster headache. If this localized sympathetic deficit played any part in the increase in orbital temperature that occurs on the painful side during cluster headache, parallel changes in frontal temperature should also have been observed. In fact there is no significant change in heat loss from the forehead but increased warmth is often noted over the ipsilateral cheek, half of the nose and temple[7]. Moreover, flushing of these areas during cluster headache does not correlate with the presence or absence of ptosis[11].

It is more logical to assume that conjunctival injection, lacrimation and nasal congestion, which correlate with increased temperature of nose, cheek and forehead[11] result from parasympathetic discharge along the greater superficial petrosal (GSP) nerve, particularly as such symptoms are abolished by section of that nerve[12].

The GSP nerve is probably also responsible for sweating over the central mask of the face that persists after cervical sympathectomy[13] and is particularly prominent after a gustatory stimulus. In our series[8] gustatory sweating and flushing were not influenced by a unilateral cervical sympathetic lesion.

Fanciullacci *et al.*[14] have challenged the concept that the pupillary changes of cluster headache are caused by a lesion of the third sympathetic neuron. They found that the intravenous injection of clonidine 0.1 mg (which activates presynaptic adrenoceptors centrally, thus reducing sympathetic outflow) produced greater miosis on the symptomatic side. However, this change was significant only at 15 minutes after administration of the drug. Possibly the withdrawal of residual sympathetic drive leads to a greater miosis because of the summation of central inhibition and a third neuron deficit.

In conclusion, the investigations reported here are consistent with the residual Horner's syndrome of cluster headache being caused by a lesion of the third sympathetic neuron. The combination of defective pupillary dilatation to tyramine and impaired flushing and sweating in an area limited to the medial aspect of the ipsilateral forehead is difficult to explain by a central (first neuron) lesion and quite unlike a second neuron lesion. There is no evidence to implicate the sympathetic nervous system in the ocular and nasal vascular changes that accompany an attack of cluster headache. The possibility remains that flushing of the lower face during an attack is caused by sympathetic overactivity on the side affected by cluster headache, and that such vasodilatation does not affect the forehead significantly because of the associated defect in the peripheral distribution of the third sympathetic neuron.

Acknowledgements — The authors are grateful to the National Health and Medical Research Council of Australia, the J. A. Perini Family Trust and the Adolph Basser Trust for their support of the research programme.

References

1 Romberg, M. H. (1840): *A manual of nervous diseases of man.* Trans. E. H. Sieveking. London: Sydenham Society.
2 Fanciullacci, M., Pietrini, U., Gatto, G., Boccuni, M. & Sicuteri, F. (1982): Latent dysautonomic pupillary lateralization in cluster headache. A pupillometric study. *Cephalalgia* **2**, 135–144.
3 Vijayan, N. & Watson, C. (1982): Evaluation of oculocephalic sympathetic function in vascular headache syndromes. Part 11: oculocephalic sympathetic function in cluster headache. *Headache* **22**, 200–202.
4 Saunte, C., Russell, D. & Sjaastad, O. (1983): Cluster headache: On the mechanism behind attack related sweating. *Cephalalgia* **3**, 175–185.
5 Ekbom, K. & Kudrow, L. (1979): Facial flush in cluster headache. *Headache* **19**, 47.
6 Horton, B. T., MacLean, A. R. & Craig, W. McK. (1939): A new syndrome of vascular headache: results of treatment with histamine: preliminary report. *Proc. Staff Meetings Mayo Clinic* **14**, 257–260.
7 Drummond, P. D. & Lance, J. W. (1984): Thermographic changes in cluster headache. *Neurology* **34**, 1292–1298.
8 Drummond, P. D. & Lance, J. W. (1987): Facial flushing and sweating mediated by the sympathetic nervous system. *Brain* (In press).

9 List, C. F. & Peet, M. M. (1938): Sweat secretion in man. IV. Sweat secretion of the face and its disturbances. *Arch. Neurol. Psychiat.* **40**, 443–470.
10 Nieman, E. A. & Hurwitz, L. J. (1961): Ocular sympathetic palsy in periodic migrainous neuralgia. *J. Neurol. Neurosurg. Psychiat.* **24**, 369–373.
11 Drummond, P. D. & Lance, J. W. (1985): Clinical symptoms and thermographic asymmetry in cluster headache. *Migraine Proceedings of the 5th International Migraine Symposium*, ed. F. Clifford Rose, pp. 156–161. Basel: Karger.
12 Gardner, W. J., Stowell, A. & Dutlinger, R. (1947): Resection of the greater superficial petrosal nerve in the treatment of unilateral headache. *J. Neurosurg* **4**, 105–114.
13 Monro, P. A. G. (1959): *Sympathectomy*. London: Oxford University Press.
14 Fanciullacci, M., Pietrini, U., Marabini, S. & Cangi, F. (1985): Enhanced miotic response to clonidine in cluster headache: a possible implication for a central sympathetic defect. In *Migraine, clinical and research advances*, ed. F. Clifford Rose, pp. 144–150. Basel: Karger.

28

IRIS SENSORY NEURONS

IN CLUSTER HEADACHE:

A RADIOIMMUNOLOGICAL

AND PUPILLOMETRIC STUDY

M. Fanciullacci, U. Pietrini,
M. Nicolodi, P. Geppetti, L. Barca* and F. Sicuteri

*Institute of Internal Medicine and Clinical Pharmacology,
*Department of Ophthalmology, Florence University,
Viale Morgagni, 85 50134 Florence, Italy*

Introduction

Bipolar sensory neurons of trigeminal nerve that convey pain sensation from the head if antidromically stimulated are able to provoke peripheral phenomena, eg miosis[1], cerebral vasodilation[2] and gland secretion[3,4]. In this perspective it has been postulated that the activation of trigeminal substance P (SP) containing fibres may cause the symptoms of cluster headache (CH)[5,6]. The eye, the preferential target organ of CH, is a rich centre of SP and other biologically active neurokinins. In fact immunohistochemical techniques have allowed the localization of SP and many other peptides to animal and human eyes[7-10], and functional studies also outline a potential role for them in ocular physiology. In particular, their miotic action has been stressed in some mammalian species[1,11,12], thus suggesting that they contribute to the neurogenic control of pupil size[13]. Because the localization of SP to tissues of human eye is interesting from the point of view of CH pathogenesis, we analyzed the distribution of SP-like immunoreactivity (SP-LI) in human ocular tissues in comparison with two animal species. In addition, pupillary responses to the conjunctival instillation of echothiophate iodide (EI), a putative releaser of neuronal SP, was evaluated in healthy volunteers to confirm in humans its non-cholinergic miotic action, and in sufferers of CH as compared to migraine controls.

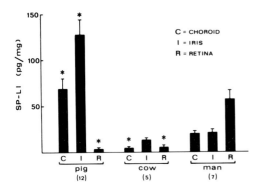

Fig. 1. *SP-LI levels (pg/mg of proteins) in choroid, iris and retina of pig, cow and man.* *P<0.01 versus human eye structures. Number of samples in parentheses.

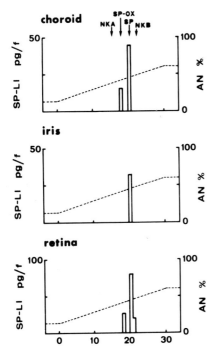

Fig. 2. *Immunochromatogram of the SP-LI content of human retina, iris and choroid.* NKA, neurokinin A; NKB, neurokinin B; SP-ox, SP sulphoxide.

Materials and methods

SP-LI measurements

Choroid, iris and retina were obtained from man, cow and pig 8–10 h after death or sacrifice. Samples were extracted with 2N acetic acid (1/10; w/v), centrifuged and the supernatant freeze-dried. SP-LI content was measured by radioimmunoassay (RIA) as previously described[14]. For HPLC analysis, a reverse phase 5 μ ultrasphere C18 (Beckman, CA) column was used. Samples were eluted with a linear gradient of 10–50% acetonitrile in a 0.1% trifluoracetic acid solution, at a flow rate of 1 ml/min for 30 min.

Statistical analysis was carried out by Duncan's test for multiple comparison.

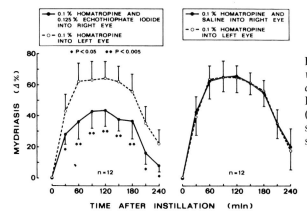

Fig. 3. *Homatropine induced mydriasis with (closed circles) or without (open circles) EI (0.125%) (left panel).* Homatropine induced mydriasis with (closed circles) or without (open circles) saline (right panel). *n*, number of treated subjects.

Pupillometric studies with EI

Pupil diameters were measured in standard light conditions, using an electronic pupillometer previously described[15]. Measurements were obtained before and every 30 min after drug instillation for 3–4 h. Conjunctival instillation was always performed with one drop of the drugs used. Pupillary diameters were expressed as percentage changes from pre-drug values.

(a) Twelve healthy volunteers ranging in age from 23–38 years (mean±s.e.m. = 27.4±2.3) received 0.1% homatropine plus 0.125% EI into the right eye. The other eye received homatropine only and served as control. Three days later the eyes of the same subjects were instilled with 0.1% homatropine into both eyes plus saline into the right eye. At the peak of homatropine mydriasis, light reflex was evaluated after 5 min of dark adaptation in infrared light. Light stimulus was obtained by photographic flash. Pupil measurements were made for 4 h.

(b) Twelve male episodic cluster patients ranging in age between 12–42 years (mean ±s.e.m. = 33.2±2.5) were tested during headache-free intervals of cluster phase. 0.125% EI was instilled into both eyes and pupil measurements were obtained for 3 h.

(c) Twelve migraine patients, four males and eight females, between the ages of 17 to 45 years (mean±s.e.m. = 35.4±3.8) with marked prevalence of unilateral headache, received during headache-free period 0.125% EI into both eyes. The period of observation was 3 h.

Statistical analysis of pupillometric values was performed using Student's *t*-test for paired data.

Results

SP-LI measurements

In man the retina contains a higher concentration of SP-LI than the two other ocular structures. Human retina also showed more elevated SP-LI level in comparison with swine and bovine retina, but the iris was the structure where SP-LI content was higher both in cow and pig (Fig. 1). The HPLC analysis of the SP-LI content in the three ocular structures examined in all the species, indicated the presence of a major fraction eluting as authentic SP or its sulphoxidated form (Fig. 2).

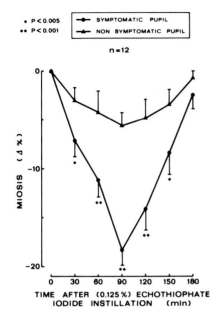

Fig. 4. *Miotic effect of EI (0.125%) instilled into both eyes of 12 CH patients.* Symptomatic pupil (closed circles); non-symptomatic pupil (closed triangles). *$P<0.005$; **$P<0.001$.

Effect of EI on homatropine-induced mydriasis

Homatropine induced a bilateral marked pupillary dilatation. As expected, homatropine abolished the response to the light (data not shown). The instillation of EI, but not saline, was able to reduce homatropine mydriasis from 30 to 240 min after instillation (Fig. 3).

Asymmetric miosis by EI in cluster patients

In CH group, EI instillation induced on the symptomatic pupil a significantly more intense miosis from 30 to 150 min after instillation. The maximum difference between the two eyes was observed at 90 min (Fig. 4).

Symmetric miosis by EI in migraine patients

EI elicited a bilateral symmetric miosis in migraine patients. The pupil on the side of predominant head pain showed a significant miosis when compared with pre-drug values, at 60 ($P<0.05$), 90 ($P<0.005$) and 120 ($P<0.02$) min after EI instillation. A significant miosis in the contralateral pupil was present at 60 ($P<0.01$), 90 ($P<0.001$) and 120 ($P<0.02$) min after administration. The peak of the miosis was at 90 min (Fig. 5).

Discussion

The underlying mechanism of the miosis occurring during a CH attack is not yet clarified, but it is likely that autonomic and/or trigeminal sensory nerves are involved. The presence of SP-LI containing fibres has been shown in animal and man[16]. The quantitative analysis of SP-LI content in ocular structures demonstrates that, although in different amounts, SP-LI is contained in human as well as bovine and swine iris. HPLC analysis indicates the occurrence of a fraction of SP-LI eluting as authentic SP in extracts of human iris. Therefore, SP must be included in the neurochemical anatomy of human iris.

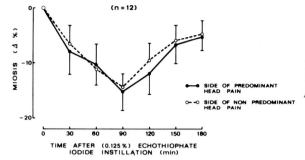

Fig. 5. *Symmetric miosis by 0.125% EI instilled into both eyes of 12 migraine patients.*

Although not fully elucidated, the efferent function of trigeminal sensory neurons in the eye seems to operate together with parasympathetic and sympathetic neurons in the control of iris motility. In the rabbit, the miotic response to the light involves parasympathetic pathways to the iris sphincter muscle, whereas the mydriasis associated with emotion or non-trigeminal painful stimuli reflects a sympathetic discharge to the iris dilator muscle. The miosis evoked by eye injury appears to be caused by local sensory reflex involving release of neurokinin-like materials, such as SP, from terminals of the sensory trigeminal fibres[13,17].

Anatomical distribution and pharmacological data indicate large differences between the species regarding the effects of neurokinins on iris[12], but it is likely that a neurogenic control of the sensory fibres is also operative in humans.

Experiments performed in the presence of homatropine appear to indicate that, also in man, EI is able to constrict the pupil through a non-cholinergic action. According to findings obtained in animal models, this action is likely to be due to the release of neurokinins from trigeminal sensory fibres[18,19]. The more intense miotic response to EI on the symptomatic side of CH patients may represent the first clue of an augmented activity of trigeminal sensory neurons. This effect could be due to an increased release of SP from neuronal store or to a receptor hyperresponsiveness to normal or even reduced release of SP. The possible occurrence of SP receptor supersensitivity is consistent with the hypothesis of a functional and partial deafferentation of trigeminal sensory neurons in CH[20]. This asymmetric response to EI seems to be peculiar to CH patients as it is not present in migraine, and suggests that the iris is not a target organ in the mechanism of migraine lateralization. The response to EI on the symptomatic pupil of CH was moderate and less intense than that observed in migraine patients but, before drawing final conclusions, it remains to compare the present data with the miotic effect of EI in healthy subjects.

Furthermore it cannot be ruled out that the excessive response to EI on the symptomatic side of CH reflects only the well documented deficiency of sympathetic tonus. Our previous data indicate that a latent Horner's-like pupil on the symptomatic side occurs in the majority of CH patients[21]. This subclinical dysfunction has been unmasked not only during headache-free intervals of the active phase but also in cluster-free periods. Ipsilateral sympathetic abnormality was demonstrated by the altered response to several autonomically active eye drops instilled into both eyes[22].

In animals, sympathetic ganglionectomy provokes a rise of SP and calcitonin-gene-related peptide levels in the homolateral iris. This rise seems to be dependent on nerve growth factor (NGF) which is essential for the development and maintenance of both sympathetic and sensory fibres[23,24]. It has been postulated that after sympathetic denervation iris elaborates NGF which may provoke peptide synthesis in sensory trigeminal neurons. The post-sympathectomy generated pain (sympathalgia), which occurs in some patients after therapeutic sympathetic ganglionectomy or block[25], is a clinical condition which, at vascular level, could hear some similarity with the sympathetic sensory interaction hypothesized in the iris. With this in mind, CH may represent a human disease due to a disturbance (genetic or acquired) of NGF, which may create an elevation and lowering, respectively, of sensory and sympathetic activities.

Acknowledgements—This work was in part supported by a grant from CNR (Roma) 'Medicina Preventiva e Riabilitativa' Sottoprogetto 'Controllo del Dolore' contratto n 85.00.559.56.

References

1 Bill, A., Stjernschantz, J., Mandahl, A., Brodin, E. & Nilsson, G. (1979): Substance P release on trigeminal nerve stimulation, effect in the eye. *Acta Physiol. Scand.* **106**, 371–373.

2 Moskowitz, M. A. (1984): The neurobiology of vascular head pain. *Ann. Neurol.* **6**, 157–168.

3 Duner-Engström, M., Fredholm, B. B., Larsson, O., Lundberg, J. M. & Saria, A. (1986): Autonomic mechanisms underlying capsaicin induced oral sensation and salivation in man. *J. Physiol.* **373**, 87–96.

4 Wells, U. & Widdicombe, J. G. (1986): Lateral nasal gland secretion in the anaesthetized dog. *J. Physiol.* **374**, 359–374.

5 Sicuteri, F., Rainò, L. & Geppetti, P. (1983): Substance P and endogenous opioids: how and where they could play a role in cluster headache. *Cephalalgia* 3 (suppl. 1), 143–145.

6 Hardebo, J. E. (1984): Involvement of trigeminal substance P neurons in cluster headache. An hypothesis. *Headache* 11, 294–304.

7 Unger, W. G., Butler, J. M., Cole, D. F., Bloom, S. R. & McGregor, G. P. (1981): Substance P, vasoactive intestinal polypeptide (VIP) and somatostatin levels in ocular tissue of normal and sensorly denervated rabbit eyes. *Exp. Eye Res.* **32**, 797–801.

8 Stone, R. A., Laties, A. M. & Brecha, N. C. (1982): Substance P-like immunoreactive nerves in the anterior segment of the rabbit, cat and monkey eye. *Neuroscience* 7, 2459–2468.

9 Tervo, T., Tervo, K. & Eranko, L. (1982): Ocular neuropeptides. *Med. Biol.* **60**, 53–60.

10 Terenghi, G., Polak, J. M., Ghatei, M. A., Mulderry, P. K., Butler, J. M., Unger, W. G. & Bloom, S. R. (1985): Distribution and origin of calcitonin gene-related peptide (CGRP) immunoreactivity in the sensory innervation of the mammalian eye. *J. Comp. Neurol.* **233**, 506–516.

11 Soloway, M. R., Stjernschantz, J. & Sears, M. (1981): The miotic effect of substance P in the rabbit. *Invest. Ophthalmol. Vis. Sci.* **20**, 53–60.

12 Unger, W. G. & Tighle, J. (1984): The response of the isolated iris sphincter muscle of various mammalian species to substance P. *Exp. Eye Res.* **39**, 677–684.

13 Wahlested, C., Bynke, G., Beding, B., Von Leithner, P. & Hakanson, R. (1985): Neurogenic mechanisms in control of the rabbit iris sphincter muscle. *Eur. J. Pharmacol.* **117**, 303–309.

14 Sicuteri, F., Fanciullacci, M., Geppetti, P., Renzi, D., Caleri, D. & Spillantini, M. G. (1985): Substance P mechanism in cluster headache: Evaluation in plasma and in cerebrospinal fluid. *Cephalalgia* 5, 143–149.

15 Fanciullacci, M., Pietrini, U. & Boccuni, M. (1982): Disruption of iris adrenergic transmission as an index of poor endorphin modulation in headache. In *Advances in neurology*, vol. 33, Headache, physiopathological and clinical concepts, eds M. Critchley, A. P. Friedman, S. Gorini & F. Sicuteri, pp. 365–374. New York: Raven Press.

16 Stone, R. A. & Kuwayama, Y. (1985): Substance P-like immunoreactive nerves in the human eye. *Arch. Ophthalmol.* **103**, 1207–1211.

17 Ueda, N., Muramatsu, I., Sakakibara, Y. & Fujiwara, M. (1981): Noncholinergic, nonadrenergic contraction and substance P in rabbit iris sphincter muscle. *Jap. J. Pharmacol.* **31**, 1071–1079.

18 Mandahl, A. (1985): Effects of the substance P antagonist (D-Arg[1], D-Pro[2], D-Trp[7,9], Leu[11]) SP on miosis caused by echothiophate iodide or pilocarpine hydrochloride. *Eur. J. Pharmacol.* **114**, 121–127.

19 Mandahl, A . (1985): Echothiophate iodide causes miosis by substance P release. In *Substance P metabolism and biological actions*, eds C. C. Jordan & P. Oehme, p. 236. London: Taylor and Francis.

20 Sicuteri, F. (1987): Quasi phantom head pain from functional deafferentation. *Clin. J. Pain.* (In press).
21 Fanciullacci, M. (1979): Iris adrenergic impairment in idiopathic headache. *Headache* **19**, 8–13.
22 Fanciullacci, M., Pietrini, U., Gatto, G., Boccuni, M. & Sicuteri, F. (1982): Latent dysautonomic pupillary lateralization in cluster headache. A pupillometric study. *Cephalalgia* **2**, 135–144.
23 Kessler, J. A., Bell, W. O. & Black, B. I. (1983): Interactions between the sympathetic and sensory innervation of the iris. *J. Neurosci.* **3**, 1301–1307.
24 Schon, F., Ghatep, M., Allen, J. M., Mulderry, P. K., Kelly, J. S. & Bloo, S. R. (1985): The effect of sympathectomy on calcitotin gene-related peptide levels in the rat trigeminovascular system. *Brain Res.* **348**, 197–200.
25 Loh, L. & Nathan, P. W. (1978): Painful peripheral states and sympathetic blocks. *J. Neurol. Neurosurg. Psychiat.* **41**, 664–671.

29

CONNECTION BETWEEN CLUSTER

HEADACHE AND ACTIVATION

OF HERPES SIMPLEX INFECTION

Jan Erik Hardebo

Departments of Neurology and Histology,
University Hospital of Lund, S-221 85 Lund, Sweden

Summary

Some cluster headache sufferers with regional and temporal coincidence between trigeminal herpes simplex virus and exacerbations of cluster headache are presented. Further, a beneficial effect in such cases by the antiviral agent acyclovir, if given early in the period, is demonstrated. A theory on herpes viral activation of pain pathways in cluster headache is presented.

Introduction

The mechanisms behind cluster headache are poorly understood but some coupling to infectious diseases exists. Upper airway infections often precede a period of attacks, and sinusitis and endonasal lesions (eg septum deviation) is often found in sufferers[1-3]. Generally, cellular immunity is activated by viruses. Cell-mediated immunological abnormalities (in subpopulations of T-lymphocytes and monocytes) are present in some cluster headache sufferers[4-7], and the immunological abnormality is probably linked to the HLA-DR5 antigen[5]. The periodicity of attacks, reports on increased number of mast cells in facial skin[8-9], and the beneficial effect of steroid treatment may indicate infection, recurrent in character, as a causative factor.

Herpes virus, taken up by axon terminals in the skin or mucosa, and subsequently transferred via axonal transport in sensory fibres, may reach the cranial sensory ganglia—the trigeminal ganglia in particular—and establish a latent infection there. The virus may also travel further into the central nervous system by neuron to neuron transmission[10]. Cluster headache has been reported to start a few months after an ipsilateral herpes zoster ophthalmicus[11]. Ipsilateral blisters of labial herpes simplex occurred in the middle of periods in one sufferer from cluster headache[12]. Theoretically, the well-known intermittent recurrence of herpes simplex infections, due to reactivation of latent ganglionitis, may initiate a period of cluster headache. Cold sores in the mucosa or skin may not necessarily appear during each of such reactivation periods.

Acyclovir (Wellcome) prevents replication of herpes virus during reactivation. The metabolite, acyclovirtriphosphate, blocks a substrate for herpes-specific DNA-polymerase in the virus. This enzyme is of vital importance for the virus to replicate and, when DNA-synthesis is prevented if acyclovir is given early enough, eruption periods are shortened, but the risk for recurrence remains. As shown in mice, reactivation of a latent herpes simplex infection in the trigeminal ganglion is not prevented by this or similar drugs[13]. Acyclovir has virtually no side-effects in the dose given.

Case material

Two patients with secondary chronic cluster headache for 9–13 years, experienced eruptions of ipsilateral herpes labialis (usually caused by herpes simplex virus type 1), starting a few days before severe periods of headache. One further patient experienced infraorbital skin eruptions of herpes simplex about once a year for 10 years. With maximum pain within the same area, but so far not coincident with the eruption periods, this patient had periods of cluster headache for 12 years. This provides additional argument for a link between trigeminal herpes simplex ganglionitis and cluster headache, and justified trials with acyclovir treatment in these patients.

Patient no. 1

A 33-year-old man had secondary chronic left-sided cluster headache since 1973, with attacks occurring once or twice each day. A typical attack consists of severe retro-ocular pain, radiating posteriorly towards the ear and to the eyebrow, lasting for 1–1½ h, and associated with ipsilateral conjunctival injection, lacrimation, nasal congestion, rhinorrhea, reddening and swelling of eyelids, and dilatation of the superficial temporal artery. He eventually became unresponsive to all medical treatment except high dose steroids. Therefore, supraorbital and sensory zygomatico-facial nerve branches were cut, and finally in March 1983 retrogasserian glycerol injection was performed to achieve a marked, reversible trigeminal analgesia. Within one month after a second glycerol injection, performed in February 1984, herpes labialis appeared on the ipsilateral half of the upper lip, recurrent for seven periods so far. The analgesia has gradually subsided and is now normalized (except in areas supplied by supraorbital and zygomatico-facial nerve branches). Coincident with these eruptions of herpes labialis, except for the first and third time, the patient experienced attacks of cluster headache: mild pain during the first period, when marked analgesia was still present; prominent pain, with all the ordinary signs of autonomic dysfunction, during the second period, when about half analgesia remained: severe pain with autonomic dysfunction during the last three periods, when little or no analgesia was present. Pain was felt also in the analgesic supraorbital and zygomatic areas, indicative of pain projection or referred pain. The labial cold sores appeared 1 day to 1 week before the headache attacks began. On all five occasions attacks ceased within 1–2 days of medication with 200 mg tablets of acyclovir (Wellcome) five times daily for 5 days, which is the recommended dose to be effective against herpes simplex (Fig. 1, showing attacks during the third and fourth periods). In the fourth period one weak attack appeared after acyclovir treatment (Fig. 1).

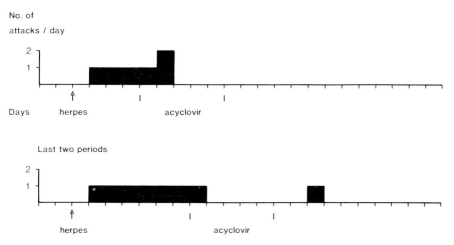

No. of
attacks / day

Days   herpes   acyclovir

Last two periods

herpes   acyclovir

Fig. 1. ♂ *C.A.S. 33 years. Secondary chronic cluster headache, again apparently periodic, linked to eruptions of herpes labialis, when sensibility returned after retro-gasserian glycerol injection.*

The treatment started after 3–6 days of daily attacks, at the most 7 days after the appearance of cold sores. The labial wound healed on this treatment combined with unguent acyclovir locally.

It may be argued that the viral infection in this patient was implanted into CSF, thus reaching the trigeminal nerve, in conjunction with the injection of hyperosmolar glycerol in the trigeminal cistern surrounding the Gasserian ganglion. However, no symptoms of meningeal irritation appeared, and normal CSF/serum quotients for antibodies against herpes simplex, varicella-zoster and cytomegalic viruses were measured in CSF, sampled after (October 1985) the glycerol injections. A more likely explanation is that an already present, latent trigeminal herpes infection was activated by manipulation of the nerve, as is often noticed by an eruption of herpes labialis a few days after neurosurgical intervention of the trigeminal nerve root or ganglion, irrespective of diagnosis.

Patient no. 2

This 28-year-old woman has a secondary chronic right-sided cluster headache since 1977, with an attack frequency of 1–3 per day. Her attacks comprises severe pain in the medial eye angle, radiating frontally, and with pain also occipitally, lasting for 1 h, and associated with ipsilateral conjunctival injection, lacrimation, nasal congestion and rhinorrhea. She has eventually become unresponsive to all medical treatment except oxygen inhalation combined with ergotamine. The patient has experienced eruptions of ipsilaterial herpes labialis (upper lip) a few days before a period of enhanced attack frequency. Such cold sores have recurred several times for about 10 years, but not necessarily in connection with cluster headache exacerbations. In the only exacerbation period tested so far, acyclovir treatment, starting on the 17th day of enhanced frequency and 20 days after the appearance of cold sores, attacks transiently subsided during the treatment period (Fig. 2).

Patient no. 3

This 35-year-old woman suffers from right-sided episodic cluster headache about once yearly for 12 years, with an attack frequency of one per day. The pain is localized just behind or above the eye, radiating parietally and to the upper jaw, lasting for 1–4 h, and associated

185

Fig. 2. ♀ *L.F. 28 years. Secondary chronic cluster headache with periods of enhanced attack frequency lasting for 2–3 months.*

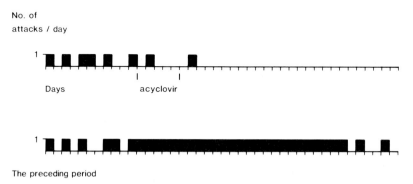

Fig. 3. ♂ *T.I.E. 41 years. Periodic cluster headache, started after ipsilateral uveitis.*

with ipsilateral lacrimation, nasal congestion, rhinorrhea, miosis and ptosis. For 10 years she experiences ipsilateral cold sores laterally infraorbitally, combined with local continuous aching pain and hyperalgesia, with no symptoms of autonomic dysfunction, for a few weeks — now about every second year, initially more frequently — but so far not coincident with the cluster headache periods. Therefore, she has not been given acyclovir during periods with cluster headache, but treatment given against cold sores in May 1986 shortened that period.

Acyclovir was also tested in some other cluster headache sufferers without any relationship to cold sores anamnestically. One male patient had his disease starting within a few months after an ipsilateral uveitis in 1971. The infectious agent behind the uveitis is not known, but herpes virus is not likely as causative factor, since the uveitis was not preceded by a keratitis. His periods normally lasts for 5–8 weeks, occurring over intervals of a few years. His rightsided attacks, lasting for 2 h, comprises severe retro-ocular pain, radiating to the maxilla and with accompanying ipsilateral conjunctival injection, lacrimation, ptosis, miosis and feeling of nasal congestion. Following acyclovir treatment, starting after 11 days, the period was brought to an end within a few days (Fig. 3).

Acyclovir was also tested in some cluster headache sufferers that were without obvious connection to infections within the ipsilateral trigeminal territory. In one male patient with episodic cluster headache, this treatment, starting on the 8th day, reduced attacks to less than half of the expected frequency for the remaining 2 months period. During medication in the middle of the period in one female patient with episodic cluster, attacks transiently subsided for a few days, beginning on the 3rd day of medication. The same effect was noticed in three male patients with chronic cluster headache, whereas no effect was seen in two male chronic sufferers. In none of these chronic patients was the medication given in conjunction with an exacerbation of the disease.

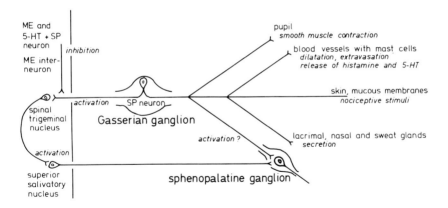

Fig. 4. *Schematic illustration of possible reflex arch and axon reflexes involving trigeminal substance P neurons.*

The present findings provide evidence that exacerbations of cluster headache, at least in some patients, is linked to activation of a latent trigeminal herpes simplex infection, and furthermore, offers a plausible treatment. It also indicates that the anti-herpes medication with acyclovir, in order to be effective, should be given in the beginning of such exacerbation periods. From this limited material it appears as if no dramatic positive effects can be expected in cases without a coupling to ipsilateral infections within the trigeminal territory but, before such conclusions can be drawn, further tests should be performed early in the periods in episodic cluster headache sufferers, ideally in double-blind studies.

Whether cluster headache sufferers had traces of present or previous herpes infections was studied by measurements of IgG antibody activities in serum and lumbar CSF by ELISA, in samples taken during cluster periods. To detect activity, such samples should be taken within a few months after an infection (or a few years in case of CNS infection). As indicated above, patient no. 1 had no elevated serum levels or CSF/serum quotient of herpes simplex or cytomegalo virus in samples from 1981 and October 1985 (onset of attacks 1973, of attacks coincident with herpes labialis, March 1984), whereas serum antibody activity of varicella-zoster was high in both samples. In one further patient, who displayed 16 monocytes in CSF taken 3 weeks before the start of left-sided attacks (the cell count was virtually normalized 1 month later), normal antibody activities were found in both samples. This patient had suffered from right-sided cluster periods since 1958, and continued to do so at times independent of the left-sided periods. CSF taken 1 month earlier, in the middle of a right-sided period, showed normal cell count and normal antibody activity.

In this patient, sampling of serum together with CSF from Meckel's cave surrounding the Gasserian ganglion, in conjunction with retrogasserian glycerol injection, revealed only an expected generalized elevation of the various CSF/serum quotients of virus antibodies, due to the defective blood- nerve barrier of the Gasserian ganglion[14].

The findings lend support to the following hypothesis on cluster headache: trigeminal and other cranial sensory fibres become activated by inherent herpes virus infection. This involves pain fibres[10] with substance P, and sometimes neurokinin A and calcitonin gene-related peptide (CGRP) as transmitters, both centrally at the spinal cord synapse in the spinal trigeminal nucleus and peripherally at motor terminals around eg glands, vascular smooth muscle and mast cells (axon reflexes). An irritative focus is established, which upon activation gives rise to exacerbation periods of cluster headache. Release centrally activates central pain pathways to produce the pain during attacks and, by virtue of a reflex arch to the superior salivatory nucleus, a parasympathetic release over the greater superficial petrosal nerve and sphenopalatine ganglion occurs[15]. Due to synapses also between the postganglionic autonomic neuron and trigeminal substance P fibres in the sphenopalatine ganglion (Fig. 4), this autonomic activation is enforced.

Intraneuronal resynthesis and subsequent axonal transport of a peptidergic transmitter, to sufficiently refill emptied nerve terminals, is a process that will probably take several hours, which may account for the refractory period between individual attacks, during which new attacks cannot be provoked. Horner's syndrome and forehead anhidrosis will follow if sympathetic fibres in the wall of the internal carotid artery are damaged against the bony carotid canal when this artery becomes dilated and edematous due to release of substance P, neurokinin A, CGRP, and substance P-induced release of histamine and serotonin from mast cells, and bradykinin and prostaglandin formation locally in the vessel wall[16]. Through interaction between these agents, 'pain receptors' near substance P nerve terminals in the vessel wall may also become activated, which may probably contribute to the pain of an attack. This may be especially valid for vessels dilating in narrow rigid structures like the carotid canal, where pain receptors will also become activated mechanically.

Pain in cluster headache may also have a more central origin, as eg indicated by findings of altered CSF levels of peptides involved in pain control[17]. Herpes virus, having reached beyond the cranial sensory ganglia to pain modulatory structures by neuron to neuron transmission, may become activated to cause exacerbation periods of the disease.

References

1 Loisy, C., Arnaud, J., Becaud, G., Beorchia, S., Brauchli, G. & Dussillol, P. (1985): Is cluster headache a disease of endonasal origin? *Cephalalgia* **5** (Suppl. 3), 280–281.

2 Meyer, J. S., Binns, P. M., Ericsson, A. D. & Vulpe, M. (1970): Sphenopalatine ganglionectomy for cluster headache. *Arch. Otolaryngol.* **92**, 475–484.

3 Bonaccorsi, P. (1972): Revaluation of ethmoido-sphenectomy in some cephalagic syndromes. *Res. Clin. Stud. Headache* **3**, 343–377.

4 Giacovazzo, M. (1986): Antigenic characterization in cluster headache. Abstract at the workshop on Trends in Cluster Headache, Montesilvano, Italy.

5 Giacovazzo, M., Martelletti, P., Valeri, M., Piazza, A., Monaco, P. I. & Casciani, C. U. (1986): Variations in the Leu7 + and LeuM3 + leucocyte subpopulations observed in cluster headache are dependent on HLA-DR antigens. *Headache* **26**, 315–316.

6 Thonnard, E. (1979): T and B lymphocytes in vascular headaches. *Headache* **19**, 244.

7 Martelletti, P., Alteri, E., Rinaldi-Garaci, C., Pesce, A. & Giacovazzo, M. (1986): Defect of serotonin binding to manonuclear cells from episodic cluster headache patients. *Headache* **26**, 316.

8 Appenzeller, O., Becker, W. J. & Rogaz, A. (1981): Cluster headache. Ultra-structural aspects and pathogenetic mechanisms. *Arch. Neurol.* **38**, 302–306.

9 Liberski, P. P. & Prusiński, A. (1982): Further observations on the mast cells over the painful region in cluster headache patients. *Headache* **22**, 115–117.

10 Kristensson, K., Nennesmo, I., Persson, L. & Lycke, E. (1982): Neuron to neuron transmission of herpes simplex virus. *J. Neurol. Sci.* **54**, 149–156.

11 Sacquegna, T., D'Allessandro, R., Cortelli, P., DeCarolis, P. & Baldrati, A. (1982): Cluster headache after herpes zoster ophthalmicus. *Arch. Neurol.* **39**, 384.

12 Joseph, R. & Clifford Rose, F. (1985): Cluster headache and herpes simplex: an association? *Br. Med. J.* **290**, 1625–1626.

13 Svennerholm, B., Vahlne, A. & Lycke, E. (1981): Persistent reactivable latent herpes simplex virus infection in trigeminal ganglia of mice treated with antiviral drugs. *Arch. Virol.* **69**, 43–48.

14 Arvidsson, B., Kristensson, K. & Olsson, Y. (1973): Vascular permeability to fluorescent protein tracer in trigeminal nerve and Gasserian ganglion. *Acta Neuropath.* (Berl.) **26**, 199–205.

15 Lance, J. W., Lambert, G. A., Goadsby, P. J. & Duckworth, J. W. (1983): Brain-stem influences on the cephalic circulation: experimental data from cat and monkey of relevance to the mechanism of migraine. *Headache* **23**, 258–265.
16 Hardebo, J. E. (1984): Involvement of trigeminal substance P neurons in cluster headache. An hypothesis. *Headache* **24**, 294–304.
17 Hardebo, J. E. & Ekman, R. (1987): Substance P and opioids in cluster headache. In *Trends in cluster headache*, eds F. Sicuteri & L. Vecchiet. Amsterdam: Elsevier. In press.

30

INCREASED IMMUNE COMPLEXES

AND IMPAIRED PATTERNS OF CELL-

MEDIATED IMMUNITY IN CLUSTER HEADACHE

M. Giacovazzo and P. Martelletti

Headache Service, Medical Pathology,
Institute of Medical Clinic 2°, Rome University 'La Sapienza', Italy

Summary

Circulating immune complexes (CIC) and leukocyte subsets have been studied in 19 patients affected by episodic cluster headache during and between cluster periods. The presence of CIC was determined in a further five patients between cluster periods.

Circulating immune complexes were evaluated using two techniques based on different principles revealing different types of CIC: the solid phase C1q method and the conglutinin radioimmune assay. Monoclonal antibodies have been used to phenotype total T-helper/suppressor, K and NK leukocyte subsets and monocytes.

The findings demonstrate an increased incidence of CIC in the 19 patients followed with time (37%) compared to control subjects (10%), and an increase in Leu7-positive cells (killer and natural killer cells) and in LeuM3-positive cells (monocytes). Interestingly, when patients were grouped according to the presence of CIC, only CIC-positive patients showed the above described abnormalities. This would suggest that the cell-mediated immune alterations present in these patients may interact with the presence of CIC.

Introduction

The demonstration that a number of immunological abnormalities are present in patients affected by cluster headache (CH) has resulted in renewed interest. An important genetic finding in this disease has been the lower phenotypical frequency of HLA-B14 antigen and the increased frequency of the HLA-DR5 antigen on the major histocompatibility complex[1,2]. A strong correlation between the efficacy of lithium therapy in these patients and the presence of the HLA-B18 antigen has been described[3,4]. Increased values of killer/ natural killer, large granular lymphocytes and monocytes were found during the cluster period[5,7]. Moreover these mononuclear cells lacked the serotonin high affinity binding site on their surface independently of the painful phase[8].

Associated hyperergic pathologies are frequent in CH patients[9], and in many of these disorders circulating immune complexes (CIC) have been found to play a role in the pathogenetic sequence. These clinical observations and laboratory findings have led us to study the humoral immunological aspects of CH and to verify the possible interrelationships with the well-established alterations occurring in cell-mediated immunology. The presence of CIC was evaluated in a group of episodic CH (ECH) patients, both during attacks and during the pain-free phase. Since different types of complexes are detected according to the principle of the technique used, two methods to detect CIC have been chosen: solid phase C1q binding test and the conglutinin RIA. The pattern of the leukocyte subsets was also assessed during the study.

Methods

Patients

Those who gave informed consent for these investigations were 24 ECH patients (22 males, two females; age range 23–40 years). No patients had received therapy for at least 90 days.

The presence of CIC and the levels of leukocyte subsets were evaluated in 19 patients both during and between cluster periods, the remaining five patients being sampled for CIC only in between and not during ECH attacks. Samples between cluster periods were collected at least 3 months after the disappearance of the last cluster period. One hundred and eighty-nine blood donors, age range 18–59, were considered as controls for the limits of positivity in the CIC assay[9].

Methods to assess CIC

The solid phase C1q binding test (C1qSp)[11] and the conglutinin binding test (KgBt)[12] were used to detect CIC. C1qSp is based upon the affinity of the first component of complement (C1q), bound to polysterene tubes, for the Fc region of complexed immunoglobulins. The ability of staphylococcal protein A, labelled with ^{125}I, to interact with $IgG_{1,2,4}$ was used to reveal CIC bound to C1q. The affinity of conglutinin, fixed to polypropylene tube walls, for the complex bound C3 is the basis of KgBt. Again ^{125}I-labelled staphylococcal protein A was used to reveal tube-bound CIC. These methods reveal different types of complexes: C1q detects mainly medium size CIC in antigen excess, whereas conglutinin detects large size CIC near the equivalence point. Results were expressed in micrograms of aggregate equivalents per millilitre of undiluted serum (μg AHG Eq/ml). Values greater than 6 μg AHG Eq/ml were considered above the limit of positivity in the C1qSp assay, whereas 4 μg AHG Eq/ml was the limit in the KgBt assay. A patient was considered positive if at least one of the methods gave a positive reading.

Methods to assess leukocyte subsets

Samples of 20 ml venous blood were collected from each subject during and between attacks. The blood was heparinized and the mononuclear cells isolated on a Ficoll-Hypaque gradient ($d = 1.077$). The cells were washed twice in Hank's balanced salt solution (HBSS), counted and resuspended in HBSS at the appropriate concentration. Two hundred

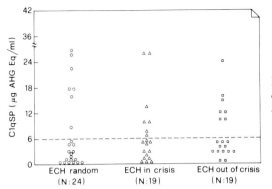

Fig. 1. *Occurrence of circulating immune complexes in episodic cluster headache patients by the C1qSp assay.*

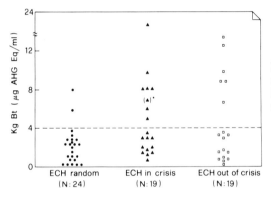

Fig. 2. *Occurrence of circulating immune complexes in episodic cluster headache patients by the KgBt assay.* *Positivity shown only in crisis.

μl cell suspension were then incubated in an ice/water bath for 30 min with 5 μl monoclonal antibodies (MoAb) (Becton-Dickinson, Ca, USA), followed by the fluorochrome second step reagent (anti-mouse IgG antibody labelled with fluorescein isothiocyanate, FITC). At least 200 cells were read in each experiment with a Leitz diavert fluorescence microscope.

A negative control was included in each preparation. The value of this control (background) was subtracted in the calculation of the results. The following MoAb were used: Leu1 (pan T), Leu2a (suppressor/cytotoxic), Leu3a (helper), Leu7 (killer/natural killer), LeuM3 (monocytes). The immunoreactivity of patients was evaluated on the basis of the helper/suppressor (Leu3a/Leu2a) ratio.

Statistical methods

Student's *t*-test, and Wilcoxon's matched pairs test were used for the statistical evaluation of the data obtained.

Results

Of 24 patients studied for CIC using the two methods described above, eight (33%) revealed the presence of CIC with at least one of the methods (one case with KgBt; six cases with C1qSp and one with both methods) (Figs 1 and 2).

Nineteen patients out of 24 were examined during ECH attacks and in normal periods. Seven (36.8%) of the 19 revealed a constant presence of CIC irrespective of their condition;

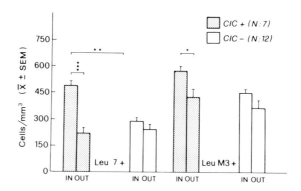

Fig. 3. *Episodic cluster headache patients divided in two subgroups: with circulating immune complexes (CIC+) and without (CIC−). *P<0.02 (Wilcoxon's matched pairs test); **P<0.01, ***P<0.001 (Student's t-test for paired and unpaired data).*

the sole exception was one patient who revealed CIC only during ECH crises. A second patient was positive to both methods during attacks, but only to one method (C1qSp) between attacks (Figs 1 and 2).

A marked increase of Leu7-positive subset (390 ± 50 *vs* 266 ± 36, $P<0.05$) and of LeuM3-positive subset (498 ± 25 *vs* 348 ± 42, $P<0.05$) was noted during the crises in the whole group of 19 ECH patients studied, confirming previous data[5,6,7].

When these 19 ECH patients, studied both for the CIC and for the leukocyte subsets, were divided in two subgroups (ie with and without CIC), the Leu7-positive and the LeuM3-positive subsets were increased only in the subgroup with CIC during ECH attacks (484 ± 24 *vs* 222 ± 26, $P<0.001$ and 571 ± 28 *vs* 451 ± 22, $P<0.02$ respectively) (Fig. 3).

The comparison of values of the same subset in the two subgroups measured during and between attacks revealed a significant increase in Leu7-positive cells in CIC-positive patients compared to the same cells in CIC-negative patients during ECH crises (484 ± 24 *vs* 293 ± 15, $P<0.01$) (Fig. 3).

Discussion

The results showed that the percentage of CIC-positive ECH patient was three or four times higher than in the normal population. In fact CIC have been reported to be present in only 10% of a normal control group[10]. No variations were observed between the incidence of CIC during crises and headache-free periods. Another point of interest demonstrated by this study is the confirmation that during the crises there is an increase of K, NK and monocyte cells but, above all, there was a striking correlation between this increase and the presence of CIC.

It is of particular interest that K cells can be directly activated by CIC via the binding to Fc-IgG receptor. Through this mechanism, K cells can release lymphokines and mediate damaging effects over the target[13]. The interaction between CIC and circulating monocytes may therefore initiate the release and/or modulation of vasoactive substances (ie serotonin)[14]. However, since the stimulating capacity of CIC has been previously reported, even on mast-cells which, as is well-known, release histamine[15], this aspect of the immunopathological status of CH may represent a profitable area for further research.

Acknowledgements—This work has been supported by grants from the National Research Council (C.N.R.) Target Project 'Preventive Medicine and Rehabilitation', Subproject 'Pain Control' no. 84.023458.56 and 85.00067.56.

References

1 Martelletti, P., Romiti, A., Gallo, M. F., Giacovazzo, M., Adorno, D., Valeri, M., Piazza, A., Monaco, P. I. & Casciani, C. U. (1984): HLA-B14 antigen in cluster headache. *Headache* **24**, 152–154.

2 Giacovazzo, M., Martelletti, P., Valeri, M., Piazza, A., Monaco, P. I. & Casciani, C. U. (1986): Variations in the Leu7 + and LeuM3 + subpopulations observed in cluster headache are dependent on HLA-DR antigens. *Headache* **26**, 315–316.

3 Giacovazzo, M., Martelletti, P., Romiti, A., Gallo, M. F. & Iuvara, E. (1985): Relationship between HLA system and clinical response to lithium therapy. *Headache* **25**, 268–280.

4 Giacovazzo, M., Martelletti, P., Romiti, A., Gallo, M. F., Iuvara, E., Valeri, M., Piazza, A., Adorno, D., Monaco, P. I. & Casciani, C. U. (1986): Genetic markers of cluster headache and the links with lithium salts therapy. *Int. J. Clin. Pharm. Res.* **6**, 19–22.

5 Giacovazzo, M. & Martelletti, P. (1985): Monocytes LeuM3 + and cluster headache: preliminary report. *Cephalalgia* **5**, (suppl. 3), 290–291.

6 Giacovazzo, M., Martelletti, P., Valeri, M., Piazza, A. & Casciani, C. U. (1986): A new immunological aspect of cluster headache: the increase of monocyte and NK cells populations. *Headache* **26**, 134–136.

7 Giacovazzo, M., Martelletti, P., Evangelista, B., Monaco, P. I., Tabilio, M. R. & Casciani, C. U. (1986): Lymphocyte and monocyte subsets in cluster headache: preliminary results. *EOS J. Immunol. Immunopharm.* **6**, 152–154.

8 Martelletti, P., Alteri, E., Rinaldi-Garaci, C., Pesce, A. & Giacovazzo, M. (1986): Defect of serotonin binding to mononuclear cells from the Episodic Cluster Headache patients. *Headache* **26**, 316.

9 Kudrow, L. (1980): *Cluster Headache: mechanisms and management*, pp. 67–68. London: Oxford Medical Publication.

10 Di Mario, U., Iavicoli, M. & Andreani, D. (1983): Circulating immune complexes in diabetes. *Diabetologia* **25**, 392–395.

11 Hay, F. C., Ninehan, L. J. & Roitt, I. M. (1976): Routine assay for the detection of immune complexes of known immunoglobulin class using solid state C1q. *Clin. Exp. Immunol.* **24**, 396–400.

12 Casali, P., Bossons, A., Carpentier, N. A. & Lambert, P. H. (1977): Solid phase enzyme immunoassay or radioimmunoassay for the detection of immune complexes on their recognition by conglutinin: conglutinin binding test. A comparative study with I labelled C1q binding and Raji cell RIA test. *Clin. Exp. Immunol.* **29**, 342–354.

13 Neville, M. E. & Lischner, H. W. (1981): Activation of Fc receptor bearing lymphocytes by immune complexes: killer limphocyte mediate Fc ligand induced lymphokine production. *J. Exp. Med.* **154**, 1868–1876.

14 Alteri, E. & Leonard, E. J. (1985): Serotonin: a possible modulator of human monocytes function. *J. Immunopharmacol.* **7**, 319–320.

15 Foreman, J. C., Garland, L. G. & Mongar, J. L. (1976): The role of calcium in secretory mast cells; model studies in mast cells. *Symp. Soc. Exp. Biol.* (Calcium Bio. System) **30**, 198–218.

31

IN VITRO BASOPHIL DEGRANULATION TESTS

AND NEUTROPHIL CHEMOTACTIC FACTOR

ACTIVITY IN CLUSTER HEADACHE PATIENTS

Jacek J. Rożniecki*, Beata Kuźmińska†,
Janina Grzegorczyk† and Antoni Prusiński*

*Department of Neurology, Medical School, 22 Kopcińskiego St.,
90–153 Lodz, Poland and †Clinical Immunology Laboratory of
Department of Allergology and Pneumonology, Medical School,
22 Kopcińskiego St., Lodz, Poland*

Summary

Human basophil sensitivity and releasability have been studied in some groups of patients suffering from cluster headache. We used basophil degranulation tests with Polymyxin B, nitroglycerine and D_2O (heavy water). We also estimated spontaneous basophil degranulation as well as the influence of plasma on basophil degranulation. Afterwards, neutrophil chemotactic factor activity as a basophil degranulation marker has been examined. We found significant increase of basophil degranulation to Polymyxin B, D_2O, and especially to nitroglycerine. Elevated neutrophil chemotactic factor activity in plasma during attacks confirmed the phenomenon of hypersensitivity and releasability of basophils in cluster headache attacks.

Introduction

The histamine hypothesis of cluster headache has been considered since 1939[1]. Increased whole blood histamine and histamine platelet rich plasma level[2] have been detected but there is still no evidence for an explicit role of histamine in the pathomechanism of cluster headache (CH). Basophils and mast cells contain a large amount of histamine and other mediators having vasoactive potency, so these cells might play an important role in this condition. Degranulating mast cells regarded as basophil equivalent in tissue, have been observed in the skin of the painful temporal area in CH subjects[3,4,5,6]. We tried to estimate basophil releasability and sensitivity using certain tests.

Patients and methods

In vitro spontaneous basophil degranulation after
incubation in comparison with the period before incubation

The study was carried out in 28 patients suffering from CH. The control group consisted of 22 healthy or CH subjects without attacks after nitroglycerine challenge. Partly using Benveniste's technique[7], blood from each patient was mixed with anticoagulant. Then 1.5 ml of blood was placed in two separated tubes. Blood plasma was separated by centrifugation and retained. Cellular elements of the centrifugation sediment were washed with buffer (pH 7.35) and then resuspended at the initial volume, in buffer solution. Ten μg of the suspension was placed in each of two wells of 'Microtiter Cooke System' plate. Toluidine blue (0.025%) solution (90 μl per well) was added to the first well and the number of basophils counted in a Fuchs-Rosenthal's chamber. After that, basophils on Cook plates were incubated at 37°C for 30 min and toluidine blue was added to the second well with basophil suspension. The number of basophils after incubation was counted and we assessed the degree of basophil degranulation during incubation. Only degranulation exceeding 30% in comparison with the control before incubation was considered to be positive and significant.

Spontaneous basophil degranulation during CH
attack in comparison with the period before attack

Patients and methods as previously.

Plasma influence on basophil degranulation

Twenty-four CH patients and 24 control subjects were admitted to the study. Basophils were obtained using the same technique as before. Plasma was added to basophils in the following way:
(1) Plasma obtained before attack or before nitroglycerine challenge in control group, to basophils obtained before attack or nitroglycerine challenge.
(2) Plasma obtained during attack or after nitroglycerine challenge to basophils obtained before attack or challenge.
(3) Plasma obtained before attack or challenge to basophils obtained during attack or after challenge.
(4) Plasma obtained during attack or after challenge to basophils obtained also during attack or after challenge.
   Basophils suspended in buffered saline was considered to be control. After same proceedings such as incubation and dye adding, basophils were counted in chamber and we compared final effect of serum influence on basophils with controls.

Basophil sensitivity to Polymyxin B (non-specific histamine and other mediators liberator)

We used formerly described Benveniste's technique with Polymyxin B in concentration 0.001 μg per ml added to basophils before incubation. Proceeding next as previously. Basophils incubated in buffered saline were considered as the control.

Table 1. *Spontaneous basophil degranulation after incubation in comparison with the period before incubation.*

	No.	Cluster headache Positive	Negative	No.	Control Positive	Negative
B_1 + NaCl	28	1 (4%)	27	22	0 (0%)	22
B_2 + NaCl	29	6 (21%)	23	22	1 (4%)	21

Table 2. *Spontaneous basophil degranulation during attacks in comparison with period before attacks.*

	No.	Cluster headache Positive	Negative	No.	Control Positive	Negative
B_2 + NaCl	28	4 (14%)	24	22	0 (0%)	22

Table 3. *Basophil degranulation depending on serum.*

	No.	Cluster headache Positive	Negative	No.	Control Positive	Negative
$B_1 + S_1$	25	1 (4%)	24	25	0 (0%)	25
$B_1 + S_2$	24	2 (8%)	22	24	2 (8%)	22
$B_2 + S_1$	24	7 (29%)	17	24	0 (0%)	24
$B_2 + S_2$	25	15 (60%)	10	25	0 (0%)	25

In vitro sensitivity of basophils to nitroglycerine, regarded as substance of provocative potency for CH attack

Parallel to the previous test, in place of Polymyxin B, we used nitroglycerine in three concentrations: 1, 0.1 and 0.01 μg per ml. The examination has been carried out in 19 CH patients and nine control subjects.

Basophil sensitivity to D_2O (heavy water)

Twelve patients suffering from CH and six healthy subjects were examined for basophil sensitivity to D_2O (44%), which is known as degranulation accelerator[8,9,10], all methods as previously.

Neutrophil chemotactic activity

The activity of neutrophil chemotactic factor (NCF) is well-known as a significant, characteristic marker of basophil and mast cell degranulation. Our study population consisted of 17 CH patients and 17 healthy subjects. The Nelson technique[11] was used. Blood from patients was obtained twice: first, before nitroglycerine challenge; second, during the attack or after challenge in the control group. Leucocytes were isolated from

Table 4. *Basophil reaction to polymyxin B.*

		Cluster headache			Control	
	No.	Positive	Negative	No.	Positive	Negative
B_1 + Poly-myxin B	21	5 (24%)	16	10	0 (0%)	10
B_2 + Poly-myxin B	21	12 (57%)	9	10	0 (0%)	10

Table 5. *Basophil reaction to nitroglycerine.*

		Cluster headache			Control	
	No.	Positive	Negative	No.	Positive	Negative
B_1 + Nitro-glycerine	19	11 (58%)	8	9	1 (11%)	8
B_2 + Nitro-glycerine	19	17 (90%)	2	9	1 (11%)	8

donors blood on high molecular dextran (2.2×10^8). Amounts were placed on the plate, in an eyelet of agarose gel mixed with Parker liquid, horse serum and antibiotic. Then, on both sides of leukocytes, at same distance and in similar eyelets, buffered saline and patients serum was placed. After a period of incubation we estimated index of NCF activity which was the proportion between distance covered by neutrophils in plasma direction to the distance covered to another, buffered saline direction. A ratio of at least 1.5 was considered as significantly increased. Then we repeated this procedure with plasma obtained during attack or after nitroglycerine challenge in control group. Our main purpose was to compare index before, with one during, the attack.

Results and discussion

In spontaneous basophil degranulating tests, we did not obtain any significant reaction of basophils during incubation in CH patients before attack but there was degranulation of basophils in six patients (21% of group) during attacks. We found no degranulation in control group of patients (only one patient expressed degranulation) (Table 1).

In comparing spontaneous basophil degranulation during CH attack with the period before attack, we found significant basophil degranulation only in four cases (14%) but there was no degranulation in controls (Table 2).

In tests of plasma influence on basophil degranulation we found significant degranulation of basophils obtained during attack, incubated with plasma obtained before attack in seven donors (29% of group). Even greater effect was found in the case of basophils obtained during attacks incubated with plasma also obtained during attacks. Significant degranulation occurred in 15 patients, ie 60% of CH group. We did not find any significant basophil degranulation in homologous arrangement in the control group (Table 3).

In the study with Polymyxin B, we found degranulation of basophils obtained before attack in five donors—24% of CH group. Degranulation of basophils obtained during attacks occurred in 12 cases—57% of CH patients. No degranulation was seen in the control group (Table 4).

Table 6. *Basophil degranulation depending on nitroglycerine concentration.*

		Cluster headache			Control	
	No.	Positive	Negative	No.	Positive	Negative
B$_1$ + 1 μg Nitro-glycerine	19	11 (58%)	8	9	1 (11%)	8
B$_1$ + 0.1 μg Nitro-glycerine	19	9 (47%)	10	9	0 (0%)	9
B$_1$ + 0.01 μg Nitro-glycerine	19	5 (26%)	14	9	0 (0%)	9
B$_2$ + 1 μg Nitro-glycerine	19	17 (90%)	2	9	1 (11%)	8
B$_2$ + 0.1 μg Nitro-glycerine	19	11 (58%)	7	9	0 (0%)	9
B$_2$ + 0.01 μg Nitro-glycerine	19	11 (58%)	7	9	0 (0%)	9

Table 7. *Basophil reaction to D$_2$O.*

		Cluster headache			Control	
	No.	Positive	Negative	No.	Positive	Negative
B$_1$ + D$_2$O	12	5 (42%)	7	6	0 (0%)	6
B$_2$ + D$_2$O	12	7 (58%)	5	6	0 (0%)	6

Table 8. *Index of neutrophil chemotactic activity in relation to period of attack.*

	Cluster headache			Control	
No.	Positive	Negative	No.	Positive	Negative
17	13 (77%)	4	17	3 (18%)	14

In tests with nitroglycerine, we found significant degranulation of basophils obtained before attacks in 11 donors (58%) and degranulation of basophils obtained during attack even in total group—in 17 patients ie 90% of CH group. With the exception of one case, there was no *in vitro* degranulation in any concentrations of the drug, neither before nor after nitroglycerine *in vivo* challenge in the control group (Tables 5 and 6). Degranulation was the most expressed with the highest concentration of drug.

In D$_2$O examinations we found that heavy water has the ability to potentiate (or provoke) basophil degranulation, especially cells obtained during attack. We observed significant basophil degranulation in five patients (42%) before attacks and in seven patients (58%) of CH group during attacks. There was no degranulation in controls (Table 7).

In the study of neutrophil chemotactic factor activity, there was significant increase of index during attacks in comparison with index from previous period in 13 patients (77%) of CH group. Only in three donors in control group was there an increase of NCF activity after nitroglycerine challenge but all those three patients had strong, very long-lasting headache the day following challenge (Table 8).

All these results lead to the following conclusions:

(1) We noted definite, albeit small, spontaneous releasability of basophils during attacks in CH patients.

(2) Plasma of CH patients, obtained especially during attacks, has the ability to increase degranulation of basophils obtained during attacks. Plasma does not exert this influence on basophils obtained before attacks.

(3) Non-specific histamine liberator (Polymyxin B) causes degranulation of CH patients basophils, especially those from patients during attacks. Polymyxin has no effect on basophils of donors from control group.

(4) Nitroglycerine, besides its *in vivo* cluster headache inducing action, causes *in vitro* significant degranulation almost in all CH patients, before as well as during attacks. In spite of this, it has no influence on basophils of patients from control group.

(5) D_2O (heavy water) an accelerator of basophil degranulation, significantly increases CH basophil degranulation, especially during attacks.

(6) Significant increase of NCF activity during CH attacks supports the concept regarding basophil degranulation phenomenon in pathological mechanism of cluster headache. However, we should remember that lymphocytes also produce some NCF. Our studies point to, after various stimulations, significant, spontaneous releasability and hypersensitivity of basophils of patients suffering from CH. It is still unknown whether this is due to endogenous or exogenous stimulus, excretion of certain amounts of histamine, serotonin, bradykinin, leukotrienes, prostaglandins etc, all of which can play an important vasoactive role. Increased releasability and hypersensitivity of basophils might also be caused, or elevated, by a kind of 'bath' of basophils in mediators released in serum. It still remains unknown whether this is a primary or secondary phenomenon.

Acknowledgements — This work was partly supported by grant of Psychoneurological Institute in Warsaw (1986). We thank Dr Pawel Górski and Dr Krzysztof Selmaj for their suggestions and advice.

References

1   Horton, B. T., Maclean, A. R. & Craig, W. M. (1939): A new syndrome of vascular headache: results of treatment with histamine: preliminary report. *Proc. Staff Meetings Mayo Clin.* **14**, 257–260.

2   Anthony, M. & Lance, J. W. (1971): Histamine and serotonin in cluster headache. *Arch. Neurol* **25**, 225–231.

3   Appenzeller, O., Becker, W. & Ragas, A. (1978): Cluster headache. Ultrastructural aspects. *Neurol.* **28**, 371.

4   Joseph, R., Dhital, K., Adams, J., Burnstock, G., Appenzeller, O. & Clifford Rose, F. (1985): In *Migraine, clinical and research advances*, ed F. Clifford Rose, pp. 162–165. Basel: Karger.

5   Prusiński, A. & Liberski, P. P. (1979): Is the cluster headache local mastocytic diathesis? *Headache* **19**, 102.

6   Liberski, P. P. & Prusiński, A. (1982): Further observations on the mast cells over the painful region in cluster headache patients. *Headache* **22**, 115–117.

7   Benveniste, J. (1981): The degranulation test as *in vitro* method for the diagnosis of allergies. *Clin. Allergy* **11**, 1.

8   Gillespie, E. & Lichtenstein, L. M. (1972). Histamine release from human leukocytes: studies with deuterium oxide colchicine and cytochalasin. *Br. J. Clin. Invest.* **51**, 2941.

9   Findlay, S. R. & Lichtenstein, L. M. (1980): Basophil 'releasability' in patients with asthma. *Am. Rev. Respir. Dis.* **122**, 53.

10 Editorial (1986): The concept of basophil releasability. *J. Allergy Clin. Immunol.* **77**, 291–294.

11 Nelson, R. D., Guic, P. G. & Simmon, L. (1975): Chemotaxis under agarose; a new and simple method for measuring chemotaxis and spontaneous migration of human polymorphonuclear leukocytes and mastocytes. *J. Immunol.* **115**, 6.

32

LEUKOTRIENE B$_4$ LEVELS IN MIGRAINE

AND CLUSTER HEADACHE

K. Selmaj*‡, J. de Belleroche*, I. Das*, E. Ansell†*, T. Fazzone†,
M. Wilkinson† and F. Clifford Rose*

*Academic Unit of Neuroscience,
Charing Cross and Westminster Medical School,
London and †The City of London Migraine Clinic, London, UK

Summary

Leukotriene B$_4$ (LTB$_4$) levels in plasma and its generation *in vitro* from isolated polymorphonuclear leukocytes (PMN) were measured in migraine and cluster headache (CH) patients during and between attacks. The LTB$_4$ plasma levels in CH patients during an attack were significantly higher than in patients between attacks. There was a positive correlation between the time of sampling from the beginning of attack and the LTB$_4$ level. The LTB$_4$ plasma levels in migraine patients during and between attacks did not differ significantly from control levels. The results suggest that LTB$_4$ appears rapidly in the circulation at the beginning of a cluster attack and thereafter declines in amount. Leukotriene B$_4$ release from PMN was induced by stimulation with the calcium ionophore A23187. The release of LTB$_4$ was significantly higher in migraine patients during attacks on stimulation with the lowest applied dose of A23187 (0.5 μM). Leukotriene B$_4$ release induced by A23187 in migraine patients during symptom-free intervals and cluster headache patients did not differ from healthy controls. Leukotriene B$_4$ release was not affected by 5HT and noradrenaline in concentrations up to 10^{-4} M. The results suggest that LTB$_4$ is more easily generated in migraine patients during attacks. These studies on isolated cells proved to be suitable model for the investigation of the metabolism of lipoxygenase derivatives in headache patients.

‡Permanent address: Department of Neurology, Medical Academy of Lodz, Poland.

Introduction

Leukotrienes (LTs) are a novel group of highly potent proinflammatory mediators derived from arachidonic acid (AA) via the lipoxygenase pathway[1]. LTs can be divided into two groups, both derived from unstable LTA_4, peptidyloleukotrienes (LTC_4, LTD_4 and LTE_4) previously known as $SRS-A_1$ and LTB_4. Leukotriene B_4 is a potent chemotactic factor, but also induces hyperalgesia[2], enhances vascular permeability[3] and adhesion of polymorphonuclear leukocytes (PMN) to endothelial cells[4]. All these properties prompted us to investigate the role of LTB_4 in the pathogenesis of migraine and cluster headache.

Methods

Assay of plasma levels of LTB_4-immunoreactivity (LTB_4) in patients
during attacks and in symptom-free intervals as well as in control subjects

The subjects were 14 patients with migraine and eight patients with cluster headache attending the Princess Margaret Migraine Clinic, Charing Cross Hospital, London, and the City of London Migraine Clinic, the diagnosis being made on the basis of accepted clinical criteria[5].

The migraine group consisted of five males and nine females, age ranging from 27 to 40 years (mean 32); three patients suffered from classical migraine and the others from common migraine. Ten patients were studied during their attacks and ten during symptom-free intervals at least 3 days after the end of last attack; nine of them were studied both during and between attacks.

The cluster headache group consisted of six males and two females, age ranged from 24–40 years (mean 33). All suffered from the episodic form of cluster headache and all were studied during a cluster period. Blood samples were taken during spontaneous attacks, six cluster headache patients being sampled a second time in the subsequent pain-free interval after at least 4 h. Two patients were sampled three times: twice during attacks and a third time after attacks. No patient received either prophylactic treatment or symptomatic treatment during the study. All were well apart from having headache and no patient suffered a cold for at least 2 weeks before sampling.

The control group consisted of eight healthy subjects, three males and five females, age 27 to 51 years (mean 34).

Peripheral blood was collected into EDTA tubes and centrifuged at 600 g for 10 min at 4°C. Plasma was collected and stored at −20°C before assay. Partial purification of plasma samples was carried out using Sep-Pak C_{18} cartridges (Water Associates, Millipore, UK)[6]. Samples were then assayed by radioimmunoassay using a Leukotriene-B_4 /^{3}H/ radioimmunoassay kit (Amersham International, UK).

Release of LTB_4 from PMN isolated from cluster
headache and migraine patients compared to controls

The subjects were 13 migraine patients and six cluster headache patients attending the Princess Margaret Migraine Clinic, Charing Cross Hospital, London, UK, the diagnosis being made on the basis of accepted clinical criteria[5].

The migraine group consisted of three males and nine females, age ranging from 24 to 44 years (mean 32). Six suffered from classical migraine and six from common migraine. Nine patients were studied during symptom-free intervals at least 3 days after the attack.

Four patients with common migraine were studied during typical migraine attacks at the peak of pain. One patient was studied both during and between attacks.

The cluster group consisted of six males, age ranging from 28 to 50 years (mean 42). All suffered from the episodic form of cluster headaches and were studied between attacks during a cluster period.

The control group consisted of three males and four females, age 25 to 32 years (mean 29). No patient of the control group received prophylactic or symptomatic treatment during this study and all were well apart from having headache. No subject suffered a cold for at least 1 month before sampling.

Blood was taken into EDTA tubes for preparation of PMN[7]. The cells were next incubated in Krebs buffer (0.4 ml) at 37°C with calcium ionophore A23187 (0.5–10.0 μM), 5HT (10^{-5} and 10^{-4} M) and noradrenaline (10^{-5} and 10^{-4} M) for 5–30 min. Incubation was terminated by centrifugation at 12 000 g for 30 s and the cell-free supernatants collected and stored at -20°C before radioimmunoassay of LTB$_4$.

LTB$_4$ immunoreactivity released during incubation was determined by radioimmunoassay using LTB$_4$/^{3}H/assay kit (Amersham, UK).

Results

Plasma levels of LTB$_4$

Plasma levels of LTB$_4$ were detected in all groups investigated (Fig. 1). In control subjects the levels ranged from 0.253 nM to 0.476 nM with a mean value of ($\pm$s.e.m.) of 0.311 ± 0.024. No correlation was observed between LTB$_4$ levels and sex or age in the control group.

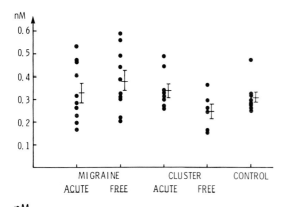

Fig. 1. *Plasma levels of i-LTB$_4$.* Each point represents an individual subject. The mean value for each group is shown and the s.e.m. indicated by a bar.

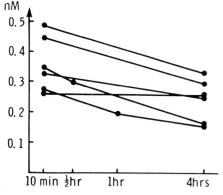

Fig. 2. *Plasma levels of i-LTB$_4$ in cluster headache patients during and after headache.* Plasma samples were taken from each subject both during an attack (first point) and after the attack (final point).

Levels of LTB$_4$ in migraine patients, both during attacks and in symptom-free intervals, were not significantly different from controls but tended to be higher, being 0.334 ± 0.04 nM and 0.385 ± 0.043 nM respectively. Samples taken at different times after the onset of attack showed no correlation between levels of LTB$_4$ and the time of sampling. In contrast, in cluster headache patients, plasma levels of LTB$_4$ during attacks were significantly elevated ($P < 0.05$) when compared with the levels in symptom-free intervals (Fig. 2) showing a clear decline after the attack (duration up to 2 h).

Release of LTB$_4$ from isolated PMN

The LTB$_4$ release from unstimulated PMN was 8.6 pg ± 8.6/10^6 cells in the control group, whilst in the other groups the release of LTB$_4$ from unstimulated PMN was higher, although not significantly: migraine free (21.8 ± 15.0), migraine acute (22.7 ± 17.1) and cluster headache (20.7 ± 12.0).

At a concentration of 0.5 μM A23187-induced LTB$_4$ release from PMN was greatest in acute migraine (8856 ± 640 pg/10^6 cells) compared to control subjects (4634 ± 620 pg/10^6 cells: $P < 0.02$) and was also significantly greater than the release evoked in migraine patients between attacks (4816 ± 865 pg/10^6 cells; $P < 0.05$). The LTB$_4$ release in migraine patients in symptom-free periods and in cluster headache patients (5480 ± 1487 pg/10^6 cells) were comparable with the release in control subjects (Fig. 3).

At a dose of 1.0 μM A23187 the release of LTB$_4$ showed a similar trend. The release of LTB$_4$ from PMN was unaffected by incubation in the presence of 5HT or NA up to a concentration of 10^{-4} M in all groups investigated.

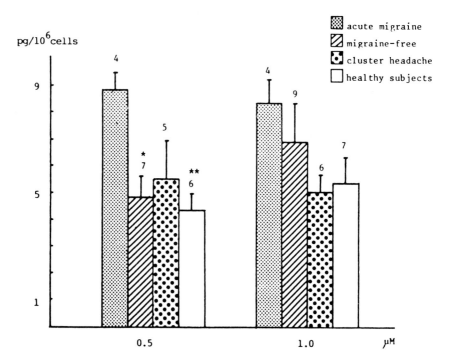

Fig. 3. *Values are means with s.e.m.s shown by bars and the number of subjects indicated and *, ** indicates that the value is significantly less than for acute migraine patients, $P < 0.02$, $P < 0.05$ respectively.*

Discussion

We found significantly increased level of plasma LTB$_4$ in cluster headache patients during attacks. The positive correlation between the time of sampling from the beginning of the attack and the LTB$_4$ levels suggests that LTB$_4$ appears rapidly in the circulation at the onset of the attack. In contrast, plasma LTB$_4$ in migraine patients during attacks did not differ from LTB$_4$ levels during symptom-free intervals. These results suggest that no changes occur in circulating levels of LTB$_4$ in migraine, but we were unable to study migraine patients immediately after the onset of the attack. Since the time of sampling ranged from 1¼ to 10 h into the attacks, any rapid and transient effect on LTB$_4$ levels could have been missed.

Leukotriene B$_4$ release from PMN upon stimulation with the calcium ionophore A23187 was not different in cluster headache patients during the active stage of the condition from that of control subjects. As we had found a positive correlation between the high LTB$_4$ plasma level and the time of blood sampling from the beginning of cluster attacks, this suggests that the source of elevated plasma LTB$_4$ levels in cluster headache patients is not PMN. Leukotrienes can be generated by a wide variety of cells and tissues, including blood vessels,[8] so that a local production of LTB$_4$ within the region of pain might be indicated. The increased ionophore stimulated release of LTB$_4$ *in vitro* from PMN in migraine patients during attacks may reflect the state of activation of these cells during migraine attacks. Calcium ionophore induced changes in calcium concentration in the cell may be responsible for activation of phospholipase A$_2$ and lipoxygenase[9] which in turn results in de novo LTB$_4$ synthesis and release[10]. Physiological cell activation via receptors also finally leads to a calcium influx[11]. The greater release of LTB$_4$ at submaximal doses of A23187 would suggest that PMN had already been activated during migraine attacks by unknown factors. It is well-known that platelet hyperaggregability occurs in migraine patients during attacks[12], a process which is also calcium dependent and a similar basis for both these phenomena could be postulated. Similar explanations could also apply to the increased release of histamine from basophils in migraine patients[13]. Alternatively, platelet derived arachidonate may serve as a precursor for the PMN-derived LTB$_4$[14]. It is difficult at the moment to assess the role of activated cells (platelets, basophils, PMN) in peripheral blood during migraine attacks, but platelet hyperaggregability is probably not important for migraine genesis[15]. Although activated PMN could well be associated with sterile inflammation as one possible mechanism causing migraine attacks, more studies are needed to elucidate this point. The use of isolated PMNs in this study proved to be a suitable model for the investigation of the metabolism of lipoxygenase derivatives in headache patients.

The pathophysiology of cluster headache is unknown but several data suggest that extracranial arteries are the site of the pain[16]. Various vasoactive and pro-inflammatory mediators are therefore candidates as possible causative agents. Non-steroidal anti-inflammatory drugs are not effective in cluster headache[17] suggesting that prostanoids are not of primary importance, but steroids, which inhibit AA formation, can be very effective in terminating the cluster period[18], indicating that lipoxygenase derivates might be involved. Leukotriene B$_4$ mediates hyperalgesia in animals[3] and humans[19], achieving a maximum level at 20 min and then reducing slowly, which correlates well with the duration of a cluster attack. The vasoactive properties of LTB$_4$ such as vasoconstriction and increasing plasma leakage[20], could easily contribute to the other clinical features of cluster attack, such as rhinorrhoea and lacrimation. Whether the increase of LTB$_4$ levels at the beginning of cluster attacks represents a genuine pathophysiological mechanism or is yet another epiphenomenon related to pain must be a subject for further study.

References

1 Piper, P. J. (1984): Formation and action of leukotrienes. *Physiol. Rev.* **64**, 749–761.
2 Levine, J. D., Lau, W., Kwiat, G. & Goetzel, E. J. (1984): Leukotriene B$_4$ produces hyperalgesia that is dependent of polymorphonuclear leukocytes. *Science* **25**, 743–745.
3 Bray, M. A., Cunningham, E. M., Ford-Hutchinson, A. W. & Smith, M. J. H. (1981): Leukotriene B$_4$: a mediator of vascular permeability. *Br. J. Pharmacol.* **72**, 483–486.
4 Gimbrone, M. A., Brock, A. F., Schafer, A. L. (1984): Leukotriene B$_4$ stimulates polymorphonuclear leukocyte adhesion to cultured vascular endothelial cells. *J. Clin. Invest.* **74**, 1552–1555.
5 Clifford Rose, F. (1985): Definition of headache. In *Handbook of clinical neurology* Vol. 34. eds G. W. Bruyn, P. Vinken & F. Clifford Rose. Amsterdam: Elsevier.
6 Das, I. (1984): Improved sample preparation and rapid extraction of prostacyclin and thromboxane metabolites from biological samples by using reversed phase octadecylsilyl-silica cartridges. *Biochem. Soc. Trans.* **12**, 834–835.
7 Dooley, D. C., Simpson, J. F. & Meryman, H. T. (1982): Isolation of large numbers of fully viable human neutrophils: A preparative technique using percoll density gradient centrifugation. *Exp. Hematol.* **10**, 591–599.
8 Piper, P. J., Letts, L. G. & Galton, S. A. (1983): Generation of a leukotriene like substance from porcine vascular and other tissues. *Prostaglandins* **25**, 591–599.
9 Lapetina, E. G. & Cuatrecasas, P. (1979): Stimulation of phosphatidic acid production in platelets precedes the formation of arachidonate and parallels the release of serotonin. *Biochem. Biophys. Acta* **573**: 394–402.
10 Borgeat, P. & Samuelsson, B. (1982): Arachidonic acid metabolism in polymorphonuclear leukocytes: Effect of ionophore A23187. *Proc. Natn. Acad. Sci.* **43**, 115–118.
11 Lapetina, E. G. (1982): Regulation of arachidonic acid production: role of phospholipases C and A$_2$. *Trends Pharmacol. Sci.* **43**, 115–118.
12 Hanington, E. (1978): Migraine: a blood disorder? *Lancet* **ii**, 501–502.
13 Selmaj, K. (1984): Histamine release from leukocytes during migraine attack. *Cephalalgia* **4**, 97–100.
14 Marcus, A. J., Broekman, M. J., Safier, L. B., Ullman, H. L., Islam, N., Serhan, C. N. & Weissman, G. (1984): Production of arachidonic acid lipoxygenase products during platelet-neutrophil interaction. *Clin. Physiol. Biochem.* **2**, 78–83.
15 Steiner, T. J., Joseph, R. & Clifford Rose, F. (1986): Migraine is not a platelet disorder. *Headache* (In press).
16 Kudrow, L. (1986): Cluster headache. Mechanism and management, pp. 99–126. London: Oxford University Press.
17 Lance, J. W. (1982): Mechanism and management of headache, pp. 205–226. London: Butterworth.
18 Jammes, J. L. (1975): The treatment of cluster headache with prednisone. *Dis. Nerv. Syst.* **36** 375–376.
19 Lewis, R. A., Soter, N. A., Corey, E. J. & Austen, K. F. (1981): Local effects of synthetic leukotrienes on monkey and human skin. *Clin. Res.* **29**, 492A.
20 Rosenblum, W. I. (1985): Constricting effect of leukotrienes on cerebral arterioles of mice. *Stroke* **16**, 262–263.

33

PLASMA METHIONINE-ENKEPHALIN LEVELS

IN PATIENTS WITH CLUSTER HEADACHE.

LONGITUDINAL AND ACUTE STUDIES

Seymour Diamond*†, Aron Mosnaim*, Frederic Freitag†,
Marion Wolf‡, Gerald Lee* and Glen Solomon†

*University of Health Sciences/The Chicago Medical School,
3333 Green Bay Road, N. Chicago, IL 60064, USA;
†Diamond Headache Clinic, 5252 N. Western Avenue, Chicago,
IL 60625, USA and ‡Loyola University, Stritch School of
Medicine, Maywood, IL 60153, USA

Summary

In a longitudinal study and when compared to controls, chronic cluster headache patients showed a wider variation of plasma methionine-enkephalin levels with single values usually below or at the lower end of the controls range. The average peptide concentration for individual patients (repeated measurements, four out of four) were statistically significantly lower than those of controls. In general, an acute cluster headache crisis is associated with important and rapid changes in the circulating levels of methionine-enkephalin. Using each patient as its own control, our results show a dramatic increase in this peptide during the 'precluster' period, rapidly decreasing to 'basal' values in the 'during crisis' phase and falling even farther during the 'postcluster' period.

Introduction

The onset of the active period of a cluster headache (CH) is associated with changes in the plasma and cerebrospinal fluid levels of a number of endogenous chemicals, the biological activities of which cover a wide range of physiological functions (see review by Edmeads[1]). Whereas most published research has been directed towards the elucidation of the possible role of circulating vasoactive substances and their regulatory enzymes in the aetiology of CH[1-5], some recent work has attempted to dissect out the

209

vascular events from the mechanisms involved in the abnormal modulation of the pain response observed in these patients[6,7]. As a model for this work, several authors have studied the endogenous opioid peptides system(s) in these subjects, as these substances (enkephalins, endorphins and dynorphins) have different degrees of antinociceptive properties and show agonist activity at the 'opiate receptor' site(s)[8,9] (review by Frederickson[10]). We now present the results of a longitudinal study of the plasma methionine[5] enkephalin (MET) levels in a group of successfully drug treated chronic CH patients (CCH). We have also analysed this peptide in the plasma of active CCH patients immediately prior to, during, and rapidly after, an acute CH episode.

Patients and methods

Longitudinal study

Subjects participating in this blind protocol were white, male outpatients ($n = 4$) of the Diamond Headache Clinic, Chicago, Illinois, diagnosed as suffering from CCH[11], and race and sex-matched, drug-free, healthy controls ($n = 3$). Single blood samples of a similar group of controls ($n = 19$) were also analysed for MET concentration; blood was always collected, between 10:00 a.m. and 2:00 p.m. During the course of this study, patients, free of other illness [age and age of onset of CCH; (1) 25 and 27, (2) 34 and 41, (3) 18 and 46, (4) 20 and 28 years of age, respectively], were taking nimodipine (30–40 mg twice daily) and one or more drugs which included non-narcotic analgesics, lithium and antidepressants. Blood samples were drawn once or twice a month during a period of 182 to 298 days; patients were in remission of their CCH, and subjects 3 and 4 suffered daily headaches and 'headaches between clinic visits', respectively.

Episodic study

Subjects ($n = 8$) participating in this blind protocol were white, male inpatients of the Diamond Headache Treatment Unit of Weiss Memorial Hospital, Chicago, Illinois, suffering from CCH. At the time of this study, patients were on Eskalith (A,B,C,D and E), verapamil + aminotriptyline (F), reserpine (G), or ergotamine tartrate + thorazine (H) (see Fig. 4). Blood was drawn prior to, during, and rapidly after, an acute CH crisis.

Blood drawn for either study (approximately 20 ml into EDTA-containing vacutainer tubes) was immediately centrifuged ($780 \times g$, 10 min), and one-half of the supernatant centrifuged again ($3000 \times g$, 10 min). The platelet pellet and both the platelet rich and platelet poor fractions, each divided into two equal aliquots, were stored in plastic tubes ($-20°C$) until analysed for MET by radioimmunoassay[12] (Fig. 1). Values reported in this study were obtained from the platelet poor plasma samples. Results are the average of the same sample analysed in duplicate, and have been individually corrected for percentage of recovery (range of 59–91%). Intra-assay and inter-assay coefficients of variation were 8.4 ± 0.1 and 10.4 ± 1.3, respectively.

Results

Figures 2 and 3 (longitudinal study) are representative of the 'basic profile' of plasma MET levels in CCH patients (during remission, drug treated) and race, and sex-matched controls ($n = 4$ and 3, respectively; more detailed results to be published elsewhere). Figure 3 also shows the results obtained from a single blood drawing from a group of 19 similarly matched

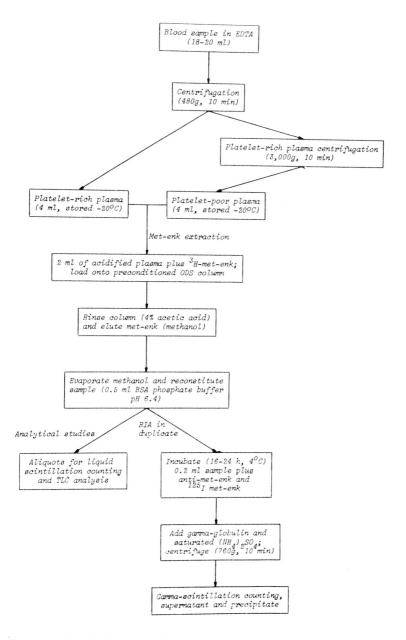

Fig. 1. *Determination of plasma methionine-enkephalin by radioimmunoassay.*

controls (range and mean ± s.d. of 57–119 and 89 ± 18 pg MET/ml platelet poor plasma). When compared to controls, headache patients showed a wider variation of the plasma MET concentration, with single values (longitudinal study) usually below or at the lower end of the controls range. Furthermore, the average peptide concentration for individual patients (four out of four, repeated measurements over a 9 to 12 month period) are statistically significantly lower than those of controls (Figs 2 and 3).

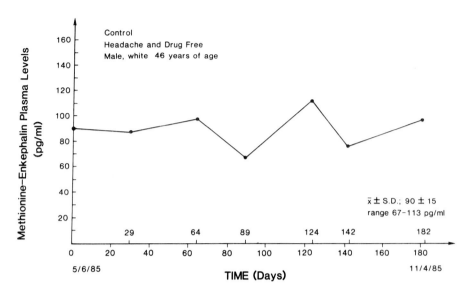

Fig. 2. *Plasma methionine-enkephalin levels.* Longitudinal study, control.

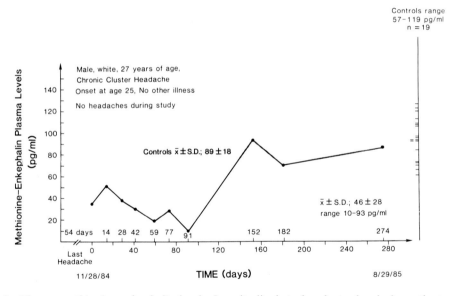

Fig. 3. *Plasma methionine-enkephalin levels.* Longitudinal study, cluster headache patient.

Figure 4 shows the changes in plasma MET levels accompanying an acute episode of CH in CCH patients. Samples were drawn closely prior to (precluster), during (acute pain), and soon after, the acute painful phase (postcluster) of the headache. Five out of the eight subjects studied (A,B,C,F and H) showed 'precluster' plasma MET levels significantly higher than their own values obtained during the 'acute pain' phase. Whereas one subject (E) had the latter value higher than its 'precluster' MET concentration, all six subjects presented 'precluster' plasma MET levels significantly higher than the baseline MET concentration showed by both CCH and controls (Figs 2, 3 and 4). During the 'acute pain' phase, peptide

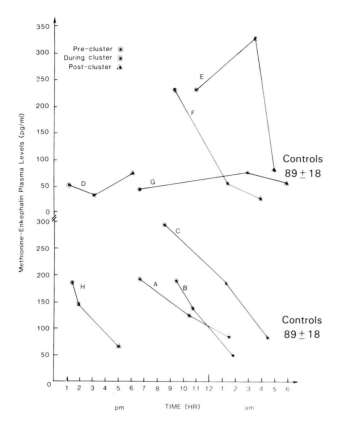

Fig. 4. *Plasma methionine-enkephalin levels during a cluster headache crisis (eight patients).*

levels showed a wide range with patients having values significantly higher than (A,B,C,E and H) or falling within baseline range (F) for CCH (Fig. 2). In seven out of eight patients (see D) studied, the 'postcluster' plasma MET levels were lower than corresponding 'acute pain' concentration, falling within the baseline range values for CCH (Fig. 2). In two of the eight subjects (D and G) we failed to detect significant changes in plasma peptide concentration during the different stages of the cluster attack, with MET concentration remaining within baseline levels (Figs 2 and 4).

Discussion

The naturally occurring families of peptides, endorphins, dynorphins and enkephalins, are widely distributed in the central nervous system and peripheral tissues and fluids[10,13], where their pathways of biosynthesis and degradation, as well as the mechanisms regulating their storage and release, are under vigorous investigation[10,13,14]. Similarly to what has initially happened with other emergent areas of research, these substances have been postulated to play a number of physiological roles, exert a variety of pharmacological actions and be of some importance in the mechanisms involved in the pathophysiology of several disease conditions (for reviews see Frederickson[10] and Watson[13]). Based largely on their antinociceptive properties[13,15,16] and the agonist activity shown by these peptides at the opiate receptor site(s)[8,9,13], it has been suggested that these substances play a role in the modulation of the pain response. In this framework, the hypothesis (Sicuteri and others) that alterations in the endogenous opioid-like peptide system(s) are responsible for the pain observed during vascular headaches has received a great deal of attention. Testing this hypothesis has produced, however, conflicting results[6,7,12,17-22].

In a longitudinal study we have now analysed the 'basic' profile of plasma MET levels in CCH patients and compared it with that of controls (both, studied over time, $n = 3$, or single samples, $n = 19$). Patients consistently showed a wider variation of the plasma peptide concentration, with single values (same patient, over time) usually below or in the lower end of the controls range (Figs 2 and 3; similar results were obtained for the other subjects studied). Furthermore, plasma MET concentration in cluster patients (average of repeated measurements in same individual, four out of four patients) were significantly lower than those of migraineurs either during a migraine attack or when 'pain-free'[12,21], reflecting perhaps, a basic difference in the functional state of the MET system between cluster and migraine headache patients.

Results from the 'episodic study' suggest that the occurrence of a CH crisis in a population of CCH patients could be generally expected (six out of eight subjects) to be accompanied by important changes in plasma MET levels. Using each patient as its own control and by comparing plasma peptide levels with those of CCH in a remission state (Fig. 3) it can be seen that plasma MET values are usually dramatically raised closely before the 'acute pain' stage, falling during this phase to levels still higher or similar to baseline, and in every case decreasing further during the post 'acute pain' period to values within the range for CCH patients. In discussing these results it should be kept in mind that, due to the very nature of this research protocol, the timing of blood drawing is set with a different degree of subjectivity, therefore making it rather imprecise to relate the results obtained to the different 'phases' of the cluster headache. As seen in Fig. 4, there is considerable time variation between the taking of 'precluster' and 'during crisis', and 'during crisis' and 'postcluster', samples for the different patients. Although it is tempting to speculate that the observed changes in plasma MET levels associated with the different stages of the cluster attack have some direct relationship to the pain accompanying the headache, there is still no firm evidence to substantiate the hypothesis that circulating MET concentration reflects either the intensity or the nature of the pain suffered by these patients; obviously more work is needed in this area of research.

Acknowledgements—We wish to thank Mr Jorge Chevesich, Ms Kathy Lazzara and the staff of Weiss Memorial Hospital involved in this project for excellent technical assistance. This project was funded, in part, by the National Migraine Foundation.

References

1 Edmeads, J. (1984): Pathophysiologic aspects of cluster headache. In *Cluster headache*, ed. N. Mathew, pp. 57–67. New York: SP Medical & Scientific Books.

2 Horton, B. T., MacLean, A. R. & Craig, W. M. (1939): A new syndrome of vascular headache: result of treatment with histamine: Preliminary report. *Proc. Staff Meet. Mayo Clin.* **14**, 257–260.

3 Anthony, M. & Lance, J. W. (1971): Histamine and serotonin in cluster headache. *Arch Neurol.* **25**, 225–231.

4 Medina, J. L., Diamond, S. & Fareed, J. (1979): The nature of cluster headache. *Headache* **19**, 309–322.

5 Bennett, A., Magnaes, B., Sandler, M. & Sjaastad, O. (1974): Prostaglandins and headache. In *Background to Migraine, Sixth Migraine Symposium*, London: Heinemann.

6 Anselmi, B., Baldi, E., Casacci, F. & Salmon, S. (1980): Endogenous opioids in cerebrospinal fluid and blood in idiopathic headache sufferers. *Headache* **20**, 294–299.

7 Mosnaim, A. D., Wolf, M. E., Freitag, F. G. & Diamond, S. (1986): Differences in plasma methionine-enkephalin levels between migraine and cluster headache patients. *Headache* **26**, 315.

8 Lord, J. A., Waterfield, A. A., Hughes, J. & Kosterlitz, H. W. (1977): Endogenous opioid peptides: Multiple agonists and receptors. *Nature* **267**, 495–499.

9 Wood, P. L. (1982): Multiple opiate receptors: Support for unique mu, delta and kappa sites. *Neuropharmacol.* **21**, 487–497.

10 Frederickson, R. C. (1977): Enkephalin pentapeptides — A review of current evidence for a physiological role in vertebrate neurotransmission. *Life Sci.* **23**, 23–42.

11 Diamond, S. (1984): Variants of cluster headache. In *Cluster headache*, ed. N. Mathew, pp. 21–23. New York: SP Medical & Scientific Books.

12 Mosnaim, A. D., Wolf, M. E., Chevesich, B. S., Callaghan, O. H. & Diamond, S. (1985): Plasma methionine enkephalin levels. A biological marker for migraine? *Headache* **25**, 259–261.

13 Watson, S. J., Akil, H., Khachaturian, H., Young, E. & Lewis, M. E. (1983): Opioid systems: anatomical physiological and clinical perspectives. In *Opioids: past present and future*, eds J. Hughes, H. Collier, M. Rance & M. Tyers, pp. 145–170. London: Taylor & Francis.

14 Hersh, B. (1982): Degradation of enkephalins: the search for an enkephalinase. *Mol. Cell. Biochem.* **47**, 35–43.

15 Hill, R. G. (1981): The status of naloxone in the identification of pain control mechanisms operated by endogenous opioids. *Neurosci. Lett.* **21**, 217–222.

16 Sicuteri, F. (1982): Natural opioids in migraine. In *Advances in neurology*, eds M. Critchley, A. Friedman, S. Gorini & F. Sicuteri, p. 33, pp. 65–74. New York: Raven Press.

17 Fettes, I., Gawel, M. Kuzniak, S. & Edmeads, J. (1983): Endorphin levels in headache syndromes. *Headache* **23**, 142.

18 Facchinetti, F., Nappi, G., Savoldi, G. & Genazzani, A. R. (1981): Primary headaches: reduced circulating B-lipotropin and B-endorphin levels with impaired reactivity to acupuncture. *Cephalalgia* **1**, 195–201.

19 Genazzani, A. R., Nappi, G., Facchinetti, F., *et al.* (1984): Progressive impairment of CSF B-EP levels in migraine sufferers. *Pain* **18**, 127–133.

20 Spillantini, M. G., Fanciullacci, M., Di Tommaso, M., Raino, L. & Sicuteri, F. (1984): Enkephalinase activity in human cerebrospinal fluid and in plasma in both physiological and pathological conditions. In *Central and peripheral endorphins: basic and clinical aspects*, eds E. E. Muller & A. R. Genazzani, pp. 309–313. New York: Raven Press.

21 Mosnaim, A. D., Chevesich, J., Wolf, M. E., Freitag, F. G. & Diamond, S. (1986): Plasma methionine enkephalin. Increased levels during a migraine episode. *Headache* **26**, 278–280.

22 Bach, F. W., Jensen, K., Blegvad, M., Fenger, M., Jordal, R. & Olesen, J. (1985): B-endorphin and ACTH in plasma during attacks of common and classic migraine. *Cephalalgia* **5**, 177–182.

V

CHRONIC HEADACHE

34

WORD PREFERENCES IN HEADACHE PATIENTS

H. Isler and M. Regard

*Department of Neurology, University Hospital,
Zurich, Switzerland*

Introduction

'Operative' attitudes: emotional defence?

Attempts to quantify characteristic behaviour patterns of headache patients by traditional psychologic test batteries and inventories have been inconclusive.

The 'neurotic' sign of the 'inverted V' in the Minnesota Multi-Phasic Inventory (MMPI) and its successors is found less often in headache than in various chronic functional pain syndromes, and in dependency on instant relief medication. Discriminance analysis of test battery results allowed a special locus to primary headache as compared with heavy metal poisoning, vertebrobasilar insufficiency, and post head-trauma syndrome only with the help of the clinical symptoms[1].

On the other hand, stimulus perception appears to be modified in headache patients[2,3,4,5], and analgesic effects have been shown to be as sex-dependent[6] as the prevalence of primary headache syndromes. Both sets of observations indicate modifications of higher cerebral strategies. This led us to expect that characteristic behaviour patterns associated with primary headache could be defined by less complicated neuropsychological methods.

From our observations of synchronous unilateral headache associated with hemispheric dysfunction recorded by depth probe EEG[7] we inferred that changes in specific hemisphere functions might correspond to headache lateralization. Such correlations had been reported in 1984[8].

We first looked for differences of handedness between headache patients and the general population but we found only a trend towards more right-handers in headache patients. We went on to compare lateralization of hemicrania with handedness but there was no correspondence.

Tradition has it that migraine patients, and headache patients in general, are perfectionistic. A comprehensive clinical study by Wolff (1948, 1963)[9] showed that this was only one of many personality features and life situations related to migraine but this insight was subsequently diluted into routine application of personality inventories originally designed for rapid detection of gross psychotic illness or organic brain damage in recruits.[10] However, Wolff's study, which has not been surpassed despite its age, clearly shows the paramount importance of emotional responses in the course of migraine.

In our own clinical assessment of behaviour patterns, the one salient feature among many less specific traits was the tendency of headache patients to prefer impersonal, detached, 'objective' answers and technicalities without emotional connotations over more personal, 'subjective' answers with emotional connotations. Similar attitudes had been described in headache patients as 'pensée opératoire'[11], and in 'psychosomatic' patients as 'alexithymia'[12].

Sifneos, who coined the latter term in 1973[12], used a short questionnaire where he pointed out 8 of 17 questions as 'key alexithymic questions', namely: 'does the patient
(1) Describe endless details rather than feelings?
(2) Use appropriate words to describe emotion?
(6) Have a rich fantasy life?
(7) Use action to express emotion?
(8) Use action to avoid conflicts?
(12) Tend to describe circumstances surrounding an event rather than feelings?
(13) Have difficulty to communicate?
(16) Is the thought content associated more with external events than with fantasy or emotion?'

Nemiah *et al.* (1975)[13] then went on to explain 'alexithymia' in terms of absence of neuronal connections of the palaeostriatal dopaminergic tract, obviously feeling that their observations must be correlated to modified cerebral function which they simply equated to hypothetical structural deficit.

Sifneos' questionnaire appears more realistic than the personality inventories since it is more concerned with emotional attitudes but the hypothesis of structural deficit proposed by his group shows that his concept is quite static. His approach to the patient relied on highly controlled, indirect verbal description, leaving little room for spontaneous on-the-spot decisions. His explanation of his own term 'alexithymia' is 'from the Greek, a = lack, lexis = word, thymos = mood or emotion': inability to read one's own emotions. (This interpretation is linguistically untenable since in ancient as well as in modern 'purified' Greek, alexi—means something that wards off, as in alexikakos, a talisman to ward off evil, or in alexibrschion, an umbrella that protects from rain.) Understanding 'alexithymia' as 'defence against emotions' agrees better not only with Greek usage but also with common clinical experience.

We concluded that 'alexithymia' and similar concepts could be understood as defensive patterns designed to ward off emotions by avoiding potentially emotional topics, and preferring the safety of objective, 'operative', non-committal expressions.

A word preference test

In order to assess the attitude of headache patients towards their emotions more directly we designed a simple word preference test.

We gave the patients a list of ten pairs of one 'operative' and one 'emotional' word in randomized order. The 'operative' words were simple terms from technical and administrative common usage, with strict and limiting connotations, whereas the 'emotional' words were selected from common usage in household or leisure for lack of limiting or strict qualities. The twenty words were selected according to personal experience with prevailing attitudes of headache patients towards emotional connotations. The language

Table 1. *Word preference test (Isler/Regard).*

Original German		Translation	
unregelmässig	planmässig	irregular	planned
präzis	grosszügig	precise(ly)	liberal
Fotografie	Wolldecke	photography	woollen blanket
anbieten	feststellen	to offer	state
Technik	Roman	techniques	novel
ins Blaue	exakt	into the blue	exact(ly)
ordentlich	zeitlos	orderly	timeless
Müesli	Anlage	müsli	setup, installation
freibleiben	durchführen	remain free	perform, execute
modellieren	konstruieren	to model	to construct

was the standard modern German which is the common written language in the region of Zurich, where the spoken language of the majority is a variant of middle (medieval) Southern German.

We then asked the patient: 'Please underline, on each line, the word that suits you better' ('Bitte unterstreichen Sie in jeder Zeile *das* Wort, das Ihnen besser passt'), adding that this was not important for individual diagnosis or treatment, only for research on headache patients as a group.

Preferred 'operative' words were counted as positive (+), 'emotional' ones as negative (−), and the sum of these points was used as a score or word preference index ranging from − 10 for the maximum of 'emotional' choices through 0 to + 10 for the maximum of 'operative' choices.

Patients and controls

The test was presented to all German-speaking patients attending our headache dispensary (Kopfwehsprechstunde) for treatment-resistant cases. This report concerns a first group of 32 male and 50 female patients with frequent or chronic headache. 'Tension' headache was found in 55% of the males and in 30% of the females, migraine in 36% of the males and in 70% of the females, while 9% of the males had cluster headache. There were 18 male and 54 female controls.

Results

There was no correlation between handedness (Oldfield index), diagnoses of primary headache syndromes (common or 'classical' migraine, tension headache), laterality of hemicranic headaches, and word preference indices.

The maximum of ten 'operative' choices was reached by a few headache patients of both sexes whereas the maximum of 'emotional' choices was found only in two female controls. There were significant differences of word preference index between headache patients and controls, and between males and females, and there was significant interaction of both variables in the analysis of variance.

The mean index of male patients was high in the 'operative' (+) range while that of male controls was in the 'emotional' (−) range. The mean index of female patients remained within the 'emotional' (−) range, closer to the 'operative' values than that of female controls but not significantly so (Fig. 1).

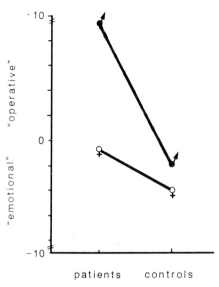

Fig. 1. *Mean word preference index in headache patients and normals.*

Search for hemisphere specificity: the Breskin Rigidity Test

We inferred that our findings resulted from modifications of higher cerebral function, or strategies.

On a more general level, some evidence of ipsilateral headache connected with hemispheric dysfunction had been presented earlier[7,8]. Regard & Landis[14] had shown in a tachistoscopic study of Szondi faces how 'affective decisions (preferences) may be overridden by cognitive decisions for which the two hemispheres compete for relative dominance', with a tendency of the left hemisphere to like, and of the right, to dislike. Similar results had been found in tachistoscopic presentation of the Rorschach plates[15] where results were interpreted in terms of perceptual defence of the left hemisphere against emotional stimuli; the standard Rorschach test has been proposed as still the most useful tool in the investigation of pensée opératoire[16] despite severe methodological disadvantages.

In the search for further evidence of modifications of higher cerebral function associated with frequent headache, the obvious direction would be to look for evidence of modified hemispheric functions. The theoretical framework for this was provided by the theory of alternating cerebral dominance established, long before Broca, by A. L. Wigan in 1844[17], supported by the split-brain investigators of the nineteen-seventies, especially J. Bogen[18], and later, from investigations of the intact brain, by Regard *et al.*[14,15] and Landis[19]. Wigan wrote in 1844 that usually one hemisphere would be less powerful so that the other could 'block its expression' while this power balance could shift from one hemisphere to the other[17]. This is now called functional hemispheric balance[14]. Defence against emotions appeared likely to involve modifications of this balance, so we intended to assess hemispheric responses to visual stimuli with differences similar to those between 'operative' and 'emotional' words.

In the tachistoscope, figure outlines were presented supraliminally to one hemisphere at a time so as to allow evaluation of its response in the intact brain. The Breskin Rigidity Test[20] figures consist of two groups, 'rigid' outlines of traditional, well-known, 'prägnant'and closed geometrical figures, and 'non-rigid', less regular, partly open and more haphazard outlines (Fig. 2); again, patients had to choose one preferred outline out of each pair of one 'rigid' and one 'non-rigid' figure. We assumed that the contrast between the two

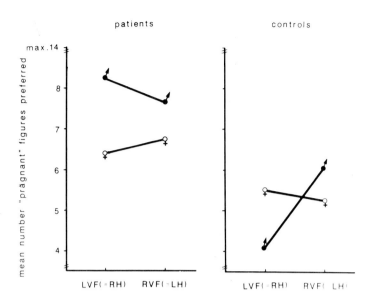

Fig. 2. *Stimulus examples of the Breskin Rigidity test.*

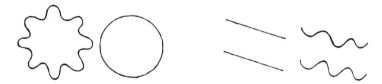

Fig. 3. *Mean number of 'rigid' (=prägnant) Breskin figures chosen by patients and by a previous group of healthy controls.*

groups approximated that between 'operative' and 'emotional' words; if there was a divergence between male and female patients and controls, and between patients and controls, similar to that found in the word preference test, both sets of observations could be related to the same underlying process, and we could develop our hypothesis of emotional defense according to eventual observations of modified processing in one hemisphere.

Again, the Breskin Rigidity Test was presented, by tachistoscope, to a series of 20 male and 20 female consecutive patients of the headache dispensary. The distribution of headache syndromes matched that in the previous groups. The results of the word preference test in both groups replicated the results of the previous groups, while the results of the Breskin Rigidity Test showed similar differences between male and female patients, and were consistent with the results of the word preference test since male patients preferred significantly more 'rigid' figures as compared to normal values of the test.

The tachistoscopic presentation showed that choosing of the Breskin figures in males occurred predominantly in the right hemisphere, with a significant difference against previous tachistoscopic Breskin test presentations in a healthy volunteer group where males had preferred rigid figures presented to the left hemisphere (Fig. 3).

Discussion

Word and figure preference tests show that patients with difficult primary headache problems, irrespective of the syndrome, generally prefer 'operative' words and 'rigid' geometrical shapes as against 'emotional' words and uncertain shapes without proper limits and obvious properties. Some results indicate that increased processing in the right hemisphere is involved in these preference decisions. This supports our concept of defence against one's own emotions as a typical behaviour pattern associated with frequent or chronic headache, since the right hemisphere has been shown to specialize in emotional responses, and especially, in negative, rejecting responses.

Our headache patients are heavily pre-selected. In order to eliminate this bias, our experiments should be repeated in a group selected by epidemiological methods. The responses of headache patients, especially our problem patients, may be unspecific for headache, and occur in any functional disorders, prolonged pain problems, or neurotic disorders. This should be investigated by comparing results in the latter groups. Nevertheless the present results indicate that primary headache problems are associated with modified patterns of hemispheric balance that express themselves as 'rigidity', 'alexithymia', or as a preference for 'operative' as against potentially emotional words and figures.

References

1 Eskelinen, L., Luisto, M., Tenkanen, L. & Mattei, O. (1986): Neuropsychological methods in the differentiation of organic solvent intoxication from certain neurological conditions. *J. Clin. Exp. Neuropsychol.* **8**, 239–256.

2 Klein, S. (1983): Perception of stimulus intensity by migraine and non-migraine subjects. *Headache* **23**, 158–161.

3 Appenzeller, O., Atkinson, R. & Kohner, J. (1984): Oral kinesthesia in scalp muscle contraction and vascular headache of the migraine type. In *Progress in migraine research 2*, ed. F. Clifford Rose, pp. 257–264. London: Pitman.

4 Eich, E., Reeves, J., Jaeger, B. & Graff-Radford, S. (1985): Memory for pain: Relation between past and present pain intensity. *Pain* **23**, 375–379.

5 Isler, H., Solomon, S. & Spielberg, S. (1984): Impaired time perception in patients with chronic headache. *Headache* **24**, 160.

6 Classen, W. & Netter, P. (1985): Sex differences in perceiving analgesic drug effects as measured by subjective pain ratings: a concealed signal detection theory analysis. *Percept. Mot. Skills* **61**, 761–762.

7 Isler, H., Wieser, H. & Egli, M. (1986): Hemicrania epileptica: Synchronous ipsilateral seizure headache with migraine features. In *Migraine and epilepsy*, eds F. Andermann & E. Lugaresi. London: Butterworths.

8 Puca, F., Antonaci, F., Savarese, M., Covelli, V., Tarascio, G., Bellizzi, M., Lamorgese, C. & Musmeci, G. (1984): Memory impairment and pain side: neuropsychological and electrophysiological study on 21 classic migraine sufferers. *Abstracts, 5th International Migraine Symposium*, pp. 43–44. London: The Migraine Trust.

9 Wolff, H. (1963): Headache and other head pain. (1st ed. 1948), pp. 399–431. New York: Oxford University Press.

10 Adler, C. & Adler, S. (1985): Pitfalls in the interpretation of psychometric testing of headache patients. *Cephalalgia* **5** (Suppl. 3), 212–213.

11 Marty, P. & de M'Uzan, M. (1963): La pensée opératoire. *Revue psychoanalytique* **27** (Suppl), 1963, 345.

12 Sifneos, P. (1973): The prevalence of 'alexithymic' characteristics in psychosomatic patients. *Psychother. Psychosom.* **22**, 255–262.

13 Nemiah, J., Freyberger, H. & Sifneos, P. (1975): Alexithymia: A view of the psychosomatic process. In *Modern trends in psychosomatic medicine 3*, ed. O. Hill, pp. 430–439. London: Butterworths.

14 Regard, M. & Landis, T. (1986): Affective and cognitive decisions on faces in normals. In *Aspects of face processing*, eds H. Ellis, M. Jeeves, F. Newcombe & A. Young, pp. 363–369. Dordrecht: Martinus Nijhoff.

15 Regard, M., Landis, T. & Bash, K. (1984): Affektivität: Tachistoskopische Nachweise von Hemisphärenunterschieden (Eine Studie mit dem Rorschach — Test). Beiträge zum V. Kongress '*Psychologie in der Medizin*'. München: Institut für Medizinische Psychologie der Ludwig-Max-Univesität.

16 Vogt, R., Thomas, G. & Wirsching, M. (1985): Zur Spezifität der 'pensée opératoire' bei psychosomatischen Störungen. *Psychother. med Psychol.* **35**, 160–166.

17 Wigan, A. (1944): A new view of insanity: The duality of the mind proved by the structure, functions, and diseases of the brain and by the phenomena of mental derangement, and shown to be essential to moral responsibility. London: Longman, Green, Brown, and Longmans. Reprint (ed. J. Bogen) Pasadena: J. Simon, 1985.

18 Bogen, J. (1968): The other side of the brain: an appositional mind. In *The nature of human consciousness*, ed. R. Ornstein, pp. 101–125. San Francisco: W. Freeman.

19 Landis, T. (1986): Right hemispheric reading: A clinical experimental approach to dual brain interaction. Unpublished habilitation thesis, University of Zürich.

20 Regard, M., Landis, T., Wieser, H. & Hailemariam, S. (1985): Functional inhibition and release: unilateral tachistoscopic performance and stereoelectroencephalographic activity in a case with left limbic status epilepticus. *Neuropsychologia* **23**, 575–581.

21 Breskin, S. (1968): Measurement of rigidity, a non-verbal test. *Percept. Mot. Skills* **27**, 1203–1206.

35

METHIONINE-ENKEPHALIN AND SEROTONIN

IN MIGRAINE AND TENSION HEADACHE

Michel D. Ferrari*, Marijke Frölich[†], Jacobus Odink[‡],
Carlo Tapparelli[§], Johanneke E. A. Portielje* and George W. Bruyn*

Department of Neurology and Chemical Pathology[†],
University Hospital Leiden, The Netherlands;
Department of Clinical Biochemistry[‡], TNO-CIVO Toxicology and
Nutrition Institute, Zeist, The Netherlands and
Department of Preclinical Research[§], Sandoz AG, Basle, Switzerland*

Summary

As part of an extensive study on biochemical differences between classic migraine (CLM), common migraine (COM) and tension headache (TH), serotonin (5HT) and methionine-enkephalin (MET) were simultaneously determined in platelets and platelet-poor-plasma (PPP) in nine healthy controls and a group of strictly defined and categorized, medication-free patients, with TH ($n = 9$), CLM ($n = 10$) or COM ($n = 21$). Migraine patients were studied both during and between attacks. In addition, incubation experiments were done to investigate whether migraine-attack plasma releases platelet-MET and/or 5HT, and whether this effect is restricted to platelets from migraineurs only. The following changes and differences were found:
(1) Plasma-5HT levels in attack-free migraineurs were half those found in TH or controls.
(2) During migraine attacks, compared with attack-free periods, plasma-5HT was higher in both COM and CLM, but platelet-5HT was lower only in COM.
(3) TH patients had high plasma-MET levels, with low to normal platelet-MET levels.
(4) Migraineurs, notably COM, had high platelet-MET levels which like plasma-MET, increased during an attack.
(5) The platelet/plasma-MET ratio appears to discriminate between COM and TH.
(6) Migraine-attack plasma released MET, but not 5HT, from platelets, exclusively in migraineurs.
It is suggested that platelet-MET increases during the prodromal stage of a migraine attack, and is released during the headache phase, presumably by a plasma factor.

Introduction

Methionine-enkephalin (MET) and serotonin (5HT) were studied as part of an extensive biochemical survey, the main aims of which were to investigate whether, and to what extent, classic (CLM) and common migraine (COM) as well as COM and tension headache (TH) differ pathophysiologically[1-10]. Related aims were to define possible diagnostic markers and to analyse biochemical changes during both COM and CLM attacks.

Serotonin was studied because of (a) its recently postulated headpain-causing effect[11-14b], (b) the speculative statements on shifts of 5HT from the platelet into the plasma during a migraine attack, which are based merely on extrapolation instead of on experiments in which 5HT in both platelets and PPP are measured simultaneously[15-19], (c) the fact that studies on the presumed platelet-5HT-releasing effect of migraine-attack plasma were dealing with relatively small numbers of patients[15-18].

Methionine-enkephalin was studied because of its putative analgesic, monoamine-modulating and 5HT-neutralizing effects[20-22]. In addition, as in the nervous sytem, MET in the platelet seems to be co-stored together with 5HT and other monoamines and is released concomitantly with 5HT. It was hypothesized that MET might serve as a natural antagonist for the pain-producing effect of 5HT[23].

We present in this chapter the results of simultaneous measurements of MET and 5HT in platelets and PPP from medication-free patients with CLM ($n = 10$), COM ($n = 21$) or TH ($n = 9$) and controls ($n = 9$). Migraine patients were investigated both between and during attacks which enabled us to study differences between the various clinical entities, as well as to verify whether, during migraine attacks, 5HT and/or MET levels in platelets and PPP change. In addition, incubation experiments were done to investigate whether the shift of 5HT and/or MET is caused by a releasing effect of migraine-attack plasma and whether only platelets from migraineurs are sensitive to this effect.

Subjects and methods

Subjects

Forty-nine female patients and controls were studied. To select patients and to divide them into groups, as homogeneous as clinically possible, we used, in addition to the diagnostic criteria of the Ad Hoc committee[24], much more rigid definitions. When tested, all subjects had to have been free of any medication for at least 12 days.

Samples

K2EDTA blood was collected from a cubital vein and immediately placed on ice. Blood was collected when the patient had been free of attacks for at least 12 days. Platelet rich plasma (PRP) and PPP were prepared by differential centrifuging within 1 h and kept frozen at $-20°C$ until assayed or (PPP) used for incubation experiments. Platelets were counted in whole blood as well as in PRP.

Incubation experiments

From every CLM ($n = 11$) and COM ($n = 19$) patient, six platelet-pellets were prepared by centrifuging aliquots of 1 ml PRP, obtained from blood freshly collected during an attack-free period. From these six pellets, two pellets were each resuspended in 1 ml distilled water; the next two pellets were each incubated for 60 min at 37°C, with 1 ml PPP, obtained

Table 1. *Mean levels of serotonin (5HT) and methionine-enkephalin (MET) in platelets and platelet-poor-plasma, and whole blood (WB) platelet counts in classic and common migraine patients during attack-free periods as well as tension headache sufferers and healthy controls. s.d. and P values according to one-way ANOVA.*

	Classic (n = 10)	Common (n = 21)	Tension (n = 9)	Control (n = 9)	s.d. (df = 45)	P
5HT(amol/platelet)	3.9	4.4	4.1	3.5	1.8	NS
5HT(nmol/1 plasma)	13.1	12.2	33.2	30.1	18.4	<0.01
MET(10^{-21}g/platelet)	34.3	57.3	7.6	12.8	32.3	<0.001
MET(ng/1 plasma)	33.3	28.3	68.1	39.6	7.5	<0.001
Platelets/nl WB	243	271	268	266	75.9	NS

Table 2. *Mean levels of serotonin (5HT) and methionine-enkephalin (MET) in platelets and platelet-poor-plasma, and whole-blood (WB) platelet counts in classic (CLM) and common (COM) migraine patients during attack (+) and attack-free (−) periods.*

	Attack	Classic (n = 10)	Common (n = 21)	s.d. intra (df 29)	s.d. between (df 29)	P diag- nosis	P attack	P diag. attack
5HT	−	3.9	4.4	1.5	2.1	NS	<0.005	<0.02
(amol/platelet)	+	4.1	2.5					
5HT	−	13.1	12.2	20.5	24.9	NS	<0.02	NS
(nmol/l plasma)	+	27.8	25.6					
MET	−	34.3	57.3	22.5	38.9	<0.03	<0.001	NS
(10^{-21}g/platelet)	+	46.1	88.5					
MET	−	33.3	28.3	3.2	7.7	NS	<0.001	NS
(ng/l plasma)	+	39.5	35.8					
Platelets	−	243	271	39.4	63.8	NS	<0.05	NS
(per nl WB)	+	227	248					

s.d. and *P* values according to split-plot two-way ANOVA. Diagnosis: difference between CLM and COM; attack: difference between attack-free and attack; diag. attack: difference in change during attack between CLM and COM; s.d. intra: s.d. for intra-individual change; s.d. between: s.d. for differences between CLM and COM.

from their own blood between attacks and the final two pellets were each incubated with 1 ml PPP, obtained from their own blood during an attack.

From every TH patient ($n = 10$) and control ($n = 9$), eight platelet-pellets were prepared. From these eight pellets, two pellets were each resuspended in 1 ml distilled water, two were incubated with 1 ml PPP obtained from their own blood, two were incubated with 1 ml PPP obtained from blood of a migraineur between attacks and the final two pellets were incubated with 1 ml PPP, obtained from blood from the same migraineur during an attack.

After incubation, platelet-pellets and the supernatants belonging to them were separated by centrifuging and kept frozen at −20°C until analysed. In this way, from every subject, each time two separate pellets were incubated with the same particular incubation-medium. One of these two pellets served for the determination of MET, the other for 5HT.

Table 3. *Mean platelet and supernatant methionine-enkephalin (MET) and serotonin (5HT) concentration after incubation of platelets from 11 classic and 19 common migraine patients with distilled water or with plasma obtained either during an attack or during an attack-free period.*

	After incubation with	Platelets from classic (n = 11)	common (n = 19)	s.d. (within) (df 28)	P
MET in pellet (10^{-21}g/platelet)	Water	122.5	139.4	11.1	NS
	Attack-free plasma	122.3	136.5		
	Attack plasma	87.0	107.3	11.8	<0.001
MET in supernatant* (pg/ml)	Attack-free plasma	4.4	17.9	8.7	<0.001
	Attack plasma	23.6	31.5		
5HT in pellet (amol/platelet)	Water	2.94	2.87	0.25	<0.02
	Attack-free plasma	2.74	2.72		
	Attack plasma	2.81	2.61	0.34	NS

*Change in supernatant, calculated by subtracting plasma values used for incubation.
s.d. and *P* values according to split-plot two-way ANOVA for differences between effects of various incubation media.

Biochemical assays

Methionine-enkephalin was determined by RIA (Immunonuclear Corp. Stillwater MN)[25]. Serotonin was quantitated by HPLC coupled to electrochemical detection (modification after Koch & Kissinger[26]).

Data analysis

Platelet-MET and 5HT levels were calculated by dividing the difference between their concentration in PRP and PPP by the platelet-count in PRP. Platelet/plasma-MET ratios were calculated by dividing the MET concentration in platelets by the MET concentration in PPP. The changes of MET levels in the supernatants, caused by the various incubation media, were calculated by subtracting their concentration in the PPP used for incubation from the concentration found in the supernatant after incubation.

Differences between groups (for migraine only attack-free) were analysed with one-way ANOVA. Differences between attack and attack-free periods as well as differences between the MET/5HT concentrations in the supernatants or in the platelets, after incubation with the various media, were analysed with two-way ANOVA (type split-plot). A *P*-value less than 0.05 was considered statistically significant.

Results

Serotonin in platelets and plasma (Tables 1 and 2)

Mean basal platelet-5HT levels were the same in all groups. Mean basal plasma-5HT levels in both CLM and COM were half those found in TH and controls ($P<0.01$). During both COM and CLM attacks, mean plasma-5HT increased 100%, up to the same levels as found in TH and controls ($P<0.02$). In contrast, during attacks, mean platelet-5HT dropped about 43% only in COM and not in CLM ($P<0.005$).

Table 4. *Mean platelet and supernatant methionine-enkephalin (MET) and serotonin (5HT) concentration after incubation of platelets from controls and tension headache patients with distilled water, own plasma or with plasma from a migraineur obtained during an attack or during an attack-free period.*

	After incubation with	Platelets from control (n = 9)	tension (n = 10)	s.d. (within) (df 17)	P
MET in pellet (10⁻²¹g/platelet	Water	79.0	136.4		
				13.5	NS
	Own plasma	82.6	148.1		
	Attack-free plasma	79.6	146.1		
				11.2	NS
	Migraine-attack plasma	82.0	136.7		
MET in super-natant* (pg/ml)	Own plasma	− 4.1	− 4.9		
				7.9	<0.001†
	Attack-free plasma	5.2	28		
				7.9	NS
	Migraine-attack plasma	− 5.0	23.3		
5HT in pellet (amol/platelet)	Water	3.33	4.13		
				0.30	NS
	Own Plasma	3.34	4.06		
	Attack free plasma	3.27	4.16		
				0.33	NS
	Migraine-attack plasma	3.71	4.05		

*Change in supernatant, calculated by subtracting plasma values used for the incubation. s.d. and P values according to split-plot two-way ANOVA for differences between effects of various incubation media.
†Only for tension headache.

MET in platelets and plasma (Tables 1 and 2)

Mean attack-free platelet-MET content in CLM and COM was 3–7 times higher than in TH or controls ($P < 0.001$). Mean plasma-MET levels in TH was twice as high as in controls or attack-free migraineurs ($P < 0.001$). During an attack, migraineurs showed substantially higher platelet-MET levels than during an attack-free period ($P < 0.001$). Platelet-MET levels in COM were higher than in CLM patients ($P < 0.03$). Plasma-MET levels during migraine attacks were higher than outside attacks ($P < 0.001$). No difference was found between CLM and COM plasma-MET levels.

Mean platelet/plasma-MET ratios in controls (0.37) and TH (0.11) were significantly lower than mean ratios in CLM (1.12) and COM (2.23) ($P < 0.002$; s.d.: 1.47). The mean ratio in COM was higher than in CLM ($P < 0.03$).

MET and 5HT after incubation of platelets from migraineurs (Table 3)

Platelets from migraineurs after incubation with attack-free plasma had about the same platelet-MET concentration as platelets exclusively resuspended in water. In contrast, platelets after incubation with attack-plasma had about a mean 24% lower MET concentration than platelets only resuspended in water or incubated in attack-free plasma ($P < 0.001$). In fact, platelet-MET content dropped in all (except one) migraineurs. The corresponding supernatants showed an equally significant increase in MET content after incubation with attack-plasma with respect to supernatants after incubation with attack-free plasma ($P < 0.001$). This strongly suggests a shift of MET from the platelets into the supernatant. No difference was observed between platelets from CLM or COM.

Mean 5HT content in platelets after incubation with either attack-plasma or attack-free plasma showed a slightly (about 7%) lower mean value than platelets only resuspended in water. No difference was observed between platelet-5HT after incubation with attack-plasma or with attack-free plasma, nor between CLM and COM.

MET and 5HT after incubation of platelets from TH and controls (Table 4)

For both platelet- 5HT and MET, no relevant differences were found between the various platelet-pellets after incubation with either of the several incubation media.

Discussion

In vivo results

The first conspicuous finding is that plasma-5HT in migraineurs was less than half that of TH and controls.

Second, during both COM and CLM attacks, plasma-5HT increased more than 100%, while at the same time platelet-5HT decreased (43%) only during COM and not during CLM attacks. Obviously, at least in CLM attacks, the rise in plasma-5HT is not likely to be explained by a mere shift of 5HT out of the platelets.

Third, in contrast to what was established for 5HT, the platelet-MET content during a migraine attack was significantly higher than during attack-free intervals. Likewise, plasma-MET levels during an attack were higher, without however reaching the levels found in TH patients, who had by far the highest plasma-MET levels.

Fourthly, TH and migraine patients seem to have a quite opposite, and possibly specific, distribution of MET between platelets and plasma. TH had very high plasma-MET and low to normal platelet-MET levels whilst, in contrast, migraineurs had low to normal plasma-MET but high platelet-MET levels. The platelet/plasma-MET ratio promises to be a useful diagnostic marker, notably to distinguish between COM and TH. All TH patients and all (except one) controls had ratios smaller than 0.55 whilst, in contrast, all (except two CLM) migraineurs had ratios (mostly considerably) higher than 0.55.

Earlier reports on MET in migraine have produced controversial results, even between sequential studies by the same group and show important methodological differences compared with our study[25,26-30]. The most striking are the use of antidepressive medication, known to increase platelet-MET[27], and a less rigid separation of migraine and TH patients. Consequently, a clear comparison with our results is not feasible.

Pathophysiological interpretation of our results must remain speculative. The role of MET in migraine may be related to its analgesic or monoamine modulating effects[20-22] but, since plasma-MET is probably partially derived from pro-enkephalin from adrenal medulla and sympathetic ganglia, its level might reflect adrenergic activity[20-22]. Similarly, in the platelet, as in the nervous system, MET seems to be co-stored and concomitantly released with monoamines, platelet-MET might reflect monoaminergic activity, or function as an antagonist, eg for 5HT[23,27].

Incubation experiments

Plasma from migraineurs did not release platelet-5HT in a relevant way. Presumably, 5HT release by migraine-attack plasma was found by chance in earlier studies on patient-series of limited size[16,18].

In contrast to the non-release of 5HT, migraine-attack plasma (but not attack-free plasma) induced a substantial release of MET from platelets of all (except one) migraineurs, but not from platelets of TH or controls. Apparently, during both COM and CLM attacks, a 'MET-releasing factor' circulates in the plasma, for which only platelets from migraineurs are sensitive.

The absolute platelet-MET levels in the incubation experiments were higher than in-vivo measurements. Possibly, the experimental set up, with incubation and additional centrifuge steps, promotes the formation of MET, eg by conversion from a precursor but, since the incubation experiments were merely meant to study the relative effects of the various incubation media, we feel this phenomenon has not materially influenced our results.

To integrate both 'in vitro' (release of platelet-MET by migraine-attack plasma) and 'in vivo' observations (increase of platelet- and plasma-MET during an attack), we hypothesize that platelet-MET increases already before the clinical start of the attack, eg during the promonitory sign phase, and is partially released during the headache phase, by a putative 'MET-releasing factor' circulating in the plasma.

Acknowledgement — The authors are grateful to Mrs Jenneke Ferrari-Muns for typing the manuscript.

References

1 Wilkinson, M. & Blau, J. N. (1985): Are classical and common migraine different entities. *Headache* **25**, 211–212.
2 Olesen, J. (1985): Reply to 1. *Headache* **25**, 213.
3 Dalessio, D. J. (1985): Is there a difference between classic and common migraine. *Arch. Neurol.* **42**, 275–277.
4 Ziegler, D. K. (1985): The headache syndrome. *Arch. Neurol* **42**, 273–274.
5 Manzoni, G. C., Farina, S., Granello, F., Alfieri, M. & Bisi, M. (1986): Classic and common migraine, suggestive clinical evidence of two separate entities. *Funct. Neurology* **1**, 112–122.
6 Featherstone, H. J. (1985): Migraine and Muscle contraction headaches a continuum. *Headache* **25**, 194–198.
7 Martin, P. R. (1985): Classification of headache. The need for a radical revision. *Cephalalgia* **5**, 1–4,
8 Clifford Rose, F. (1986): Headache: Definitions and classification. In *Handbook of clinical neurology*, Vol 4 (48): Headache, ed. F. Clifford Rose, pp. 1–12. Amsterdam: Elsevier Science Publishers.
9 Nappi, G. & Savoldi, F. (1985): Headache: Diagnostic system and taxonomic criteria. London: John Libbey.
10 Kudrow, L. (1986): Muscle contraction headaches. In *Handbook of clinical neurology* vol. 4 (48), ed. F. Clifford Rose, pp. 343–352. Amsterdam: Elsevier Science Publishers.
11 Moskowitz, M. A., Henrikson, B. M. & Beyerl, B. D. (1986): Trigeminovascular connections and mechanisms of vascular headache. In *Handbook of clinical neurology*, vol 4 (48): Headache, ed. F. Clifford Rose, pp. 107–115. Amsterdam: Elsevier Science Publishers.
12 Richardson, B. R. & Engel, G. (1986): The pharmacology and function of 5HT^3 receptors *TINS* **9**, 424–428.
13 Loisy, C., Beorchia, S., Centonze, V., Fozard, J. R., Schlechter, P. J. & Tell, G. P. (1985): Effects on migraine headache of MDL 72, 222, an antagonist at neuronal 5HT-receptors. Double-blind placebo controlled study. *Cephalalgia* **5**, 79–82.
14a Richardson, B. P., Engel, G., Donatsch, P. & Stadler, P. A. (1985): Identification of serotonin M-receptor subtypes and their specific blockade by a new class of drugs. *Nature* **316**, 126–131.
14b Scatton, B., Duverger, D., L'Heureux, R., Serrano, A., Fage, D., Nowicki, J. P. & MacKenzie, E. T. (1985): Neurochemical studies on the existence, origin and characteristics of the serotonergic innervation of small pial vessels. *Brain Res.* **345**, 219–229.
15 Eadie, M. J. & Tyrer, J. H. (1985): *The biochemistry of migraine*. Lancaster, England: MTP Press.

16 Anthony, M. (1986): The biochemistry of migraine. *Handbook of clinical neurology vol 4 (48): Headache*, ed. F. Clifford Rose, pp. 85–105. Amsterdam: Elsevier Science Publishers.

17 Dvilanski, A., Rishpon, S., Nathan, I. & Zolotowz Korczyn, A. D. (1976): Release of platelet 5-hydroxytryptamine by plasma taken during and between migraine attacks. *Pain* 2, 315–318.

18 Muck-Seler, D., Deavonic, Z. & Dupelj, M. (1979): Platelet serotonin (5HT) and 5HT-releasing factor in plasma of migrainous patients. *Headache* 19, 14–17.

19 Fozard, J. R. (1982): Serotonin, migraine and platelets. In *Progress in pharmacology 4/4*, pp. 135–141. Stuttgart, New York: Gustav Fisher Verlag.

20 Kiser, R. S., Gatchel, R. J., Bhatia, K., Khatami, M., Huang, X -Y. & Altshuler, K. Z. (1983): Acupuncture relief of chronic pain syndrome correlates with increased plasma MET-Enkephalin concentrations. *Lancet* ii, 1394–1396.

21 Grossman, A. & Clement-Jones, V. (1983): Opiate receptors: Enkephalins and Endorphins. *Clin. Endocrinol. Metab.* 12, 31–56.

22 Millan, M. J. & Herz, A. (1985): The endocrinology of the opioids. In *International review of neurobiology vol 26*, ed. J. R. Smythies and R. J. Bradley, 1–62.

23 Di Giulio, A. M., Picotti, G. B., Cesura, A. M., Paneraj, A. J. & Mantegazza, P. (1982): MET-enkephalin-immunoreactivity in blood platelets. *Life Sci.* 30, 1605–1614.

24 Friedman, A. P., Finley, K. M., Graham, J. R., Kunkel, E. C., Ostfeld, A. M. & Wolff, H. G. (1962): The classification of headache. *Arch. Neurol.* 6, 173–176.

25 Mosnaim, A. D., Wolf, M. E., Chevesich, J., Callaghan, O. H. & Diamond, S. (1985): Plasma methionine enkephalin levels. A biological marker for migraine? *Headache* 25 259–261.

26 Koch, D. D. & Kissinger, P. T. (1979): Determination of tryptophan and several of its metabolites in physiological samples by reverse phase liquid chromatography wave electrochemical detection. *J. Chromat.* 164, 441–445.

27 Boiardi, A., Picotti, G. B., Di Giulio, A. M., Bussone, G., Galva, M. D., La Manta, L. & Mantegazza, P. (1984): Platelet MET-enkephalin immunoreactivity and 5-Hydroxytryptamine concentrations in migraine patients: effects of 5-Hydroxytryptophan, amitriptyline and chlorimipramine treatment. *Cephalagia* 4, 81–84.

28 Mosnaim, A. D., Wine, R., Diamond, S. & Wolf, M. E. (1984): Plasma methionine enkephalin levels during migraine episodes. In *Progress in migraine research 2*, ed. F. Clifford Rose, pp. 155–161. London: Pitman.

29 Mosnaim, A. D., Chevesich, J., Wolf, M. E., Freitag, F. G. & Diamond, S. (1986): Plasma methionine enkephalin increased levels during a migraine episode. *Headache* 26, 278–281.

30 Mosnaim, A. D., Wolf, M. E., Freitag, F. G. & Diamond, S. (1986): Differences in plasma methionine-enkephalin levels between migraine and cluster headache patients. *Headache* 26, 315.

36

ARTERIAL AND VENOUS PLASMA

ENKEPHALINASE AND ACE ACTIVITIES

IN PRIMARY HEADACHE SUFFERERS

M. G. Spillantini, P. L. Del Bianco and A. Panconesi

*Institute of Internal Medicine and Clinical Pharmacology,
University of Florence, V. le Morgagni, 85 50134 Florence, Italy*

Summary

Opioid peptide levels are altered in blood of primary headache sufferers. This variation could be due to alteration in their metabolism, since the activity of enkephalinase, an enzyme involved in enkephalins breakdown, is also changed in venous plasma of these subjects. In this study we have investigated the activities of enkephalinase and of angiotensin converting enzyme (ACE), both cleaving the gly-phe bond of the enkephalin molecule, in venous and arterial blood of chronic headache and common migraine sufferers.

We report no difference in ACE activity in venous and arterial plasma of both common and chronic migraine sufferers. Enkephalinase activity is increased in venous plasma of chronic migraine sufferers but not in common migraine when compared with arterial blood. The increased enkephalinase activity in venous blood of chronic migraine sufferers could be related to a release of the enzyme consequent to the stress of continuous pain.

Introduction

Primary headache has been described as a dysfunction of the antinociceptive system[1]. Opioids are involved in the modulation of pain[2] so that impairment in their function was investigated in primary headache sufferers. Previous results indicate that an alteration of the endogenous opioid system was present in these subjects, since morphine-like factors or enkephalins were decreased in cerebrospinal fluid[3,4]. Other variations have been found in plasma[5,6] and the responsiveness to various stimuli of opioid receptors was also altered[7]. The alterations in opioid levels could be attributed to a defect of either degradation or synthesis. Among various enzymes involved in enkephalin breakdown, enkephalinase (neutral metallo endopeptidase 3.4.24.11) has been considered to be related to the turnover of enkephalins because of its affinity for these pentapeptides *in vitro*, and to the ability of its specific inhibitor thiorphan to induce naloxone-reversible analgesia and increase of met-enkephalin *in vivo*[8-11]. Angiotensin converting enzyme (ACE) is also able to cleave enkephalins and different peptides other than angiotensin I, but with less affinity[12,13]. Plasma enkephalinase activity in chronic migraine sufferers and in cluster headache patients during the cluster period was increased when compared to control subjects[14]. Conversely the enzyme activity is lower in migraine sufferers when pain is not present and increases during the attack[15]. The increase that we found in venous plasma of chronic migraine patients, when compared to control subjects or common migraine sufferers in the pain-free period, prompted us to also investigate the enkephalinase activity in arterial plasma. The impossibility of obtaining arterial blood from control subjects led us to compare chronic migraine patients with common migraine sufferers in between attacks, when they are symptomatologically similar to normal control subjects. Angiotensin converting enzyme activity was also measured in both venous and arterial plasma to see whether the two enzymes have the same behaviour.

Materials and methods

Arterial and venous blood samples were obtained from ten chronic migraine sufferers (five females, five males; age 28–52 years) and 12 common migraine sufferers (seven females, five males; age 25–50 years) in between attacks[16]. No subjects had history of heart disease. Patients were hospitalized and drug-free for at least 2 days, and were required to maintain an overnight fast and to remain in a resting position 30 min prior to the sampling time (performed between 9–12 a.m.). In each subject, blood was taken from an antecubital arm vein and the humeral artery of the contralateral arm. The blood was collected in heparinized glass tubes, immediately centrifuged at $2100\,g$ for 15 min and plasma stored directly at $-20°C$ until assayed.

Enkephalinase activity assay

Enkephalinase activity was measured by a fluorimetric method[17].

One hundred and fifty μl of plasma (diluted $1/30$) were added to Suc-ala-ala-phe-AMC dissolved in Hepes/NaOH 50 mM pH 7.4 for 60 min at 37°C. After stopping the reaction by addition of 10^{-6} M thiorphan to the samples and heating at 95°C, 0.75 μg amino-peptidase M were added and further incubated at 56°C for 1 h. Fluorescence released from the substrate was compared with that of the standard obtained incubating Suc-ala-ala-phe-AMC with 3 μg thermolysine. Blanks were obtained adding 10^{-6} M thiorphan.

Angiotensin converting enzyme activity assay

Angiotensin converting enzyme activity was measured as previously reported by Yang and Neff[18]. Fifty μl of plasma (diluted $1/10$) were added to $50\,\mu l$ of Hip-His-Leu dissolved in 50 mM pH 7.4 Hepes/NaOH + NaCl 2N. Blanks were obtained by adding 10^{-6} M captopril. The reaction was stopped adding 2N NaOH and fluorescence was obtained including orthoptaldehyde in the incubation medium. Fluorescence of each sample was compared to that of the standard curve obtained with different concentrations of His-Leu.

Protein and haematocrit evaluations

Protein content of each sample was evaluated according to the method described by Lowry *et al.*[19], while haematocrit was measured by routine analysis.

Reagents

The following reagents were used: Suc-ala-ala-phe-AMC (Bachem, Switzerland), Hepes, His-Leu, Hip-His-Leu and thermolysine (Sigma, USA). Orthoptaldehyde (Merk, West Germany). Thiorphan and captopril were kind gifts of Dr J. C. Schwartz (INSERM, France) and Squibb Co. (USA) respectively.

Statistical analysis

Statistical analysis of the data was obtained using paired Student's *t*-test.

Results

Enkephalinase activity was significantly higher in venous plasma of chronic migraine sufferers (1.79 ± 0.3 pmol/mg protein/min) as compared to arterial plasma (0.95 ± 0.3 pmol/mg protein/min; $P < 0.005$). In common migraine sufferers no differences of enkephalinase activity were found between venous (1.4 ± 0.6 pmol/mg protein/min) and arterial (1.1 ± 0.6 pmol/mg protein/min) plasma (Fig. 1). In chronic migraine sufferers a difference in ACE activity was not observed between venous (0.17 ± 0.01 nmol/mg protein/min) and arterial (0.16 ± 0.01 nmol/mg protein/min) plasma. The activity of this

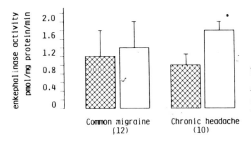

Fig. 1. *Enkephalinase activity in venous and arterial plasma of common migraine (left) and chronic migraine (right) sufferers.* In parenthesis numbers of the subjects. *$P < 0.005$.

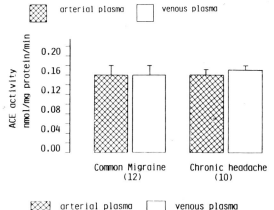

Fig. 2. *ACE activity in venous and arterial plasma of common migraine (left) and chronic migraine (right) patients.*

enzyme in venous (0.16 ± 0.02 nmol/mg protein/min) and arterial (0.16 ± 0.02 nmol/mg protein/min) blood of common migraine patients was not significantly different (Fig. 2). The same results were obtained when enzyme activity levels were expressed in terms of haemodilution after haematocrit evaluation, rather than protein concentration.

Discussion

These data confirm a difference between enkephalinase activity in venous plasma of chronic migraine and common migraine sufferers[15]. Furthermore, in chronic migraine, enkephalinase activity is different between venous and arterial plasma in the same subject while this difference does not exist in common migraine sufferers. Enkephalinase activity also has the same mean value in arterial plasma of chronic and common migraine sufferers. The lack of arteriovenous gradient of ACE activity is in agreement with previous studies[20].

It is very difficult to explain the increase of enkephalinase activity in venous plasma of chronic migraine sufferers. Damage of the vascular wall cannot be the cause of the increase of enkephalinase activity because ACE (which is also present in the vascular wall) is not released. One hypothesis is that in these patients the enzyme is selectively released from the vascular wall of the microvessels of the arm. The turnover of a neurotransmitter (as for cathecolamines and angiotensin) can generally be correlated to the enzyme involved in its synthesis or metabolism. The activity of enkephalinase could be related with the enkephalin concentrations as was suggested in animal brain and in human cord blood and newborns[21,22]. Peptidases are located in endothelial cells of the vascular wall and are believed to regulate the levels of neuropeptides as is the case for kinins[23]. At the microvessel level enkephalinase activity in venous plasma could represent a clearing system for enkephalins (and perhaps other peptides); in the case of chronic migraine its activity seems to be altered resulting in low amount of opioids in their plasma[5]. In these patients a change of opioid receptor activity in the vein has been found[7] indicating a more general alteration of the opioid system which can involve hyperreactivity of the degradating enzyme as well.

Acknowledgement — The study was supported by Progetti finalizzati 'Chimica fine e secondaria' and 'Controllo del dolore' of CNR (Rome).

References

1 Sicuteri, F. (1979): Headache as the most common disease of the antinociceptive system: analogies with morphine abstinence. In *Advances in pain research and therapy, vol. 3*, ed. J. Bonica, F. Liebeskind & D. Albe-Fessard, pp. 358–365. New York: Raven Press.
2 Martin, W. R. (1984): Pharmacology of opioids. *Pharmacol. Rev.* **35**, 283–323.
3 Sicuteri, F., Anselmi, B., Curradi, C., Michelacci, S. & Sassi, A. (1978): Morphine-like factors in CSF of headache patients. *Adv. Biochem. Psychopharmacol.* **18**, 363–366.
4 Genazzani, A. R., Nappi, G., Facchinetti, F., Micieli, G., Petraglia, F., Bono, G., Monittola, C. & Savoldi, F. (1984): Progressive impairment of CSF B-EP levels in migraine sufferers. *Pain* **18**, 127–133.
5 Baldi, E., Salmon, S., Cappelli, G., Brocchi, A., Spillantini, M. G. & Sicuteri, F. (1982): Intermittent hypoendorphinemia in migraine attack. *Cephalalgia* **2**, 77–81.
6 Facchinetti, F., Nappi, G., Savoldi, F. & Genazzani, A. R. (1981): Primary headaches: reduced circulating B-lipotropin and B-endorphin levels with impaired reactivity to acupuncture. *Cephalalgia* **1**, 195–201.
7 Sicuteri, F. (1982): Opioid receptors in human iris and vein: their impairment in migraine and similar disorders. In *Advances in migraine research and therapy*, ed. F. Clifford Rose, pp. 145–152. New York: Raven Press.

8 Schwartz, J. C. (1983): Metabolism of enkephalins and the inactivating neuropeptidase concept. *Trends Neurosci.* **6**, 45–47.

9 Malfroy, B., Swerts, J. P., Guyon, A., Roques, B. P. & Schwartz, J. C. (1978): High affinity enkephalin-degrading peptidase in mouse brain and its enhanced activity following morphine. *Nature* **276**, 523–526.

10 Roques, B. P., Fournie'-Zaluski, M. C., Soroca, E., Lecomte, J. M., Malfroy, B., Llorens, C. & Schwartz, J. C. (1980): The enkephalinase inhibitor thiorphan shows antinociceptive activity in mice. *Nature* **288**; 286–288.

11 Zhang, A. Z., Yang, H. Y. T. & Costa, E. (1982): Nociception, enkephalin content and dipeptidyl carboxypeptidase activity in brain of mice treated with exopeptidase inhibitors. *Neuropharmacology* **21**, 265–290.

12 Erdos, E. G., Johnson, A. R. & Boyden, N. T. (1978): Hydrolysis of enkephalin by cultured human endothelial cells and by purified peptidyl dipeptidase. *Biochem. Pharmacol.* **27**, 843–848.

13 Erdos, E. G. (1984): Multiple functions of human 'converting enzyme' and 'enkephalinase' in peptide metabolism. *Jap. J. Hypertension* **6**, 71–81.

14 Sicuteri, F., Fanciullacci, M., Geppetti, P., Renzi, D., Caleri, D. & Spillantini, M. G. (1985): Substance P mechanism in cluster headache: evaluation in plasma and cerebrospinal fluid. *Cephalalgia* **5**, 143–149.

15 Spillantini, M. G., Fanciullacci, M., Michelacci, S., Baldi, E. & Sicuteri, F. (1985): 'Enkephalinase' activity in plasma and cerebrospinal fluid in primary headache. In *Updating in headache*, ed. V. Pfaffenrath, P. O. Lundberg & O., Sjaastad, pp. 264–268. Berlin: Springer Verlag.

16 Ad Hoc Committee on classification of Headache (1962): Classification of Headache. *J. Am. Med. Ass.* **179**, 717–718.

17 Spillantini, M. G., Geppetti, P., Fanciullacci, M., Michelacci, S., Lecomte, J. M. & Sicuteri, F. (1986): In vivo 'enkephalinase' inhibition by acetorphan in human plasma and CSF. *Eur. J. Pharmacol.* **125**, 147–150.

18 Yang, H. Y. T. & Neff, N. H. (1972): Distribution and properties of angiotensin converting enzyme of rat brain. *J. Neurochem.* **19**, 2443–2450.

19 Lowry, O. H., Rosebrough, F., Farr, A. L. & Randall, R. J. (1951): Protein measurement with folin phenol reagent. *J. Biol. Chem.* **193**, 265–275.

20 Faymonville, M. E., Drese, C., Radermeker, M. & Lamy, M. (1984): Arterial and venous serum levels of angiotensin converting enzyme (ACE) during non-pulsatile cardiopulmonary bypass in man. In Abstract Book '*Kinin '84*', Savannah, USA, p. 42.

21 Malfroy, B., Swerts, J. P., Llorens, C. & Schwartz, J. C. (1979): Regional distribution of high affinity enkephalin degradating peptidase (enkephalinase) and effects of lesions suggest localization in the vicinity of opioid receptors. *Neurosci. Lett.* **11**, 329–333.

22 Baldi, E., Spillantini, M. G., Cosenza-Biagioli, E., Mainardi, C., Cianciulli, D., Carbone, C. & Panero, C. (1986): Met- enkephalin-like immunoreactivity (MELI) and enkephalinase activity (EKA) in cord blood and newborns in the first hours of life. *Biol. Res. Pregnancy* **2**, 84–88.

23 Sicuteri, F., Franchi, G., Del Bianco, P. L. & Fanciullacci, M. (1966): Some physiological and pathological roles of kininogen and kinins. In *Hypotensive peptides*, eds E. G. Erdos, N. Back & F. Sicuteri, pp. 522–535. New York: Springer Verlag.

37

TRANSFORMED OR EVOLUTIVE MIGRAINE

Ninan T. Mathew

Houston Headache Clinic, Houston, Texas 77004, USA

Summary

Traditional teaching considers migraine as a purely episodic phenomenon, whilst daily headaches are categorized as muscle contraction or tension headache. Clinical observation by Dalsgaard-Nielsen[1] indicated that 73% of patients with migraine get frequent low grade headaches between their attacks. He concluded that headache is not just an episodic phenomenon, but a permanent deviation from normal because of a biological threshold for headache lower than in the normal population.

Discussing the natural history of migraine, Graham[2] observed that in some individuals headache may show an increasing frequency of attack until they become a daily occurrence. In 1982, Mathew et al.[3] reported a series of patients who had a clear-cut history of episodic migraine but whose headaches, over the years, transformed into a daily or near daily headache. This chapter extends that paper with additional observations and a larger number of patients.

Materials and methods

The history and clinical features were analyzed in detail of 630 chronic daily headache patients who were selected from a series of 1600 patients seen in a headache clinic population between the years 1982 and 1985. The diagnostic breakdown of the 1600 patients of whom 39% had chronic daily headaches is given in Table 1.

The diagnostic criteria for migraine is shown in Table 2, where certain points are allocated for individual clinical features of migraine. A minimum of 5 points out of 10 was considered essential to meet the diagnostic criteria for migraine. Chronic daily headaches were divided into three types: Type I, starts as daily or near daily headache with no change in the severity and lack migrainous features; Type II, starts as daily or near daily headaches with occasional more severe headache with some migrainous features; Type III, (transformed or evolutive migraine) starts as a clear-cut occasional episodic migraine (common or classic) in the teens or twenties, with increasing frequency over the following years, and regular menstrual aggravation of headache in the 30's and early 40's, evolving into chronic

Table 1. *Diagnostic breakdown of a series of 1600 patients.* (Headache clinic population).

Diagnosis	Number	Percentage
Cluster	117	7
Classic migraine	30	2
Common migraine	451	28
Intermittent mixed headache	295	18
Chronic daily headache (CDH)	630	39
Post-traumatic headache	69	4.3
Psychogenic	6	0.3
Temporal arteritis	2	0.1

Table 2. *Diagnostic criteria for migraine.*

	Points
Aura	3
Prodrome	1
Trigger factors	1
Unilaterality	1
Gastro-intestinal symptoms	1
Family history	1
Menstrual aggravation	1
Response to ergotamine	1
Total	10

Should score a minimum of 5 points to meet the diagnostic criteria for migraine.

daily headaches. The majority of this form of chronic daily headaches still retain some migrainous features.

While obtaining the details of the clinical features and natural history of the headache, age, sex, age of onset of episodic migraine, age of transformation, type of headache pain, location, and timing of the headache, was recorded. Details of the types, quantity and frequency of the symptomatic medication usage were obtained. Separate inquiries into the use of simple analgesics, and analgesic/sedative combinations, caffeine containing analgesics, ergotamine/caffeine combinations, nasal decongestants and antihistamine combinations, and benzodiazapine were made. Detailed history of sleep and sleep habits were obtained, including difficulty in initiating sleep, maintaining sleep, and early morning awakening. The role of head and neck trauma and associated hypertension in transforming episodic migraine into daily headache was assessed.

In assessing the psychological and behavioural aspects, the following items were looked into:

(1) Depression using history, symptoms, and depression scales including Zung's scale and Beck depression scale.

(2) Minnesota Multiphasic Personality Inventory (MMPI).

(3) Anxiety scales.

(4) Stress prone behavioural patterns including Type A behaviour and non-assertiveness.

(5) Psychological interview, psycho-social and family dynamics were also included in the evaluation.

In the therapeutic field, observations were made on the effects of withdrawal of daily symptomatic medications. Beneficial effects of anti-migraine agents used prophylactically were assessed and the role of behavioural treatment in the overall management of the patient was also evaluated. All patients had a thorough neurological and systemic examination, and appropriate laboratory and neurodiagnostic tests to exclude structural causes for headache. Post-traumatic chronic daily headaches and temporomandibular joint (TMJ) dysfunction were excluded from the series.

Results

The number of cases in each category of chronic daily headache, along with sex distribution and age of onset of daily headache are shown in Table 3. Table 4 deals with the transformed migraine group, and includes the age at first visit, the age of onset of episodic migraine, duration of episodic migraine before the transformation occurred, age of transformation to chronic daily headache, and duration after the transformation. The figure is the graphic representation of the chronology of episodic migraine and chronic daily headache in the transformed migraine group. Between the age of 30 and 40, the incidence of chronic daily headache supersedes the incidence of episodic migraine in this group.

The diagnostic categorization of the types of migraine before chronic daily headache developed revealed 45 (9.2%) patients with classic and/or complicated migraine, and 444 (90.8%) patients with common migraine. Among the classic migraine, 21 out of 45 (4.2% of

Table 3. *Chronic daily headache.* (Total 630 cases).

Type	Number	Percentage	Male	Female	Age of onset of daily headache
Type I	84	13.33%	36	48	29.5 ± 9.5
Type II	57	9.04%	18	39	32.4 ± 10.5
Type III (Transformed migraine)	489	77.61%	105	384	39 ± 11.2

Table 4. *Transformed migraine.*

Age at first visit	Mean age of onset of episodic migraine	Mean duration of episodic migraine before transformation occurred	Mean age of transformation to chronic daily headache	Mean duration after transformation
Mean 41 ± 12 Range 11–64	Mean 22 ± 9.2 Range 3–53	Mean 16 ± 11 Range 1–51	Mean 39 ± 11.2 Range 12–65	Mean 6 ± 5

Figure. *Graphic representation of the chronology of episodic migraine and chronic daily headache in the transformed migraine group.*

the total transformed migraine patients) showed a clear history of transformation from classic to common migraine and then to chronic daily headache.

Positive family history of headache was obtained in 73.5% of cases with transformed migraine compared to 32.1% in Type I and 31.5% in Type II ($P<0.01$). Percentage of females who showed a history of menstrual aggravation of headaches are as follows; Type I, 25, Type II, 30 and transformed migraine or Type III, 60 ($P<0.01$), thereby showing significant increase in the number of patients with a history of menstrual migraine in this transformed migraine group.

Identifiable trigger factors occurred in significantly larger numbers in the transformed migraine group compared to the Type I and Type II chronic daily headaches, the figures being Type I, 21%, Type II, 31% and transformed migraine 88% ($P<0.001$) (Table 4a). Associated gastro-intestinal symptoms such as nausea, vomiting, diarrhoea, were seen in a higher proportion of patients with transformed migraine, compared to Type I and Type II chronic daily headaches. Seventy-six per cent of patients with transformed migraine showed associated gastro-intestinal symptoms, compared to 26% and 35% for Type I and Type II respectively. Similarly, visual and neurological symptoms were seen in 36% of patients with transformed migraine as opposed to 15% for Type I and 14% for Type II ($P<0.01$) (Table 4b).

The incidence of hypertension (10%) was higher in the transformed migraine group than in the others.

Table 4a. *Trigger factors.*

Type of headache	Percentage of patients with identifiable triggers
CDH Type I	21
CDH Type II	31
Transformed migraine	88*

*($P<0.001$).
CDH, chronic daily headache.

Table 4b. *Chronic daily headache accompanying symptoms.*

Type	Gastro-intestinal symptoms	Visual and neurological symptoms
Type I	26%	15%
Type II	35%	14%
Transformed migraine	76%*	36%*

*($P<0.01$).

Table 4c. *Chronic daily headache time of onset of headache.*

Type	Early a.m.	Nocturnal	Afternoon or evening
Type I	29%	7%	64%*
Type II	42%	36%	10%
Transformed migraine	73.6%*	33%	32%

*($P<0.01$).

The time of onset of headache

Waking up with a headache was significantly higher in patients with transformed migraine than in the other groups. On the other hand, Type I chronic daily headache patients had worse headache during the afternoon or evenings, differences that are statistically significant at a level less than 0.01 (Table 4c). In heavy analgesic/sedative/caffeine/ergotamine users, a predictable early morning headache, usually between 2:00 a.m. and 5:00 a.m. occurred on a daily or near daily basis.

Location of the headache

Even though statistical significance could not be obtained, analysis of the location of headache revealed that Type I chronic daily headache and Type II chronic daily headache had bilateral headaches in 92% and 80% respectively, the posterior regions of the head and neck being predominantly involved. In transformed migraine, on the other hand, headache tended to be mainly unilateral in 58% of patients and mostly frontal or fronto-temporal in 54% of patients. Chronic low grade headaches also tended to be on the side and site of the migrainous attacks in cases of transformed migraine.

Use of symptomatic medication

Daily use of analgesics was common in chronic daily headaches, especially in the transformed migraine group, while Type I and Type II chronic daily headache groups also used excessive amounts of analgesics on a daily basis (Type I, 67%, Type II, 66%, transformed migraine, 87.2%). All consumed at least 14 analgesic tablets per week, most patients averaging 21 per week (3 per day) and some as high as 10 to 12 per day. Thirty two per cent of patients used two types of analgesic tablets, and 3% used three types of analgesic medications daily. The daily medications for symptomatic relief used by patients with transformed migraine are given in Table 5.

Table 5. *Daily medications for symptomatic relief transformed migraine — 489 cases.*

Type of medications or preparations	Number	Percentage
Analgesic/sedative/caffeine/codeine combination	150	30
Excessive caffeine or analgesic/caffeine combination	141	28
Simple analgesics — aspirin or acetaminophen	114	23
Antihistamine with or without decongestants	63	13
Ergotamine	54	11
Proproxyphene	36	7

Table 6. *Behavioural scales.*

Type of headache	Zung depression scale score	Beck depression scale	Type A behaviour pattern[4]
CDH Type I $n = 84$	$53 \pm 9.9^*$	$11 \pm 8.6^*$	42 ± 4.7
CDH Type II $n = 57$	$63 \pm 12.7^{**}$	$16 \pm 5^*$	47 ± 7.6
CDH transformed migraine $n = 489$	$52 \pm 10.8^*$	$13 \pm 10.3^*$	$50 \pm 9.2^*$
Episodic common migraine $n = 100$	34 ± 4.2	8 ± 2.4	42 ± 4.8

CDH, chronic daily headache.

Behavioural scales including Zung depression scale, Beck depression scale, Type A behaviour pattern[4] are tabulated in Table 6. All groups of patients with chronic daily headaches, including transformed migraine, showed significantly elevated depression scales compared to episodic migraine patients. In addition, the transformed migraine patient showed an elevated Type A behavioural pattern score.

MMPI scales

Based on the MMPI, abnormal personality profile was found in 61% of patients with chronic daily headache compared to 12.2% in the episodic migraine group ($P<0.01$). Fifty-six per cent showed elevations of scales 1, 2, and 3, ie hypochondriasis, depression and hysteria, with the majority showing a typical V configuration. Thus 'neuroticism' was found to be significantly higher in patients with chronic daily headaches. There was no statistical difference between the various types of chronic daily headaches. Twenty-one per cent also had various combinations of elevated scales of 6, 7, 8, and 9. Elevated scales 6, 7, 8, and 9 were more often seen in Type I and Type II chronic daily headache patients.

Treatment

Treatment will be mentioned only in passing. All patients were treated by:
(1) withdrawal of daily symptomatic medication,
(2) institution of low tyramine, low caffeine diet,
(3) initiation of prophylactic pharmacotherapy using beta-blockers or tricyclic anti-depressants or calcium channel blockers, or methysergide. In some cases non-steroidal anti-inflammatory agents were also used. Co-pharmacy using two or three medications was instituted in many,
(4) biofeedback and behavioural therapy including individual and family counselling.

The results can be summarized as follows: 76% showed more than 75% reduction in headache index during an average follow-up period of 36 months. Eighteen per cent showed between 50 and 70% reduction in headache index. Six per cent of cases were intractable and continued to have near daily headache, and most of these showed extremely abnormal personality profiles in the MMPI and other behavioural scales.

Discussion

From this study it is obvious that a large majority of patients who present with chronic daily or near daily headache have had a previous history of clear-cut episodic migraine which over the years has transformed into a chronic daily headache. The group of patients with this particular form of chronic daily headache appear to have certain characteristics such as: family history of migraine, menstrual aggravation of headache, frequent presence of identifiable trigger factors, predilection for unilaterality of headache and predominance in fronto-temporal and retro-orbital areas, and early morning awakening with a headache. They also show increased incidence of gastro-intestinal and neurological symptoms compared to other groups of chronic daily headaches. Because of these distinct clinical features and natural history, it may be logical to refer to them as 'transformed' or 'evolutive' migraine. This term is used not to confuse the already controversial classification of headaches, but to emphasize the importance of recognizing this group of migraineurs who otherwise are categorized as 'tension headache'.

246

In a previous paper[3] we have argued that the majority of this form of chronic daily headache is a continuum of the migraine process, influenced and perpetuated by a number of factors such as: excessive use of medication, abnormal personality profile, depression, stress, traumatic life events and hypertension, and that diagnosis of a separate entity of tension headache is not justified under those circumstances.

In a paper on status migrainosus, Couch and Diamond[5] found that most frequent precipitating factors for continuous migraine were psychiatric factors, medication abuse and withdrawal, diet and changes of oestrogen levels. Iatrogenic worsening of migraine through analgesic and ergot abuse is known to be a major cause of migraine chronicity[6,7,8], and withdrawal of symptomatic analgesic medications[9] and ergotamine[10,11] often lead to marked lessening in frequency and severity of headache.

It can be argued that excessive use of analgesics is a consequence of the worsening of the headache, and not a cause of worsening. In one study there was no significant difference in the consumption of symptomatic analgesic medications between the controls and the chronic group before the chronicity occurred[12].

There are a number of unanswered questions about this particular group of chronic headache patients. Why are migraineurs prone to frequent or daily headaches as time evolves? Is this due to a depletion of central antinocioceptive neuro-chemical factors[13-15] or is it an abnormal sensitivity of the peripheral vascular receptors? What is the role of daily symptomatic medication in the perpetuation of the daily headache? What is the mechanism of their action? Kudrow[7] suggested that analgesics may suppress the activity of central serotonergic pathways concerned in pain regulation. Are the behaviour abnormalities such as 'neuroticism' and depression the result of chronic pain or vice versa? Or are they also due to the same central neuro-chemical abnormalities which lead to chronic headache? Future research and observations should find answers to all these questions.

References

1 Dalsgaard-Nielsen, J. (1970): Some aspects of the epidemiology of migraine in Denmark. Kliniske Aspekter i Migraereforskningen, Copenhagen.
2 Graham, J. R. (1968): Headache and cranial neuralgias. In *Handbook of clinical neurology*, Vol. 5, eds P. J. Vinken & G. W. Gruyn, p. 48. New York: Elsevier Publishing Co.
3 Mathew, N. T., Stubits, E. & Nigam, M. P. (1982): Transformation of episodic migraine into daily headache: analysis of factors. *Headache* **22**, 66–68.
4 Friedman, M. & Rosenman, R. (1974): *Type A behavior and your heart*. New York: Knopf.
5 Couch, J. R. & Diamond, S. (1983): Status migrainosus: causative and therapeutic aspects. *Headache* **23**, 99–101.
6 Isler, H. (1982): Migraine treatment as a cause of chronic migraine. In *Advances in migraine research and therapy*, ed. F. Clifford Rose, pp. 159–163. New York: Raven Press.
7 Kudrow, L. (1982): Paradoxical effects of frequent analgesic use. In *Advances in neurology*, ed. M. Critchley *et al.*, Vol. 33, pp. 335–341. New York: Raven Press.
8 Diener, H. C., Dichgans, J. & Gerber, W. D. (1983): Drug induced chronic headache. In *Proceedings of the 1st International Headache Congress* (abstracts), Munich.
9 Rapoport, A. M., Weeks, R. E., Sheftell, F. D., Baskin, S. M. & Verdi, J. (1986): Analgesic washout period, a critical variable in the evaluation of headache treatment efficacy. *Neurology* **36** (Suppl. 2), 100–101.
10 Saper, J. R. (1976): Migraine: II Treatment. *J. Am. Med. Ass.* **239**, 2480–2483.
11 Lippman, C. W. (1955): Characteristic headache resulting from prolonged use of ergot derivatives. *J. Nerv. Ment. Dis.* **121**, 270–273.
12 Baldrati, A., Bini, L., D'Alessandra, R., Cortelli, R., Capoa, D., Carolid, P. & Sacquegna, T., (1985): Analysis of outcome predictors of migraine towards chronicity. *Cephalalgia* **5**, (Suppl. 2), 195–199.

13 Appenzeller, O. (1975): Pathogenesis of vascular headache of migrainous type: The role of impaired central inhibition. *Headache* **15**, 177–179.

14 Anselimi, B., Baldi, E., Cassacci, F., *et al.* (1980): Endogenous opioids in cerebrospinal fluid and blood in idiopathic headache sufferers. *Headache* **20**, 294–299.

15 Sicuteri, F. (1978): Opiate receptors and migraine headache. *Headache* **17**, 253–257.

38

HEADACHE ASSOCIATED WITH FLUID RETENTION IN WOMEN: MISDIAGNOSIS AS MIGRAINE

W. F. Durward*, I. K. Hart* and M. G. Dunnigan†

*Department of Neurology, Institute of Neurological Sciences
Southern General Hospital, Glasgow G51 4TF, UK and †Department of
Medicine, Stobhill General Hospital, Glasgow, G21 3UW, UK

Summary

Fluid retention (idiopathic or cyclical oedema) in women is frequently unrecognized and commoner than most practitioners appreciate. There is a significant risk of misdiagnosis as migraine and in this chapter the authors offer examples of cases so misdiagnosed initially, together with the results of a postal survey of 141 women with fluid retention. The survey confirms, with high significance, potential for misdiagnosis with 72% of the respondents reporting headache as a significant component of symptoms of fluid retention prior to treatment.

Diagnosis of fluid retention is discussed, risk factors described and principles of management recommended.

Introduction

There is a lack of adequate teaching on the subject of fluid retention. The practitioner may first encounter this condition when he enters general practice and is confronted by patients with apparently bizarre symptoms who regularly present themselves for repeat prescriptions for diuretics. Standard textbooks, including endocrinological and gynaecological monographs, make little reference to the problems of fluid retention, and articles on the subject are scattered in specialist journals.

Most women with fluid retention do not show gross dependent or pitting oedema. While the mechanisms of fluid retention remain uncertain, causal factors can often be evaluated by analysis of precipitating risk factors. In most women, fluid retention shows no relationship to the menstrual cycle, although some patients show premenstrual exacerbations with true premenstrual fluid retention, accompanied by other features of premenstrual

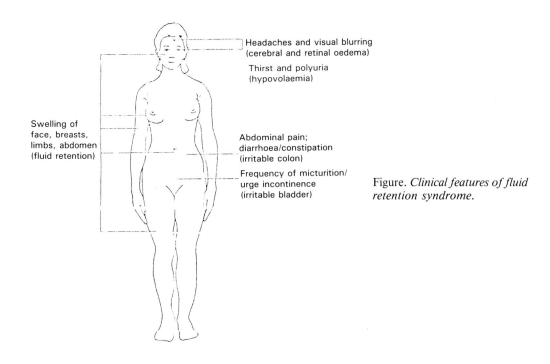

Headaches and visual blurring
(cerebral and retinal oedema)

Thirst and polyuria
(hypovolaemia)

Swelling of
face, breasts,
limbs, abdomen
(fluid retention)

Abdominal pain;
diarrhoea/constipation
(irritable colon)

Frequency of micturition/
urge incontinence
(irritable bladder)

Figure. *Clinical features of fluid retention syndrome.*

syndrome. The term 'fluid retention syndrome' offers a more accurate description, implying the presence of significant fluid retention in a woman in the absence of cardiac, renal or hepatic disease or of hypoproteinaemia from any cause.

In considering the problems of fluid retention in women two general points should be borne in mind. Firstly, many women are fluid-retaining to a variable degree, with some swelling of ankles in hot weather or on prolonged standing; in contrast, men almost never show 'physiological' fluid retention of this kind and the presence of ankle oedema in a man usually indicates definite underlying pathology. The reason for the female propensity to fluid retention is uncertain, but it may be related to the need to conserve sodium and water during menstruation, lactation and pregnancy[1]. Secondly, the aetiology of excessive fluid retention in women is multifactorial and the basic biochemical defect remains uncertain. It is not one of a deficiency or excess of a single hormone but should be viewed as an abnormal response to a number of differing humoral, metabolic and autonomic mechanisms, some or all of which may be present in individual patients. For this reason the condition should be considered as a syndrome rather than as a single entity. Consideration of fluid retention as a multifactorial syndrome allows a risk-factor approach to causes and management and eliminates the fruitless search for a single 'cause'.

The main symptom of the fluid retention syndrome is swelling of the face, hands, abdomen and legs (Figure). Swelling is usually least marked in the morning, except for the face, but becomes more marked as the day advances with maintenance of the upright posture. The swelling is usually more apparent to the patient and her relatives than to the examining physician. Abdominal swelling distresses the patient since it is unsightly and abdominal girth may increase by as much as five or six inches from morning to evening leading to the patient requiring to change into loose-fitting clothes, or even into night-clothes, by early evening. Swelling of the fingers and hands may be troublesome and lead to the removal of rings. Swelling of the lower limbs rarely produces gross pitting oedema, but the generalized increase in limb volume makes it difficult to put on or remove shoes or boots.

The swelling which characterizes fluid retention is accompanied by diurnal weight gain. Normal women can gain up to 3 lb from morning to evening but fluid-retaining patients observe diurnal weight gain up to as much as 15 lb daily. The recording of morning and evening weight provides the best single estimate of the severity of the syndrome.

Many fluid-retaining patients experience intense thirst, which results in the consumption of large quantities of fluid during the day. Polyuria does not occur in the upright posture but becomes evident when the patient lies down or retires to bed. The thirst of severe fluid retention may continue during the night with the patient keeping a supply of fluid at the bedside. The patient who retains much fluid may spend the day drinking and gaining weight, then spend the evening and night passing urine because of the diuresis produced by the assumption of the recumbent posture. Fluid-retaining patients with severe thirst may be regarded as hysterical water-drinkers, or investigated for diabetes with negative results.

Many patients with fluid retention suffer from headaches, probably due to a degree of cerebral oedema. They may be misdiagnosed as having migraine, including migrainous neuralgia, and this possibility is discussed further below. Alternatively the patients may be regarded as possibly having brain tumour and be investigated accordingly; indeed a significant number of these patients will be finally diagnosed as having benign intracranial hypertension (pseudo-tumor cerebri). Visual symptoms occur in fluid-retaining patients and vary from mild blurring to true amblyopic episodes lasting from a few seconds to several minutes and often related to change in posture. The obscurations may be related to increased intra-cranial pressure associated with cerebral oedema and may lead to the patient presenting to ophthalmologist or physician who pursues the possibility that these are transient ischaemic episodes. Fluid-retaining patients often report non-specific symptoms of fatigue and many patients complain of slowing of cerebration.

Many fluid-retaining patients suffer from functional or autonomic disorders of the bowel and/or bladder. One of the authors (M.G.D.)[2] reports that about one third of cases give a history suggestive of irritable bowel syndrome with lower abdominal pain located in the right or left iliac fossa associated with altered bowel habit. Such patients often find their way to surgeon or gynaecologist and are then liable to be subjected to unnecessary investigations and surgical intervention. About one fifth of the patients suffer from functional bladder disturbance and complain of diurnal frequency of micturition, with occasional urge incontinence, and may be referred to urologist or gynaecologist.

Some fluid-retaining patients suffer from vasovagal symptoms with episodes of hypotension leading to faintness or transient loss of consciousness with pallor and sweating on assuming the upright posture. Such vasovagal symptoms show a poor correlation with the severity of fluid retention. They may suffer from a variety of psychiatric problems, demonstrating anxiety states or depressive illnesses of varying severity, and a minority suffer from severe personality disorders.

A significant number of patients with fluid retention are referred from one specialist to another, acquire thick case records and consider that they are suffering from an illness which defies diagnosis, a situation that compounds anxiety, needless over-investigation and, occasionally, unnecessary surgery.

The symptoms of fluid retention tend to far outweigh objective features, especially to the clinician who is not familiar with the syndrome. The most obvious sign is abdominal distension which may give the patient the appearance of being pregnant. This cause of the distension has not been established precisely but may be partly due to a decrease in abdominal wall tone and partly to oedema of small and large bowel. Evidence of ascites is absent and the abdomen is tympanitic on percussion. Radiology of the alimentary tract during abdominal distension shows no abnormality.

The second reliable sign of fluid retention is the patient's facial appearance with puffy features which are easily recognized with experience. Care should be taken to distinguish the facies of hypothyroidism and the nephrotic syndrome.

Marked pitting and dependent limb oedema is not found in the fluid retention syndrome and the presence of gross oedema of the lower limbs usually implies an alternative diagnosis.

As stated above, the most reliable objective evidence of fluid retention is the diurnal weight variation which all patients exhibit and without which the diagnosis should not be entertained. The keeping of a weight chart is an essential part of diagnosis and management. Weight variation usually shows little or no correlation with the menstrual cycle and, in the majority of patients, the assumption of a recumbent posture at night leads to a diuresis and a return to normal weight by next morning. This is not true of all patients and severe cases may show periods of fluid retention extending over several days, followed by diuresis.

Many, but by no means all, fluid-retaining patients are obese. On examining the abdomen particular attention should be paid to the presence of an irritable or spastic colon. The blood pressure in fluid-retaining patients is variable. A small number show a degree of postural hypotension but the onset of vasovagal symptoms is irregular and may not be readily demonstrable on first encounter in an out-patient clinic.

Patients with severe fluid retention may show ophthalmological abnormality on fundoscopy — ranging from fullness of the veins with indistinct disc margins, to a minority of patients who show frank papilloedema and constitute a sub-group of the condition known as benign intracranial hypertension.

Case studies

The prevalence of the fluid retention syndrome is uncertain. Most general practitioners will have a number of female patients who regularly demand diuretics for fluid retention. One of the authors (M.G.D.)[2] found 29 of 107 women (29%) interviewed consecutively in one general practice to give a history of mild to moderate fluid retention. In 16 patients the symptoms were mild, but 13 women had experienced symptoms which were sufficiently severe to lead them to consult their general practitioner at least once. One general practitioner in Lanarkshire, Scotland reported treating 51 patients for moderate to severe fluid retention over a 10-year period[2], figures which give some idea of the prevalence of the more severe forms of the syndrome in a large industrial general practice.

The majority of women with severe fluid retention syndrome are in the 20–50 age group, but patients may present after the menopause and this diagnosis has been made for the first time in a patient aged more than 70 years. Children have also presented with the syndrome, with onset well before the menarche and commonly occurring in families. The symptoms in children were identical to those of adults. Some patients diagnosed in adult life with fluid retention give a history of fluid-retaining symptoms going back to early childhood. Fluid retention is often familial. One of the authors (M.G.D.) has seen two male patients over a ten-year period who demonstrate typical features of this syndrome, but it is overwhelmingly a condition of women.

One of the authors (W.F.D.) is a consultant neurologist who became convinced by experience of cases that fluid retention was underdiagnosed and also misdiagnosed in neurological or general practice as migraine. The following three sample case histories demonstrate this point.

Case 1

E.G., 62-years-old, female and overweight. Patient complaining of intermittent headache, tendency to periods of relapse and remission, headache throbbing in character, associated

Table 1. *Features of headache responding to treatment of underlying fluid retention.*

	Yes (%)	s.e.%	P
Throbbing in character	91	4.3	< <0.001
Associated with nausea and/or vomiting	80	6.0	< <0.001
Associated with visual upset	96	2.9	< <0.001
Severe enough to wake from sleep	78	4.6	< <0.001
Severe enough to interfere with normal life	91	4.3	< <0.001

N = 45

N, total within group; n, subset of group answering yes or no.

$$\text{s.e.\%, standard error of percentage} = \frac{\text{subset answering yes} \times (100 - \text{subset answering no})}{N}$$

$$\text{Calculation of } P \text{ from formula} \frac{\%\text{ answering yes} - \%\text{ answering no}}{\text{s.e.\%}}$$

Table 2. *Was headache a prominent symptom of fluid retention before treatment?*

	n	%	s.e. %	P
Yes	59	72	4.96	< <0.001
No	23	28		
Total(N)	82			

Did headache improve with treatment of fluid retention?

	n	%	s.e. %	P
Yes	45	76	6	< <0.001
No	14	24		
Total(N)	59			

Were migraine remedies successful in treating headache before fluid retention was dealt with?

	n	%	s.e. %	P
Yes	17	77	6.7	< <0.001
No	5	13		
Total(N)	22			

For key see footnotes to Table 1.

nausea, often awakening in the middle of the night with headache, crocodile tears associated with headache, also eyes and one cheek becoming red during headache. Reported daily weight gain 5–6 lb, nocturia. Migraine remedies failed. Remission with weight loss, carbohydrate restriction and spironolactone.

Case 2

M.McI., 38-years-old, female. Patient describing headaches of migrainous neuralgia type with onset coinciding with weight gain about 2 years previously. Additional weight gain each day. Pizotifen (Sanomigran) prescribed without benefit and the patient was taking pethidine regularly. An experienced consultant neurologist was contemplating cerebral angiography. Remission with weight loss, carbohydrate restriction and spironolactone.

Case 3

S.M., 53-years-old, female, and overweight. Patient complaining of headache which was worse towards evening, slurring of speech also worse towards evening and abdominal pain with distension. Weight gain towards evening. Remission with weight loss, carbohydrate restriction and spironolactone.

Method

The authors decided to conduct a postal survey of 141 patients with fluid retention seen over a 10-year period by one of the authors (M.G.D.). The results of this survey are given in the accompanying tables (Table 1 and Table 2). A study of the questions and answers demonstrate how a misdiagnosis of migraine could readily be made. The answer to each question is shown to be statistically significant.

Attention is drawn to the high response rate in this postal survey—65%. Eighty-five replies were received and 14 questionnaires were returned 'gone away'. It is assumed that 127 questionnaires were received. This response rate is very high for a postal survey and, per se, reflects the very real nature of the symptoms coupled with the difficulty experienced by the patients in obtaining appropriate advice and their consequent willingness to co-operate in a research project.

Results and discussion

It is beyond reasonable doubt that fluid retention syndrome is a significant and under-diagnosed problem in the community, but the diagnosis is not difficult once it occurs to the attending physician.

A single aetiology has not been established but major risk-factors may be metabolic/endocrine or psychiatric, and minor risk-factors can also be identified.

Weight gain and/or obesity appears to be the commonest precipitating cause of fluid retention. About two-thirds of patients can relate onset of symptoms to weight gain which need not be sufficient to produce formal obesity (defined as 20% or more above ideal weight). Many fluid-retaining patients have relatives with diabetes mellitus or may themselves be diabetic[3].

Endocrine factors which may be relevant in fluid retention include the premenstrual state, non-toxaemic oedema of pregnancy, oral contraceptives, hypothyroidism or thyrotoxicosis.

Many patients with fluid retention show psychiatric abnormalities which may include anxiety, depression or personality disorders[1,4]. The last group may be especially difficult, with the patient often manipulative, showing hysterical features and tending to disrupt the lives of those close to them. Some patients have been recognized to have developed symptoms of fluid retention abruptly after stress—some even become bloated within minutes of acute stress.

Minor risk-factors which may aggravate pre-existing fluid retention include upright posture, severe physical exertion, fever, warm weather[5], steroids (especially oral contraceptives and danazol) and analgesics (including phenylbutazone, indomethacin and even aspirin). Undiagnosed fluid-retaining patients are especially liable to receive a variety of hormones, analgesics and anti-depressant drugs, many of which make the condition worse.

The principles of management can be summarized as suspecting and then confirming the diagnosis, reassuring the patient, evaluating risk factors, advice on diet and diuretics.

A few severely disabled patients benefit from a period in hospital, especially if they have been taking large doses of loop diuretics which can have a paradoxical effect on fluid restriction, that is, cause worsening. Other patients who may be admitted include those who show severe psychiatric disturbance or who cannot lose weight at home.

The main element of treatment is diet with restriction of carbohydrate. Even those patients who are not formally obese, that is, the majority, derive considerable benefit from weight reduction. Weight loss of 15–30 lb will ameliorate or abolish the symptoms of fluid retention in many patients. An initial diet of 800–1000 k cal is recommended with particular restriction of carbohydrate intake to give about 40% of calories.

The role of diuretics in the treatment of fluid retention is controversial. There is little doubt that some patients with fluid retention abuse diuretics or become dependent on them. Diuretics are often ineffective in the obese fluid-retaining patient. A patient who initially responds to diuretics may find that these become ineffective and then try to increase the dose, or to abandon the diuretic when it becomes obvious that it has become ineffective. Spironolactone is the drug of first choice but chlorthalidone or bendrofluazide may also be effective; the latter drugs should be prescribed with a potassium supplement, as fluid-retaining patients appear especially vulnerable to potassium depletion. In fluid-retaining patients who require a diuretic the authors usually begin treatment with spironolactone 100 mgm daily. Diuretics are not to be regarded as a permanent treatment for fluid retention and the patient should be persuaded to discontinue treatment from time to time and to attempt to achieve control by dietary means alone, if possible. Patients may require diuretics at times of stress, during intercurrent infections, or in warm weather and may be able to discontinue them at other times.

Sodium and water restriction in fluid-retaining patients seems reasonable at first sight but is usually ineffective.

A small minority of patients remain fluid-retaining despite the above measures, and these often show psychiatric abnormalities. A large number of other drugs have been used in the management of fluid retention, including bromocriptine, L-dopa, sympathomimetic amines and chlorpropamide. All of these drugs have produced benefit in individual patients, but many have unpleasant side-effects and their use should be restricted to specialist referral centres. A small minority of fluid-retaining patients remain refractory to all therapy.

All patients with fluid retention should be provided with an explanation of the nature of the syndrome. Anxious patients may require a minor tranquilliser. Patients with severe depression or a personality disorder should be referred to a psychiatrist. Some patients require treatment for an associated irritable bowel syndrome which should be managed initially on conventional lines with a high-fibre diet and an anti-spasmodic drug. Patients with persistent bladder symptoms in spite of treatment may benefit from an anti-spasmodic drug. If bowel or bladder symptoms persist, referral should be made to an appropriate specialist.

References

1 Thorn, G. W. (1968): Approach to the patient with 'idiopathic edema' or 'periodic swelling'. *J. Amer. Med. Assoc.* **206**, 333–338.
2 Donnigan, M. G. (1985): Recognition and management of the fluid retention (idiopathic or cyclical oedema) and premenstrual syndromes. In *Medical gynaecology*, ed. M. C. MacNaughton, pp. 27–54. London: Blackwell Scientific Publications.

3 Sims, E. A. H., MacKay, B. R. & Shirai, T. (1965): The relation of capillary angiopathy and diabetes mellitus to idiopathic oedema. *Ann. Int. Med.* **63**, 972–987.
4 Edwards, O. M. & Bayliss, R. I. S. (1976): Idiopathic oedema of women. *Quart. J. Med., New Series XLV* **177**, 125–144.
5 Streeten, D. H. P. (1979): Idiopathic oedema. *Lancet* **i**, 775–776.

39

THE ROLE OF THE OCCIPITAL

NERVE IN UNILATERAL HEADACHE

Michael Anthony

*The Department of Neurology, Prince Henry Hospital,
and the School of Medicine, University of New South Wales,
Sydney, Australia*

Introduction

It has been previously reported[1] that attacks of chronic cluster headache can be arrested for varying periods following injections of methylprednisolone acetate in propylene glycol (Depomedrol, Upjohn) into the region of the ipsilateral greater occipital nerve (GON). The explanation put forward for this effect was that the injection interrupted impulses arriving along the GON at the cervico-trigeminal relay, which forms the pain centre for the head. This centre is made up of the descending spinothalamic tract and nucleus of the trigeminal nerve, which become both morphologically and functionally associated with the upper cervical segments, its cells forming a continuous column with the cells of the posterior horn of the spinal cord as far down as C_4[2]. As a result, the centre acts as a basis for overlap of impulses arriving along both the trigeminal nerve and the upper cervical roots. The main sensory nerve arising from these roots is the GON, formed by the medial branch of the C_2 dorsal ramus with a small communicating branch from that of the C_3 root[3].

The pain of cluster headache is felt predominantly in the fronto-temporal and ocular areas of the head, but not infrequently it also spreads to the occipital region. At the same time migrainous headaches are mostly hemicranial and are also felt in the above areas, whilst the pain of occipital neuralgia is experienced mainly in the occipital region, though it may spread to the temporal and frontal areas of the head[4].

Since attacks of cluster headache can be stopped for a period by injecting the ipsilateral GON with Depomedrol, it was decided to study the ability of such injections to prevent attacks of unilateral migraine recurring on the same side of the head and of occipital neuralgia, which is always unilateral.

Table 1. *Steroid injection of the occipital nerve in unilateral headache. Clinical details of patients.*

	Number	Male	Female	Age range	Mean age	Headache duration (years)	Headache frequency
Cluster headache	20	19	1	26–64	42.5	1–23	1–4/day
Unilateral migraine	20	4	16	27–69	45	4–36	1–4/week
Occipital neuralgia	20	4	16	35–78	56.3	1/4–32	2–7/week

Patients and methods

Three groups, each of 20 patients and suffering from (1) chronic cluster headache, (2) frequent attacks of unilateral migraine recurring on the same side of the head, and (3) occipital neuralgia, were selected for study. Clinical details of the patients can be seen in Table 1. None of the patients demonstrated any abnormality of the nervous system, nor were any of the investigations performed abnormal. The majority of patients demonstrated greater tenderness of the GON on pressure on the side of the headache than on the non-affected side. All patients suffering from occipital neuralgia had marked tenderness of the ipsilateral GON, 12 had hyperalgesia, and 2 hypoalgesia, in the distribution of the nerve. None of the patients with cluster headache or migraine showed similar sensory signs on the scalp.

Every patient received first 4 ml, 1% lignocaine local anaesthetic into the region of the GON during an episode of headache, for the purpose of assessing the effectiveness of the procedure in relieving the pain of the attack. Ten patients with cluster headache and ten with unilateral migraine received similar injections whilst headache-free, and subsequently 160 mg Depomedrol by intramuscular injection, for the purpose of assessing whether either local anaesthetic alone or systemic steroids are capable of altering headache frequency at all. Finally, all patients received an injection of 160 mg Depomedrol into the region of the GON ipsilateral to the headache, when headache-free. The date of the injection was recorded on a card, on which the patient also recorded the date of the first and subsequent headaches, and which formed the basis of assessment of headache freedom following the injection of the steroid. Patients with unilateral migraine and occipital neuralgia received only one injection of steroid into the region of the GON, whilst those with chronic cluster headaches received a second injection soon after the return of their attacks, as most patients found this to be an effective treatment of their condition.

The technical details of injecting the GON were similar to those described previously[1].

Ten patients with severe chronic cluster headache, who had already received several injections of Depomedrol, were eventually subjected to surgical division of the greater and lesser occipital nerves or of the C_2 and C_3 sensory roots, on the side habitually affected by the headache.

Results

Control observation

Injection of local anaesthetic into the region of the GON during attacks of headache, arrested the headache in the majority of patients in each group. Local anaesthetic injected into the region of the GON, or intramuscular Depomedrol when patients were headache-free, failed to prevent headache in every case. Results are summarized in Table 2.

Table 2. *Steroid injection of the occipital nerve in unilateral headache. Control observations.*

	Headache type		Result	
1. LA during HA	Cluster headache	20	Arrested	16
	Occipital neuralgia	20	Arrested	18
	Unilateral migraine	20	Arrested	16
2. LA during HAF	Cluster headache	10	HA return (4–24 hrs)	10
	Unilateral migraine	10	HA return (1–4 days)	10
3. Depomedrol IM	Cluster headache	10	HA return	10
	Unilateral migraine	10	HA return	10

LA, local anaesthetic; HA, headache; HAF, headache-free; IM, intramuscular.

Table 3. *Steroid injection of the occipital nerve in unilateral headache.*

	Result of treatment			
	Number of patients	*Number responded*	*HA relief range (days)*	*HA relief mean (days)*
1. Chronic cluster HA	20	18	5–73	20.3 (1st resp.) 32.0 (max. resp.)
2. Unilateral migraine	20	18	13–66	30.1
3. Occipital neuralgia	20	19	28–140	47.7

1st resp., first response; max. resp., maximal response; HA, headache.

Chronic cluster headache

Eighteen of the 20 patients experienced periods of headache freedom varying from 5 to 73 days following the first injection of steroid, the mean duration of relief being 20.3 days (Table 3). One patient failed to respond at all, whilst another was headache-free for only 2 days, but he was also classified as treatment failure due to the brevity of the response. Both patients responded when the injection was repeated at a later date, experiencing relief from headaches for 35 and 22 days, respectively (Table 4). When maximal responses were only considered, following either the first or second injection, mean duration of relief was 32.0 days (Table 3).

Unilateral migraine

Eighteen of the 20 patients experienced periods of headache freedom following injection of steroid ranging from 13 to 66 days, the mean duration of relief being 30.1 days (Table 3).

Occipital neuralgia

Nineteen of the 20 patients experienced relief either from attacks of headache or continuous headache following the injection. The period of relief ranged from 28 to 140 days, the mean duration of relief being 47.7 days (Table 3). If the patient with the longest response of 140 days is excluded, the mean duration of relief was again considerable, 35.3 days.

Table 4. *Chronic cluster headaches. Clinical details of patients and response to steroid injection of the occipital nerve.*

Patient no.	Age	Duration disease (years)	HA side	HA frequency (per day)	HA duration (hours)	Response (HAF days)
1	64	8	L	1–3	1–3	5, 10
2	30	8	L	1	½–1½	20, 56
3	30	10	R	1–3	½–¾	36, 28
4	26	10	L	1–5	½–1	15, 21
5	55	11	L	2	½–1	31, 15
6	49	1	R	1	½	30, 73
7 F	29	1	R	1–4	3–4	5, 10
8	58	6	L	2	¾–1	40, 33
9	47	6	L	1	1–2	23, 27
10	53	2	L	1–3	2–4	49, 13
11	34	2	R	1	½–1	4, 14
12	28	9	L	1	1–2	12, 68
13	60	8	L	1–2	½–1	21, 3
14	53	3	L	1	1–1	12, 3
15	41	2	R	1–2	¾–2	2, 22
16	41	21	R	2–3	¼–2	0, 35
17	26	12	L	2	1½–2½	37, 0
18	52	1	L	1–4	¼–½	29, 16
19	43	23	R	2	¼–2	14, 29
20	31	7	L	1–2	1	21, 10

HA, headache; HAF, headache-free; L, left; R, right.

Side-effects of steroid injection

The commonest side-effect was a sensation of soreness or dull ache in the region of the occiput and the upper neck, varying in duration from a few hours to 3 days. This was complained of by 37 of the 60 patients. Three patients complained of a sensation of destabilization, as though walking on soft ground and being uncertain of their step, a symptom which lasted 2 days in one patient and about 5 days in the other two. The symptom was attributed to blockade of proprioceptive impulses from the head produced by the injection. Finally, one patient became mildly confused, with disordered thought processes and clouded sensorium and these symptoms, which were thought to be psychological side-effects occasionally induced by steroids, persisted for 1 week.

Occipital neurectomy — Cervical rhizotomy

Seven patients were subjected to neurectomy of the ipsilateral greater occipital and lesser occipital nerves. In 4, relief was short lived (7, 10, 15 and 20 days), two were headache-free for 12 and 18 months before the headaches returned, whilst the remaining patient continues to be headache-free to date, 4 months after the operation.

Five patients were subjected to C_2 and C_3 intra-dural, preganglionic division of the sensory roots ipsilateral to the headache. Two patients had the operation after a previous surgical neurectomy failed to control the headaches, whilst in three rhizotomy was the initial surgical procedure. In only one patient was relief short-lived (20 days), whilst in the remaining four it ranged from 3 to 20 months. In fact the patient with the longest period of relief continues to be headache-free to date.

Table 5. *Chronic cluster headache occipital neurectomy/cervical rhizotomy. Clinical details of patients and results of surgery.*

Patient no.	Sex age	Duration HA(years)	HA side	Frequency HA(daily)	Duration HA(hours)	Occipital neur- ectomy	HAF	Cervical rhizotomy	HAF
1	M 33	12	R	1–3	½–¾	May. 84	10 Days		
2	M 46	11	L	1	1–2	Dec. 84	15 Days		
3	M 43	20	R	2–3	1–2	Dec. 84	18 Months		
4	M 54	4	L	1	1–½	Oct. 84	20 Days		
5	M 28	9	L	1	1–2	May. 86	4 Months		
6	M 67	10	L	1–3	1–3	Aug. 82	12 Months	Mar. 84	20 Days
7	M 38	6	R	3–4	1–3	Aug. 84	7 Days	Sep. 84	3 Months
8	F 31	1	R	1–4	3–4			Aug. 84	20 Months
9	M 31	10	L	1	½–1½			Oct. 84	10 Months
10	M 52	2	R	1	½–2			Oct. 84	3 Months
						Mean duration of HA relief (days)	153		222

HA, headache; HAF, headache free; L, left; R, right.

Mean duration of headache freedom for the seven patients subjected to neurectomy was 153 days, and for the five subjected to rhizotomy 222 days. Details of patients and results of the two procedures are summarized in Table 5.

Discussion

The results of this study demonstrate that attacks of unilateral headache — cluster headache, unilateral migraine and occipital neuralgia — can be arrested by anaesthetising the ipsilateral GON with local anaesthetic, and that recurrent attacks can be prevented for some weeks by steroid injection (methylprednisolone acetate, Depomedrol) into the region of the GON. Control observations consisting of injecting local anaesthetic into the region of the nerve when patients were headache-free or intramuscular injection of Depomedrol, had no preventive effect on the course of the headaches. Finally, the fact that in all cases the headaches returned after a variable period of headache freedom, confirms that this was entirely due to the effects of the steroid injected into the region of the GON.

The mechanism whereby Depomedrol produces relief from recurrent headaches in the categories investigated in this study remains at best conjectural. It has been suggested that both methylprednisolone acetate and its suspended medium, propylene glycol, are capable of causing demyelination of nerve fibres when injected near nerve trunks, as has been shown in the rat[5]. In any case the steroid must disrupt conduction along the GON, since relief of an acute attack of unilateral headache can be arrested within minutes by blocking conduction of the nerve with local anaesthetic, and surgical division of the nerve or of its sensory roots (C_2 and C_3) also produces relief from recurrent headaches for periods ranging from a few weeks to several months, as shown in this study.

The question as to what exactly causes irritation of the GON leading to the production of headache has been the source of considerable debate. The suggestion that this is due to compression or trauma of the nerve[6] as it passes between the posterior arches of the axis and the atlas, or as it traverses the numerous muscle planes before its emergence onto the scalp, has not been sustained[7]. In fact, between the axis and the atlas, there is no intervertebral disc, no facetal joint and therefore no intervertebral foramen. There is no reason why the nerve should be irritated easily or frequently. It is far more likely that irritation of the GON occurs as a result of displacement, abnormal movements or osteo-arthritic changes in the atlanto-axial, or facetal joints, which are richly supplied by sensory nerve endings. Pain arising from facetal joints of the upper neck may also be secondary to nerve root irritation at a lower level, causing abnormal muscle spasm[7]. Since all these joints fall within the receptive field of the cervico-trigeminal relay, pain can also be referred to the trigeminal territory, producing occipito-frontal or hemicranial headache of the types investigated in this study; these statements are based on scattered observations available in the literature, and both extensive and reliable studies are necessary to validate the views put forth in this discussion.

References

1   Anthony, M. (1985): Arrest of attacks of cluster headache by local steroid injection of the occipital nerve. In *Migraine: clinical and research advances*, ed. F. Clifford Rose, pp. 168–173. Basel: Karger.
2   Carpenter, M. B. (1976): Human neuroanatomy, 7th edn, pp. 354–357. Baltimore: Williams & Wilkins.
3   Bogduk, N. (1982): The clinical anatomy of the cervical dorsal rami. *Spine* **7**, 319–330.
4   Bogduk, N. (1985): Greater occipital neuralgia. *Current therapy in neurological surgery*, ed. D. M. Long, pp. 175–180. Philadelphia: Decker.
5   Selby, R. (1983). Complications of depomedrol. *Surgical Neurol.* **19**, 393–394.
6   Hunter, C. R. & Mayfield, F. H. (1949): Role of the upper cervical roots in the production of pain in the head. *Amer. J. Surg.* **78**, 743–751.
7   Sluijter, M. E. & Koetsveldt-Baart, C. C. (1980): Interruption of pain pathways in the treatment of the cervical syndrome. *Anaesthesia* **35**, 302–307.

40

CLINICAL EXPERIENCES WITH

EPERISONE HYDROCHLORIDE

IN MUSCLE CONTRACTION HEADACHE

Shukuro Araki, Makoto Uchino, Shinichi Ikegawa and Hiroshi Sato

The First Department of Internal Medicine,
Kumamoto University Medical School, Kumamoto, Japan

Introduction

Muscle contraction headache is probably the most common type of chronic headache in Japan. The immediate source of pain in this type of headache is claimed to be sustained contraction of the muscles of the neck, face and scalp which may produce pain of extra-cranial muscles. This is commonly psychosomatic and associated with psychogenic stress.

Various therapies have been used for the treatment of this condition including physical therapy and psychotherapy. With drug therapy, antidepressants, sedatives and muscle relaxant agents are commonly used in addition to analgesics[1].

In patients with muscle contraction headache, pain itself increases muscular tonus, and may cause local circulatory involvement of compression or peripheral nerves, resulting in secondary pain. Analgesics and muscle relaxants are commonly used together in order to break this vicious cycle[2].

1 : Structural Formula :

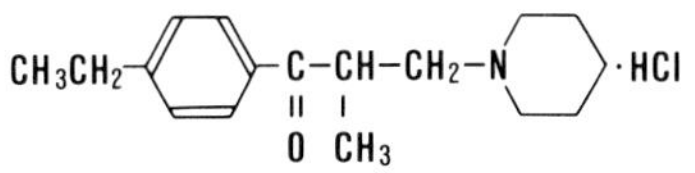

$C_{17}H_{25}NO \cdot HCl$

Fig. 1. *Chemical characteristic of eperisone hydrochloride.*

2 : Molecular weight : 295.85

3 : Chemical name : 4'-Ethyl-2-methyl-3-piperidinopropiophenone hydrochloride

Table 1. *Background data of the patients.*

Parameters	Category	Number of the cases
Sex	Male	19
	Female	31
Age (years)	20–29	3
	30–39	6
	40–49	10
	50–59	10
	60–69	15
	70–79	6
Setting	Outpatients	44
	Inpatients	6
Diagnosis	Muscle contraction headache	50
Duration of illness	3 months	10
	6 months	9
	1 year	15
	3 years	6
	5 years	4
	10 years	4
	> 10 years	2
Other disorders	Absent	13
	Present*	37

*Hypertension (14); hypotension (4); depressive state (3); cervical spondylosis (3); hepatic disorder (3) and others.

Eperisone hydrochloride (Fig. 1), which was developed as a result of extensive pharmacological screening of beta-aminopropiophenone derivatives, is thought to suppress spinal reflexes by inhibiting alpha and gamma-motoneurons and suppressing the pain reflex[3].

The muscle relaxing effect of eperisone hydrochloride has been shown in patients with spastic paralysis due to cerebrovascular disease[4], spastic spinal paralysis, postoperative sequelae, and cervical syndrome as well as in lumbago[5] and periarthritis of the shoulder[6].

In the present study, we administrated a new muscle relaxant, eperisone hydrochloride, and evaluated its efficacy and safety in patients with muscle contraction headache.

Subjects and methods

The present series consisted of fifty patients, of whom 19 were males and 31 were females. They consisted of 44 outpatients and six inpatients, and were suffering from chronic muscle contraction headache and examined by neurologists at Kumamoto University Hospital from December 1984 to August 1985.

Differential diagnosis of muscle contraction headache and migraine is sometimes difficult, even to the neurologist, and the diagnosis was made by medical history and clinical symptoms such as long-sustained contraction of the skeletal muscles of scalp, face, neck and shoulders. The diagnosis was confirmed by the examination of CSF, skull and neck X-ray and cranial CT scan.

Table 2. *Precipitating factors of muscle contraction headache.*

Psychogenic problems	16 (32%)
Psychosomatic stress	9 (18%)
Neurotic character	6 (12%)
Organic neurological disorders (eg cervical spondylosis)	4 (8%)

Table 3. *Clinical symptoms (n = 50).*

Headache	
Bilateral, occipital, frontal and suboccipital pain	50 (100%)
Neck stiffness	46 (92%)
Neck pain	43 (86%)
Shoulder stiffness	47 (94%)
Shoulder pain	40 (80%)
Back pain	21 (52%)
Dizziness	13 (26%)
Tinnitus	7 (14%)
Numbness of upper extremities	11 (22%)
Numbness of lower extremities	3 (6%)
Nausea	11 (22%)
Vomiting	6 (12%)

The test drug preparation used in this study was white sugar coated tablets, each of which contained 50 mg of eperisone hydrochloride. We withheld all other muscle relaxants, sedatives, analgesics and antidepressant drugs for at least 1 week before the treatment. Each patient was given three tablets (150 mg) divided into three. In addition, no physical therapy was used. The drug was administrated for 2–4 weeks, and the changes in subjective and objective symptoms were evaluated weekly by the same physician. At the beginning of drug treatment and at the end of 4 week study, the following tests were performed: haemoglobin, haematocrit, blood urea nitrogen, AST, ALT, lactic dehydrogenase, alkaline phosphatase and urinalysis. At each weekly visit, blood pressure and pulse rate were also measured. Finally, the overall improvement and overall safety were determined. This clinical trial was not conducted according to double-blind or cross-over design.

Background data

The background data of the patients of this study is listed in Table 1. They consisted of 19 males and 31 females, whose ages ranged from 22 to 75 years-old (with an average of 53.6). The duration of headache was 3 months or less in ten cases, from 3 to 6 months in nine cases, from 6 months to 1 year in 15 cases, from 1 to 3 years in six cases, from 3 to 5 years in four cases, from 5 to 10 years in four cases and 10 years or more in two cases. Other disorders were absent in 13 cases and present in 37 cases, viz hypertension in 14 cases, hypotension in four cases, depression in three cases, cervical spondylosis in three cases, hepatic disorders in three cases and other conditions in ten cases.

Precipitating factors in our patients were psychogenic or psychosomatic stress in 50%, neurotic personality in 12% and organic neurological disorders such as cervical spondylosis in 8% (Table 2).

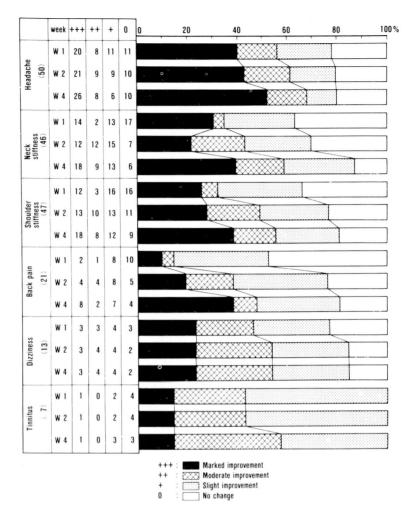

Fig. 2.

Clinical symptoms before treatment

Clinical manifestations observed before treatment are shown in Table 3. Headache of muscle contraction type, which consisted of dull, aching and non-pulsating pain, was seen in 100% of the patients. Other symptoms were shoulder stiffness in 94%, neck stiffness in 92%, neck pain in 86%, shoulder pain in 80%, back pain in 52%, and dizziness in 26%.

Results

Subjective symptoms such as headache, neck and shoulder stiffness, back pain, dizziness and tinnitus were evaluated according to the following four categories by the physician's impression; marked, moderate, or slight improvement, and no change.

Table 4. *Overall improvement.*

						Improvement rate	
Overall improvement	+ + +	+ +	+	0	–	A	B
Total (47 cases)	9	16	14	8	0	53%	85%

+ + +, Marked improvement; + +, moderate improvement; +, slight improvement; 0, no change; –, exacerbation; improvement rate A, (+ + +) and (+ +); B, (+ + +), (+ +) and (+).

Table 5. *Overall safety.*

Overall safety	Number of cases	Types
No side-effects	40 (89%)	
Mild effects requiring no discontinuation of treatment	1 (2%)	Anorexia
Treatment temporarily discontinued or dosage reduced due to side-effects	0 (0%)	
Treatment definitely discontinued or should have been discontinued	4 (9%)	1 angular stomatitis 2 general fatigue 3 stomach pain 4 nausea
Total	45	

Headache was significantly improved in the first week of the treatment and in the second and fourth weeks, improvement became increasingly marked. A similar pattern was observed in neck and shoulder stiffness and back pain. Dizziness and tinnitus were improved in the first week, especially the latter which was improved in all cases (Fig. 2).

Improvement of objective symptoms is shown in Fig. 3, and was evaluated in the same way as subjective symptoms by neurologists. Tenderness in the neck and shoulders was improved in 58% and 65% of the patients respectively in the first week. In the fourth week, the improvement rate of neck and shoulder tenderness increased to 79% and 83% respectively.

At the conclusion of the study, the physician indicated the clinical impression of treatment as rated by the objective and subjective symptoms. The degree of change was rated according to five categories: marked, moderate, and slight improvement, no change and exacerbation. The final overall improvement rate was 53% with 'marked and moderate improvements', and increased to 85% when slight improvement was included. No exacerbation of symptoms was observed (Table 4).

The results of the overall safety based on the presence or absence of the side-effects and their severity are shown in the Table 5. Side-effects occurred in five cases: anorexia, angular stomatitis, general fatigue, stomach pain and nausea in one case, respectively. In the case of anorexia, treatment was not stopped because this side-effect was so mild, but in the other four cases, treatment was discontinued and these symptoms subsided. No severe side-effect was observed.

Discussion

The mechanism of chronic muscle contraction headache is similar to that of chronic muscle contraction in any area of the body. Degeneration of bones and joints, fatigue of muscles and various kinds of stress produce muscle spasm. Subsequently, sustained muscle

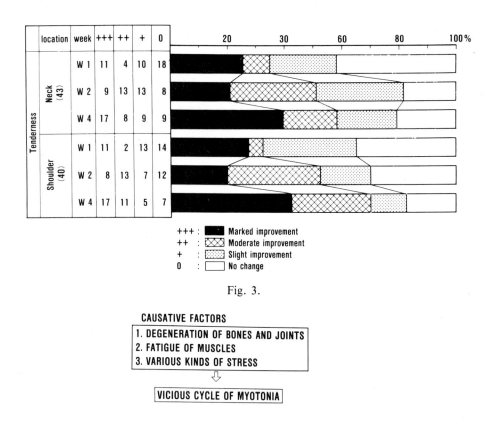

	location	week	+++	++	+	0
Tenderness	Neck (43)	W 1	11	4	10	18
		W 2	9	13	13	8
		W 4	17	8	9	9
	Shoulder (40)	W 1	11	2	13	14
		W 2	8	13	7	12
		W 4	17	11	5	7

+++ : ■ Marked improvement
++ : ▨ Moderate improvement
+ : ▦ Slight improvement
0 : □ No change

Fig. 3.

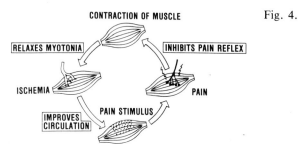

CAUSATIVE FACTORS
1. DEGENERATION OF BONES AND JOINTS
2. FATIGUE OF MUSCLES
3. VARIOUS KINDS OF STRESS
⇩
VICIOUS CYCLE OF MYOTONIA

Fig. 4.

CONTRACTION OF MUSCLE

RELAXES MYOTONIA   INHIBITS PAIN REFLEX

ISCHEMIA   PAIN

IMPROVES CIRCULATION   PAIN STIMULUS

contraction causes circulatory insufficiency of the muscle and noxious stimulation of pain by deposition of lactate, kinin and substance P. There then arises the cycle of pain, spasm and ischemia[2].

Eperisone hydrochloride might disrupt this vicious cycle by acting at three sites (Fig. 4). Suppressing spinal reflex potentials by inhibiting alpha and gamma motor-neurons, it relaxes muscle spasm[3], and improves local circulation by suppressing vascular smooth muscle contraction. It also has an inhibitory effect on pain reflex potentials.

This drug has been reported to be relatively effective in patients with spastic paralysis, cervical syndrome and lumbago[4-6]. In evaluating the efficacy of this drug in patients with muscle contraction headache, the physician's global impression of symptomatic improvement at the final examination showed an overall improvement rate (marked and moderate improvement) of 53%. The improvement rate increased to 85% when slight improvement was included. High improvement rate (more than 60%) was observed both in objective and subjective symptoms.

Laboratory tests showed no drug-related abnormalities, and significant effects on blood pressure and pulse rate were not observed during the course of this study. Side-effects occurred in five cases (10%); four patients discontinued the administration of the drug due to side-effects such as angular stomatitis, gastric discomfort and general fatigue, but, no severe side-effect was observed.

The findings presented here indicated that eperisone hydrochloride is an effective and well-tolerated drug in relieving many of the symptoms of hypermyotonia in patients with muscle contraction headache.

Conclusion

The clinical efficacy of eperisone hydrochloride was evaluated in 50 patients with muscle contraction headache, who received 150 mg of this drug daily for 4 weeks.
(1) The drug was effective on subjective symptoms such as headache, neck and shoulder pain, the improvement rate being 82%.
(2) Objective symptoms such as tenderness of the neck, shoulder and back were improved, the improvement rate being 68%.
(3) The final overall improvement rate was 58% with 'marked and moderate improvement', which increased to 85% when 'slight improvement' was included.
(4) Side-effects occurred in five cases; anorexia in one, gastric discomfort in two, general fatigue in one and angular stomatitis in one. None of these was severe.
(5) Eperisone hydrochloride is considered to be useful for the relief of headache and the hypermyotonia of muscle contraction headache.
(6) This clinical trial was a randomized study, but was not conducted according to double-blind and cross-over design, further precise evaluation of this drug is required.

References

1 Lance, J. W. (1982): *Mechanism and management of headache.* London: Butterworths.
2 Saper, J. R. (1983): Headache disorders. In *Current concepts and treatment strategies* pp. 1–305. Boston: John Wright, PSG Inc.
3 Otake, S. *et al.* (1981): Effects of 4-ethyl-2-methyl-3-piperadino-propiophenone on experimental rigidity and spinal cord activities. *Folia Pharmacol. Jap.* **77**, 511.
4 Kuroiwa, Y. *et al.* (1980): Clinical experiences with eperisone hydrochloride in spastic paralysis. *Jap. J. Clin. Exp. Med.* (Rinsho to Kenkyu) **57** (12), 4033–4038.
5 Hanai, K. *et al.* (1983): Clinical experiences with eperisone hydrochloride in lumbago. *Jap. J. Clin. Exp. Med.* (Rinsho to Kenkyu) **60** (6), 2049–2053.
6 Tahara, T. *et al.* (1983): Clinical experiences with eperisone hydrochloride in cervical syndromes. *Prog. Med.* (in Japanese) **3** (9), 1703–1713.

41

ANTIDEPRESSANTS IN THE TREATMENT OF MIXED HEADACHE: MAO INHIBITORS AND COMBINED USE OF MAO INHIBITORS AND TRICYCLIC ANTIDEPRESSANTS IN THE RECIDIVIST HEADACHE PATIENT

Frederick G. Freitag, Seymour Diamond and Glen D. Solomon

Diamond Headache Clinic, Visiting Lecturer, Department of Family Medicine, Chicago College of Osteopathic Medicine, Chicago, USA and Diamond Headache Clinic, Adjunct Professor of Pharmacology, The Chicago Medical School, Chicago, USA and Staff Physician Diamond Headache Clinic, Chicago, USA

Summary

In the treatment of pain and especially headache the use of the tricyclic antidepressants has been well established. Monoamine oxidase inhibitors (MAOIs) have been minimally used in the treatment of headache, and the combined use of MAOIs and tricyclic antidepressants have not been previously studied. This chapter examines the results of the use of MAO inhibitors alone and in combination with tricyclic antidepressants in the treatment of the recidivist headache patient.

Study design

The charts of the Diamond Headache Clinic were reviewed for patients treated with either MAOIs or combination therapy with MAOIs and tricyclic antidepressants. Forty-three patients with diagnoses of migraine, muscle contraction, or mixed headaches were included

Table 1. *Reduction in headache parameters.*

	Migraine		Mixed		Muscle contraction	
	MAO	MAO/TCA	MAO	MAO/TCA	MAO	MAO/TCA
>90%	1	—	4	2	2	2
50–90%	7	—	8	4	—	—
<50%	5	—	2	1	2	—
No change	6	2	2	1	—	—

in this study. The charts of these patients were reviewed for the following: (1) diagnosis; (2) demographic characteristics; (3) previous medications for the treatment of headache and response to these agents; (4) headache parameters of frequency and severity of headaches prior to treatment; and (5) headache parameters during treatment. Safety parameters, including physical examination, laboratory evaluation, and reporting of side-effects, were included in this retrospective survey.

The side-effects were classified according to their area of involvement, such as the autonomic nervous system, the central nervous system, or effects on other body organs or functions. The MAOIs used in the study were phenelzine or isocarboxazid, although only four patients were treated with the latter. Amitriptyline, doxepin, trimipramine, and trazodone were the tricyclic antidepressants used in the study.

Results

A group of forty-three patients comprised seven males and thirty-six females. The patients with migraine headache ranged in age from 30 to 61 years (mean 43.3), the mixed headache patients from 20 to 66 years (37.6 mean), and the patients with pure muscle contraction headache from 27 to 70 years (mean 57.4).

Fifty-one various combinations of therapies were tried with these patients. One patient was treated with two different MAOIs alone and then with each of the two MAOIs in combination with a tricyclic. Another four patients were treated with an MAOI, followed by combination therapy with the same agent and a tricyclic. Other therapeutic regimens included two patients treated with two different MAOIs followed by one MAOI in combination with a tricyclic agent, two patients using two different MAOIs, and the remaining patients were treated with MAOI therapy alone. Patients receiving treatment with MAOIs, prior to being seen at the Diamond Headache Clinic, were given combination therapy.

Three of eighteen migraine patients had classical migraine while the remaining fifteen experienced common migraine. One migraine patient experienced an excellent response with complete amelioration of her headaches (Table 1). Another seven patients demonstrated at least a 50% reduction in the headache parameters, and five other patients had at least a partial response. No improvement was noted in the remaining five patients, including one who received treatment with both MAOIs and a tricyclic in two different combinations.

In the treatment of mixed headache, fifteen patients were treated with an MAOI alone. Four of these patients experienced excellent results and an additional eight patients had at least a 50% reduction in headaches, including one patient who was subsequently treated successfully with combination therapy. One patient experienced fair results with phenelzine, and poor results with isocarboxazid. Another patient demonstrated poor results on combination therapy with phenelzine but fair results with isocarboxazid alone. The remaining patient responded poorly to singular MAOI therapy. Combination therapy in mixed headaches resulted in two patients achieving complete remission of their headaches,

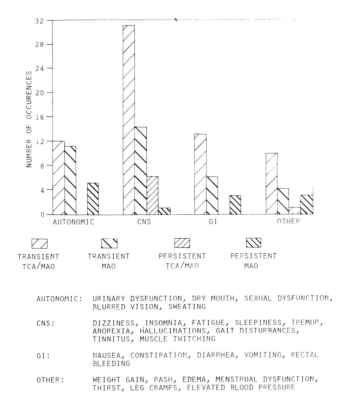

AUTONOMIC: URINARY DYSFUNCTION, DRY MOUTH, SEXUAL DYSFUNCTION, BLURRED VISION, SWEATING

CNS: DIZZINESS, INSOMNIA, FATIGUE, SLEEPINESS, TREMOR, ANOREXIA, HALLUCINATIONS, GAIT DISTURBANCES, TINNITUS, MUSCLE TWITCHING

GI: NAUSEA, CONSTIPATION, DIARRHEA, VOMITING, RECTAL BLEEDING

OTHER: WEIGHT GAIN, RASH, EDEMA, MENSTRUAL DYSFUNCTION, THIRST, LEG CRAMPS, ELEVATED BLOOD PRESSURE

Figure. *Side-effects, time of occurrence and treatment.*

including one patient who had a good result with MAOI therapy alone. Four additional patients experienced a good response, and, one patient with pure muscle contraction headache had an excellent response for over 1 year during treatment with phenelzine, but eventually required combination therapy in order to maintain the response. Because of side-effects to the tricyclics, combination therapy was discontinued. The patient was continued on isocarboxazid and experienced partial improvement in her headaches. The other two patients treated with MAOIs alone had an excellent and a fair response respectively. Only one patient with muscle contraction headache received combination therapy and experienced almost complete relief from the headaches.

One reason that MAOI therapy became unpopular was the potential for interactions between a variety of foods and other medications with these agents, thus causing a bias against using MAOIs and tricyclics in combination. Our experience with this therapy revealed no significant occurrences of food or drug reaction while on MAOI or combination therapy. None of our patients involved in this study experienced hypertensive crisis or hyperpyrexia, and there were no reports of significant adverse effects on any of the laboratory parameters. On physical examination, rare abnormalities, gait disturbance and edema were demonstrated, but these symptoms were transient and resolved with either adjustment of medication dosage, discontinuation of the drug, or the passage of time. In the majority of cases, the therapy was continued.

Side-effects occurred in most patients upon initiation of either type of therapy (Figure) but, in the majority of these patients, they resolved with appropriate management of the medications. In comparing the occurrence rate of side-effects with MAOIs in combination with the tricyclics, against singular MAOI therapy, there is a marked increase in the occurrence of side-effects in the former. A careful review of this increased rate revealed that this occurrence is typical of any form of tricyclic therapy. We believe that the increase in side-effects with combination therapy does not suggest a potentiation of one group of agents, but is representative of the side-effects of tricyclic therapy. In patients receiving singular MAOI therapy, the majority who continued to have persistent side-effects were those patients who also experienced the least degree of improvement in their headaches. However, in those patients treated with combination therapy, this pattern was not as distinct. Several patients who had achieved good or excellent results with combination therapy, had to be discontinued from further treatment because of persistent side-effects.

Discussion

Sicuteri[1] has advanced the hypothesis that central depletion of monoamines may be responsible for migraine headaches. Similarly, the role of monoamine depletion has been advanced as a possible mechanism in muscle contraction headache[2,3]. Others[4,5] have suggested that there is a link between depression and headache, including migraine and muscle contraction. Diamond[4] has demonstrated effectiveness of amitriptyline in the treatment of headache as well as in the treatment of depression. Lance and Curran[5] found that both amitriptyline and imipramine were of significant benefit to patients with chronic muscle contraction headache.

Tricyclic antidepressants have proven beneficial in the treatment of migraine eg amitriptyline[6]. Another tricyclic, doxepin, has been used in a study of patients with mixed headaches[7]. Anthony and Lance[8], found that using the MAOI, phenelzine, in migraine prophylaxis, resulted in at least a 50% reduction in headaches in 80% of 25 patients who had been refractive to currently available medications for migraine treatment.

A co-pharmaceutical approach to headache has been demonstrated as more beneficial than treatment with single agents alone[9]. This approach, using several pharmaceutical agents together with each aimed at specific aspects of the treatment problem, is well established in the medical community.

The use of MAOIs and tricyclics for the treatment of resistant depression has recently been gaining acceptance[10], based on evidence suggesting synergism between the agents[11], despite warnings against their combined use from pharmaceutical firms and the FDA. The safety and effectiveness of combined therapy has been reported in an extensive report[12] which included a review of all reported cases of morbidity or mortality associated with their use. In this review, the authors found that the combination of any of several MAOIs with the tricyclic, imipramine, were responsible for the morbidity associated with each of the cases. Another report[13] suggested that the tricyclic, amitriptyline, may prevent the reaction between MAOIs and tyramine containing foods.

Conclusion

In this current study, we were able to partially confirm the results of previous studies on MAOIs in the treatment of migraine, and demonstrate that MAOI therapy was effective in the treatment of both pure muscle contraction and mixed headache.

This is also the first report on the use of MAOIs and tricyclics in the treatment of several types of headache. Our results suggest that combination therapy may prove beneficial in a substantial number of patients. We also confirmed the results of previous papers dealing with the safety of MAOI and tricyclic therapy, as none of our patients experienced any significant reactions.

Patient selection is of primary importance in choosing the appropriate form of therapy, especially in treatment with MAOIs singly or in combination with a tricyclic antidepressant. Since the potential for serious drug and food interactions does exist, the patient should have adequate trials on more standard therapies before MAOI therapy is utilized, and should receive adequate trials on singular MAOI therapy before combination therapy with MAOIs and tricyclics is considered. Patients selected for MAOI therapy should be clearly motivated to maintain strict adherence to the necessary dietary and medication restrictions essential in using these agents. Patients should receive thorough education on these restrictions as well as periodic reinforcement of instructions. It is essential that the physician be cognizant of the need to carefully select patients who will be compliant with the necessary medication restrictions and dietary prohibition while on MAOIs. In following these precautions, we feel that the MAOIs singly or in combination with tricyclics can be used safely. Admission to an inpatient headache treatment unit should be considered for initiation of combination therapy with an MAOI and a tricyclic antidepressant.

References

1   Sicuteri, F. (1976): Migraine, a central biochemical dysnociception. *Headache* **16**, 145.
2   Sicuteri, F. (1981): Opioid receptor impairment-underlying mechanism in pain diseases. *Cephalagia* **1**, 77.
3   Rolf, L. H., Wiele, G. & Brune, G. G. (1981): 5 Hydroxytryptamine in platelets of patients with muscle contraction headache. *Headache* **21**, 10.
4   Diamond, S. (1964): Depressive headaches. *Headache* **4**, 255–259.
5   Lance, J. W. & Curran, D. A. (1964): Treatment of chronic tension headache. *Lancet* **i**, 1236.
6   Gomersall, J. D. & Stuart, A. (1973): Changes in the pattern of attacks during a controlled trial. *J. Neurol. Neurosurg. Psychiat.* **36**, 684.
7   Morland, T. J., Storli, O. V. & Mogstad, T. E. (1979): Doxepin in the prophylactic treatment of mixed 'vascular' and tension headache. *Headache* **19**, 382–383.
8   Anthony, M. & Lance, J. W. (1969): Monoamine oxidase inhibition in the treatment of migraine. *Archs. Neurol.* **21**, 263.
9   Mathew, N. T. (1981): Prophylaxis of migraine and mixed headache. A randomized controlled study. *Headache* **21**, 105–109.
10 White, D. & Simpson, G. (1981): Combined MAOI-tricyclic antidepressant treatment: A re-evaluation. *J. Clin. Psychopharacol.* **1**, 264–282.
11 Schildkraut, J. J. & Kety, S. S. (1967): Biogenic amines and emotions. *Science* **156**, 21–30.
12 Schuckit, M., Robins, E. & Freighne, J. (1971): Tricyclic antidepressants and monoamine oxidase inhibitors, combination therapy in the treatment of depression. *Arch. Gen. Psychiat.* **24**, 509–514.
13 Pare, C. M. B., Hallstrom, C., Kline, N. & Cooper, T. B. (1982): Will amitriptyline prevent the 'cheese' reaction of monoamine oxidase inhibitors? *Lancet* **ii**, 183–186.

AUTHOR INDEX

SUBJECT INDEX